STEPTOE AND SON

STEPTOE AND SON

Ray Galton & Alan Simpson
with Robert Ross

Published by BBC Worldwide Ltd,
80 Wood Lane, London W12 0TT

First published 2002
© Ray Galton, Alan Simpson and Robert Ross 2002
The moral right of the authors has been asserted

ISBN 0 563 48833 6

Commissioning Editor: Ben Dunn
Project Editor: Rebecca Kincaid
Copy Editors: Hugh Morgan and April Warman
Book Design: Sarah Ponder
Production Controller: Christopher Tinker

Set in ScalaSans
Printed and bound in Great Britain by Butler & Tanner Ltd, Frome
Jacket and plate sections printed by Lawrence-Allen Ltd, Weston-super-Mare
Colour separations by Radstock Reproductions Ltd, Midsomer Norton

Contents

The Story of Ray Galton and Alan Simpson's *Steptoe and Son*

By Robert Ross

Dedicated to Harry and Willie

Thanks to: Ben Dunn, Rebecca Kincaid and Vicky Thomas at BBC Worldwide, Malcolm Chapman, Dick Fiddy, Tony Lang for his 1987 paper *The Steptoe and Son Saga*, Mark Pearson of The Official *Steptoe and Son* Appreciation Society, Trevor Bannister, Graham Stark, Frank Thornton, June Whitfield, the ever-reliable Tessa Le Bars, and, of course, the 'governors', Ray Galton and Alan Simpson.
Also thanks to: the BBC Archives at Caversham, the Colindale Newspaper Library, and the British Film Institute.

Chapter 1

Any Old Iron?

'We were literally made an offer we couldn't refuse,' remembers writer Alan Simpson. 'Nobody, before or since, has ever been given such freedom, and I doubt it will ever happen again.' The offer was simple. In 1961 Ray Galton and Alan Simpson, British television's most celebrated and prolific comedy scriptwriters, were presented with the opportunity to make their own series of one-off, half-hour plays. The title for the series was *Comedy Playhouse*, and as Ray Galton continues: 'It was amazing. We were told we could do absolutely anything. We could write them, direct them, edit them, even star in them if we wanted to!' Galton and Simpson had a strong desire to break away from writing comedy that was geared towards the persona of an established comedian, so they were delighted with this opportunity to flex their writing muscles with a string of self-contained projects. Fate and fortune stepped in, however. The fourth offering in the series was a two-handed dialogue between rag 'n' bone men in London's Shepherd's Bush. The show proved an instant success, recognized by both the viewing public and the powers that be at the BBC as something very special indeed. The very thing the writers were hoping to get away from – another long-running comedy series – was the result.

That wonderfully cluttered set, with the ever-present skeleton and stuffed grizzly bear, and the accumulation of rubbish from a thousand totting trips, are now etched on our consciousness. The thin, ailing father full of patriotic pride, and the downtrodden son struggling to find his feet away from parental pressure, complete the snapshot of a London that is both thankfully and regrettably gone for ever.

The series enjoyed national popularity from the outset. Moreover, it broke new ground in situation comedy on British television. Described by one critic as being 'like Harold Pinter but with shorter pauses', the socially aware scripts and highly convincing performances placed the series in the England of the 1960s just before the decade started to swing. Yet there were still reminders of the despair and hardship of war.

The scripts utilized subtle one-liners, extremely unsubtle comic hooks for guaranteed laughs and displayed a rare understanding of the poverty-stricken situation many families faced in Macmillan's 'never had it so good' Utopia.

The influence of *Steptoe and Son*'s skilful combination of new ideas and established elements remains as strong as ever. The series has become a television landmark and the situation comedy by which every other must be judged. With this definitive single-set, claustrophobic sitcom, Ray Galton and Alan Simpson's writing ushered in a whole new set of codes and conventions for television comedy. For the first time on British television, characters from a working-class environment were allowed to instigate the humour, where previously they had been restricted to earthy, often patronized roles. With the success of *Steptoe and Son* writers gained a freer hand to explore and extend the boundaries of the sitcom format. Within a few short years almost every new British sitcom chose to display a close familiarity with the lower classes, and employ a lifelong loser as its central character.

In 1964, writers Dick Clement and Ian La Frenais were among the first to follow the lead of Galton and Simpson. Instead of examining the ins and outs of London's working classes, they chose to tackle the gritty realities of industrial England and the wage-slave youth of *The Likely Lads*. At around the same time, Johnny Speight delved even deeper into the London mire to create his anti-hero Alf Garnett in *Till Death Us Do Part*. From 1973 Clement and La Frenais put the comic situation into closer confinement, and addressed even more sensitive issues, with their classic prison-based situation comedy *Porridge*. The following year Eric Chappell created ITV's premier sitcom favourite, *Rising Damp*, celebrating the grim, ill-fated social climbing of landlord Rigsby.

John Sullivan's much-loved *Only Fools and Horses*, first broadcast in 1981, returned to the roots of *Steptoe* by investigating the lives and loves of London street traders. In among the family tensions and the failed scams, there are reminders of *Steptoe* in the constant sense of confidence in a brighter future – though there is none of the ambition for social respect and cultural understanding that we recognize in Harold. It is a 'greed is good' and 'money is power' mentality. 'This time next year we'll be millionaires' struck a chord, some 20 years after *Steptoe*'s first appearance. It is this optimism, together with the viewer's certainty that any success will be short-lived, that produces the tragic-comic element of both sitcoms.

Towards the end of the 1980s, when the art of situation comedy had moved light years away from the basic structure that *Steptoe* had blueprinted, the Galton and Simpson rag 'n' bone saga was still a reference point for critics. The intergalactic banter of Chris Barrie's Arnold Rimmer and Craig Charles's Dave Lister in the sci-fi sitcom *Red Dwarf* was described by one reviewer as being nothing more than '*Steptoe* in space'. Whether characters are sitting in the gutter and looking at the stars, or sitting in the stars and looking back to the gutter, *Steptoe*'s influence has permeated the history of the working-class sitcom. Even contemporary comedy sees *The Royle Family* treading the familiar path first trod by Harold and Albert as the Royles vegetate through their slovenly, one-set existence. Indeed, without the Steptoes Bob and Terry, the Trotters, Fletch, the Royle family and the 'silly old moo!' of classic situation comedy would probably never have got past the commissioning stage.

Steptoe's clout in British sitcom history is even more far-reaching in that the work of Galton and Simpson pioneered a casting strategy that has been used and reused ever since: the employment of theatrically trained actors to add extra weight to the more dramatic elements of the comedy. Coming as this does from an era that was accustomed to simply tailoring situations to comedians and their established comic baggage, one cannot overestimate the revolutionary importance of the central casting in *Steptoe and Son*. Without the series' popularity and effectiveness, firmly rooted in the minds of the new generation of programme-makers, the history of the sitcom would have been very different indeed. Without it, respected actors such as Arthur Lowe, Richard Briers and Nigel Hawthorne would never have found fame and immortality in *Dad's Army*, *The Good Life* and *Yes, Minister* respectively. While the subject matter of these reflected more on the middle and upper classes of Britain, and the writing was suitably readjusted to encompass slapstick, regular ensemble playing and convoluted satire, the shadow of *Steptoe and Son* still loomed large over their success.

Of course, *Steptoe and Son*, greeted with huge applause on its first appearance in 1962, was the critical pinnacle of a writing partnership that had first caught the imagination of the public nearly 10 years previously, and had moulded the foundations of Britcom during its formative years. Interestingly, the bulk of Galton and Simpson's most celebrated writing before *Steptoe and Son* is attributed to Alan Simpson and Ray Galton. By the time *Steptoe and Son* returned in 1970 the order had changed and history, the public and the writers themselves acknowledge the Galton and Simpson brand as definitive. As Alan Simpson points out: 'I couldn't care less ... I've always had half the money and that's the important thing!'

With the benefit of a brand-new canvas on which to work, Galton and Simpson were free to write without reference to any previously established rules of the genre. 'We would think of ideas on our own and if they were acceptable to the other we would go ahead along those lines,' remembers Ray Galton. 'If an idea met with silence, we would drop it and think of something else.'

Alan Simpson adds:

> I reckon it would take us, in actual fact, about five months to write a series of seven. We weren't quick writers, generally speaking. Every word was torn from our bodies! We would hear that Barry Took and Marty Feldman could knock out a *Round the Horne* in two days. It was very, very rare for us to write that quickly, although we did write one *Comedy Playhouse*, 'Impasse', in four hours. We started at 9 o'clock Saturday morning and at 1 o'clock I typed in 'The End'. We couldn't get the words down fast enough, but that was so rare as to be a land-speed record for us. Other times we would take three weeks to chip out a half-hour, with days and days going by in which we couldn't write a single word. The art to it was to make sure that when you read a three-week script and you read a three-day script, you couldn't tell the difference – we had the technical ability to make a script flow even if it was just a word a day.

The 'Impasse' script was a rarity in more ways than one, as Ray Galton continues: 'As a rule, we were weekday writers and we got weekends off – it was our job. My goal was to have a whole week to write each programme. That was our aim, our luxury.' Alan Simpson agrees: 'We weren't trained writers and we didn't have the journalistic background of having to write at the touch of a button with an editor screaming, "Quick, 500 words on a train accident". We didn't have that – not like Keith Waterhouse, for example. He wouldn't dream of agonizing over anything. He had the ability to bang it out. We wrote because we wanted to.'

Galton and Simpson's joint contribution to British television is colossal, ranking them among the small handful of comedy writers whose names are recognized by a large section of the viewing public.

Alan Simpson was born in Brixton on 27 November 1929 and Ray Galton a few months later, in Paddington, on 17 July 1930. Both had a passion for words but also an assumption that they would spend their working lives very much as each previous generation had spent theirs. As a teenager, Simpson, with a leaning towards nautical endeavour, worked as a shipping clerk in London. Galton got a job with the Transport and General Workers' Union. It was a near-tragedy that brought about their meeting. When they were still only in their late teens Galton and Simpson met in the Milford Sanatorium, Surrey. The year was 1948 and both were being treated for tuberculosis. Half a century ago TB was rife and, with the fledgling health service still finding its feet, was an almost assured death sentence. Ray Galton was admitted first; just under a year later Alan Simpson arrived, and a friendship was begun.

> Ray and I had had the same kind of upbringing, and in particular we were both mad about movies. The cinema had been a way of life. We could just chat about films all the time because we both knew all the old stars. I mean, Mary Beth Hughes – nobody else had ever heard of her! The only thing we didn't have in common was sport. Ray used to go to the Saturday morning pictures when he was young, but for me Saturdays were football days. It used to take three and a half hours to get to Brentford from where I lived in those days, so when Ray was at the pictures I was on the 6.30 a.m. trolley-bus to make sure I was in time for the 3 o'clock kick-off. Oh, and Ray didn't like Randolph Scott. I liked him because he looked like my dad a bit! Randolph Scott and sport are the only things we have ever differed on. Everything else – food, wine, entertainment – we share.

The two of them quickly discovered that they shared a similar background, a common frustration with their condition, and an interlocking sense of humour, and to relieve the boredom of complete inactivity during their recovery they began writing and performing comedy programmes. As Galton remembers: 'We were lucky in so far as there was a guy on another ward who had a great big RAF 1155 radio. If he liked you he would let you listen to it on his headphones. In the end there were about a dozen of us who switched on the radio and listened to all those wonderful channels you couldn't get from the dear BBC.' BBC radio comedy had already begun a tradition of surreal-sketch humour and recurring comic characterization with Tommy Handley's wartime morale booster *ITMA*, which would run until its star's death in 1949. However, it was the slicker, American programmes with more of a base in reality that really caught the imagination of Galton and Simpson. 'We heard all the American comedy shows of the time and that was, of course, a big plus,' Simpson recalls. 'And the sitcom, as it has become known, was popular in America from the 1930s. We would listen to Jack Benny, Phil Harris, Bob Hope, George Burns and Gracie Allen, all of them. It was an American tradition that all of the great comedians had their own shows. We were light years behind them in this country.'

The writing partnership was cemented thanks to the same man with the radio set. 'He had set up an internal radio circuit and, after joining in with all sorts of weird and wonderful programmes, Ray and I got together, wrote some comedy scripts and then broadcast them ourselves over the hospital network.' Despite the importance of the American influence it was the very British talents of Frank Muir and Denis Norden that inspired Galton and Simpson: 'They were our gurus,' remembers Simpson. 'We thought that they were just wonderful.' The radio series that fully utilized the writing of Muir and Norden was *Take It From Here*. Although best remembered for Jimmy Edwards' imposing performance as Pa Glum, the bombastic head of the Glum family, the show pioneered the use of elaborate wordplay in British comedy. It used sophisticated language to create credible situations, and supplanted the simple 'I say, I say, I say' variety-show humour that merely extended a comedian's stage persona to the radio. Within *Take It From Here* a new, challenging field of comic expression in British comedy was beginning to develop: the situation comedy.

Galton maintains: 'Muir and Norden were the first scriptwriters over here to treat the audience as intelligent. They assumed that people knew something about the arts and could understand bigger words. That was what we loved – words and intelligent humour.'

Simpson had been discharged from the sanatorium in 1950, much to the chagrin of his writing partner: 'I got there a year before him and it was a year after he got out that I finally escaped!' Galton 'escaped' to an offer from Simpson to help him write new material for his local concert party. Then, in a bid to reach a wider audience, the two decided to write to the only people they 'knew' in the business: Frank Muir and Denis Norden. As Galton points out:

> We had never met them. We wouldn't have known them if we'd tripped over them in the street, but we loved their writing. I suppose we thought that if the BBC employed them, then other people with writing aspirations like us might stand a chance. We wrote to them for advice, and they wrote back and gave us the classic cop-out line: 'We liked what you wrote, we thought it was very funny but why don't you send it to the script editor of the BBC because they are always on the look-out for new material.' In other words, don't bother sending it to us because we can't help you. Once we'd got established, if anyone sent us something to look at, we always wrote back saying exactly the same

thing that Frank Muir and Denis Norden had said to us! You are warned! It worked for us, so why shouldn't it work for you?

Muir and Norden had, in fact, recommended that the two budding writers send their material to a BBC script editor by the name of Gale Pedrick. The year was 1951, and Ray Galton and Alan Simpson were about to become professional writers: 'We agreed from the start of the partnership that we should both take the blame!' remembers Ray Galton. To begin with they simply adapted and anglicized all the puns and wordplay they had picked up from the American radio shows they had loved listening to in the sanatorium. 'We were really rewriting Bob Hope gags,' admits Simpson, 'or at the very least trying to write material which sounded like his sort of style.' Derek Roy, one of the biggest show-business names in the country, was the first comic to employ their services on a regular basis. Consciously modelling himself on the slick American tradition, Roy was the alternative host of the hugely successful radio revue *Variety Band-Box*. The other host was a fresh-faced comic by the name of Frankie Howerd. When Howerd suddenly rose to fame, Galton and Simpson rose too, scripting the early 1950s radio hit, *The Frankie Howerd Show*. They would write for the comedian for many years afterwards. 'He really was unique,' remembers Alan Simpson. 'There is simply nobody like him. We were always writing small bits and pieces for him, right up to the end. It was always good fun writing for Frank.'

But it was the universally slated 1951 radio disaster, *Happy-Go-Lucky*, that introduced Galton and Simpson to their greatest comic muse: Tony Hancock. Drafted in to salvage the sinking ship, they eventually found themselves writing practically all of *Happy-Go-Lucky*. 'Alan and I were at rehearsals,' recalls Ray Galton, 'and this figure wandered over to us with the script and muttered, "Did you write this?" We nodded. The figure said, "Very good!" and wandered off again. That was Hancock.'

Galton and Simpson would write several stage and radio spots for Tony Hancock, and later they suggested a radio sitcom format tailored especially for the star. The first series of *Hancock's Half Hour* was broadcast from November 1954 and rocketed Galton and Simpson to the top echelon of comedy scriptwriters. 'That show was a joy from start to finish,' remembers Ray Galton. 'We had four of the biggest laughers in the business: Sid James of course; Kenneth Williams, who was forever snorting and cackling; Bill Kerr, who would just explode; and Hancock himself, who would often end up on the floor helplessly holding his sides, aching with laughter at what the others were doing. It was probably the happiest part of our professional life.'

A television version, with regular radio colleague Sid James in tow, had its debut in 1956 and quickly became a favourite with the nation, honing the two-hander playlet format that would become the speciality of its writers. By the time the final series was transmitted in 1961 it had been shortened by five minutes, aptly renamed simply *Hancock* and had seen the parting of the ways for Hancock and Sid James. It also contained Galton and Simpson's undisputed masterpiece 'The Blood Donor'. There had been a feature film with Tony Hancock, *The Rebel*, that same year and an alternative television series, *Citizen James*, for Sid James in 1960. Clearly, Galton and Simpson were relishing these opportunities to write for Britain's finest comic talent, but the Hancock association was facing an extended break, so it was lucky that the offer that couldn't be refused came in the autumn of 1961.

By 24 October 1961 Tom Sloan, the Head of BBC Television Light Entertainment, had announced the *Comedy Playhouse* collaboration with Galton and Simpson: 'This is an idea of mine which I have fully discussed with them and with which they are in full agreement.'

As the *Radio Times* commented, the 'Ray Galton and Alan Simpson Presents *Comedy Playhouse*' series was designed as a 'tribute to their talents. A showcase for their writing rather than for the acting of one particular star as usually happens'.

Ray Galton remembers:

> The man who has to be thanked for *Steptoe and Son* is Tom Sloan. He rarely, if ever, gets the credit he deserves, and a lot of people took the mickey out of him, thinking he was just another one of those military men at the BBC without any idea of the business. That's rubbish. When we split with Hancock, Tom Sloan called us into his office and said, 'Now what are you going to do?' We said, 'Well, we'd like to write a series for Frankie Howerd.' He said, 'No, you're not!' We weren't under contract mind you, but he said, 'No, Frankie Howerd's finished in this business.' He was quite wrong about that, of course, and we knew it. We kept saying, 'Look, don't be daft. Frank's a genius,' but it did no good. He said, 'Howerd's last series for the BBC was an absolute disaster.' He buzzed for his secretary and asked her for all these charts of audience appreciation for previous shows. The viewing figures were pretty lousy for Frankie and the appreciation was even worse. So this was his proof that Frankie was finished in the business.

'Mind you,' continues Alan Simpson, 'if Sloan had said, "All right, then, give us 10 Frankie Howerd shows" when we suggested it, we would have done that series instead of 10 *Comedy Playhouse* episodes and, therefore, no *Steptoe* so, thank you, Tom Sloan, again!' But, as Ray Galton confirms:

What Tom Sloan actually said was, 'I want you to fulfil a programme title that I've thought up.' He explained: 'I've got a spot for a series called *Comedy Playhouse* and I've got 10 half-hour slots, and what I'm asking you to do is fill them. You can do anything you want with them.' He gave us total freedom, and nobody, but nobody has ever been given that opportunity. To be fair to him, he even said, 'If you want to put Frankie Howerd in one of them, that's fine,' and eventually we did use Frank.

Howerd starred in a single effort, 'Have You Read This Notice?', in the second batch of *Comedy Playhouse* shows in 1963, the same year that saw his career enjoy a complete resurgence.

Galton remembers: 'Sloan gave us five hours of television time with which we could do what we wanted. He said, "The only thing I insist on is using my title, *Comedy Playhouse* – that's all. The rest is up to you two." Of course, we jumped at the chance. It was a golden opportunity to fulfil an ambition: to write for actors. It really was emancipation from being a comedian's scriptwriters.'

The Tony Hancock shows had recruited a 'local repertory company' of straight actors who were accomplished at playing comic authority figures. The touch of realism that this added gave weight and credibility to Hancock's observational comedy. The success of these shows had shown the way forward for sitcom, particularly in the minds of Galton and Simpson. A straight performance could, as often as not, make a funny line even funnier. More important, a straight actor could give equal conviction to a line written for straight effect.

Talking to the *Radio Times* in 1961 both Galton and Simpson were aware of the significance of *Comedy Playhouse*: '[It] represents an important departure. This series can be a real turning point in our writing career. In these half-hour shows – they're really one-act plays – we dream up our own characters, and the actors playing them have to fit the writing instead of the other way round. If the series succeeds, this is the kind of thing we want to do from now on.' The first *Comedy Playhouse*, 'Clicquot et Fils', was screened on 15 December 1961 and cast Eric Sykes as an underemployed undertaker in the France of 1926. Warren Mitchell co-starred. In that week's issue of the *Radio Times*, Tom Sloan penned an appreciation of the series:

In the last six years one of the most distinctive contributions to light entertainment has been in the field of situation comedy. Tony Hancock, Eric Sykes, Jimmy Edwards, Charlie Drake, Sidney James, Harry Worth and now *The Rag Trade* have all raised this type of humour to a level which is unsurpassed in this country. It is a record of which we in the BBC are very proud. In all these series the same stars have played the same roles or a variety of roles in scripts written by crafts-men who have allied their particular talents to these stars over a long period. For writers this can generally be a wholly satisfying experience but I have often wondered how certain of them would react if they were invited to write exactly what they wanted to write – with no particular star in mind. To this end I have asked Alan Simpson and Ray Galton to launch a new series called *Comedy Playhouse*. I am glad to say they have jumped at the assignment, and the first of their original comedy plays will be shown tonight.

'In effect,' remembers Ray Galton, 'we became the stars. For once, the writers were the major attraction in a comedy series. I don't think that's ever been repeated.'

Thus, the situation and scripting of the series reassuringly followed the criteria of intelligence, humour and realist situation comedy. However, the internal BBC memo made a point of suggesting actors who exhibited comic talents, such as Terry-Thomas, Ian Carmichael, Kenneth Williams and Kenneth Connor, for the *Comedy Playhouse* series

The comic two-hander that Galton and Simpson had pioneered with the Tony Hancock and Sid James dialogues was extended within the *Comedy Playhouse* format. The historical tale of a bigamist, 'The Private Lives of Edward Whiteley', starred Tony Britton and Raymond Huntley. Peter Jones and June Whitfield teamed up for 'The Telephone Call', while a recognized Galton and Simpson classic, 'Sealed with a Loving Kiss', saw its first interpretation with Ronald Fraser and Avril Elgar. The eighth show, 'Visiting Day', saw Bernard Cribbins as a hospital patient. As if to prove that the stars of 'The Offer' were jobbing actors, Wilfrid Brambell co-starred as his father. Under producer Barry Lupino, Brambell enjoyed the challenge of altering his appearance: 'I went to make up and put in for a flat 'at, stiff starched collar, string tie and a drooping beer-sodden moustache.'

The final *Comedy Playhouse* of the series, 'The Channel Swimmer', broadcast on 16 February 1962, once again recruited Warren Mitchell, this time playing alongside Sid's *Citizen James* co-star, Sydney Tafler. Michael Brennan played the eponymous swimming hopeful.

However, by the end of the series, everybody was talking about just one of the 10 commissioned programmes. The fourth show was called 'The Offer' and saw an extended argument between a father and son, partners in a rag 'n' bone business in London's Shepherd's Bush. Graham Stark, who starred with Alfred Marks in the seventh show, 'The Status Symbol', had reason to be furious, albeit with tongue very firmly in cheek:

> The script was absolutely brilliant. It was set in a garage with me playing the assistant to Alfred Marks. It was probably the funniest thing I ever read and Alfred and I clicked immediately. I seriously thought it had 'series' written all over it. Anyway, I watched the *Comedy Playhouse* series as it was transmitted, eagerly waiting for our show to turn up and send shockwaves through the business. After the fourth programme I telephoned Alan Simpson and said: 'Thank you very much!' He said: 'What have I done now?' 'You've just ruined our chance of a series!' I said. 'What do you mean?' he spluttered. 'That show that's just been on,' I continued, 'is a guaranteed series and I want a part in it!' Alan dismissed the idea, but I wasn't wrong was I? Oh, and I was never cast in any of the television episodes!

Graham Stark wasn't the only one who saw the show's potential.

Chapter 2

Make Me an Offer!

Tom Sloan's pet project, *Comedy Playhouse*, had been assigned a string of four producers to oversee the 10 self-contained plays. Duncan Wood, who had produced the Tony Hancock shows for television, had been allotted four of the *Comedy Playhouse* series, including the opening episode and what turned out to be the all-important fourth programme, 'The Offer'.

Various television reference books have reported that both Alan Simpson and Ray Galton worked as rag 'n' bone men in their youth. 'That,' Ray Galton recalls, 'isn't entirely true. The family who lived next door to me were involved in all sorts of business. The father never did any proper work as such. He would do all sorts of strange things to earn a crust. The son got hold of a horse and cart and went totting round the Mitcham area. I went out with him once or twice until my mother found out and I got a walloping! He used to take his stuff down to Sparrowhawk's.'

'Jack Sparrowhawk was a big rag 'n' bone centre where all the local totters would take their pickings,' confirms Alan Simpson. 'It was a huge scrap-metal depot, and it was right next door to the school I used to go to. But I can't claim that that had any bearing on *Steptoe and Son* because it didn't.' However, the pair had certainly used the industry before *Steptoe*: in 1958 it was the starting point for radio's *Hancock's Half Hour*, 'The Junk Man'. 'The idea of rag 'n' bone men certainly appealed to us,' remembers Alan Simpson. 'It was part of our youth. They did literally go round the streets ringing their bell and shouting out: "Any old rags, bottles and bones ... rags and bones." They were wonderful characters.'

Ray Galton agrees: 'I got into trouble with my mother one day because I gave one rag 'n' bone man something from the house. They were giving out balloons and windmills on sticks. I ran in to see my mother with this wind-mill on a stick and proudly said, "Look what I got!" She hit the roof. God knows what I gave for it!'

In June 1962 the *Radio Times*, in a feature promoting the first series of *Steptoe and Son*, related: 'Several years ago in a Shepherd's Bush eel-and-pie shop, scriptwriters Alan Simpson and Ray Galton became intrigued by the strange slang that two men sitting nearby were using. They were, it turned out, junk dealers, and Alan and Ray made a note to do something about such characters some day.'

In reality, the genesis of the concept was not so easy, as Ray Galton remembers: 'People often ask us how we came up with the idea of rag 'n' bone men and the answer is simple – desperation!'

'We had quite literally dried up,' continues Simpson. 'After all that excitement and keenness about writing individual pieces for actors, we had run out of fresh ideas by number three. About four days went past and we couldn't think of a thing. When that happened, instead of just chatting about the weather or sitting there saying nothing, we would try to make each other laugh and hopefully get something we could use at the same time. We had a silly sort of private joke for our own amusement where we would come up with ridiculous ideas and conversations, like:

"What's George Sanders doing now?"
"He's now at Wimbledon dog track. He's just doing an up and down cross double on the one and three dog!"'

This game was the basis for the Galton and Simpson 'dialogue' style. There is an intriguing parallel between much of the writers' work and the writing situation the partnership found itself in. As often as not, the two men were 'locked' away in a room together desperately trying to coax fictional dialogues out of their imaginations. The frustration of the writing process and the frustration of being confined together for so long would, naturally, spill out on to the written page. Simpson remembers:

'When the ideas wouldn't come and the silly jokes weren't very silly, we would just muck about with the concept of two people in a room. Ray and I would try to think of the most outrageous ideas possible just to make each other laugh. For example, I would say, "There were two rat catchers at Buckingham Palace ...". It was always two of something! Anyway, after the fourth unproductive day during the painful process of thinking of the next *Comedy Playhouse*, Ray happened to say, 'There were two rag 'n' bone men ...', and I said, "Yeah, yeah – you'll never get a half-hour show out of two rag 'n' bone men." Famous last words!'

However, the throwaway notion was not dismissed so easily, as Simpson recalls:

> Another two or three hours of nothing went by and I said, 'Ere, what about those two rag 'n' bone men?' I think Ray had forgotten about them by then, but he said, 'Let's start!' It was an unusual occupation and as far as we knew it had never been done before, apart from by Syd Walker in his variety act. It was always about deadlines to beat with us, so we started: First rag 'n' bone man. Second rag 'n' bone man. We just had them arguing about the day's business. We didn't know who they were or what their relationship was. We just started writing. After about 10 pages it was flowing very nicely. We were getting a few jokes in, and Ray said, 'Well, we can't just go on like this. Who are they and what's going to happen? What's the story?' So we stopped and reread what we had done. It became clear that one of them was older than the other one. The older man was staying at home and not working because of his arthritis, and the one who'd been out on the round and was talking about getting another job was clearly a lot younger. Suddenly, it hit us – father and son. That was the breakthrough! It gave what we'd written a whole new meaning, and everything seemed to click into place. It really was like a shaft of light had come in through the window and made those previous 10 pages come alive. We were literally halfway through writing when the father and son notion came to us. We could then take an element from the first 10 pages, where the young man has picked up a golf club on the round, and return to that. This one golf club was his symbol of a better life, a tangible symbol of his need to get away from his father and improve himself with a higher class of person.

The all-important name of Steptoe was inspired by a real shop that Ray Galton knew well:

> Although the first one wasn't called *Steptoe and Son*, we did have to call the rag 'n' bone business in 'The Offer' something. The name Steptoe came from a little shop in Richmond, by the graveyard, just off Red Lion Street. Anyway, down this lane there were a few old Victorian shops, and one was a photographer's shop called Steptoe and Figge. I just thought that Steptoe was a wonderful name to use at some point and 'filed' it away. The rag 'n' bone men seemed to fit it perfectly.

In a schools' edition of *Steptoe* scripts that were published in 1971 Galton and Simpson observed, with the benefit of hindsight, that, 'We decided to make the son in his late thirties as this would heighten the tragic element in the situation of a son still tied to a dependent parent. If the son had been a young man, one would have the feeling that his life was still in front of him, that there was hope that he would eventually get away and create a new life for himself. Furthermore, this happened to be our own age as well, and a writer is always at his best writing about things and people he is familiar with.' Although both Galton and Simpson were actually only just into their thirties at the time, the young man's fate at the hands of his domineering father is clearly written from the heart. It introduces a darker note than had previously been seen within the fledgling sitcom format.

One thing was certain. When it came to casting 'The Offer', the original policy of the writers had to be rigorously adhered to. As Simpson comments:

Although we had used Eric Sykes and Stanley Baxter along the way, we didn't try to tailor the roles to their established comic strengths. It was, in effect, the use of a recognized comic in a 'proper' acting job. But for 'The Offer' we were determined to use two serious character actors. The material couldn't have been played by a familiar comic personality; it simply wouldn't have worked. A well-loved comedian has far too much baggage to lug around. For instance, you couldn't seriously have Eric Morecambe opening the door and finding a woman eight months pregnant on his doorstep saying, 'You are the father of my child.' If you did it, it would be a cheap gag. If Eric Morecambe played that situation it would lose its reality.

Galton agrees:

With actors you can convey true situations much more easily. In those days because of the constraints of their persona, no comedian would dare declare his or her political affiliation or sexuality. You couldn't do a comedy script with Tony Hancock raving on about serious socialism or expressing his personal opinions. To the public he was Tony Hancock on the screen and he was Tony Hancock off the screen. Actors could be anything and be anybody, whether it's Adolf Hitler or a cleaning lady, or even Adolf Hitler's cleaning lady.

The casting for 'The Offer' therefore needed good, experienced actors without any fixed television personas. These two players had to become Steptoe and Son in the eyes of the public. They should not end up merely as a couple of favourite actors playing the parts.

For the old man, both Galton and Simpson were agreed. They were keen to employ an actor by the name of Wilfrid Brambell. 'I had been called Wilfrid (with two 'i's) after my uncle, and Brambell after Wilfrid,' the actor often noted, although he was still frequently billed as 'Wilfred' on film and stage. Even his blue commemorative plaque, unveiled in 2000, continued to credit him incorrectly as Wilfred Brambell. Although only 49 years old at the time of casting for 'The Offer', Brambell was a prolific character player on television. But, he had never become a star name.

He was born on 22 March 1912 in Dublin, Ireland. His father was a cashier with the Guinness brewery, while his mother was an amateur opera singer. Brambell made his acting debut at the tender age of two, entertaining the wounded troops of the First World War on their return from the front line. On leaving school, the young Brambell worked as a cub reporter for the *Irish Times*, juggling this job with a burgeoning acting career, which began with him receiving the princely sum of 10 shillings a week for performing at the legendary Abbey Theatre in Dublin. 'The Abbey Theatre was born of a happy fusion of brilliantly wealthy Anglo-Irish brains, and magnificently malleable Irish talents,' he commented. 'Had those two forces never met and joined, Dublin would never have become at that time the centre of the world theatre.' Brambell was a regular in pioneering productions of the works of George Bernard Shaw at the Abbey, and he later appeared at the Gate Theatre, also in Dublin. Music was equally important to the young Brambell: 'My audience wanted numbers like "The Vicar" and "I Will Be There" rather than oratorio. For far too long I blindly persisted. I even won a gold medal in 1938 for singing oratorio. It was an aria from St Paul and it was years before I realized that perhaps the reason for my award was because the aria was entitled "Oh God have Mercy".'

During the Second World War Brambell toured with the Entertainments National Service Association, delighting hundreds of servicemen: 'I am grateful for the fact that our little company gave pleasure to fellows that needed it more than we did.' Following his demobilization, he continued his acting career with various repertory companies across England and Wales. He performed in Swansea, Bristol and Chesterfield, and at the same time started to write to radio producers. Desperate for regular work, and explaining that he couldn't afford the fare to come to London for auditions, he asked for guaranteed assignments. In the meantime, he was forced to accept a variety of jobs to support himself. On the brink of television stardom in 1962, Wilfrid Brambell reflected on his early struggle: 'I washed dishes, worked in radio cabs, took a job in a food office, helped with a car census ... and became a temporary postman in Mayfair.'

Luckily, Brambell made his first inroad into feature films soon after the end of the war, making his debut in Carol Reed's harrowing IRA drama *Odd Man*

Out, with James Mason, in 1947. He subsequently took a minor role in the Charles Crichton-directed Ealing comedy, *Another Shore*, with Stanley Holloway. Brambell eventually had his big theatrical break as one of four tailors in the revue *Happy-Go-Lucky*, written by Donal McDonagh and Liam Redmond. It marked his West End debut when it opened at the Mercury Theatre in 1950, later transferring to the Criterion, and also saw his television debut when a production was especially staged from Alexandra Palace. He subsequently secured regular touring work during the early part of the decade, notably turning his hand to a Shakespearean role as Grumio in the 1954 Hornchurch production of *The Taming of the Shrew*.

Despite his theatrical training, it was early television work that set him on the road to stardom. Brambell struck up a fruitful association with the respected producer Rudolph Cartier and appeared in his three BBC serials scripted by Nigel Kneale. He was a drunk in *The Quatermass Experiment*, a prisoner and an old man in *Nineteen Eighty-Four*, and a tramp in *Quatermass II*. All of these productions afforded Brambell only supporting roles, but the programmes instantly became national talking points and remain some of television's most celebrated drama productions.

For the actors involved, they proved extremely useful CV points. Almost immediately after the second *Quatermass*, Brambell was signed up by the fledgling commercial television company ATV. By the late 1950s he was appearing in classic BBC serials, with parts in *Our Mutual Friend* and *The History of Mr Polly*. Wilfrid Brambell was, in his own words, happy to accept 'loads of old men parts' despite not yet being 50.

However, the pivotal role of his career came when he was cast as an old tramp in *No Fixed Abode* for Granada's *Television Playhouse* series. As the actor remembered: 'A five-hander written by Clive Exton, it took place in a dosshouse dormitory where, for some eight hours, four social dropouts met and fused. It was a deep-thinking play with tremendous impact.' Indeed, it was this particular performance that clinched the casting of Albert Steptoe. Ray Galton remembers: 'This was exceptionally well acted by Brambell and fitted our ideas for Albert perfectly. We had also seen him in *Widowers' Houses*, George Bernard Shaw, all the other Clive Exton stuff, so we knew Brambell was good. There was no fear of his letting us down.'

Brambell's prolific output had led to his being dubbed, by less fortunate actors, as 'Old Neverstop', and fortunately he was also no stranger to comedy, with TV and film experience alongside old hands such as Arthur Askey, Brian Rix and Sid James. Galton and Simpson had found their perfect old man.

If anything, the casting of the old man's son in 'The Offer' was even more crucial. The character was, after all, the frustrated voice of the writers themselves. Again, both Ray Galton and Alan Simpson were immediately certain who they wanted to play the part. 'It seems strange to think it now,' remembers Simpson, 'but in the late 1950s Harry Corbett was the business. Whenever Harry was on television, every out-of-work actor – and that's more than most – would be in front of a television to watch him. I remember going to Gerry's Club. They had a television set, and the place was packed to the rafters with actors watching Harry Corbett. He had a great reputation as a method actor.' Galton continues: 'At the time, Harry Corbett was considered to be the Marlon Brando of this country. He was the actor's actor.'

'The public had never heard of him,' Simpson adds. 'He was known by the public as a supporting actor who played countless dreadful foreigners in English B-pictures. He was great at Spaniards and Italians because he looked swarthy, but the acting profession absolutely adored him. He was the crown prince of Joan Littlewood's Theatre Workshop Company.'

Corbett first met Joan Littlewood in 1952 and always considered it a life-changing experience. Talking in the late 1960s, he reflected on his early stage work:

> You suddenly discover that the audience believes you. They believe you really feel the thing you're playing. I was playing to people who were of the same origin as myself, and they firmly believed that this was the way working-class people should be portrayed on the stage, even though they themselves could see the evidence all around them that it was wrong and a lie. I wanted to get out of this completely. So I searched around for somebody else who reflected my point of view. Joan Littlewood was just starting Theatre Workshop and she held the same kind of views as I did.

Living in a house with the other members of the group, the actors bonded naturally and completely: 'We were doing a tour of the Northeast in the middle of February, playing to miners, miners' welfare homes. We played *Henry IV, Part 2*, *The Overcoat* by Gogol, and a mining documentary, of all things, to miners. Marvellous things came out of it, like the release of their everyday tensions.' As it toured with one-night stands, played the Edinburgh Festival and finally found a home at Stratford East, the Theatre Workshop was Corbett's passion: 'We went into this freewheeling atmosphere of the East End theatre, run-down and disreputable ... it suited our atmosphere perfectly, cocking a snook!' He made his West End debut as Sir Andrew Aguecheek in Shakespeare's *Twelfth Night* and went on to enjoy a multitude of parts, including Bob Cratchit in *A Christmas Carol* and Sir Politic Would-Be in *Volpone*: 'We did *The Dutch Courtesan* and *Hobson's Choice*. We did what we considered were the classics of different periods – we didn't care. We just threw them on, gave them a new slant.'

Eventually becoming a director of the company, Corbett graduated to leading roles, giving unique contemporary interpretations of the works of Shaw and Shakespeare: '*Richard II* was one of the happiest plays I've ever been in … all about truth, absolute searching truth.' The Workshop had deliberately and liberatingly staged it as a mockery of the concurrent staging of the play at the Old Vic. These reworkings of the classics sat easily with the Workshop's more experimental documentary pieces like Ewan MacColl's *Uranium 235*. By the end of 1961 Harry Corbett was one of the hottest stage actors in the country.

Born in Rangoon, Burma, at that time a province of India, on 28 February 1925, Corbett was the son of an officer in the British army. After his mother died, in 1928, Harry was raised by an aunt in Manchester, and caught the acting bug after seeing comedian Leslie Henson at the Manchester Opera House. During the last days of the Second World War he served in the Royal Marines and trained as a radiographer. Anxious to begin his acting career following his demob, he became an understudy at the Chorlton Repertory Company, and was awarded his first part – as the front legs of a cow – in *Dick Whittington*. Corbett stayed with the company for four years.

It was during this time that he added the 'H' to his stage name to distinguish himself from the creator and co-star of Sooty, Harry Corbett. In later years, when his comedy work had completely swamped his acting career, Corbett would happily tell interviewers that 'the "H" stands for "Hanything"'. It also proved useful shorthand for fellow actors. Wilfrid Brambell noted that, 'To his friends – one of which I hope I am – he is affectionately and monosyllabically known as H.'

Corbett's last role for the BBC before the *Comedy Playhouse* assignment had been a critically acclaimed appearance in *A Matter of Conscience*. But it was, naturally, his stage reputation that appealed to the *Comedy Playhouse* writers. Corbett was making big waves in the industry, both in the West End and in fringe theatre, with Stratford East, the Bristol Old Vic and the Langham Experimental Group. At the time that he was offered the *Comedy Playhouse* script, he was starring in a two-week season as Macbeth at the Bristol Old Vic. Alan Simpson chuckles:

> Ray always says he was doing *Henry IV* and I always say he was doing *Richard III*, but he was doing one of the classics, that's for sure …

maybe he was doing *Richard IV*! Anyway, he was doing a two-week engagement. He got the script, said he would love to do it and they let him off the second week. We really were writing 'The Offer' with Harry H. Corbett in mind to play Harold. We wanted Wilfrid, of course, but he was very much a jobbing actor. We were pretty convinced we would get Willie but we didn't really think we would get Harry. Corbett was this wonderfully experimental actor, and both Ray and I thought he was ideal for the part.

Galton and Simpson, having decided on their 'wish list' casting for 'The Offer', told producer Duncan Wood to put an availability check on Wilfrid Brambell and Harry H. Corbett and to offer them the parts. 'We were only about halfway through the script at that time,' remembers Ray Galton. The letters to both actors were dated 5 December 1961. Wood's correspondence with Brambell reflects the fact that the role had pretty much been accepted: 'I spoke to Joan Reddin [Brambell's agent] this afternoon and she tells me that you would like to see a script of the *Comedy Playhouse* episode in which, I gather, all is well for you to appear. Here it is. The part obviously is that of Albert, and Harry Corbett, we hope, is going to play Harold. I hope you like the part.' The letter addressed to Harry H. Corbett finalized the casting. It acknowledged Corbett's current run in classical theatre: 'We would like you to play Harold, with Wilfrid Brambell as Albert. I understand from your agent that all will hinge on whether you like the script or not. I hope you do. Perhaps you would let me know as soon as you can. PS: I am sure the script is over-long, and we can probably cut it to the equivalent of *Macbeth*.'

'We only discovered years later,' recalls Ray Galton, 'that both of them were signed up under a drama contract and thus got drama rates, which were, in those days, notoriously minuscule in comparison with light entertainment rates. They were actually offered something like 90 guineas each for "The Offer".'

The writers did have alternatives in mind should Brambell and Corbett turn out to be unavailable, as Alan Simpson recalls: 'If Harry had said he couldn't do it, then we would have gone with Ronald Fraser. Our second choice for old man Steptoe was J. G. Devlin.' Devlin would later be cast as the convict 'reflection' of Albert in the 1972 episode 'The Desperate Hours'.

'He was another actor well known for playing old-men parts,' continues Simpson, 'although the fact that both he and Willie Brambell were Irish character actors was purely coincidental. They just both fitted the bill. Devlin, if cast, would have been asked to play it cockney, as Brambell did, as would Ronnie Fraser, and he was a Scotsman! He had just played a cockney prisoner in a prison drama, *Slopping Out*, an Alun Owen piece, and he had been excellent in that and would have been ideal as Harold.'

In the event, Corbett and Brambell both accepted the roles with alacrity. Brambell delighted in the work of 'those overtalented writers Ray Galton and Alan Simpson'. For Corbett, 'The Offer' was the fulfilment of an acting ambition. As he said, he

> ... had met Galton and Simpson slightly and told them how much I really admired their work. I really did, and I said if ever they felt like writing anything ... of course, I never envisaged in a thousand years coming over into light entertainment. Anyway, I looked at television, and all I saw that was making any kind of good social comment was the Hancocks, the Eric Sykes ... Oh, I did envy them. So Galton and Simpson remembered this conversation, obviously took me at my word, and this thing about the rag 'n' bone men thumped through the door. I read it and immediately wired back: 'Delicious, delighted, cannot wait to work on it.' I thought, this is brilliant. Good work is always easy. You don't even have to learn the lines. They're there, they're right, and they're the lines you should say.

The rehearsal schedule was set from 10.30 a.m. on Thursday 28 December 1961 through to 3 January 1962 at the Sulgrave Boys' Club. From the moment the cast and crew met for the first time, it was clear that something special was being brought together. Ray Galton remembers:

> Tom Sloan, the guy who had given us the chance to do the *Comedy Playhouse* series in the first place, was obviously aware of how good this programme could be. On the very first day of rehearsals he quietly came over to us, cleared his throat conspiratorially, and said, 'You know what you've got here, don't you?' And we said, 'No, no, no ...' with sincere innocence. We knew it was good, but you never imagine how good someone else may think it is. Anyway, Tom Sloan said, 'Oh, come on, there's a series here. This is wonderful, it's a series!' We were horrified. We blurted out, 'Oh, no ... no, no, no, there's not a series!' It was the last thing we wanted. We had just done 10 years with Hancock and got away from all that. If we were contracted to do a series of the rag 'n' bone men we thought it would be a case of being back on the treadmill. For a whole week Sloan continually tried to persuade us to change our mind. The offer for a series was there on a silver platter even before 'The Offer' had been screened.

At the rehearsal stage, however, one of the leading actors certainly wasn't prepared for the filming requirements of a *Comedy Playhouse* episode. As

Galton recalls:

> Because we were rehearsing in scout huts and boys' clubs and the like, you never got into the studio until the day of recording. Anyway, Harry Corbett – very much the actors' laddie, dear boy – came into the studio and said, 'What are all these seats doing here?' We said, 'Well, they're for the audience.' He was absolutely appalled. He said, 'Audience – what audience?' He thought he was doing a television drama, and he didn't realize that us chaps at BBC Light Entertainment did things a little differently ... like invite a load of unpaying punters into the studio to watch it being recorded. Like most of our performers, he wasn't expecting any laughs, you see! He said, 'I shall have to rethink my entire performance.' He thought it was a piece of drama for television and thus wouldn't have an audience. Mind you, whatever he did to change his performance worked. It was beautiful to watch ... it still is.

As for Wilfrid Brambell, Alan Simpson remembers: 'The most memorable thing about that first rehearsal for me was the sight of Wilfrid Brambell turning up for work. He was in the full old actor gear: beautifully dressed, cut-glass accent, expensive cigarette case, immaculate manners. Of course, when he started reading the old man dialogue it was hilarious. This wonderful contrast between the man and the part – this was real acting!'

The pre-filming Costume and Make-up sheet for 'The Offer', dated 11 December 1961, details the quintessential 'look' of Harold and Albert from the outset. Harry H. Corbett was to be clothed in a 'tatty old overcoat – torn in places. Very dirty and battered. Playing age is about 38. He hasn't shaved. Sideboards – a bit gypsyish', while Wilfrid Brambell was to wear a 'dirty old torn black overcoat too long for him. Dirty old black homburg. Playing age is about 60. A scruffy old man unshaven for about a day and a half.' And so the iconic image of Steptoe and Son was established.

The day after the rehearsal period, the play was recorded 'as live' at BBC Television Centre, and 'The Offer' was first broadcast the following day, 5 January 1962, between an episode of Dr Kildare and the evening news. Although the Radio Times trumpeted the show, it was no more or less gushing than it had been for the three previous Comedy Playhouse efforts. Alan Simpson told the magazine that, 'In half an hour you can't really develop more than one or two characters'. The Radio Times continued: 'Tonight's play has the kind of shape within which they really like to work. There are only two speaking parts – a rag 'n' bone man and his son – the third character being a horse.' Wilfrid Brambell, also interviewed by the journal, commented:

'I suppose every actor has to get into dustbin drama sooner or later nowadays!' After rather incongruously describing the show as 'gentle humour', the *Radio Times* summary revealed that, 'Conducting a rag 'n' bone business means two things – collecting the stuff and flogging it. The old-established firm of Steptoe and Son are doing quite well on the first count, but on the second ...' Nothing would change for the next 10 years or so.

Viewing 'The Offer' as the first of a series rather than as a one-off play it is amazing how complete both the characters and the performances were from the outset. Both Brambell and Corbett hit the floor running. The beginning – the energetically upbeat *Comedy Playhouse* theme, and the maniacally active, unmanned typewriter banging out the latest Galton and Simpson offering – is disorientating for the general *Steptoe* viewer, but the essence of the series is in evidence from the very first frame of the programme proper. Indeed, once the credit sequence is completed, Ron Grainer's immortal *Steptoe and Son* theme plods out over a grainy, pitiful image of a depressed and exhausted Harry H. Corbett clip-clopping through Shepherd's Bush on his horse and cart.

Such was the popularity of 'The Offer' that Pye records released a single of 'Old Ned' and 'Happy Joe' – the *Comedy Playhouse* theme – in 1962, even before a *Steptoe* series was commissioned.

The bleakness of the opening scene, with its pioneering use of rather murky location filming, and the exhaustion of the totter after a hard day's work contrast with the buoyancy of Grainer's 'Old Ned' signature tune. And Corbett's weary performance is perfect. With the atmosphere of gloom and dejection already in place, the appearance of Brambell's wiry old man completes the picture, and provokes the initial burst of – albeit almost inaudible – querulous banter between the two. Brambell claims an iconic moment in television history as he closes the junkyard gates behind him. His action reveals the shabbily painted legend 'Steptoe and Son Scrap Merchants'.

The two actors were an instant and perfect match. 'They seemed to click into place in the first show,' recalls Alan Simpson. 'And they stayed like that.' Wilfrid Brambell and Harry H. Corbett had performed on television together before, both appearing in the 1959 adaptation of Turgenev's *Torrents of Spring*, with Corbett in the juvenile lead as Sonny, and Brambell as Mr Connor. Speaking in 1967, Corbett recalled the making of *Torrents of Spring*:

> We started with the idea of translating the story into contemporary life. Then we said, here's something that's usually done in a serial over a long period of time. But we wished to do it in a single play, get the essence of it. We'll call this the new television we wish to go for. So we

more or less got hold of the content and bones of the thing, and threw them away; then we got everybody together in the room, improvized it, and we taped it. It was the beginning of what I believe I'm known for, working with cameras.

The actors' experience with each other is clearly at play in 'The Offer'. The chemistry between Brambell and Corbett is evident from the very beginning. They have a split-second sense of each other's timing, inflections and dramatic pauses, and their partnership goes beyond simply the polish of immaculate rehearsal, into the realms of instinctive mutual awareness. This is all the more amazing given that no one at the time believed this to be anything other than a one-off encounter.

The first exchange of the script is representative of what is to come: the tone is set by the resentment and discord caused by the generation gap. The old man, showing more concern for the horse than for his own flesh and blood, is vindictive, nit-picking and dissatisfied. Asserting his authority as the head of both the business and the family, he immediately voices his dismay at the shortage of brass and lead on the load. He attacks his offspring's lack of business sense and bemoans the next generation with a bile-ridden, 'What sort of totter are you?'

But Harold emerges from his apparent dejection with mischievous glee, and announces his piece of news – he has been offered another job. The old man is completely winded by this long-dreaded revelation: his son is leaving home. Harold enjoys the old man's reaction and plays on it throughout the episode using the threat of his escape to countermand the lack of respect and responsibility he suffers from his father. We gather almost from the beginning that the offer is insubstantial, possibly illusory, but for Harold it is a psychological lifeline, a last chance to get away while the going is reasonably good.

Harold's preoccupation with self-improvement is shown from the beginning, as he hazards ill-informed opinions on Chinese vases and porcelain. Throughout the episode, his aspiration to be a man of letters and his attachment to the precious symbols of sophistication that he has scraped together reveal his antecedents in Galton and Simpson's previous 'creation', Tony Hancock. But Corbett provokes pity rather than mockery as he boasts of the contents of his library only to reappear with a scant collection of four volumes neatly tied with string. All he has is his tattered chair, his half-completed wine collection and his pitiful four books. The fruits of his struggle for freedom, individuality and respectability are all loaded on to a handcart that is going nowhere.

Despite the clear similarities between Hancock and Corbett – in their expressive, mournful eyes, their vocal intonations and their flights of fantasy – Ray Galton maintains: 'We never consciously cast Harry in the wake of Hancock, but obviously the set-up was similar. The yearning for a better life, the aspirations above his station, all that sort of thing was very much like Hancock – that *Sunday Times* colour supplement knowledge of life.'

'And the old man was there to bring him down to earth,' continues Simpson. 'Just like Sid did with Hancock. He was the voice of reality, the "with all these big ideas, you're being too grand" reasoning.' Throughout *Steptoe*, Harold often uses vintage Hancock terminology. There are suggestions of Hancock in the episode 'Upstairs, Downstairs, Upstairs, Downstairs,' and in the film *Steptoe and Son Rides Again* Harold is even heard to mutter the immortal exclamation, 'Stone me!' Indeed, Alan Simpson reveals: 'At one time we were discussing a remake of all the Tony Hancock shows with Harry. That would have been after *Steptoe* had finished. Intriguing, isn't it?'

Writing in 1971, Galton and Simpson acknowledged their debt to their earlier series: 'Steptoe Junior and his father are in many ways an extension of the characters of Tony Hancock and Sidney James in the old *Hancock's Half Hour* series. The conflicts between the two sets of characters are also often based on common ground. However, the *Steptoe* series explores its characters in more depth.' Indeed, Corbett's moment of optimism in 'The Offer' is nigh impossible to watch when the viewer knows beforehand that this will be as good as it gets for a long, long time.

Wilfrid Brambell also comes to his role with the essence of his character fully formed. The old man's ethos is in place from the first heart attack he fakes in order to get his own way. It is a trick in which, the script tells us, his son is already well versed. Indeed, as we become privy to the old man's miraculous recoveries and recurrent attacks as his son wanders in and out of the scene we get an immediate insight into his manipulative character. But Harold doesn't need to see the old man's sudden improvements and deteriorations. He's seen it all before. This knowledge of the Steptoes' strained, knowing relationship makes the characters familiar and appealing from the moment we meet them. Although we have never seen the characters before, the superb performances allow us to experience their humdrum existence as something that has been played and replayed many times. The occasional fumbled line or lost expression, as Brambell the actor is glimpsed behind the befuddled Albert Steptoe, is endearing in itself.

Ray Galton admits: 'Later we did get very exasperated with Willie Brambell for stumbling on a line during a performance, as we couldn't go back and do it again unless it was a total disaster. The takes were just so long, sometimes as much as 20 minutes, that you couldn't justify rerecording for the odd fumbled word. Brambell fluffed dialogue quite often and I would scream, "He's ruined it!" We were very precious in those days! In my mind any stumble on a line meant the joke was lost, and if it happened at all it was the old man doing it, but seeing the shows now you think, what was our problem? There's a little fluff, so what?' Alan Simpson remarks: 'He was playing an old man, so you can forgive it within the characterization, and apart from that Willie was always very professional. He was a good actor and could recover very well and very quickly.'

Old man Steptoe's hoarding instinct and his pathetic love of 'beautiful' things – actually worthless pieces of junk – soften the harshness of the character. The plate that he values so highly is painfully apt in its shabby appearance. The script does not specify that it should be particularly dilapidated, but the props department's offering allows Brambell to get excited over a cracked and broken 'find'. However, Corbett's flight of educated fancy as he appraises the item is at best short-sighted, and at worst completely inaccurate. As he chastises the old man's ignorance, Harold's own 'expertise', the very quality that he believes will free him from this shoddy business, is exposed as lacking. Although the old man is convinced by Harold's opinions and is hurt by the dismissal of his old, experienced 'eye' for a bargain, Corbett's performance suggests that he knows he himself is walking on very thin ice. Harold knows as little about antiques as his father does. The audience, picking up his faux pas, realizes it too.

The cluttered grandeur of the Steptoe home adds further depth to the performances. As Corbett enters the living room, realizing from the haphazard display of 'precious things' that his father is up to something, he removes his cap and places it on the stuffed head of a leopard. It gets a laugh, but it isn't consciously a bit of funny business. For both Harold Steptoe and Harry H. Corbett, this is the most natural thing in the world: 'Although I've put a lot of myself into Harold Steptoe,' Corbett reflected, 'we had a lot in common right from the start.'

As the episode draws to a close, it is a testament to both the writers and actors that the viewer's sympathy shifts from one character to the other with almost every line of dialogue. We can, regardless of age or experience, empathize with both of them.

Albert Steptoe's vindictive joy in refusing to allow his son the use of the 'family' horse reveals his essential selfishness, but the frailty and helplessness that

Brambell brings to his performance suggests a frightened, lonely person who hides insecurity with a ruthless streak. Brambell embodies the vulnerability of impending age in his hunched posture, shuffling walk and wounded expression. The leers and grunts – which would become assured and often overused crowd-pleasers in the years to follow – are used sparingly here. The pathetic gesture with which he offers his son the plate is poignantly played. The son's dismissive rejection of this most prized possession symbolizes his rejection of his father, and Brambell's performance shows that the character realizes this only too well. And so our attachment shifts from the junior to the senior member of the household. The script gives no conclusive indication as to whose side the audience should be on, and that is the real beauty of the piece.

This was very much a new sort of comedy and, indeed, a new sort of television. Attention to the working classes was a rarity, but actually making them the heroes of a sitcom was ground-breaking in the extreme. The audience for this landmark production was still very much tuned in to a more unsubtle, lowbrow style of comedy. During this first half-hour of *Steptoe* perhaps the biggest laugh comes from the sight of a lavatory lugged off the cart by the disgruntled young man. By the end of the programme, great swathes of the emotionally charged dialogue are met with complete silence.

Brambell's desperate cunning and Corbett's determination to cut loose are interspersed with just the occasional comic line. Indeed, by the close only the odd member of the studio audience can produce a subdued chuckle at Brambell's tearful, affectionate reassurances. The near-tragedy of the last scene, as Brambell looks on helplessly while the son he loves seems to collapse with despair, is as powerful as *Steptoe* ever got. The audience is speechless. One can imagine why series potential was seen in 'The Offer': it is powerful, meaningful and, above all, real.

Alan Simpson was delighted not to get any laughs during the conclusion:

> We watched that closing scene as Harry literally crumbles. He's trying to push his meagre belongings away and start a new life, and he can't do it. We were watching this scene and Harry actually broke down and cried and I thought, real tears! This is what it's all about ... this is acting! We weren't used to it with writing for comedians. Usually it would be stylized, shoulder-lurching sobs when comics cried. Harry really got hold of that final scene. It was real drama to him.

The writers' avoidance of the easy-laugh conclusion marked the start of a new sensitivity. This wasn't just comedy any more; this was real life. 'In *Steptoe and Son*, Ray Galton and Alan Simpson have evolved a character drama entirely new to television: deeper, truer, sadder, funnier than anything that has gone before. It's really tragicomedy, which is the essence of everyday life,' intoned Harry H. Corbett in 1965. As Ray Galton comments as regards comic portrayal of the working classes: 'I can't think of anybody else who was trying to make you laugh and cry at the same time like we were trying to do.'

Chapter 3

Money is the Root
of all Evil

The first recorded reaction to 'The Offer' within the BBC was typical of the corporation's bureaucratic reputation. It was the show's producer Duncan Wood's official defence of the show's unusually long running time of 30 minutes and 10 seconds. In a memo of 6 January 1962, Wood explained that the programme had been 'practically uneditable. There are only two people in the cast, and the running shots necessary make editing very difficult indeed.' But the initial reaction to the show which began to filter through a week later was enough to justify his decision. On 11 January, Wood was delighted to hear from the Information Office, Manchester, that 'Mrs Jack La Rue, widow of the famous film actor [in fact, he was very much alive], who was over here from California for Christmas, rang to say how much she enjoyed *Comedy Playhouse* on 5 January – quite the finest thing she has seen on television in this country.'

The Audience Research Report, published on 25 January, expressed nationwide appreciation of 'The Offer'. Although some audiences preferred the flippant, purely comic elements of the show, seeing 'nothing more than "a jolly good laugh" and a "most amusing sketch" about two "terribly comic characters"', it is clear that it 'meant far more to others'. Many viewers believed it 'had the hallmarks of comedy at its very best, in that tears were never far from laughter', and that the actors gave 'extremely sensitive and sympathetic interpretations of the two characters, which marked them as character actors of exceptional perception and talent'. The dental surgeon who perceived it as 'a hateful, nasty play. A sordid, inconsequential interlude between a rogue and a fool' was clearly in the minority. Tom Sloan, keen on the concept since the first day of rehearsal, was still pushing for a series based on the trials and tribulations of the rag 'n' bone partnership.

Despite all the public and critical acclaim showered on the programme, Ray Galton and Alan Simpson were still reluctant to concede to the idea of a series. For them 'The Offer' had been a very good script and, undoubtedly, the pick of the *Comedy Playhouse* series, but it was designed and executed as a one-off. It was simply 'an exploration of the relationship between two people of different generations, trapped in their own environment and completely interdependent' and, as Alan Simpson continues: 'With "The Offer" we thought, "We've written a little piece of Pinter here and we can't repeat it." We actually didn't want to try to repeat it, but still Tom Sloan badgered us.' So insistent was Sloan that, as early as 12 January 1962, a standard information sheet instructed that 'The Offer' 'must be retained longer than 24 hours after transmission because of "possible repeat". Please therefore hold the tape until June 30 1962'. Clearly, 'The Offer' was being earmarked for 'pilot' position. Sloan would not drop his suggestions for a series.

Duncan Wood wrote personally to both Brambell and Corbett on 15 January 1962. His note to Corbett said: 'Now that I am clear of the *Comedy Playhouse* factory for a couple of weeks, just a line to congratulate you on an outstanding performance in "The Offer". It is a long time since we had such reaction to an individual show. Quite apart from this, it was one of the most enjoyable rehearsal weeks I have spent. Please give me a ring when you are free and come up and have a drink.' With the actors suitably congratulated, the onus was back on the writers to agree to a series.

Finally, Galton and Simpson ran out of excuses. As Ray Galton recalls:

> We let our natural cowardice come out! For weeks and weeks we had said no. Everything we tried to put in the way of a series Sloan knocked down immediately. In the end we decided to put the emphasis on somebody else. The only excuse that seemed to be reasonable was the problem we had experienced with Harry Corbett being uneasy about television work in front of an audience. We really piled on the concern for Harry, making out that he had an absolute abhorrence of doing television with an audience, and that, of course, without Harry we couldn't possibly even consider doing a series.

Alan Simpson remembers: 'We didn't think Harry would do it. We thought he was an actor, doing his Shakespeare.'

'Foolishly, we struck a deal that if both Harry and Willie were happy about doing a series, we would do it,' continues Galton. 'The BBC thought, fair enough, and Sloan immediately got on to them, offered them a lot more money and they both jumped at it. They were only getting ninety guineas a week being legitimate actors. That's the difference between drama rates and variety rates. There's no money in being serious!'

The agents for Brambell (Joan Reddin Limited) and Corbett (Fraser & Dunlop) were duly approached with regard to the actors' availability between 30 April and 21 June 1962. On 23 January a BBC memo detailed the situation with the artists concerned:

1. Wilfrid Brambell – He has a standing commitment to go into the next Walt Disney feature film [*The Three Lives of Thomasina*]. He has recently completed one of these [*In Search of the Castaways*] and this next one is due to start production on 30 April. However, it is anticipated that he will not be required until the last half of the film and the Disney production office is letting us know. Apart from this he has no other commitments over the period in question and both he and his agent are in favour of his acceptance. 2. Harry H. Corbett – Over this same period Harry Corbett has no commitments whatsoever. His agent, Gordon Black, is in favour of his acceptance, but so far has not spoken to Harry Corbett himself. This conversation will take place within the next 24 hours and we will be informed as soon as possible.

On 24 January 1962 Duncan Wood commented on the expected expenses of the production: 'We must assume, I suppose with regret, that we shall be asked for special fees from these two. Would you please let me know what we eventually get away with.' Wood also revealed, in a letter dated 29 January 1962, that 'I learnt from Mary O'Brien this afternoon that she is having some trouble in the contracting of Harry H. Corbett and Wilfrid Brambell for this series. Apparently the situation is that for 'The Offer' we paid Corbett 75 guineas and Wilfrid Brambell 100 guineas in both cases plus rehearsal and filming fees, which totalled approximately 25 guineas each. After initial negotiation, these artists' agents are asking 150 guineas plus rehearsal/filming for Corbett and 175 guineas all-in for Brambell.' Having come up against opposition to this settlement, Wood asked Tom Sloan to 'liaise with Bush Bailey in the very near future, otherwise we might stand a chance of losing both these artists. We surely *must* recognize that we are now casting these two actors in *star* parts.' Wood even exaggerated somewhat, saying that 'scripts are commissioned' to add to the sense of urgency. In the end, the artists got their fee.

Financial benefits apart, Corbett was apparently delighted to return to the character. Interviewed by the *Radio Times* as part of the June 1962 promotion for the series, he said: 'To get the chance of building a character like Harold in "The Offer" was wonderful – to be able to develop this character for a further five episodes is paradise for an actor.' Interestingly, this belief in the series was reflected in the BBC's reverential treatment of *Steptoe and Son*. In the *Radio Times* it wasn't billed as Light Entertainment but came under the more weighty heading of Plays and Films. However, in retrospect, Corbett revealed that his initial thoughts were pretty much akin to those of the writers. Speaking in 1972, he explained: 'When I first heard they wanted to make it into a series, my immediate reaction was that the BBC wanted as usual to kill something good that they had got. We moaned and groaned but eventually agreed and the BBC were proved dead right as usual.'

In public, Wilfrid Brambell was cheerfully philosophical about re-creating Albert Steptoe in a series. For him it was just another 'old man job' and one, at the tender age of 50, that he had already perfected long ago. His private concern was that the series might overexpose him: 'I shied off, terrified by the prospect of that man-eating medium. So many actors who had won success in popular television serials had already slipped silently into anonymity when their writers' inspiration died. In fear of following them I staunchly refused Tom Sloan's offer. The BBC upped the ante and eventually I reluctantly succumbed, as do we all to the tempting, beckoning finger of Mammon.' Swallowing his professional pride and taking the job, Brambell told the *Radio Times*: 'Today it takes me longer to look 50 than it does to look 80. I don't use make-up, I just stop shaving for a few days, they dirty me down a bit, and that's it. Where other actors get film parts that take them to glamorous places like Bermuda and Tahiti, my broken-down characters always seem to end up somewhere like Shepherd's Bush or the Elephant and Castle.' Both actors were comfortable and assured in their roles, and almost overnight Brambell and Corbett became Steptoe and Son, sacrificing their own identities for the characters. The notion of mistaken identities became something of a joke to the two, as when Corbett was almost thrown out of BBC Television Centre because he was considered an undesirable, or when Brambell was recognized by the only two other British travellers on the Greek island of Aegina and was greeted with 'Albert Steptoe, I presume!' In the first flush of success, the actors revelled in the nation's recognition of the programme.

On 9 February 1962 Ray Galton and Alan Simpson signed the contract for a series of *Steptoe and Son*. They agreed to write five more half-hour scripts to add to 'The Offer', which was to be repeated the week before the new episodes were screened, and Alan Simpson recalls: 'All five were mostly set in and around the rag 'n' bone yard and the Steptoe house. We were just trying to extend the relationship we had already tackled in the *Comedy Playhouse* carry-on with the same claustrophobic existence.' As Ray Galton remembers: 'There was never anything grand about our plan for *Steptoe*. We just shut those gates and there they were, just talking together.'

'That's all we needed.' Simpson continues: 'We would start afresh each morning. We would work through the day, go out, switch off, have a drink, go home and come back the next day to start again.' Galton adds: 'I very rarely switched off, to be honest. I had ideas floating around most of the time. I would then come in the next morning and say to Alan, "How about so and so for this episode?" and we would work from there.'

Duncan Wood returned to the helm for the first series of *Steptoe and Son*. Simpson remembers Wood as 'a wonderful man … we had been working with him since the very first days of the television *Hancock's Half Hour* shows. We learnt how to do television together. He was a good judge of what should and what should not stay. Very often it meant losing some of our favourite lines, but it was ultimately his decision and invariably he was dead right about the parts that had to go.' Wood was aware of how much further *Steptoe and Son* could go in comparison with *Hancock's Half Hour*. '*Steptoe* is comedy in depth – high comedy with a flow of tragedy underneath. It is a more dramatic type of show than *Hancock*; it's strong meat. *Hancock* is more innocuous … the Steptoes produce a more violent reaction – be it for or against.'

By 9 April 1962 Duncan Wood was in a position to instruct Brambell and Corbett: 'Please find enclosed the first script of the new series. As you will see it is again slightly longer than *Macbeth* for both of you. However, I think it is another good piece of material and I can therefore only wish you both the very best of luck.' Wood proposed to keep the series very much in the vein of 'The Offer'. On 16 February he had written: 'Since I would like to achieve continuity in the design style, I would be most grateful if you could allocate Malcolm Goulding to design these shows.' Goulding was assigned the job, but almost immediately Wood had a fight on his hands over the show's running time. The powers that be thought that, like the last series with Tony Hancock, the show should be made up of 25-minute episodes. Furthermore, it was again suggested that 'The Offer' be edited down, this time to fit the time slot for the new series. On 21 February Wood explained: 'I do not think this can possible [sic] be edited to the extent required.' Tom Sloan agreed, although it wouldn't be the last time that the 25-minute *Steptoe* idea would be considered.

Although it was agreed that everything about 'The Offer' had been nearly perfect, even the location, there was still room for small improvements, and the *Steptoe* house later found itself on Oil Drum Lane. 'That,' remembers Galton, 'was our little homage to the fact that in Victorian times anything to do with modernity was captured and put on street signs. You had names like Electricity Lane, and there was a place in Hammersmith called Pumping Station Lane, which I loved. Oil Drum Lane sounded worse!' Simpson remembers it slightly differently: 'I've always said that it was actually called Oil Drum Lane. Where the Cromwell Road extension is cut into two halves in Hammersmith, I'm sure one of those was Oil Drum Lane, but I could be wrong. We certainly used Oil Drum Lane in one of the television *Hancock* shows, "The Missing Page". It's such a wonderful name.'

The actual junkyard location for 'The Offer' was at 147 St Anne's Road, London W12, a stone's throw from Duncan Wood's office. The owners, T. & E. Watts, were paid £10 10s for use of the yard. For the series, their other premises, at 25 Norwood Lane, Shepherd's Bush, were used as the exterior of the Steptoes' business. As the *Radio Times* reported, this site was 'just round the corner from BBC TV Centre, London, and sections of the yard were duplicated in the studio'. The authentic-looking cobblestones on the studio set were made out of rubber to make things more comfortable for the actors.

Sydney Lotterby, Duncan Wood's assistant, recontacted genuine rag 'n' bone man Chris Arnold with regard to the *Steptoe* series. On 24 April 1962 he wrote requesting that 'the cart has to be the same one as we used previously, and could your brother [Arthur Arnold] be with us to look after the horse. Incidentally, it would help us if the horse could be a little less frisky than the one we had last time.'

The rehearsal schedule for the first series of *Steptoe and Son* was set from 7 May to 12 June 1962, at the billiard room of the Sulgrave Boys' Club. Composer Ron Grainer was retained for the series' incidental music. The theme was newly recorded by Grainer and his musicians, and a memo of 8 June also noted that 'a new opening title sequence was edited on to the front of the tape [for "The Offer"], which included the new signature tune'. This had clearly sent Duncan Wood into confusion, for on 7 June he was reprimanded by the presentation editor for informing him that that day's rescreening of 'The Offer' would run to 30 minutes and 5 seconds when 'in fact it ran to 29 minutes and 36 seconds and did not help us to make a tidy junction into the *News* as planned'.

Galton and Simpson explained in 1971 that 'we had no preconceived ideas of how the series would develop. It was not necessarily about two rag 'n' bone men. They could be two bankers, two doctors, two anything. The important factor is the way they react to each other, although the rag 'n' bone yard does provide a bizarre lower-depths type of background which not only gives an added source of comedy but also has the effect of making us all feel safer, and superior to them, though not, we are pleased to say, without compassion.' For Harry H. Corbett:

> ... the rag 'n' bone trade didn't mean a thing; I wasn't interested in a documentary about rag 'n' bone men. It gave a perfect format and a set-up to range and slash all over the place. I mean, with Harold the domestic work is over and done within five or ten minutes. Then it's all politics, sex, general economics, the Church; it's about a thousand and one things, but it's certainly not about the rag 'n' bone business. That was of no interest to us.

Frank Muir, one of Galton and Simpson's scriptwriting heroes, firmly believed that they set the whole thing in a junkyard merely 'to annoy the props department'. But quite apart from the visual pleasure that the cluttered living room affords, it also complements the frustrated dialogue of the protagonists, and provides a real sense of the father and son firmly embedded in their social and cultural heritage.

Harry H. Corbett caught the flavour of the scripts immediately and identified with Harold's predicament:

> He has his dreams all day, and so do we; it's in all of us, and we never lose it. And he's a man in the grip of that terrifying dilemma – how long do you stand by your duties and let life slip away from you? There are so many people in the same situation. A lot is written about the problems of teenagers and old folk, but the thirties have their troubles too, and to me *Steptoe* is basically an exploration of this theme. It's a marriage of light entertainment and drama, it's a tragicomedy – and that's life.

Galton and Simpson, blessed with an actor of the calibre of Harry H. Corbett, found it relatively easy to script these vicissitudes of thirty-something life: 'We were able to have Harold draw on experiences, memories and nostalgia that we shared with him: the 1930s, Munich, the war, rationing, the fervent desire for a socialist Utopia that never came, and the inhibitions of his generation towards the opposite sex.'

The first series brilliantly built on the expectations that 'The Offer' had established. Wilfrid Brambell's old man Steptoe, for the first time credited as 'Albert' though not initially referred to as such in the dialogue, is revealed to be even more cunning and wicked than we at first thought. But still his pathological fear of being left alone imbues his cantankerous persona with feeling and pathos.

Unlike in the 'pilot' episode, where the outcome of Harold's job offer is very much in the lap of the gods, in the first official episode of *Steptoe and Son*, entitled 'The Bird' and recorded on 16 May 1962, the old man has a hand in his own destiny. Once again Harold is talking about leaving the family business and home, but this time the major threat to the old man's peace of mind is, predictably, a girlfriend. Albert's reaction contains the usual mixture of suspicion, pathetic acceptance and, more unexpected, genuine consideration for his son. At one point he practically pleads with him to bring the young lady back for supper. But, behind the goodwill, the old man is shamelessly interfering and he ultimately scuppers Harold's chance of happiness, however fleeting that chance might have been. Having arranged a slap-up meal for three, Harold endures Albert's relentless commentary on the girl's late arrival, his suggestions that she's out with another man and his satisfaction over the fact that she has humiliated his son. But, goaded past breaking point, Harold eventually loses his temper, smashing up the dining arrangements and greeting the arrival of the lady in question very coldly. The relationship is brutally severed when he presents her with a plate of fish and chips, picked up off the floor. Harold's evening is completed as the old man puts the clock back an hour, revealing that the girlfriend had not been late after all. For Ray Galton, 'That was the nastiest thing the old man ever did. Such cruelty!'

'But a good ending,' offers Alan Simpson. 'A very good ending. One of the best we ever did.'

It had been four months since 'The Offer' was broadcast, but the cast and crew worked meticulously for a perfect re-creation of the characters. Wardrobe mistress Jane Roberts and make-up supervisor Jean Lord used original publicity photographs to reproduce exactly their look, and were given the option of running through the tape of 'The Offer' in case they wanted to take notes for continuity.

Elements first introduced in the pilot – the disgusted cry of 'You dirty old man!' and the old man's obsession with the horse – were resurrected and the sight gag of Harold brushing horse manure off his shoe and giving a look of sophisticated indignation is repeated at the very start of 'The Bird' episode. Albert's miserly cunning is reintroduced as he heats old torch batteries for that extra bit of power, while his wistful reflections on 'fighting for my king and country' further widens the gulf of experience that divides the two.

In this opening episode, humour arises naturally from the situation and no consciously 'funny' lines are used. Instead, the dialogue dips into darker areas than sitcoms can normally cover, sometimes revealing uncomfortable memories. It is extremely rare, and was completely unheard of in 1962, for a sitcom character to berate his father for domestic violence, but Harold does so here as he painfully recalls the blows he received as a seven-year-old. As with 'The Offer', the script manages to convey both points of view with equal validity. Harold's resentment and anger appear reasonable and justified, yet the old man, with his mournful expression and his regret for his 'spare the rod and spoil the child' upbringing of his son seems somewhat forgiveable in his brutality. Harold can, in turn, appear callous and uncaring towards his father. To welcome Harold's girlfriend, the old man has proudly donned 'the suit I was married in' and his collection of medals, but his efforts are imme- diately belittled as Harold manhandles him to the sink and washes his 'dirty old man' neck. However, as the relationship develops, the viewer can feel that their bickering is founded as much on their care and solicitude for each other as on their more evident mutual irritation.

Brambell's performance is loaded with pathos, as the old man attempts to conceal his own deep need for company beneath a forced cheerfulness and a casual suggestion of a quiet night in in front of *Perry Mason*: 'Why don't you stay in and watch him?' His appeal to Harold's enjoyment of the programme is to no avail. *Perry Mason* or not, Harold is going out. The poignancy of Albert's harrowing reaction to Harold's murderous inclinations is lightened by Corbett's performance on an imaginary violin. Brambell, staring wildly and genuinely outraged, conveys the desperation of a man for whom such threats cannot be a joke. His technique in visual comedy is also excellent, as he blows a speck of dust off the dinner table while all around him is muck, and absent-mindedly wipes the grease from the fish-and-chip paper on to his sur- prisingly well-groomed hair.

Harold's mounting frustration and eagerness to get away are developed fur- ther than they were in the pilot. The one-liner, 'I might have to dig a tunnel to get out of here soon', is almost thrown away within the strained conversa- tion, but it perfectly sums up his fate. He resents being treated like a child while he struggles to assert his manhood, but his sulky and destructive behaviour as he pulls the foam rubber out of his chair is undeniably childlike, and is challenged by his father accordingly.

For Harry H. Corbett the character of Harold had already been compro- mised through his watching of the first episode:

> I envisaged him as a romantic lead, but Harold looks nothing like that to me. I can see me in there. I envisaged what the authors intended this man to be. Now the authors are stuck with me, and I play him for that. He changes in the sense that they wrote further facets of the same man. Take the girl I meet in the early episode. I am waiting for the idealized dream. This was still to do, remember, with getting away

from the rag 'n' bone trade, the going into some other business. And I see now that something curious took over which I wasn't aware of, an almost bourgeois approach to marriage, the playing it quietly, the deference, the cosy table not set out like the table in the restaurant, but set out like a kind of little home we'll have in the suburbs with the little motor car to wash every weekend like everybody else – and it's all played out on a very gentle level.

Chapter 4

Steptoe and Sun

With the repeat of 'The Offer' on 7 June 1962 preceding the new batch of programmes, a comparison between the *Comedy Playhouse* episode and the first series of *Steptoe and Son* could be made. The Audience Research Report proves that viewers did just that. The new episode, it seems, had the 'same qualities that were enjoyed' and contained 'most lively and piquant comedy writing'. 'The Bird' was 'a combination of humour and pathos' and 'a winner' for entertainment value. A 'must for future viewing', the series had moved away from the original two-hander format, albeit only just. Valerie Bell, in the title role, is only ever seen from behind, and her fleeting performance comes at the very end of the piece. The actress would reappear on several occasions as various players in Harold's ill-fated love life.

For the second episode, 'The Piano', Galton and Simpson dropped the established format. The old man is completely absent for the first few minutes of the action, as Harold natters with a refined, haughty gentleman who wishes to rid his luxury flat of the title instrument. In the Wardrobe, Hair and Make-up Requirements file, the character is called simply 'The Man' and decribed as 'a Noel Coward type, sophisticated, art connoisseur'. For the role, Galton and Simpson turned to the character actor Brian Oulton, who had already appeared in a similarly pompous turn in *Carry On Nurse* and had long been a valued member of the *Hancock* company on television. The pivotal comic device of the episode, the attempted removal of a piano from an impossibly small room, is reminiscent of the 1932 Oscar-winning Laurel and Hardy short, *The Music Box*.

However, even though, as Ray Galton explains, 'the idea may be nicked', its execution contains a unique moment in *Steptoe* history. As Galton continues:

'"The Piano" was the first time that anybody swore on television. It was pretty mild by today's standards – "What goes up can bleeding well stay there!" – but a barrier was broken down. When Muir and Norden were writing comedy series for the BBC, they had to ask if they could use the word "strewth". We never put language in for shock value; it just came naturally.' Alan Simpson remembers that, 'Tom Sloan's attitude was that this was a dramatic piece. If it had been a purely comedy production, we would probably have had to put "flipping" or "blinking" or something, but it was accepted as a comedy drama.'

'The line was referred to upstairs,' recalls Ray Galton. 'But Sloan said, "This will be changed over my dead body!" So "bleeding" stayed!'

'It seems ridiculous today,' reflects Simpson. 'But this was 1962 and a very big deal. Questions were asked in Parliament about the filthy language being used on the BBC because of that "bleeding"!' According to Galton, the writers still had to compromise: 'If we were writing realistic dialogue – and I'm not saying we were – and we were using a load of working-class chaps, every other word would be an expletive, and a much, much stronger one than "bleeding"! You would even split words up and put a swear word in. That's the reality. So the occasional "bleeding", although it may have been groundbreaking, certainly wasn't true to life. Nobody, not even us, could get away with the language that was really being used.'

The opening, a class-conscious discussion between Harold and the gentleman, rapidly exposes the shortcomings of both. Harold is initially suspicious and unnerved by the house-proud, foppish client. The man's abundance of slippers (to lend to visitors in an attempt to protect his carpet) is greeted with an amazed, 'I'm not stopping. I've got work to do!' Harold, conscious of his own pretensions to grandeur, is insulted by the gentleman's condescending manner and in the end blurts out, 'I've got a place of my own, you know!' The toff's preconceptions concerning the lower classes are revealed by his amazed, 'Really?' The boundaries of accepted discussion for television are then pushed further as Harold's initial explanation for the absence of the gentleman's wife, that she has died, receives the reaction, 'Unfortunately, no!' Clearly, television was being forced to change and adapt to a more cynical and more permissive age. Harold's humiliating mistake over the gentleman's wife doesn't deter him from letting his disguise as a refined man-of-the-world slip as he lets out the suggestion that the gentleman's luxury flat is an ideal bird-pulling property.

Harold's behaviour wavers between pride in his no-nonsense cockney identity, and emulation of the sophisticated charm of his client. When he brings

Albert to the flat, he even offers him Turkish slippers and makes a show of calm acceptance of the 'kinky' behaviour of the client. Brambell's portrayal of the old man's bewildered moment of insight into the upper classes contrasts brilliantly with Harold's attempt to conceal his own fascinated reaction to the sordid secrets of the successful.

The old man is happy to make use of his war years, as he convinces the gentleman that he is doing all the exhausting work while his son stands idle. Harold, however, shows real concern for his father. Corbett almost whispers, 'You all right now?' after the breathless old man has climbed the stairs. The moment is subtle and touching. Grim tales of the trenches manipulate the gentleman into providing a drop or two of something harder, and Albert makes a cheeky recovery to chant: 'Beer if it's here, brandy if it's handy.' Brambell lends him all his own acting ability as he switches from bewildered and pained old man, to subservient dogsbody, to grinning, conniving vagabond moment by moment. We, unlike Brian Oulton's gullible gentleman, may not be taken in as once we were, but we can retain some affection for the old rogue. Through his shameless knavery, the character loses its original edge of surprise and empathy, but such barefaced cheek can nevertheless be endearing. Still, all Albert's feverish chatter and cynical struggle for self-preservation are balanced by an almost innocent unworldliness. His discovery of the newspaper headline 'Ghandi's dead' isn't played for laughs but in a tone of sincere disbelief. Even Harold being better informed isn't mocked or attacked; the old man is simply hurt: 'You knew? And you never told me?'

The 'wiggling' of the grand piano takes up very little of the actual action, and does not even come to a successful conclusion. A day's work is wasted, a prized item is abandoned and the pair receive a ticking off from another *Hancock* regular, Roger Avon, as a policeman concerned about the horse and cart being parked without lights. The dejected admission of defeat makes for a beautifully downbeat finale.

The production schedule was punishing but rewarding, as Wilfrid Brambell revealed:

> Television light entertainment is, I think, more tense than provincial weekly rep. *Steptoe* rehearsals start at 10 in the morning on Monday. The director, the writers, the floor manager, 'H' and I sit around a table and read the script together for the first time. There are laughs, slight alterations, suggestions, and the occasional confrontation, all of which have been sorted out before going home at about 5 o'clock. Tuesday mornings are the beginnings of 'getting down to it'. One Monday evening in the early days, dear old Duncan Wood, our original producer,

flippantly told 'H' and me to be back at 10 in the morning DLP, which in our language means 'dead letter perfect'. In the language of the uninitiated it simply means 'know it'. Despite the fact that it was a 68-page foolscap script, I, in an evil moment, decided to take the mickey out of Duncan and old 'H'. I stayed up with black coffee until the wee small hours of the morning and arrived at rehearsal dead on time, and dead letter perfect. How was I to know that my equally evil playmate Harry H. would have thought of doing precisely the same thing? He also arrived at rehearsal minus script. 'H' and I expressed surprise. Duncan expressed nothing. So, for ever after, Harry and I were obliged to 'know it' at 10 o'clock on Tuesday mornings. One of the many things which amazed me, and made me admire Duncan, was that unlike many other producers he had done his homework before the morning call. He knew it before we did – his musical arrangement and all!

Ray Galton remembers:

There was always the odd cut for time reasons and the odd reworked bit of dialogue, but not very much at all. On the day of recording we were actually asked not to add anything because it was hard for the actors to relearn material having already learnt a great chunk. In America they rewrite after the commercial break sometimes – we were kinder. The producer would plead, 'No more lines at this stage ... they've got enough to think about! Don't give them any more, lads.' And that still applied to script cuts. The actors didn't want to learn what not to say because that was difficult too. Harry and Willie did have a lot of lines to learn, but that's their job, isn't it? ... and they did it brilliantly well.

There were certainly a lot of lines to learn for the next episode, 'The Economist', which to all intents and purposes was another two-hander based around disagreement and business acumen. Indeed, the only other actor to appear was Frank Thornton, making his *Steptoe and Son* debut. A Galton and Simpson regular, Thornton had chatted with Tony Hancock's 'Blood Donor' and appeared in the very first *Comedy Playhouse*, 'Clicquot et Fils', in November 1961. Thornton pre-filmed his brief but pivotal *Steptoe* perform-ance outside the labs at Modernair Processes Limited on 10 May 1962. His cynical, no-nonsense purveyor of false teeth crops up halfway through the episode and skilfully splits the father and son confrontation into two halves. Harold, the struggling bookworm and student of capitalism, faces Albert, the know-your-place worker, with the father doggedly rebuffing comments on the importance of learning and famine relief with ill-conceived but determined opinions. The old man's almost Nazi-style assault on books, professing a desire to burn literature and allow the working class to stay working class, is so outlandish that the horror of his thoughts only retains humour through ridiculous flights of fancy such as 'reading leads to communism!'. Harold, of course, can never win, but at least his thinking is steered away from communism and on to capitalism. His theories of bulk buying to improve the business's cash flow may go pear-shaped almost immediately, and his motives may be questionable (he wants to retire and play golf), but his earnest attempts to better himself and to improve his lot in life are painfully endearing. The *Steptoe and Son* production team was also making inroads into Britain's bastions of respectability. For one scene in the programme, Harold's ill-timed investment in 4000 dentures called for an advertisement in the *Times* newspaper. A BBC memo recorded: 'I am glad to hear that you think there is unlikely to be any objection to our using a fictitious advertisement in the *Times* in one of our *Steptoe and Son* programmes.' It remains a mystery as to whether anybody tried to take up the offer of 4000 dentures.

The next episode, 'The Diploma', continued the argumentative two-hander format and Harold's dedication to book-reading, with the canvas slightly widened to include both him and the old man in totting scenes shot on location. These sequences were pre-filmed on 23 May 1962 but the majority of the programme was reassuringly tethered in the studio. The script manages to be both funny and slightly political, incorporating Albert's misunderstanding of the Common Market and Harold's prophetic reflection that the threatened tunnel under the Channel could destroy the little firms of Britain. Indeed, as he reflects, 'You can't get any littler than us'. His surprisingly frank rant, 'British junk for the British', although tongue in cheek and half-hearted, suitably illustrates the fear that had spread throughout the country in the shadow of change and the European Community. In another early example of Harold's desperate bids to improve himself – he leaves the business to study for a diploma in television repair – Harry H. Corbett gives a mesmerizing performance, sending up the old man's suggestion that business is poor because Harold looks scruffy with a colourful vignette as 'Harold Steptoe, the totting toff!'. Later, as Harold is deep in concentration over his television wires and blueprint, Corbett rolls over from his working position to answer a nagging query from his father, rather than unnecessarily disturb his flow of work. Still, the highlight is really irrelevant to the actual narration, as Corbett brilliantly mouths to his father's oft-told story of how the firm acquired an old pair of spectacles. Every expression, pause and sickened grimace perfectly balances Wilfrid Brambell's gleeful retelling. Brambell's reaction to change is deadly earnest, of course, and contrasts the old man's political and commercial naivety with a proud determination to keep his family business (started by his father in 1894, we learn) from going to the wall. The crux of the dispute is Harold's resignation to change and resignation from the totting firm's board of directors in favour of the diploma course and his dawning career in television repair. The father, naturally, cracks the intricate workings of the television Harold has constructed and which has failed to work, scuppers his son's dreams and reinstates the status quo. An unfairly neglected episode, the climactic inevitability in Corbett's voice as he sighs 'I'll go and feed the 'orse' sums up his fixed place in life.

The final instalment of the first series of *Steptoe and Son* was transmitted on 12 July 1962, a month after its recording. In many ways 'The Holiday' remains the most moving episode of the series. 'It is a fact that the funniest comedy often comes from situations that, treated dramatically, would be tragic in the extreme,' Galton and Simpson comment.

With the relationship between father and son cemented in the previous five encounters, this half-hour again tackles Harold's need for freedom. The issue is all the more emotive because he questions the very thing that Albert believes has given the two a shared sense of freedom over the years: the family holiday in Bognor. The son's aspirational desire for a holiday abroad and the old man's stick-in-the-mud insistence on an English holiday was used several times during the series and, as the *Radio Times* noted: 'With holidays very much in vogue just now nothing could be more natural.' From the outset, the dreary location footage gives Harold's dreams a sense of impractical optimism, as he lovingly gazes at exotic holiday posters from his horse and cart. The familiar *Steptoe* theme tune even lilts and rearranges itself into a calming, relaxing interpretation by Ron Grainer, all strings and promises of sun-kissed beaches.

The dialogue begins as the Steptoes' perpetual bickering includes a daring dig at the outrageous price of a television licence. This was not only near-revolution at the BBC, but also shows how believable the characters had become. When Albert labels the TV licence as 'a clout round the back of the nut every January', much of the audience would be thinking exactly the same thing, while his description of his son's indiscriminate viewing habits, 'from Cliff Michelmore to Gawd Save the Queen', is now a nostalgic time capsule of 1960s television schedules.

Again, the old man's ignorance (amazed that Greece is so popular as a holiday destination considering that most of it is falling to bits) and patriotism (vowing not to return to Europe following his First World War experiences) are bleakly tinged with comedy, but it's the sense of the family unit in collapse that is the focal point for the dramatic tension of the episode.

Harold is made to feel guilty about his dreams of escaping, even if only for a fortnight. Corbett's impassioned performance is leavened by an earnest desire to see the old man suitably cared for during his absence. However, Brambell's pathos as he quietly tries to put a brave face on things is almost mesmerizing. He rejects the £15 offered to him from his son's holiday money with an amazing lack of self-indulgence. As all the previous holidays he has enjoyed are denounced as mere shams, his tearful lament, explaining how much he always looks forward to the holiday he spends with his son, is poignant beyond words. It's a masterly piece of work from Brambell, rounded off by his repeated, 'I don't want it!' as Albert continually refuses Harold's conscience money.

Corbett, rising to the challenge, allows Brambell space and time to deliver his piece. As the old man departs for bed, with a meek, 'See you in the morning, Gawd willing', Corbett's pause and the comic inevitability of his closing aside round off the scene perfectly.

Harry H. Corbett was delighted with his working relationship with Wilfrid Brambell:

> Not one of our scenes, surprisingly enough, relies on double takes, grimaces or whatever you wish to call them. They rely on words and timing. The pace is delightfully slow and true to the subject matter. In the hands of a couple of hack charlatans, they'd have said, 'Come on, now, speed, speed, speed, bang it out, lads, get the laughs; kick high and smile at the gallery'. But we had the time to play it properly. The lift of an eyebrow or the twist of a face can get a laugh on a fairly serious line if you wish it to. It's the control of this that is important. Look at the contact between Willie Brambell and me. Willie is holding it, but the point has to go over without a laugh getting in the way, and I'm holding back certain things. Remember, the dialogue isn't screamed out, and you've got gales of laughter sometimes, so it takes playing. The thing must register but not look as if we're shouting over our laugh.

Frank Thornton, the most prolific of *Steptoe* guest stars who had made his debut earlier in the series in 'The Economist', recalls:

> Wilfrid Brambell told me about filming 'The Holiday' during one of my later appearances. He said: 'Alan and Ray had written this as a fake heart attack; that is Albert manipulating Harold for his own ends. I said, "No, I'm going to make it a *real* heart attack!" Alan and Ray were

horrified, saying that you couldn't have anything like *real* illness or death in a sitcom! I said, "You boys don't know how good you are. It is perfectly feasible to have a real heart attack. My mother was exactly like that. Whenever any of her children faced her with a problem she didn't want to face, she would promptly retire to her bed with a genuine attack of asthma, which would miraculously disappear when the unpleasant situation was resolved the way she wanted it. And *that* is what I'm going to do with Albert."' Apparently, after transmission Alan and Ray went to Wilfrid and said, 'You were absolutely right!' Wilfrid knew that Albert *must* believe in his sickness. It was real to him and thus real to the audience.

The doctor tending this psychosomatic attack is played by Colin Gordon, another regular from the old *Hancock* days, and one of the scriptwriters' favourite actors. 'We loved Colin and we always tried to use him whenever possible,' remembers Ray Galton. 'He had this wonderfully petulant face, and in "The Holiday" he managed to convey so much understanding for Harold in just a minute or two of screen time. He had such control as an actor.' Indeed, Gordon's performance embraces both physical comedy and an excellent portrayal of understated empathy. The delivery of the line 'There's no cure for loneliness, Harold' is subtle and calm but hard-hitting. The doctor can do nothing but shake his head in helpless understanding as Harold ponders the fact that he will be on his own after sacrificing his life to his father's well-being. Gordon's 'We're all trapped by something' is played with sympathy and grace. The fact that after such revealing moments he can depart on a laugh – denying himself the pleasure of draining his glass of horrible whisky – marks Colin Gordon out as one of the key guests of the series.

The Bognor footage was recorded from 10.15 a.m. on 26 May 1962. The extras were ferried to the pier head on the day of filming. Two single rooms (for Corbett and Brambell) and one twin (for Wood) at the Royal Norfolk Hotel, Bognor, had been used the previous night, with the actors receiving an extra fee of £2 10s for overnight expenses. The wardrobe department delighted in creating holiday clothes for the old man, requesting that the hat be a 'typical Blackpool one – "Kiss Me Quick" or something similar on it'.

Alan Simpson remembers:

We didn't make the trip to Bognor. Most of the location filming we left in the very capable hands of Duncan Wood and, besides, it was pretty straightforward sort of stuff with a surprising lack of dialogue. But we were there a fair bit during rehearsal. Time permitting, we would probably make it to three of the six days that the cast and crew would be working on each show. We would be there for the first run-through on Monday and go along on the first day they started blocking it and then go away, back to the office as soon as possible, and leave them to it for the rest of the week. Usually, we were already writing the next episode. Then we would go back, all day long, on the day of recording. That would be the one and only day in studio. We would have a day off, the next day would be the read-through for the next one, and off we went again.

Ray Galton reveals that, 'Alan and I didn't go every day because it might have made the director look superfluous, but I wouldn't have minded being there all the time!'

Two days after the studio date for 'The Holiday' and just one day after 'The Bird' aired, producer Duncan Wood wrote a congratulatory note to Galton and Simpson '... to thank you yet again for five wonderful scripts. I think we have got a success on our hands, and I hope we get the kind of crits that you deserve. I will give you a ring next week, because I feel we ought to have a little celebration lunch.'

Perhaps more importantly, Wood was open in his praise of the entire company. On the last day of filming he had circulated a memo which recalled 'a smooth and uneventful day in the studio with no trouble. Good recording session. This has been a most rewarding series for all concerned – I hope the results on the screen will justify our confidence'. After profuse thanks to the crew, Wood concluded, 'There only remains to state the obvious. Alan Simpson, Ray Galton, Harry Corbett and Wilfrid Brambell are four of the most creative artists I have enjoyed working with. They should be contracted for ever.'

Thankfully, Wood's confidence was well placed. The first batch of episodes was critically lauded. In a review in the *Sunday Times*, published on 15 July 1962, Maurice Wiggins noted that '*Steptoe and Son* virtually obliterates the division between drama and comedy. Messrs Simpson and Galton have struck a vein so rich that one can almost speak of a major breakthrough in television comedy.' The programme had become a talking point for the nation during its run, and the *Evening Standard* of 19 July hoped and urged that 'Mr Tom Sloan can find the time to repeat the series'. Such was the impact of *Steptoe and Son* that the BBC made the unprecedented decision to do just that. As Ray Galton recalls:

It was a hit straight away. It had caught on enormously, and by the time number three or four had been out it was a huge success. People were complaining that they had missed some of the early episodes, and such was the demand for another chance to see them that they were all repeated immediately. 'The Holiday' went out on the Thursday and the following Friday 'The Bird' was on again. The series was an even bigger hit the second time round. It was the biggest thing in the country. It was amazing, and we weren't even aware of it. Alan and I were on holiday, and Harry H. Corbett joined us down in southern Spain, exclaiming: 'It's unbelievable. I can't go anywhere.' So we had no reason not to do any more!

Perhaps most charmingly of all, Tony Hancock was equally delighted with *Steptoe*'s success. 'We didn't see a great deal of Tony after we stopped working with him, but after the first series had gone out to great acclaim we saw him round at our offices in Orme Court and he said, "Congratulations, it's wonderful."'

Indeed, by the time the repeats were screened *Steptoe and Son* was being enjoyed in 4.2 million homes across the country. Wilfrid Brambell, interviewed for the 23 June 1962 issue of the *North-Western Evening Mail*, revelled in his new-found stardom: 'So long as I can earn enough to pay the rent and get in the odd bottle, I'm happy.' He need not have worried. Plans were already afoot for more episodes. A BBC memo just two days before the fourth instalment of the first series was broadcast reveals that Duncan Wood had already discussed another series with the writers. 'Following our lunch with Alan Simpson and Ray Galton yesterday, we are making a written commitment for Harry Corbett and Wilfrid Brambell between November 19 and January 19, for six more editions of *Steptoe and Son*. Since other commitments are coming in fairly fast for these two performers, I think we should make every effort to get firm recording dates as soon as possible.' Believing that a 'realistic budget would be between £1800 and £1900 per show', Wood put things in motion for the next series.

On the day before the first repeat, a memo from Wood detailed that, 'I had lunch with Harry H. Corbett today, and the final details for *Steptoe and Son* contracts have now been settled. Wilfrid Brambell is signing for a fee of 350gns. per show, this to include all filming within rehearsal period. I have given his agent an understanding that he will receive, as before, first billing in the *Radio Times*. He enjoyed this position on the first series since the artists were billed in alphabetical order and it was already my intention to adhere to this order in series two ... Harry H. Corbett has signed for a fee of 300gns., this again to include all filming within the rehearsal period.' The budget for the second series was increased by nearly £500 and would 'probably require one additional filming session' for which Brambell would receive

£36 15s and Corbett £31 10s, but the BBC happily reasoned that, as the pro- posed second series of *Comedy Playhouse* had been cut from 13 to just seven episodes, they were already making a saving of £6000 in pre-production.

Still, eager viewers didn't have to wait until the following year for brand-new *Steptoe* material. Such was the popularity of the *Steptoe* characters that Corbett and Brambell were invited by the BBC to reprise their roles for a spe- cially written sketch by Galton and Simpson. It was to be broadcast as part of the seasonal light entertainment spectacular *Christmas Night with the Stars*, scheduled as the centrepiece of Christmas Day's television attractions. The six minutes of self-contained *Steptoe and Son* were presented as the comic highlight towards the end of the programme.

The sketch was deliciously typical, with Harold, besotted by his latest girl- friend, Olive, planning a Christmas to remember. His father, of course, isn't interested in spending the day at Olive's, wanting just to stay at home with his son, eating pudding and watching television: 'No, I'm not going out. The Queen's speech is on at 3 o'clock. I never miss the Queen's speech ... I like to hear it in my own house. It's sort of more personal that way. Like she's talk- ing just to me. Sort of family to family.' The conclusion, of course, comes as heartache for Harold. A certain Neville telephones to say that he's just got engaged to Olive. Crestfallen, Harold steadfastly informs him: 'I won't be coming round. It's Christmas Day. I always spend Christmas Day with my father.' As he removes his dapper cravat – Olive's present – he settles down for a familiar Christmas with the old man.

While *Steptoe* fans gathered round their televisions on Christmas night, the Christmas sacks they had emptied that morning had probably included a prized long-playing record of *Steptoe and Son*, released by Pye Records.

Featuring a complete recording of the television soundtrack for 'The Bird' and lengthy extracts from 'The Diploma' (rechristened 'The Gentle Art of Totting'), 'The Economist' ('Choppers For Sale') and 'The Holiday', the tran- sition to audio was seamless. The single concession to the sound-only medium was the occasional newly recorded explanatory link voiced by Harry H. Corbett. Alan Simpson comments, 'We were always more concerned with the words anyway, so when the television shows were put on record there were hardly any edits needed, just the occasional snip when a character walks across the room.' Ray Galton remembers: 'They had done *Pieces of Hancock* which had worked really well, and we were drafted in to make suggestions on which *Steptoe* extracts should be used. But it was a pretty pedestrian sort of compilation. We didn't have much of an input really, but we were consulted.' Simpson continues: 'In those days some people didn't think anybody would buy a record of a whole show because they could have seen it on television. In those days the snippets approach was far more common. The show was presented in a way you couldn't see on television, in excerpt form. Then someone decided that the whole show should go out. That first *Steptoe* record was the best of both worlds really. One side had a whole show, the other side had clips.'

BBC script editor Gale Pedrick, who had given Galton and Simpson their first break more than 10 years previously, was invited to write the sleeve notes for the recording:

> In next to no time at all, Albert Steptoe and his son Harold have joined the great company of cockney characters among whom are remembered the immortal creations of Dickens, Jerome K. Jerome and W. W. Jacobs. If you think this too sweeping a flight of fancy, consider how soon the Steptoes have become inseparable from the London scene. They are as salty and British as jellied eels, Southend pier, the Old Bull and Bush, pig's ear and the Caledonian Market. In half a lifetime of writing for television and about it, I cannot remember a series which has made a firmer and more rapid impact than has *Steptoe and Son*.

Chapter 5

Steptoemania

The 1960s was a decade of major cultural upheaval. Television had come of age and was the source of the iconic characterizations that would symbolize this change. Interestingly, the most powerful – Albert and Harold; Pete and Dud's beer-swilling philosophers in *Not Only ... But Also*; Johnny Speight's bigoted Alf Garnett – came from comedy, as if the serious message – that the voice of the nation was now the voice of the working class – had to come through a medium that was not in itself too threatening. From Michael Caine to the Beatles, it was fab to be a worker. Although many viewers probably enjoyed *Steptoe and Son* simply because it was a very good comedy, Galton and Simpson were also able to use the show to address the contemporary problems of society. It was primarily funny, but if a socialist bomb or two found their targets, all the better. The rag 'n' bone protagonists could make their audience think, and reconsider the situation in which they and their countrymen were living. The 1960s weren't all miniskirts and yellow submarines. Before the hippie movement, and even before the Beatles' first LP, there was *Steptoe and Son*.

Such was the popularity of the series that the Duke and Duchess of Bedford publicly announced that anyone bearing the name of Steptoe would be welcome to take tea in their grounds, and around 400 Steptoes gathered at Woburn Abbey. 'I didn't know there were that many,' comments Alan Simpson. 'Although there was at least one famous one,' Ray Galton explains. 'The first man to create artificial insemination was Patrick Steptoe, and I met him once. I said, "I hope the show hasn't been too much of an embarrassment for you!" and he said, "No, it's been funny." Apparently he was in Birmingham, at one of the concert halls, and naturally he was on call. The public announcement bellowed, "Would Mr Steptoe please go to so-and-so hospital," and the audience erupted with laughter!'

Wilfrid Brambell attended the Woburn Abbey event as guest of honour:

> The Duke and Duchess had arranged for a car to transport me, complete with my Steptoe gear, to their stately home. After a warm welcome they escorted me to a bedroom where I changed out of my natty grey suit into my naff clothes. I was formally and individually introduced to all 400 Steptoes. They came from all walks of life.

Harry H. Corbett had declined the invitation, but he did join Brambell in the celebrated ritual of switching on the Blackpool illuminations. The old man was uncertain of their reception:

> I had thought that southern humour has always been very different from that of the north. How wrong I was. There were over 4000 people to meet us at the airport, and six helmeted cops on motorbikes accompanied our car to the hotel where, after being given drinks and time for a wash and change, we were ushered into the 'Murr's parlour'.
>
> The Lady Mayoress was resplendent on that sunny afternoon.

Not only had the nation taken the Steptoes to its heart, but the critics were charmed by the earthy reality of the scriptwriting. Galton and Simpson, lauded as never before, won the 1962 Writers' Guild Award for Best Writers. Moreover, in November 1962 Harry H. Corbett had been named Actor of the Year by the Guild of Television Producers and Directors, while Duncan Wood became Best Light Entertainment Producer at the same awards ceremony. As their creations became fully accepted by the public, Galton and Simpson could begin to add more history to the characters and delve deeper into what made the father and son tick. Series two, greeted by the *Radio Times* with 'The old firm is back in business', retained the bitter resentment and affectionate battling of the first series, but the writers had the freedom and leisure to consider where these characters had come from and where, if anywhere, they were going.

'We didn't feel any pressure to better or top the previous shows,' recalls Ray Galton. 'The only pressure we felt was the pressure we always felt: to get the material written in time. The characters and situations flowed fairly easily and, to be honest, nothing is going to live up to the public's fondness for what has gone before. As long as we were happy with the scripts, that's all we could really hope for, and because we had written so much, we always knew it wouldn't be a complete disaster. That's not to say we had a cavalier attitude, we certainly didn't. It's just that we knew we could craft some good material.'

Despite the show's high standing, Duncan Wood had to struggle to retain the original half-hour running time of the series. As it had with the first batch of programmes, the BBC had planned to cut *Steptoe* to a 25-minute slot. In a memo of 24 October 1962 Wood had to 'make a plea from the heart ... the kind of comedy we have done in the past and hope to do again in *Steptoe*, which relies heavily on character work, is not only very difficult but at times impossible to exploit fully in 25 minutes.' He continued by citing the fact that it would be 'relatively much easier in the case of a show like *Benny Hill*, where the comedy is broader and more surface. I am terribly afraid that a similar cut in the *Steptoe* timing may destroy the depth of characterization which we have achieved in the past.' Again, Tom Sloan agreed. The following day he wrote and assured Wood that he had 'always felt that this was one series that would suffer considerably by cutting to 25 minutes'. Later, Sloan noted that retaining *Steptoe* at half an hour 'had the effect of reducing the Thursday episode of *Compact* to 25 minutes and, thus, everybody was happy'.

As the new series began, with 'Wallah-Wallah Catsmeat', Duncan Wood needed only to focus on the iconic hatstand with Albert's hat and Harold's cap as his opening image to evoke *Steptoe* to the full. The studio audience, already geared up for more of the classic banter, can be heard to anticipate the arrival of the Steptoes. When Wilfrid Brambell ambles on to the set, it is as if an old friend is welcomed back. In less than 12 months, the Shepherd's Bush rag 'n' bone man had become a warmly appreciated guest in millions of homes, albeit one who disgusted as often as he pleased. The ratings for January 1963 were astronomical – well over 8.5 million households. At a conservative estimate, this meant that *Steptoe and Son* was now being watched by 22 million viewers across the country.

The show's instant fame and success didn't dent its social awareness. The sitcom had become a platform from which to air and discuss vital issues of the day. Within the opening gambit of the second series, Albert lights up and coughs up over breakfast as his son looks on in disgust. Threatening to take a photograph of the old man's morning cigarette intake and 'put it on them cancer adverts – that'll stop 'em!', Harold taps into the new health scare of the early 1960s. Couched in comedy, he addresses a fear that was bringing into question one of the nation's favourite social habits.

While it is the show's main aim to entertain, there is no denying that the writers realized the power of comedy: 'It is certainly true that serious artists carry more intellectual prestige than their comic brethren. We guarantee that Laurence Olivier's views on, say, pollution of the atmosphere and the population explosion would carry more weight than Tommy Cooper's. If, however, in the process of making people laugh you can advance a point of view or illuminate the human dilemma, so much the better. Ridicule and satire are two of the strongest weapons in man's armoury.'

Full use is again made of the cluttered junkyard's comic potential, as Albert grabs the newspaper that has been left protruding from the mouth of a stuffed eagle outside the Steptoes' door. Harold enthusiastically peruses the stocks and shares in the paper, embracing the get-rich-quick dream of the worker as he points out the old man's disastrous results in the football pools. Albert may be pictured as a slob, but the script shows him to be at ease with his lowly position. It is Harold who is trapped by his own fantasies of better things, as he casually dismisses his father as a 'mif' – milk in first. Harold, deluding himself as to his own social standing, complains that in upper-class Claridges Albert would be instantly labelled a commoner. The fact that Harold himself hasn't got a chance of being accepted into the Claridges 'community' isn't mentioned, not even by the old man. Even Albert seems to accept that Harold at times is a better class of person than he is.

Having joked about selling Hercules the horse to the catsmeat man for £25, Harold discovers the animal sweating and in apparent poor health. In the episode's pivotal scene, the unseen vet is investigating the trouble as Harold worries and Albert is philosophical. When his father suggests a cup of tea to calm his nerves, Harold launches into a tirade against the cockney sparrow stereotype, an attack on the Ealing universe, where tea is a cure for all known disasters, a marker of all known celebrations and an antidote to all known heartaches. It is a beautifully written and acted monologue. The evocation of war-torn Londoners, with their chirpy smiles, sticking their collective thumb up to the newsreel cameras and raising a cup of tea, reveals an understanding of, and distaste for, the clichéd working-class image. Still, even the ever-reliable cup of tea can't help the sick horse. Money is very short, and there's the vet's bill to pay. The old man, displaying a sense of real fear when one of their creditors 'turned quite nasty', faces the facts. Again Albert is seen to be the level-headed one, confronting the problem while Harold loses himself in a fantastic rant about mythical company returns and the chairman's fall from grace. Corbett's manic description of high finance is brilliantly complemented by Brambell's strait-laced observation, 'We should get the vet to have a look at you as well!' Harold's suggestion of a suicide pact likewise falls flat as Albert reminds him of his rush to get a fallout shelter when the Cuban missile crisis erupted. The show's ability to deal with recent and potentially world-shattering events in the sitcom context is quite breathtaking at times, and it takes true comic acting to preserve the humour of the situation as

Harold mournfully reflects that he's ready to meet his maker. A sharp knock at the door pulls him out of his morbid apathy. It's not death, of course. It's not even the vet, as expected. It's a chirpy cockney character right out of the clichéd tea-drinking image that the show has just debunked. The character, played by British film icon Leslie Dwyer, is the personification of the real optimism of London: a friendly, fellow rag 'n' bone man bearing rags to help out the poverty-stricken and horseless business of Steptoe and Son.

John Laurie, who before gaining fame as Private Fraser in *Dad's Army* was a character actor with over 30 years' experience, plays the whisky-guzzling vet. Ray Galton remembers that Laurie was 'another great favourite of ours. What a wonderful actor he was. I remember seeing him as the crofter in Hitchcock's *The 39 Steps*, so it was a real thrill to have someone of his calibre on the show.' Duncan Wood, writing to Laurie on 21 November 1962, explained: 'I am delighted that you can do this show for us ... [the vet is] a gentleman who has been mentioned in past episodes but whom we have not as yet seen.' The Wardrobe, Hair and Make-up requirements described the vet as 'a rather seedy individual: old beltless raincoat, seedy suit with waistcoat and rumpled white collar, striped shirt, nondescript tie ... old tweed hat'. Laurie clearly relished the role. The corruptible vet, having discovered that the horse is just exhausted and not sick, is more than happy to allow the Steptoes to undermine the community spirit of the Shepherd's Bush totting fraternity. Initially moved to tears by the rallying of their peers, the Steptoes sense the financial benefit and the opportunities for loafing provided by the totters' unconditional kindness. By paying the going rate for rags picked up on their behalf, and selling them on at a profit, the scam, amazingly, seems to work out well for the cunning ruffians. In retrospect it's refreshing to see success for a scheme in which both Steptoes share, and the audience can appreciate the enjoyment of father and son as life deals them a good hand.

This first episode of series two formally introduced the Steptoes' horse. Named Hercules in the script for the first time, he was, in fact, called Hercules in real life. He was also very much a working rag 'n' bone man's horse. Owned by totters Arthur and Chris Arnold, Hercules clip-clopped the streets of Notting Hill and, after enjoying television fame, was often chased by children offering carrots and sweets.

The Audience Research Report for the opening episode of the new series was eagerly read by the production team, as an indicator of *Steptoe*'s shelf life. Although many thought it was 'not quite vintage *Steptoe*', it was 'generally welcomed as signalling the return of a series which has, during its brief existence, obviously become something of a television classic'. Furthermore, praise was lavished on 'the actors, who had managed to get under the skin of their parts to such an extent that it was, apparently, "hard to imagine them as anyone other" than the Steptoes.' One viewer believed 'they go together like eggs and bacon', while the 'dialogue [was] always completely natural and comedy and pathos went hand in hand'. A few dissenting voices thought 'the theme sordid and distasteful or objected to the "colourful" language'. But one viewer was speaking for the majority of the nation when he proclaimed the new episode to be 'Marvellous! One can almost smell the junkyard'.

The audience figures were impressive as well and caught the media's attention to the extent that it invented a battle royal between Tony Hancock and the Steptoes' scriptwriters. Ray Galton recalls: 'The second series of *Steptoe* conflicted with Hancock's ITV series. Both were going out on the same night. *Steptoe* was finishing just before 8.30, and that's when *Hancock* started. It became front-page news. Who was winning the ratings war? Us without him or him without us?' Alan Simpson remembers: 'Our return, after all that success with the first series, was up against Hancock's first ITV series after quitting the BBC. It wasn't planned; it just happened. But the papers had a field day. *Hancock* got hammered by *Steptoe!*'

'The Bath', the second offering in series two, remains one of the most instantly recognizable episodes, perhaps because of, rather than despite, the fact that it allowed established *Steptoe* clichés to be deliberately played up for laughs. Corbett's entrance receives huge cheers of approval from the studio audience, as his relentless 'dirty, dirty ... dirtiness!' within this ultimate 'dirty old man' vignette becomes almost self-referential in the overuse of the catchphrase.

Singing 'These Foolish Things' from his tin bath in the living room, the puniness of the grotesque old man illustrates his pathetic qualities as much as his disgusting ones. The contrast between the two men's physiques here is a powerful one – even more so considering Harold's references to the old days when Albert would wallop him for no good reason. The residual domination of the old man over his hulking son adds a chilling dimension to the never-ending arguments.

Albert's ravenous consumption of a jar of pickled onions while he's in the bath – dropping some of them into the water along the way – has become a defining moment in our collective memory of the old man. 'Even now people come up to us and say, "Oh, that bit with the old man in the bath ... hilarious!"' says Simpson. Galton remembers: 'As a result we decided to always add some nasty habit for the old man just to please that part of the audience!'

Wilfrid Brambell retained vivid memories of the scene:

> Pickled onions have always been a favourite food of mine. I have
> ceased to relish them, although I still relish that moment of really
> revolting realism which I know that many viewers still remember. It
> was filmed in the unmentionable month of November. At the time I
> had a temperature of 103 degrees and had lost so much weight that my
> little naked body resembled a rusted wooden washboard. I was frozen
> from the waist up, but boiled from the waist down during that
> sequence – boiled because during every camera cutaway the consider-
> ate props man topped up my carefully clouded bath water with repeat-
> ed kettles of boiling water, which he considerately poured from a great
> height around my ankles. When that bath scene terminated I had a
> quick change that precluded the possibility of a shower, and so I had
> to be content with a quick rub down. During this frenzied operation
> Duncan Wood burst into the quick-change room and asked me what
> the hell I was doing halfway through the scene. I had been wriggling
> and writhing in that bathtub, so I informed him that the reason for
> these unrehearsed gyrations was that one of the larger pickled onions
> had bypassed my cache-sexe and insinuated itself into my anal orifice,
> and that I was not prepared to leave it there for the remainder of the
> episode. For at least two weeks after that short sequence, despite the
> fact that I sprayed expensive unguents all over my body even where
> they stung, I stank even to myself like an empty vinegar bottle.

The replacement of the soapy onions into the jar is just part of the scene's
powerful appeal. 'The old man wallowing in front of the fire in a tin bath was
not only visually funny, but also awoke in older viewers memories of the way
some of them once lived, and still do in too many places,' wrote Galton and
Simpson in 1971. Indeed, despite Harold's outrage at his father's behaviour,
the scene allows the characters to voice the concerns of an underprivileged
nation living under the 'never had it so good' Conservative government of
Harold Macmillan. The show brought before the national conscience the four
million homes without a bathroom and the great unwashed had a champion
in *Steptoe and Son*. Indeed, while Harold cynically quotes the Prime Minister,
Albert's futile cries of 'Harold!' could as often as not be seen as cries for
assistance directed towards a government lacking in consideration for, and
understanding of, the nation. Alan Simpson recalls, 'I lived in Brixton until
the age of about four, in a building built in the 1910s for doctors, solicitors
and the like. It was quite middle class, but it had been converted into flats
before we moved in and the floor that we were on didn't have a bathroom. So

it was a zinc bath and an outside toilet. Having said that, it wasn't like *Steptoe*. They lived in a slum, but we knew what they were going through.' Ray Galton agrees that they instilled in their scripts a social awareness that had arisen from their childhood experiences: 'That's why we eventually had the old man as a Tory and Harold as an idealistic socialist ... as we all were in those days. It balanced the argument and allowed us to expose what we felt needed exposing. The Labour government of Clement Attlee was a wonderful time of change, and we pontificated on what had gone wrong since then.'

While using commonplace and familiar political touchstones to enhance the comedy and vice versa, Galton and Simpson were also aware of the power of their own medium: television. Happy to let their characters mock, discuss or casually refer to other programmes, the writers knew full well that their television audience would get the reference and share the joke. Thus, we have Corbett chucking the old man into the cupboard under the stairs to make room for his new bathroom, with a comment about Barry's house, a reference to the television DIY expert Barry Bucknell.

As Harold continues his quest for a love life, future *George and Mildred* star Yootha Joyce makes her first foray into *Steptoe* as Harold's latest lady friend. 'Yootha had known Harry Corbett for years because she had been part of the Stratford East company,' remembers Ray Galton. 'When she first came on board it was wonderful because she was old friends with Harry and that came across on the show. They worked really well together, and she became quite a regular. At that marvellous moment when she enters the Steptoe house and she says, "Oh, my Gawd!", we both knew we had found a real *Steptoe* actress.' Indeed, Harry Corbett acting opposite Yootha Joyce moves away from the dictatorial attitude inspired by Albert and takes on schoolboy nerves as he struggles to prepare a cocktail for her. The shaky repetition of 'Go in ...' as he fumbles to get the drinks into the cocktail shaker is painfully loaded with first-date anxiety. The set-up of the scene, with Harold in the foreground and his leggy companion silently preparing herself in the background, is beautifully indicative of the potential coupling between the experienced and the hoping-to-experience.

By now, Harold's threat to leave home is seen as nothing more than an attempt to get his own way. Indeed, Harold's notion of leaving is as familiar and toothless a weapon as Albert's feigned ill health. Both know when the other is play-acting

As an actor, Harry H. Corbett felt self-conscious when he first saw himself on the television screen. Speaking in 1967, he explained:

I am conscious of the fact that I've had a broken nose. I wish this

ABOVE: Harry H. Corbett in his most famous role for the first time; a publicity pose for the *Comedy Playhouse* episode, 'The Offer'.

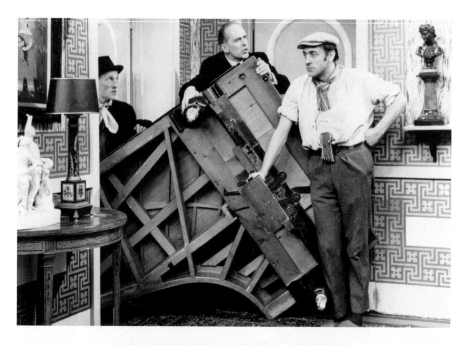

TOP: Stalemate as guest star Brian Oulton joins 'father' and 'son' in the first series episode, 'The Piano' (1962).
ABOVE: The eternal struggle to better himself! Harold unsuccessfully grapples with television engineering in 'The Diploma' (1962).

TOP: Harold has high hopes of sailing the high seas in the 1963 episode, 'Homes Fit for Heroes' ...

ABOVE: ... but, as usual, his holiday dreams of domestic escape turn sour.

RIGHT: 'There was more in there than that!' Harold suspects his father of stealing his savings in 'The Holiday' (1962).

BELOW: The Steptoes at breakfast at the start of the second series opener, 'Wallah-Wallah Catsmeat' (1963).

LEFT: An iconic moment in television comedy as Wilfrid Brambell records the ultimate 'dirty old man' sequence for 'The Bath' in December 1962.

BELOW: The party seems to be over as Joan Newell's threat to invade the *Steptoe* home fades in 'The Stepmother' (1963).

TOP: Albert is less than impressed with his son's choice of birthday celebration in 'Sixty-Five Today' (1963).
ABOVE LEFT: Brambell allows some of his inherent Irishness to invade Albert.
ABOVE RIGHT: Poignant emotion as Albert reads his birthday card from Harold.

ABOVE: Wilfrid Brambell makes a spectacle of himself for publicity during the making of the first series episode, 'The Diploma' (1962).

ABOVE: Harold is besotted by a wealthy, lonely lady on his rounds in 'Is That Your Horse Outside?' (1963). Patricia Haines plays the tempting diversion.

would have healed attractively like it did with Ian Fleming and a few others like that, but, you see, unfortunately it didn't. It's just grown big and flabby and it wobbles. I got a thorn stuck in my eye during the war which has scratched it, marking it indelibly. Shaving as a youth, I accidentally took too much skin off here and the hair won't grow there. Now I can see all these fantastic imperfections. So I envisage in my mind's eye what the author intended this man to be. It is that that gives me the ability to be able to con you, with a bit of luck, into thinking that the nose is fairly aquiline, the double chin doesn't actually wobble, and, yes, the teeth do sparkle and they are clear and white. If I were to watch any of these episodes, do a make-up test or anything, I'd be finished. I wouldn't be able to do it. I'd be so concentrating on trying to bend the character back again.

In the next episode, 'The Stepmother', it is Albert and not Harold who is threatening to break up the partnership and move on. In a crucial programme the father–son relationship, bonded by blood but continually strained by overfamiliarity, is seen in its rawest form. It is a reappraisal of the situation established in 'The Bird', in which Harold laments being 'treated like a Judy ... it's not natural'. In that moment he sets the scene for this reappraisal and reversal. Alan Simpson remembers:

After writing this stuff for years some critic or other told me that rather than us writing Albert and Harold as father and son we had, in fact, made the relationship more like that of mother and daughter. Oh, I thought, so that's what we did. I had no idea. It was one of the posh critics who after the first series likened *Steptoe* to Strindberg! Where Strindberg writes about women, *Steptoe* deals with the same themes but with men. Harold was 37 and living at home looking after his father, which, traditionally, is the job of the 37-year-old spinster daughter. Funnily enough, one of my uncles, Uncle Bob, did exactly that. This sounds like Frankie Howerd now, but my mother used to tell us that he had had a very unfortunate relationship that had gone wrong. This woman had left him in his twenties and he never got over it, so all the other children got married and left him to look after the mother. He certainly wasn't effeminate, Uncle Bob. He was just stuck in a rut, like Harold.

The ominous title, 'The Stepmother', appears over our first proper glimpse of the quiet, nose-twitching lady in question, played by one of Duncan Wood's regulars, Joan Newell. The role reversal element in the programme is quickly established with Albert's endearing 'Thanks for seeing me home' after an evening at the pictures. The old man is taking on the role of a teenage girl, and Harold, alone and waiting, becomes the furious mother, sick with worry and allowing her anger to overcome her feelings of relief when her 'offspring' finally turns up at half past eight. Ron Grainer's score, with heavy, romantic strings accompanying the *Steptoe* theme, stops abruptly as Harold demands 'Where the bleeding 'ell 'ave you been?' While Harold's anxiety has been part-ly selfish – he has been waiting for his dinner, after all – his genuine concern for the old man's welfare on finding the house empty adds emotional power to the ensuing argument. Rejecting his father's placatory peppermint creams with a defiant 'I'm not Lolita!', Harold uses the familiar threat of leaving home to make his feelings clear. But in a new twist, it proves to be a perfect opening for Albert's piece of 'good' news. Harold's anger and bitterness shift to suspicion and then panic as his father continues to talk rationally and approvingly of Harold's impending move. It becomes clear that Harold is desperate to stay with his father. His bluff, it seems, has been called, although Harold finds solace in the absurdity of the idea of Albert's marriage, and fully exploits his rich, resonant laugh at the thought of his father being 'in love': 'You're almost 65,' he repeats.

The humour, however, evaporates in an instant. Frantically skipping from hilarity to fury – 'And why haven't I been told?' – Harold goes into denial, dis-missing the unseen intended as 'an old bag'. But, with the truth sinking in, he has to face the thought of an imminent wedding. The audience can see the sick worry in his face, as after all this time complaining, and longing for a place of his own, he's now 'being kicked out'. When forced into living alone, he realizes he doesn't want it any more. The weird eulogy for his dead moth-er that follows is dangerously uncomfortable until Albert is allowed to inject a touch of comic relief as he points out that the photograph his son lovingly holds is, in fact, of his mother's sister. Albert, having promised not to marry again, reflects the spirit of this surreal interlude by wielding a sword like a madman to defend his renewed happiness.

There is only a very brief respite in this angst-ridden episode, when Harold enjoys the good grub he believes he deserves, cooked by the intended step-mother. Once he realises she has cooked it, however, the meal is quickly rejected. Harold, like Albert before him, fails to give the new woman a chance to settle. But the real cruelty comes from the old man, whose home truths about Harold's mother mean that little is left of the rose-tinted memories that her son clings to. It starts relatively innocently as Harold's memories of his mother's cooking are dismissed by Albert's fervent, 'Liar! She couldn't cook an egg!' But Albert's insinuations about Harold's mother become increasingly unpleasant, and Harold's anger betrays a secret fear that they could be true. Hackles rise as his recollection of the local chaps admiring his mother's looks is met by a disgusted, 'They did more than look, mate!', and the conversation comes to a head when Albert questions his own paternal status: 'That's never been proved neither!'

Suddenly, in a reversal of 'The Offer', it is Harold who longs to be saved from the premature closure of the family business. Letting the debate pass from being between him and his father to between his father and the lady friend, he edges out of the argument and allows them to battle on. As a breaking up and then making up of the two ageing lovebirds follows, Harold proves himself to be no less cunning and manipulative than his father, throwing in the invented fact that Albert had described his fiancée as 'mutton dressed as lamb'. The battle begins again and this time the break-up is final. Of course, Albert doesn't remember saying anything of the sort, although a poignant performance is comically balanced with a sudden, 'Well, she was'. The audience are shown two conclusions: the father and son tucking into dessert and beer, sharing a moment of masculine camaraderie broken only by an instant of sombre reflection from the old man; and the intended, dabbing her eyes, hovering at the junkyard gates and then moving on. The relationship, doomed by Harold's intervention, is suddenly revealed as a genuine love match, destroyed by the power of family ties.

The *Radio Times* commented on Corbett and Brambell's expertise, saying that, 'The actors were closely involved with the characters they have created', and Harry H. Corbett explained:

> The Steptoes are *real* to us and because, like all human beings, they're so complex, we'll never be able to say we've fully explored them. All we can do is to take snippets and present them one at a time – touching on certain facets of character, giving clues which different people will see in a different light, as they always do when assessing other people. I don't tell my friends about the Steptoes, they tell me. The first series dealt with what you might call the economic background of the Steptoes. This new one deals with their relationship with other people. In tonight's episode, for example, it's Harold's mother who suddenly dominates, and these skeletons come screaming out of the closet at the wrong time and definitely at the wrong moment.

For Wilfrid Brambell, after a lifetime struggling as a jobbing actor, his role was a delight. At the start of work on the second series, he wrote to John Willis, who had recently employed him, at the London offices of Walt Disney Productions. Willis replied: 'Dear Wilf, Sorry to read that you have joined the elite of the acting profession. I would like to thank you for your very kind note of last week and have passed on your messages. Also thank you for the note about *Steptoe*, would it be too much to ask if I could have six tickets for the January 3rd programme ['The Stepmother']?"

The third episode of the series had revealed that the old man was almost 65, and the following programme, 'Sixty-Five Today', marks Albert's big birthday. The episode (originally titled 'The Birthday') investigates such notions as the value of presents, the thought that counts ... and the thought that counts for nothing. Broadcast on 24 January 1963, it employed the biggest cast of supporting actors to date. And, for the first time, the plot moved the couple out of their familiar studio set for long sections of contrasting 'location' action.

Albert has had a miserable day on his own and is sitting at the table when Harold comes bounding in with a box in his arms. Albert's excitement at the prospect of a present is soon disappointed as his son empties the box of books, newly acquired for himself: 'Oh, yes, very erudite.' Harold lovingly reorganizes his book collection while revealing his ignorance by continually mispronouncing authors' names ('They're a funny lot, some of these writers'), and muttering, 'I'll have to get round to reading some of these one day.' He is thoroughly enjoying himself. His father, with 'a face like a squeezed lemon', is convinced that his son has forgotten his birthday, and Harold strings the old man along with childlike pleasure. We are treated to the familiar complaints of loneliness and old age, and it isn't until just before the old man prepares for an early night that Harold gleefully hands him his present and card. Albert grabs at the gift, touched that his son has remembered, but refuses to allow himself any expression of appreciation for the expensive pair of gloves he has received. Harold fishes for words of thanks, badgers Albert to put the gloves on and orders him to keep them for best. The performances and writing perfectly capture the awkwardnesses of giving and receiving – from the old man's initial, uninterested 'They're all right,' to his meek repetitions of 'Keep these for best', the script portrays a detailed arc of changing reaction within moments of screen time.

The scene is enhanced by Harold's throwaway presentation of the birthday card and Albert's misty-eyed, sentimental reading of the printed words and handwritten dedication. Performed by Brambell with impeccable lightness of touch, it's never maudlin or overly gushing but is genuine and moving. Albert's emotional reaction, and Corbett's quiet smile as he appears to be moved himself, is quickly but gently dismissed by Harold's embarrassed apology for the gushing words. But Albert is having none of it: the card is the only thing he really wanted. The present could have been forgotten, but the card is the thing, joining all previous cards, letters to Father Christmas, school reports and other mementoes of Harold's past in Albert's chocolate box. The scene works as a wonderfully sentimental prelude to a disastrous birthday treat in the West End.

Harold appears to know that it will be a disaster from the start. Even before leaving the house, he predicts that the restaurant will not meet with his father's approval. In a nervous aside he admits, 'Half the waiters you fought against!' The evening is another attempt on Harold's part to improve his father's social standing and sophistication but cocktails, Michael Redgrave at the Old Vic and Chinese food result in a steady stream of unappreciative comments. Harold, trying his hardest to blend in, isn't fooling anybody. Desperate to mask the old man's grumbles as Albert yearns for a pint at the Skinner's Arms, Harold attempts to give an upper-class slant to his father's common conversation. But the pretence is transparent, and even the cocktail barman, played by regular supporting actor Frank Thornton, cannot hide his disgust. 'It was my very favourite *Steptoe* episode,' says Frank. 'I remember with joy Albert's reaction when, as the posh cocktail bar cannot supply him with a pint of bitter, he is handed a Pimm's No. 1 and learns the price: "What? Seven and six for a bleedin' fruit salad?" Ah! Happy days!'

The cost ('You can get a pair of boots mended for that!'), boredom (Albert prefers the 'real acting' of *Z Cars*) and xenophobia (he is convinced that a Fu Manchu dope den is concealed upstairs in the restaurant) are all ammunition for the old man. Farcical behaviour with chopsticks, and Richard Caldicot's performance as a stuttering fellow diner bring the comedy to a peak. But the episode itself ends on a refreshingly downbeat note as Harold bitterly declares that he and his father don't work together socially and suggests that Albert go down to the Skinner's Arms with his mates while he salvages the evening in the West End. As the old man sadly slopes off, he accidentally loses his gloves. But still, that instant of shared affection in the birthday card sequence shines through. Wilfrid Brambell later revealed in his autobiography that the ending was originally to have been less bittersweet. In the first draft, the old man 'reached home on the brink of tears and told his son what had happened [to the gloves]. With a hug Harold replied, "Never mind, Dad. I'll get you another pair."'

Although Richard Caldicot's performance was excellent, Duncan Wood had originally cast someone of much higher stature in the profession. Galton, Simpson and Wood had recruited Terence Alexander four times for the *Hancock's Half Hour* television shows. Alexander had been a British film star of some distinction since his part in *The League of Gentlemen* in 1960, and Wood went cap in hand to offer him a role in *Steptoe and Son*. On 29 November 1962 Wood wrote: 'The part involved is small but very important. It is that of the man in the Chinese restaurant with whom Wilfrid Brambell has the brush – it runs from pages 53 to 57. I think it is a good reaction piece, but I can only reiterate that I fully realize it is using about five per cent of your talents, and if you want to sling it straight out of the window, please do!' Clearly, Alexander did just this, although Wood had made an unprecedented commitment to him and his agent, Ronnie Walter, settling that if the actor agreed to the part, 'I can only assure you that I would release you if something better were offered over these dates'.

Having recruited a huge supporting cast for 'Sixty-Five Today', the next programme, 'A Musical Evening', returned to the basic format of the series for the first time since 'The Diploma'. A two-hander throughout, Harold's intellectual aspirations are once again brought to the fore, this time through an ignorant obsession with classical music twinned with an absolute abhorrence of 1960s pop. The old man, unusually, likes the twist and the two are at loggerheads from the beginning, whether it be debating about women, work or Wagner. Harold, old before his time and picking up his father's traits, bemoans the state of kids today and mocks the intellectual credibility of the *Juke Box Jury* panel. The cultural divide between the two is so great that nothing can bridge it, even elements of their not dissimilar personalities.

The episode is also known by the original working title 'The Keys', and the musical element is only one part of the simple plot. Emphasizing the show's physical comedy and revelling in grime, the two spend much of the half-hour in the junkyard searching for the missing key to the stable, gates and safe. This interlude allows Albert's yellow streak to emerge, as he insists that mice give him 'the willies' and refuses to put his hand inside an old sofa. Harold's cavalier attitude quickly falls away to reveal his true cowardice as he viciously attacks the piece of furniture before giving the inside a cursory grope. Later, out of view behind a pile of junk, with his distinctive, world-weary voice ably conveying his nausea, Corbett milks the line: 'Oh, Gawd! What have I put my hand in?'

The title of the following episode, 'Full House', indicates both a full house in cards and a Steptoe abode resplendent with guests. At £104 15s 2d in cash, the card game was expensive for the BBC to set up, and therefore the start of the episode is marked by a sense of urgency to get through the preliminary scenes and move on to the lavish set-up – Harold's pretentious plans for a wine and cheese party are all established within minutes. The opening does include, however, Harold's succinct dismissal of his father as 'a drunken, lazy old git'. For 1963 this was pretty strong stuff. Television controller Lew Grade reputedly banned the programme from his house because of its choice vocabulary.

But the dialogue was fresh and true to the lives of millions of viewers. Albert condemns the Camembert as foul-smelling, suggesting 'a 1938 gas mask' as a suitable 'wine' to complement the flavour, and his reaction to the paper napkins – 'Oh, Gawd. Who's coming, Princess Margaret?' – is a ripe condemnation of Harold's pretensions. Harold's pleasure when he tastes the food gives him a glimpse of a more polished universe, but he immediately drags himself back to sordid reality by asking for the opinion of his ignorant and purposely obtuse father. Harold needs reassurance, even from the source of his annoyance. And, as with his favourite writers in 'Sixty-Five Today' and his favourite composers in 'A Musical Evening', he is exposed by his own ignorance as he unwittingly mispronounces his way through his prized wine collection.

However, the crux of the episode arrives with the mention of Harold's gambling plans. Albert's puritanical attitude and a promise to his late wife lead to his self-righteous dismissal of cards as '52 soldiers in Satan's army'. In a parody of this, Harold launches himself into a missionary interlude, complete with chants of 'Will you come to the mission?', a performance on the air-tambourine and a wonderfully silly conclusion to the ditty. It is these moments, amid scenes of real anger, regret or fear, that mark out *Steptoe and Son* as one of the truly great television shows of the 1960s.

The full house of Harold's friends, or 'a jailbird, a bloke on the dole and a snow clearer' as Albert cynically describes them, are brought to life by a neatly interlaced trio of performers: the weasel-faced Jack Rodney, the familiar character actor Anthony Sagar, and Dudley Foster as the oily leader of the troupe – 'As smooth as a horse's earhole', according to Albert. Foster would appear in two further *Steptoe* adventures, 'My Old Man's a Tory' in 1965 and 'Robbery with Violence' in 1970. According to Alan Simpson, 'Dudley Foster was another one of our "known actor" castings. He was dead straight at playing comedy. Drama and comedy were both the same to him. He was just a very, very good actor. He was a *Z Cars* actor, and he didn't really do comedy. These were the ones we wanted because *Steptoe and Son*, although a sitcom, was treated as a drama in terms of the casting.'

At the start of the final episode, 'Is That Your Horse Outside?', a faster-tempo version of Ron Grainer's 'Old Ned' theme tune signals Harold's impending high spirits as he is quickly entrapped in what Albert calls the 'optional hazard' of being attractive to lonely, rich women with husbands at work all day. Fully aware of the type, Albert tries to convince him that the particular lonely, rich woman he's fallen for is only after him because he's a bit of rough, but Harold's innate self-importance and his desire to improve himself mean he will not be told.

Talking in 1970, Harry H. Corbett commented:

I think *Steptoe and Son* has revived a line of British comedy which was frank about sex. The sort of thing Marie Lloyd had – straightforward vulgarity without self-consciousness. Like when the old man says to Harold, 'This bird fancies you because you're a bit rough'. Harold's knowledge is gleaned from the *Reader's Digest*. No better than that. From the Sunday colour supplements. He's terribly affected by things he reads and sees. He was affected by the James Bond films, especially the vodka and martini, unstirred and with the ice crushed.

It is clear that location work in the cold, cold January of 1963 was treacherous, with both the horse and Brambell's bicycle appearing decidedly unstable. As Alan Simpson remembers:

Location footage was the only time you actually saw the horse, and apart from showing Hercules we used it very sparingly. The simple fact was that the quality of location film just wasn't very good in those days, and it was also very expensive, so for those two reasons the BBC kept it to the minimum. We would do the odd street scene and 'Is That Your Horse Outside?' probably used more location footage than any other. It was only this episode with the old man checking out the posh flats, and the later one, 'The Lead Man Cometh', where we see them throwing the lead into the canal, that really needed location filming. Most of the other times, location was used simply to add atmosphere to an episode.

The real London locations, in and around Orme Court just off Bayswater Road, W2, captured the higher class of Shepherd's Bush and grounded the comedy drama securely within the actual locations. Once those establishing and concluding scenes had been filmed on Friday 25 January 1963, the following Sunday, 27 January, featured Wilfrid Brambell ensconced in the Miranda Café, Kensington Square, for his lonely vigil over the woman's house. The script adds to the location material's feel of fragility with Albert's junkyard-based sad lament to Harold, about the rich women he attracted in the old days when the really big houses were self-contained places and not just a load of bedsits. It's a London gone for ever, and one that was rich in style and class. Familiar and happy with his lot as a representative of the working class, Albert considers such hobnobbing a perk of the job and not a ticket to high society. With a smattering of innuendo – 'At it all the time!' and 'Did you get anything?' after Albert has observed Harold's seven-hour stint behind drawn curtains – the subject is dealt with tastefully but openly. The narrative allows Brambell the chance to offer Albert's pearls of wisdom in an understanding and caring way. His son may dismiss his advice, but the old man makes a clodhopping but gentle attempt to bring him down to earth with the minimum of pain. Harold's distress when he does come down to earth is complemented by the brilliant, two-faced performance of haughty 'princess' Patricia Haines, who replaced the indisposed Delphi Lawrence at the eleventh hour.

His realization that the affair is over – when the coalman opens the lady's door and tells him to clear off – leads to Harold chasing the old man down the road and a concession to the basic comedy of sitcom and farce. The episode succeeds, however, in its turbulent struggle to evoke real emotional pain through the very real physical pain of the situation. As the *Radio Times* wrote: '… the old-established firm of Steptoe and Son leaves the screen for the time being, they go out as they came in – fighting, patching up and fighting again.'

The friendly atmosphere surrounding the *Steptoe* crew was clearly illustrated when, on 4 February 1963, the owners of Hercules were invited to Studio 4 for the Monday evening recording of this last episode. 'We would very much like you [Chris Arnold] and Arthur and your wife to come to the show and have drinks with us afterwards,' offered production assistant R. W. Gilbreath on behalf of Duncan Wood and the cast.

The BBC were not slow to realize the international potential of its series and in March 1963 suggested selecting a *Steptoe* episode for the Montreux Festival. The undimmed enthusiasm of the home market was reflected in a repeat season of series two in July 1963, which was regularly seen in 5.5 million homes. Galton and Simpson were presented with the Writers' Guild Award in 1963 for the second year running, and Wilfrid Brambell filmed a link for the Ivor Novello Awards on 3 May 1963, in lieu of a live appearance. *Steptoe and Son* was at the pinnacle of its attraction. Other television programmes were falling over themselves to secure clips from the series in order to bask in the reflected glory of its success. An extract from 'The Stepmother' was used on *Points of View* in February 1963, while *Perspective: The Bath*, in April 1963, resurrected the sequence of the old man with his pickled onions. Even a trailer for *Juke Box Jury* utilized the Steptoes' battle over popular music in the episode 'A Musical Evening' during which the show was mentioned.

During July of the same year, Wilfrid Brambell was on the promotional circuit, plugging his latest film, *The Small World of Sammy Lee*, and happily discussing 'his career' for the enlightenment of radio listeners. But something odd was happening within the partnership of actors at the heart of *Steptoe*. On 13 June 1963 senior booking manager E. K. Wilson wrote to Brambell's agent, Joan Reddin, and openly discussed issues concerning Harry H. Corbett's availability for another series. Wilson explained that Corbett's representatives, Fraser & Dunlop, were 'unable to give us a decision until September 30 ... they talk about a very important project ... my guess is that it is a film in which he is being offered a leading role. Could it possibly be a film of *Steptoe and Son*?' Of course it wasn't (it is most likely to have been Galton and Simpson's *The Bargee*), but one would have thought that if it had been a *Steptoe* film, firstly the BBC would have known about it and, moreover, so would Brambell's agent.

Spin-off merchandising around the series continued to do well. In October 1963 World Distributors (Manchester) Limited made a bid to publish a *Steptoe and Son* annual for the end of that year. 'Provided that clearance and agreements were arranged with Messrs Galton and Simpson', the BBC were happy with the idea, although clearly someone wasn't. It was never published. The August of 1963 had seen Pye Records re-release their *Steptoe and Son* album on the budget Golden Guinea label, although Tom Sloan for one was less than happy with the 'penny a record' deal the BBC had apparently struck. Pye's Jack Fishman had also secured the release of further *Steptoe* recordings: two EP singles, *The Facts of Life from Steptoe and Son*, which featured scenes from the final episode of series two, 'Is That Your Horse Outside?', and *The Wages of Sin*, featuring an extract from 'Full House', were duly released in 1963. Indeed, both Wilfrid Brambell and Harry H. Corbett had taken advantage of the market for vinyl. *Steptoe* recordings were clearly in vogue, and both attempted solo recording ventures based around their successful television characterizations, *Secondhand* and *Junk Shop* respectively.

The signs were clear that, where these two were concerned, the great British public was beginning to merge fact with fiction, and the actors were happy to play along. Wilfrid Brambell commented:

> People seem to have a sort of love-hate relationship with old Albert. The majority loathe him for hanging on to Harold but can't help feeling sorry for him. Yet among all the letters saying 'Let him go, you crafty old so-and-so', there have been quite a few from viewers who clearly feel that Albert is the injured party, lumbered with an ungrateful son. That's the marvellous thing about these scripts. They're so

funny and yet so truthful that again and again people feel, 'Ouch. This
has happened to me.'

Still, no one could have guessed that the series would be recognized with the
highest accolade in show business. Galton and Simpson were invited to write
an original 15-minute sketch for Brambell and Corbett for the 1963 Royal
Command Performance.

The third series of *Steptoe* had already been commissioned by this stage,
but the royal seal of approval suitably concluded the golden year *Steptoe and
Son* had just enjoyed. Performed at the Prince of Wales Theatre, London, in
front of Her Majesty the Queen Mother, Princess Margaret and Lord
Snowdon, on Monday 4 November 1963, the *Steptoe and Son* section was
one of the biggest talking points of the entire show ... four fab lads from
Liverpool took pride of place. It was the same show that famously featured
John Lennon's cheeky introduction to 'Twist and Shout', in which he asked
the audience for their help: 'Will the people in the cheaper seats clap your
hands ... and the rest of you just rattle your jewellery.' It was a defining
moment in pop culture – the workers were holding court and the ruling classes ate out of their hands. '*Steptoe* was a huge success, and we were simply
asked to do it and we did it,' recalls Ray Galton. Alan Simpson continues:

> Ray and I went to the dress rehearsal, but we didn't get a look-in
> because Marlene Dietrich hogged the entire afternoon with her light-
> ing requirements. She knew her own business and what she wanted,
> so Harry and Willie didn't get on, as far as I recall. They had been hang-
> ing around since 11 in the morning, in full costume, and just as they
> were about to walk on stage Dietrich turned up and took over. She
> frightened the director ... she clearly knew more about the business
> than he did, or any of us, come to that. As for the actual performance,
> we weren't even invited to that – they didn't have room. Writers?
> You're joking!

Brambell himself later recollected that he and Corbett were working at opposite ends of the country at the time, which 'precluded the possibility of more
than one day's rehearsal. On the morning of that memorable day, we got
together in one of the many rooms of the Mapleton Hotel for a quick word
rehearsal which was not made any the more easy by the crowds of people in
the street below incessantly chanting our signature tune and demanding our
appearance on the balcony.' Following the 'La Dietrich' interlude, the *Steptoe*
section was scheduled for rehearsal:

> The director called Harry on to the stage where they both discussed
> the format of our sketch while I sat seething in the sixth row of the

darkened stalls. Eventually 'sir' enquired of Harry as to the where-abouts of, as he called me, 'your sidekick'. I don't think that my rage was justified, but when finally I was peremptorily summoned by micro-phone to mount the stage, I staunchly and silently refused to do so. Eventually, amid cries of 'Where is he?' the house lights were turned on. When I was so revealed, I was quietly angry enough to inform that director that the name of the show was not *Son and Steptoe* and that I also was in it. To add to my fury, the gentleman had the nerve to sug-gest that at the end of our dialogue, and at the fall of the curtain, 'H', on its relift, should be discovered downstage centre bowing to the royal box, long after which I was expected to make an apologetic entrance through the downstage left 'pros' arch in order to join him for my acknowledgement of the presence of royalty. This I refused to do, and when pressure was brought to bear on me I told him to apologize to the Queen Mother for my unexpected absence. I returned to my 'un-dressing' room in the hotel and re-dressed. The director came to my room and redressed. Later, I apologized to 'H' for my pomposity, to which he replied, 'I'd have done the same under the circumstances'. This, I think, is a further proof that 'H' and I work together rather than fight against each other.

The Galton and Simpson script was no less irreverent than John Lennon's comment. The vignette featured a smug Albert totting down the Mall and reflecting on the wonderful haul he has just picked up from a big house down the road – Buckingham Palace as it turns out. Harold is outraged and des-perately tries to discover the full details, getting more and more distraught with each new twist. 'It was a good little piece ... as those things go,' com-ments Alan Simpson modestly. 'Shows how long ago it was,' he continues. 'The little boy who sells Albert the Crown Jewels was Prince Charles!' That little boy handing over the royal 'junk' in exchange for a windmill on a stick was as affectionately knowing and comically disrespectful as the antics of the Crazy Gang. Needless to say, in an atmosphere of Beatlemania and Steptoemania the sketch was warmly received, not least by the royal family, as Wilfrid Brambell remembered: 'The participating artists rushed to their rooms to wash and brush up in order to look all right for a royal presentation. We were lined up in the foyer of the Prince of Wales Theatre in order of prece-dence. Harry and I were placed somewhere near the middle of the queue. I don't remember who was below us, but naturally Marlene Dietrich had justi-fiably been given first place.' The Queen Mother, a self-confessed *Steptoe* fan whose favourite episode was 'Is That Your Horse Outside?', seemed to love

'Old Steptoe totting for tat', according to Brambell. 'I shall always remember Her Majesty's appraisal: "I so enjoyed your sketch. Lovely local fun."' The newspapers were full of the Steptoes and the Beatles the following day, and when ITV televised the edited highlights on 10 November 1963 the programme attracted viewing figures of 10.4 million homes. Both the Beatles and Steptoes enjoyed a boost to their already towering popularity, and public demand for further merchandise was instant. Pye, who had already cleverly secured the distribution rights for the BBC soundtracks, now also signed up the Royal Variety extract and issued it as a single, *Steptoe and Son at Buckingham Palace*, with Harry H. Corbett adding explanatory dialogue such as, 'That's his polo mallet!' as the old man reveals his haul to gales of audience laughter.

The record stayed in the charts for 12 weeks, peaking at number 25. The number one on the day of its release was, not surprisingly, the Beatles' 'She Loves You'. The record's success was further proof of the appeal and popularity of *Steptoe and Son*. The decade that swung was shouting the house down with guitar-laden pop, and the Steptoes were holding their own in alien terrain. The music scene was packed with the Stones and the Manfreds, Dusty and Cliff, the Hollies ... and the Steptoes. The association with the Beatles was, of course, far from over for the senior member of *Steptoe*'s cast. But in the meantime, the Steptoes' 12-week stay in the charts was complemented by the seven-week run of series three on BBC television.

Chapter 6

Steptoe Through the Tulips

The BBC was keen to get at least two episodes of the third series in the can before Christmas, and rehearsals began at West Kensington Church Hall in earnest. Wilfrid Brambell and Harry H. Corbett (now represented by agent Freddie Ross) were recruited for 2 and 5 December for pre-filming on the opening episode on location at Ham House. The building was being used as the old people's home that was to be the focal point of the opening episode, 'Homes Fit for Heroes'. This initial pre-studio recording also included material destined for later episodes. Unfortunately, the format had finally been compromised by the BBC's insistence that the running time for each episode be reduced to 25 minutes. 'It was probably because of overseas sales and commercial timings,' comments Galton. 'The scripts continued to be just as long, mind you. We would just have to cut more out! We would still work to 20 pages, quite often going to 24 pages, and only once in a blue moon would we do 18 pages, which was just about the perfect length. We would hardly ever throw anything away though, it was too precious. If we lost a scene one week, we would often resurrect it some other time ... and if it was thrown away it really was crap!'

But the reduced running time wasn't the only change to be made for the new series. According to a BBC note of 9 December 1963, 'Ron Grainer is unable to undertake the composition of incidental music', so for the first time another composer, Norman Percival, was assigned. Grainer's 'Old Ned' theme was, of course, retained.

Broadcasting started almost immediately in the New Year, with the first episode of series three going out on 7 January 1964 and being watched in an amazing 9.4 million homes – impressive, given that *Coronation Street*, already well established, was falling short of these figures. The series would peak at 9.7 million homes by the end of the run in February. The *Radio Times*, featuring Corbett and Brambell as cover stars, heralded the return of *Steptoe and Son*. Gale Pedrick commented on the writers who had 'wisely ... rationed themselves – and us' thus leaving the audience begging for more *Steptoe* and finally delivering to a thunderous reaction. The opening episode is a typically poignant piece of work. The phrase 'Homes Fit for Heroes' refers to the riches and stability promised to the men returning from the trenches of the First World War – one of whom Albert patently was. However, it is also used here as a contemporary comment on the welfare of the nation's senior citizens. Although it is Harold, with his socialist tendencies, who points out the disgraceful treatment of the old people of Britain, it is his very selfishness that is pushing his father into an old people's home in the first place.

Harold is once more determined to break away from the business, this time to enjoy a two-year break on the seven seas. Albert laughing uproariously at his son's dream of foreign travel is reminiscent of Harold's incredulous dismissal of his father's planned marriage in series two. But Albert is not amused for long, and his jealousy boils over at the thought that his son is about to 'float round the world with five bits of crumpet' while he himself is 'playing dominoes and making handbags' in an old people's home.

The episode is structured as a blow-by-blow reappraisal of the series one programme, 'The Holiday'. A reference to Bognor is an obvious clue, and Harold is again trying to get away on his own – for two years now, rather than two weeks. There's an almost identical moment as Albert goes off to bed leaving a guilt-ridden Harold offering to make supper and muttering to himself about the 'hysterical month' he's about to endure before he sets sail. Still trying to kid himself, he complains that 'I could have cleared out years ago', but the fear that had dominated him in 'The Holiday' – that time is running out and that his age is against him – is echoed here. Now, though, his age has finally caught up with him as the nine other members of the proposed sailing trip, with an average age of 20, consider Harold too far outside their age group for comfortable companionship. Thus, the two rag 'n' bone men are reunited in the end. There's clearly no escape for Harold now, but the threat of the old firm breaking up had been so real and imminent this time round that Albert for once gives up his pathetic, lonely-old-man act. He is embittered, aggressive, proud and petulant, but far from frail.

The matron of the old people's home is given a condescending, schoolteacherly interpretation by Peggy Thorpe-Bates, the wife of 'The Piano' guest star Brian Oulton. Treating the old folk, who temporarily include Albert, like helpless children, she laughs off the old man's threats of wild behaviour. Wilfrid Brambell clearly relishes giving the wild-eyed warning that if there are old ladies around 'you better keep them locked up for a start', but Albert's attempts to scupper his placing at the home are short-lived. The matron is having none of it, and before long father and son are left alone to say their goodbyes. Stuck in his little room with his little washbasin, the old man remains angry and tight-lipped. When he crossly observes that he's used a washbasin before, Harold refrains from making the obvious reply. He pauses, but doesn't mock his 'dirty old man'. The scene is too tender and moving to accommodate the familiar catchphrase.

Harold cheerfully insists that Albert won't miss him at all: 'It'll be the other way around, probably.' The sober underplaying of Harold's exit line – 'I shall be thinking about you, Dad, all the time ...' is a beautiful piece of acting, enabling Brambell, on his own at last, to collapse from deadpan anger to tearful timidity. The musical score from Norman Percival, and Duncan Wood's sensitive direction, combine with Brambell's performance, as the old man crumbles to insignificance before our eyes, to create a powerful coda to the Steptoes' life together. It is an emotional moment matched only by Harry H. Corbett's monologue as he prepares for his trip. His thought that, 'I hope I don't get as old as him ... another 20 years and I'll turn it in!' is, in retrospect, poignant even beyond the original intention.

Along with 'The Holiday', the episode was Wilfrid Brambell's favourite *Steptoe* of the 1960s. For Harry H. Corbett, too, 'Homes Fit for Heroes' held a special place. For him it captured the essence of what the series was trying to do: make an audience think, laugh and cry in equal measures. 'The perfect example was when the old man was in the old people's home, alone, in tears. How sad. The next thing you know he's through the window giving an up-yours sign to get out of the place. He had the chance of an ideal set-up – thousands of lovely old birds – but he rejects it.'

George Campery and Roland Fox, the Head and Assistant Head of Publicity, made use of the recording date, 12 December 1963, for the first episode of the new series. As one of the BBC's flagship productions, the episode was utilized to form the basis of a big pre-Christmas party for the television correspondents of the London daily and evening papers, and favourable reviews followed the occasion. 'Homes Fit for Heroes' was broadcast on 7 January 1964 and the Audience Research Report for 30 January 1964 signalled clear approval for the new series. Many people were 'obviously delighted' although some felt the subject matter was 'a little too near the sad truth to be wholly entertaining'. Still, one viewer made the very good point that there was 'never any real doubt [that Harold's plans] would come to naught (particularly since this was the first rather than the last programme in the series)'. Many viewers were distressed, feeling that Harold had suffered a radical change in character and believing it unlikely that he would 'even consider such an action'. This 'put the Steptoes' entire relationship into somewhat different – and less endearing – perspective. This surely is a new Harold who plans to leave Dad with hardly a twinge of conscience. Has he altered so much in so short a time? I hope not!' Still, a hairdresser seemed to sum up the general reaction: 'While the theme of "parking" an ancient parent is not one that normally would amuse me, the knowledge that the old man would undoubtedly win in the end made the matter entirely palatable. If this particular episode was at times rather more pathetic than funny, it provides, nevertheless, yet another example of the unique blend of humour and pathos which had come to be the hallmark of *Steptoe and Son*. It was sad, and was so skilfully written as to avoid any danger of falling over the edge into sentimentality.' Many considered it 'one of the best', 'an excellent study of human problems and emotions' and 'a real gem of a script', while those who were 'slightly disappointed in the script [were] often concerned that in any other show they would have regarded it as exceptional'. *Steptoe and Son* 'had set itself such a supremely high standard'. One enthused fan wrote affectionately of the relationship: 'Oh, my Gawd. They're saying the same old things but, oh, my Gawd, I love it.' The acting was, as usual, universally appreciated. 'Viewers,' the report concluded, 'obviously found it difficult to realize that they *were* acting and their performance tonight was, apparently, as faultless as ever; together they formed a partnership that had in its short lifetime become almost a legend.' 'Galton and Simpson, Brambell and Corbett – what a combination,' thought one, while a secretary spoke for an entire nation when she remarked, 'Poor old Harry – he'll never get away (fortunately for us). It's marvellous to have them back again, and I only hope I can stay in every Tuesday to see the whole series.'

Having brought the emotional core of the Steptoes' relationship to the fore with 'Homes Fit for Heroes', the following two episodes returned to a lighter tone with two of the most hilarious and polished programmes in the series. 'The Wooden Overcoats' deals with superstition, a favourite Galton and Simpson subject, and is a farcical study in terror and its causes. 'We loved all those old wives' tales,' recalls Ray Galton, 'all that "pigeons on the roof, there'll be a death in the house" business. The coffins were just something weird and wonderful for them to collect, but they provided excellent material for the old man. Obviously, it would worry him more than it would worry Harry.'

Corbett's mocking performance is brilliantly taken down a peg by the wide-eyed, maudlin turn of Brambell, whose old character-acting skills are fully resurrected. He excels with a brilliant shaggy dog story about a man who slept in a house with coffins and ended up a 'white-haired, raving maniac'. Indicating a devil's horns with his fingers and pulling fearful faces, Brambell's physical business beautifully captures the hysteria of superstition.

Duncan Wood not only heightens the tension with shadowy images and flickering candles, but fully utilizes the familiar décor of the Steptoe home, as Harold's exotic poster of Tahiti becomes immediately suggestive of black magic. The ever-present skeleton and stuffed bear take on new menace, and the sinister, moustached Edwardian gentleman advertisement adds to the macabre atmosphere. Corbett's 'Oh, my Gawd!' as he suddenly sees his reflection in the mirror is the high point of the comedy. Norman Percival's incidental music also enhances the spooky feel of the episode, with the Steptoe theme sliding into a death march and the heart-pounding moments complemented by sinister strings and dramatic pauses.

The underpinnings of the relationship between father and son are also investigated, as, at the start of the episode, Albert believes a burglar has interrupted his session with a sunlamp. Although soon clouded by abuse and argument, the split second when the old man realizes that the burglar is Harold is a delight: he throws his arms around him in overjoyed relief. Harold may initially be cocky enough to dismiss the grotesque old man as an advert for famine relief, and he mocks both the useless sunlamp with its 60-watt bulb and parental love, but by the closing scene he is terrified. Ultimately, convinced that the coffins he has brought into the house are a bad omen, he has to share his father's bed in the stable to get a good night's sleep. He regresses so far as to demand a glass of water before bed, revealing the little boy within the man – the little boy who can never leave the family home and business.

The third series, technically fine-tuned and drawing on the expertise of Duncan Wood and his technicians, used up to six cameras for filming. This gave the show its fluidity and fly-on-the-wall realism. The approach also gave Harry H. Corbett some standing in the television industry. He said of the early episodes:

> I'm now known as a camera actor, and it's terrifyingly important to know where the camera is at all times. You could say this is being camera-conscious if you wish, but it's important to know. That camera is there all the time. Otherwise I won't get freedom, funnily enough, especially as the men will get to know me by my movements. So

consequently I'm going to lose the most important point of the play by being off shot. For instance, reaction in comedy, at least this form of comedy, is a line. It is written in. I mean, if you say to me, 'The place is burning', right, you cut to me; I've merely got to say in reaction, 'Is it?', or I've got to say, 'My God!' – with a pause. But that is the line; the camera must cut to me; you must see the reaction. Or we mustn't see the reaction. So this must be planned, and the camera and the other actor must know this and must be ready to hold it up so that this reaction can go in.

After reverting to childhood in 'The Wooden Overcoats', Harold is back to his usual self from the outset of the next programme in the series, 'The Lead Man Cometh'. He complains about working a 13-hour day: 'I'm shagged out!' He complains about the lack of food: 'I ain't got sparrow's guts like what you has!' And he complains about the flask of tea the old man has prepared: 'The monkeys that advertise it could make better tea than that!'

Albert knows that the business situation is bad and, going misty-eyed, tries to buck his son's ideas up, both by ridiculing the amount his son spends on junk and by showing concern at the fact that the business is losing money fast. Typically, Harold can suggest nothing save a facetious suicide pact. Temporary relief arrives in what must be considered one of the most unforgettable *Steptoe* guest appearances: a relatively unknown Leonard Rossiter enters stage left and gives the two leads something of a run for their money.

Rossiter's first appearance is extraordinary. With his back to the camera, he continues the *Hamlet* soliloquy from the point where Harold has broken off. The Wardrobe, Hair and Make-up sheet describes the character as wearing 'old blue trousers, old blue suit jacket. Raincoat with belt made of string, old dirty shirt with no collar, old sweater. Old woollen scarf. Old cap, cycle clips. Greasy unkempt hair, 2–3 days' growth of beard.' Indeed Rossiter, unshaven and scruffy, continually puffing on a cigarette and Welsh to boot, immediately arouses the old man's suspicions. But with Albert's harsh words about his lack of business sense still ringing in his ears, Harold takes a gamble and buys the lead Rossiter is offering. Of course the outcome – that the lead was from the Steptoes' own roof – is vengeance for their successful scam over the local totters in 'Wallah-Wallah Catsmeat'. With a title corrupting Arthur Miller's *The Ice Man Cometh*, and a supporting actor of such magnetism, this episode was an instant winner. The role call report for the cast and crew simply includes the single word 'excellent' by Rossiter's name.

'Steptoe à la Cart' shows father and son in open rivalry, over a young woman whom Harold hopes to marry. Gwendolyn Watts, an actress who had already notched up comedy roles opposite Benny Hill, Harry Worth and Michael Bentine, and Peter Jones in *The Rag Trade*, gives a real sense of youthful innocence and well-being to the central guest performance as an au pair girl from France. Harold brings the girl back to the house, but when Albert discovers that his son has been talking about him behind his back and referring to him as 'old misery guts' to his girlfriend, Albert is set for revenge. The old man reveals that he can speak fluent French, learnt during his First World War service, and effortlessly charms the young lady, much to Harold's dismay. His unsporting behaviour is in the end revealed to be irrelevant, as the plot exposes the young lady as Albert's granddaughter and thus Harold cannot marry her anyway.

Once again, *Steptoe* uses television culture to make funny and accurate observations. Finding the old man clad in African tribal gear and dancing round the living room, Harold wears an expression of pure delighted bemusement. Reflecting on whether Albert has gone mad or joined some weird organization, he makes the knowing comment: 'There's a distinct touch of *The Avengers* about you sometimes!' A reference back to Harold's obsession with gramophone records, last investigated in 'A Musical Evening' in series two, gives continuity to the character as this time he acquires a 'learn French' record. Albert's xenophobia provides an excuse to condemn his son's choice of girlfriend as he summarily dismisses the entire Gallic race as to be found only in 'some doorway'. But this is a woman Harold seriously loves, and there's a real sense of dramatic tension as the sad facts of the family connection dawn. Gwendolyn Watts brilliantly depicts a range of emotions, from happiness in finding her 'new' grandfather to unease with her 'new' uncle and disappointment and brave-faced regret at the thought of losing her boyfriend.

Harry H. Corbett, whose memoirs, *The Harry H. Corbett Story by Harold Steptoe*, were serialized in the *People* from 19 January 1964, told the *Radio Times*:

> I share with Harold – and, I suspect, most people – that marvellous daydream of being multilingual. You know how it goes: there's an international crisis and everything depends on a stranger speaking a strange language, which no one can understand. An urgent call to Corbett, the only man in London who can help – and with a few crisp phrases in an obscure Uzbekistandu dialect, he saves the situation.

Talking in 1967, Corbett reflected more fundamentally on 'Steptoe à la Cart', addressing the serious issues behind the Continental encounter:

> You see Harold's normal reaction to sex. First of all there was, 'Cor, I'm

right in it here', next you get the character he's trying to evolve within himself, the excusing of this on the ground that no, this is love. First of all there's sex and after that there's the conscience thing that makes him change it; it's got to be love. Of course, he's thrilled about it, who's been about with an au pair? That's a piece of one-upmanship, and he's got the night all worked out.

'Steptoe à la Cart' used a sizeable cast and some location filming, but the following episode went even further. A note to the restaurant manager from production secretary Liz Cranston read: 'Just a warning that the cast for next week's *Steptoe* episode will be much larger than usual. There are likely to be about 30 artists in at coffee time, and a total of 60 for tea.' The budget for additional actors was an almost prohibitive £2457, including a bunch of 'furtive old men' for the 'naughty' film queue.

Galton and Simpson explored 1930s cinema nostalgia for the episode 'Sunday for Seven Days'. Albert is the perfect voice for the maxim that 'they don't make 'em like that any more', and the old man's nostalgic fondness for vintage cinema is brought into effective contrast with his desire to enjoy the latest nude flick. With one of Galton and Simpson's sharpest scripts, and boasting one of the fullest casts, 'Sunday for Seven Days' recalls the essence of late 1950s *Hancock's Half Hour*. Both on television and radio, in shows like 'The Big Night Out' and 'The Last Bus Home', Tony Hancock and Sid James argued about the latest 'flavour of the month' or each other's poor dress sense. Here, Harry H. Corbett can invest Harold with further Hancockian pretensions. As Harold snobbishly refuses to enter the cinema when the film has started (which was common practice in the 1960s) and floats dreamily into the pretentious world of Fellini's cinema, Albert brings his aspirations tumbling down. The old man, naturally, prefers the idea of seeing 'her 48 and a half' to Fellini's *8½*.

'Cinemas are a great situation for comedy,' Ray Galton maintains. 'Like a dentist's chair or a lift, there's an atmosphere, a code of behaviour that is expected. Plus, we both loved films. When I was young we had three main circuits plus independents, so you could go four or five times a week because there would be a different programme on a Sunday: hence our title. It would be a double feature, and as often as not the minor film was better than the main attraction. You would have news, *The March of Time*, a cartoon ...'

Albert's encyclopedic knowledge of, and fanatical obsession with, classic cinema adds a real depth to the episode. Recounting 'marvellous' memories of Fred and Ginger, Ronald Colman's *Lost Horizon* and the original *Dr Kildare* series with Lew Ayres ('better than that bloke they've got on television now'),

Brambell also indulges in a flesh-creeping description of the latest fictitious radioactivity 'classic', *The Beast from the Bog*.

Harold's protective affection for his father emerges within the cinema when a beefy heavy, played by Michael Brennan, threatens to end Albert's incessant talking with a well-placed ice-cream tub. Regular *Hancock* support player Alec Bregonzi appears too, desperately trying to remove his girlfriend from the reach of Harold's unsubtle advances.

The BBC had certainly loosened up in the 18 months or so prior to this episode. Albert can disparagingly condemn Fellini's *8 ½*, hilariously misunderstanding the title: 'Maybe it's his hat size.' The old man's choice language lets rip, as Fellini's work promises to be 'a load of old cobblers', Alain Resnais' 1961 film *Last Year at Marienbad* was 'a load of old boots' and a gentleman keen to hear the film above the audience's bickering is soundly put down with: 'Oh conkers.' Moreover, it was almost inconceivable that the BBC would allow copious shots of naked young women in any show bar *Steptoe*. Ten years later, Fletch's pin-ups in *Porridge* would still shock some viewers. In *Steptoe*, the much-discussed permissiveness of society in general finally crept into the BBC. Even so, the *Radio Times* still resolutely avoided the issue and explained that the old man 'prefers a film which quickly gets down to basic facts'.

A clip from *8 ½* was used in 'Sunday for Seven Days', for which a fee of 10 guineas was paid to the British distributors, who also asked for an on-screen credit for their co-operation, a credit edited from international prints of the episode.

Soho nightclubs and the old men with more money than sense who populate them was the focal point for the following episode, 'The Bonds That Bind Us'. The old man's premium bonds come up trumps at last, and Wilfrid Brambell was given the opportunity to bring the part of Albert much closer to his own persona. The transformation from scruff to toff for the old man's foray into the West End was achieved through a montage of grooming sequences which Brambell pre-filmed with several extras. The wardrobe sheet detailed the change in Albert and reveals how the effect was managed: 'usual – scruffy & unshaven, but note hairdo below (can be hidden under hat for Take 1). A sparkling brand-new set of teeth (these he [Brambell] will supply – his "other" set). His hair should look immaculate and freshly cut with blow waves. He can wear his hat throughout Take 1 to cover this up. The whole effect is one of a complete dandy.' Newly dapper, with a new suit, a new pair of 'denches' and a new haircut, Albert refuses to give handouts to Harold. Later, when the son rejects his father's conscience-appeasing gift of an electric shaver, the situation drives another wedge between the two protagonists.

Money is the root of all evil, and if a rival suddenly has it and you haven't, it's the source of a bitterness that refuses to heal.

Originally, the casting was to embrace one of the best young actresses in the country, Billie Whitelaw, in the role of the good-time girlfriend Albert picks up in Soho. Her agent had expressed an interest in the part, although conditionally on Whitelaw's script approval. Duncan Wood wrote directly to Whitelaw, enclosing the script: 'I hope you like it because Harry, Wilfrid, the authors and myself are unanimous that you are the only person to play it.' In the event she withdrew, and the honour went to June Whitfield, an actress more naturally associated with comedy, thus slightly diminishing the dramatic impact of the part. Whitfield, described by Frank Muir as 'God's gift to scriptwriters', had been part of the radio cast of Muir and Norden's *Take It From Here* and working with her was a real treat for Galton and Simpson: 'We thought June was just wonderful. We would use her in everything if we could!'

Indeed, Whitfield had been an intrinsic part of the finely balanced comedy of the Tony Hancock classic 'The Blood Donor' in 1961. She had also starred with Peter Jones in 'The Telephone Call', part of the 1962 *Comedy Playhouse* series that spawned *Steptoe and Son*. 'The great thing about June, almost unique among comedy actresses, is that she is wonderfully funny and also very sexy and desirable,' remembers Ray Galton. 'That fitted our purpose here. She was stunning, with this marvellous comic ability.'

Whitfield's playing is perfect throughout as she desperately tries to cover up her cockney traits, happily drinks out of the bottle when the Steptoes are out of sight and crumbles at the thought of policemen, investigation and exposure when Harold pretends Albert's money is stolen. As when any interloper tries to dismantle the Steptoe relationship, one Steptoe can't function without the other. Harold's piles of washing-up and meal of cold baked beans symbolize his attempts to cope on his own as half of a couple. Wilfrid Brambell's sneer of enjoyment as he departs for the West End is loaded with knowledge, as he is well aware that the money won't last for ever and relishes Harold's distraught rambling. But this is severely contrasted with the docile wreck of a man who momentarily surfaces when his fiancée is revealed as a gold-digger. The protectiveness and love between father and son are at the heart of the episode as always, but in June Whitfield *Steptoe and Son* found one of its most memorable sources of disruption to this bond.

Viewers commented of Albert's transformation that it was 'refreshing to see him in jaunty mood rather than the downtrodden old man of recent episodes'. As a housewife observed: 'If the love-hate relationship between Harold and Albert is not to make us feel uncomfortable, Albert *must* be shown in a more sympathetic light now and again.' The leads were marked out as 'two of the best comedy actors ever seen on television'. June Whitfield, 'who excels in the London accents', received praise, as did the regular camera crew and designer 'in a variety of shots that made smooth work of showing the incumbents of the Steptoe household'.

Rehearsals for the rest of the series were held at St Michael's Hall, Commonwealth Avenue, and at this stage of production the next episode was rather grandly named 'Sweeter Than All the Roses'. This title was quickly changed to the more straightforward 'The Lodger'. If you can imagine 'The Offer' played to an audience already aware of the relationship between father and son, you have an encapsulation of 'The Lodger', a superbly scripted and warmly acted two-hander, with Brambell and Corbett crossing and double-crossing each other with zest. For most of the time each of them knows exactly what the other is up to, but never reveals his knowledge until maximum humiliation is reached. Harold is less able than Albert to bear humiliation and makes the empty threat that he will leave home if a lodger comes in to help pay the bills. The audience knows his departure will never be permanent. The threat does, however, start a vicious feud that will separate the totting pair for a week. Politics once more becomes a battleground, culminating in Albert's sarcastic rendition of 'The Red Flag'. Serious commentary concerning miners getting shot and the 1926 General Strike is delivered amidst the fast-paced dialogue while the old man reveals his Tory tendencies as he proclaims, 'We never had it so good.'

But Harold is in full flow, and in preparation for the split, the assets of the business are stripped down and assessed. Albert wants a serious discussion, but the only money-making option he can come up with is the potentially explosive solution of bringing in a lodger. Corbett relishes Harold's Shakespearean bent as a corrupted 'the most noble rag 'n' bone man ...' quotation is qualified with 'Julius Steptoe!', a reference to the noble 'Roman' himself. As in previous episodes, 'The Lodger' treads a fine line, with knowing hints as to why Harold needs a room of his own in the first place. Corbett's understated acting pushes the subject even further as he highlights the most obvious reason. His face is uneasy and sheepish as he voices the belief that privacy is even more important when a bloke is without a bird.

Like a child, Harold tries too hard to avoid eye contact with his suspiciously disgusted parent. For the first time there is a tangible shyness and coyness about his age, as his eyes flicker and falter when he mutters that he is '30 whatever I am'. The familiar format of two-way banter is also seen at its best here, with the definitive two-shot framing Albert at the table and Harold in his armchair facing his desk. It is easy for the actors to avoid eye contact within this placing. Harold's oft-repeated threat of leaving is again debated. His father, as reluctant to call his bluff as the son is to have it called, holds back before placing a shop window advertisement for a lodger. Harold removes it and the fact that the old man knows this starts the whole argument up again. In the end, neither will admit defeat and each gently eases the other into returning to the status quo. Albert, lonely and with the room turned down by 15 potential tenants, and Harold, working as a sandwich-board man for an Indian restaurant, both come to the negotiation table with nothing to lose and nothing to offer save themselves. The scene plays like the reunion of a divorced couple. Both are trying to impress each other and suppress any suggestion of their respective failures. We, the audience, are privy to the asides and subtle hints of failure – Albert secretly hoping that the knock at the door is a lodger who will accept the room, or Harold energetically blowing into his hands for warmth.

As Corbett stuffs a chip butty into his mouth, the pity on Brambell's face shows us that he knows how ravenous Harold is behind the bravura. Corbett's performance is even more powerful. He hides his knowledge of his father's inability to find a lodger from both the audience and the old man. The final burst of familiar abuse, as Harold questions Albert's language and Albert calls him 'a lazy git' is charming and affectionate, and the ad-libbed tossing of chips into the old man's mouth is vibrant. The spat-out 'good night' from the old man and the mockingly spat-out repeat from Harold, Albert's mellowing smile and wink and Harold's beaming acceptance of being back home create a joyous reunion.

Having finished the third series and unwittingly about to face an 18-month break from regular *Steptoe and Son*, Harry H. Corbett and Wilfrid Brambell were, however, reunited later in 1964 when Galton and Simpson scripted a brief sketch for the ITV Christmas Day Gala *Night of 100 Stars*. The sequence entitled 'An Evening Out' featured the rag 'n' bone men arguing before setting off to the show in style on their horse and cart.

Chapter 7

Damned Yankees!

The Audience Research Report of 20 March 1964 gave an overall favourable review of the third series, which had attracted the biggest audience the show ever received. 'With only a few exceptions, viewers were at great pains to express their regret that yet another series of *Steptoe and Son* – the undoubted king of situation comedy shows, according to most – had once again come to an end.' Only a handful expressed uninterest. A garage proprietor 'claimed to have become "very weary of seeing these far from lovable characters" in what were "only slight variations on a recurring theme". Even less impressed was a postman who declared that he was "thankful this series had ended. I never did find it in any way funny and just can't understand why everybody raves about it!" But "brilliant" was the only possible adjective to describe the uncannily perceptive interpretations of Steptoe senior and junior.' The majority of the audience certainly 'wanted more'.

It was a long, long wait for those millions who 'wanted more'. And a lot of distracting politics within and without the BBC would need to be resolved in the interim. But *Steptoe* merchandising was still a highly profitable enterprise in the spring of 1964. Gale Pedrick produced a novelization, *Steptoe and Son*, that featured adaptations of 'The Offer', 'Sixty-Five Today', 'The Stepmother', 'The Holiday' (retitled 'Holidays' in the book), 'The Economist' and 'The Bath', while World Distributors discussed publishing an annual, called simply *Steptoe and Son*. A *Steptoe* picture book and a comic-strip *Steptoe* book were also suggested. The comic-strip idea was, however, immediately dismissed. Tom Sloan would 'certainly *not* agree to publication of this standard. *Steptoe* deserves better', while Galton and Simpson would not allow anybody else to write 'stories'. The Pedrick novelization was adapted, with permission, from the original scripts, and the BBC could do nothing but agree to it, though with reservations. Evelyn M. Thomas explained to fellow BBC marketing representative R. S. Hargreaves that 'in principle I hate these parasitical ventures and I cannot see that our series can benefit in any way by this book – but it is not bad enough to do any harm. Certainly, I share your views about Galton's remarks – it is stupid to print it [the quote] when there must be a huge juvenile market for this book.' Galton's remarks, a personal endorsement on the back of the book, read 'Please buy this book, it's filthy', and although this might be acceptable Harold Steptoe dialogue the BBC felt 'it would not seem desirable for the BBC to be associated with this sort of publicity'. However, the book sold extremely well.

Wilfrid Brambell was also keen to profit from his association with *Steptoe*. On 4 March 1964 his solicitor, Maurice J. Bushell, contacted the BBC regarding the notion of Brambell setting up a 'proposed company, Steptoe and Son Limited'. An internal memo of 10 March 1964 from Holland Bennett quickly quoted chapter and verse from Brambell's contract. This clearly stated that: 'the Artist shall not be entitled to any rights in any character or pseudonym which the Corporation may provide for the Artist'. The official BBC response, from the corporation's solicitor L. P. R. Roche, explained that 'in those circumstances, therefore, the Corporation regrets that it cannot give its authorization to your client registering the name under the title of its own well-known television series'. In an attempt to keep the peace, Holland Bennett amended the response before it was sent to Brambell's solicitors on 16 March, adding the sweetener: 'There is, of course, no suggestion that in selecting this title for the company, Mr Brambell was deliberately acting in bad faith.' Brambell's representatives closed the matter on 19 March by assuring the BBC that 'we are advising our client accordingly and feel sure he must have overlooked clause 8 in his contract'.

It was in both Brambell's and the BBC's interests to keep the situation uncomplicated. *Steptoe and Son* seemed to be everywhere, and Brambell in particular was a high-profile celebrity guest on the BBC's people programmes. He went on to appear on *Open House* on 5 September 1964 and *First Impressions* on 27 October.

Despite the rumblings within the BBC the tremendous national popularity of *Steptoe and Son* continued unabated. Two further Pye records, *More Junk from Steptoe and Son* and *Steptoe à la Cart*, were released to great acclaim, and another chunk of *Steptoe* ephemera hit the stores when Tower Press, by arrangement with the BBC, produced two 240-piece jigsaw puzzles based on the series. The images featured the famous duo with their horse and cart and the breakfast-table sequence from the series two opener 'Wallah-Wallah Catsmeat'. Both remain rare collectors' items to this day.

Fortunately for the actors, the success of *Steptoe and Son* hadn't completely jeopardized the rest of their careers. For Wilfrid Brambell the popularity of Albert Steptoe had led to his being Roy Plomley's 695th *Desert Island Discs* castaway on 30 March 1964. His musical tastes ranged from Beethoven's Symphony No. 7 in A Major to Frank Sinatra belting out 'These Foolish Things'. Brambell's chosen book was an English dictionary and his luxury item was reassuringly liquid: Scotch whisky and lager. However, lasting fame in film also came his way thanks to the huge popularity of his performance in *Steptoe*. He was given a lead role in the new Beatles vehicle, *A Hard Day's Night*. All the fab four were *Steptoe* fans and enjoyed the working-class voice of Galton and Simpson's pioneering comedy. With Beatlemania sweeping the world and the British invasion of America at its peak, United Artists were swift to take up an option on a feature film starring the group. For Brambell, it was 'a schizophrenic and a marvellous experience'.

Clearly, Brambell had the national recognition for a role in this hip and trendy film. He had also recently revealed, in 'The Bonds That Bind Us', the polished image lurking beneath Albert Steptoe's 'dirty old man'. Opposite the Beatles, of course, he lost the grime and became the 'very clean' Irish grandfather of Paul McCartney. Brambell's performance as the grumpy, aggressive stirrer fitted the bill perfectly. It's easy to underestimate his contribution to the film, overshadowed as it is by Lennon and McCartney's music and Dick Lester's wacky style of direction. Still, the contrast between Brambell's charming demeanour towards McCartney and his brazen, military roar and nagging mockery of poor Ringo Starr is one of the funniest aspects of *A Hard Day's Night*. It remains, not unsurprisingly, Brambell's biggest international film success. 'I can't remember how many times fans ecstatically asked me which of the four boys was my favourite. Invariably, my reply was "whatever one I'm talking to". It was a careful but completely true answer. I have only been in theatre for a mere 60 years, but I feel that never in the history of entertainment has there been such a revolutionary change as that which those four boys made. Not only were they witty, but with it, they were serious and talented musicians, and brilliant and lasting composers. I'm sure their music will last as long as the music of Schubert or Cole Porter.'

The only film actually to make a profit while still being made, *A Hard Day's Night* gave Brambell a whole new, global fame, albeit as Paul McCartney's grandfather and not as an actor in his own right. In Roy Carr's book *Beatles at the Movies*, McCartney recalls working with the actor and comments on a problem that had affected *Steptoe* recordings: 'Wilfrid Brambell was great ... the only terrible thing for us was that Wilfrid kept forgetting his lines. And we couldn't believe it. See, we expected all the actors to be very professional and word-perfect – couldn't imagine that an actor like Wilfrid could ever do a thing like forget his lines! So, we were very shocked and embarrassed by this.'

But regardless of Brambell's memory while on set, his performance is beautiful and it fell to him to voice the huge frustration that the Beatles were then tolerating and later rebelled against, when he summed up life with the group as unrelenting confinement: 'So far I've been in a car and a room and a train and a room and a room and a room!' When the film opened in July 1964 it was an unqualified success.

Brambell was also continuing his jobbing actor career, playing the Reverend Canon Chasuble in the November 1964 BBC presentation of *The Importance of Being Earnest*. He also banked on his *Steptoe* fame in a string of supports and cameos in British film comedies of the day. Notably he had cropped up as a rascally old man in the Barbara Windsor and Ronald Fraser crime caper *Crooks in Cloisters*, and, most interestingly, agreed to a 'gag appearance' as the junkman in the 1964 Children's Film Foundation production *Go-Kart, Go*.

While his on-screen father was cavorting with the Beatles, Harry H. Corbett also ventured into big-screen comedy. His effort was firmly rooted in his *Steptoe and Son* associations. *The Bargee*, with a script by Ray Galton and Alan Simpson and directed by *Steptoe*'s Duncan Wood, cast Corbett as a romantic charmer travelling Britain's canals. The supporting cast included many *Steptoe and Son* guest stars. 'We wrote the screenplay in 1962 and it was made in 1963,' remembers Alan Simpson. 'We thought about it while Ray and I were down in the south of Spain on holiday. This was the time when Harry came down to join us and told us how well *Steptoe* was doing at home. The idea had already been suggested for us to do a film. It never occurred to us or anybody else to do a film of *Steptoe*; even if it had, it would probably have been too soon, but we did want to do a film with Harry. So we wrote *The Bargee*, which was really the Harold Steptoe character but on the barges. He was a bit more successful with the ladies, but Harry played the part exactly like Harold.' Corbett had spent several years in unremarkable comedy films in the early 1960s, and this production was anticipated as his major break into cinema. With his *Steptoe* credentials expectations were high, but the film was greeted with only moderate interest. Ray Galton recalls why: 'Maybe the critics wanted a *Steptoe* film pure and simple ... but the time, for us at least, wasn't right.' The desire for *Steptoe* on film had also affected the reception of Corbett's performance in the 1963 film *Sammy Going South*. 'After Harold the junkman ... no one would take me seriously,' lamented the actor in 1969. 'In a movie I was in with Edward G. Robinson, I was supposed to be a devil and they just fell about with hilarity. I haven't tried villainy since.' Although in 1963 he had maintained that his ambition was 'to get to grips with Shakespeare. I've reached the age when I'm beginning to understand him a little', by 1965 he had submitted to a career dominated by acting in popular comedy.

Corbett's film career blossomed with a starring role in the 1964 adaptation of *Rattle of a Simple Man*, scripted by Charles Dyer from his own play. Corbett reprised his stage role as the painfully shy football fan Percy, who agrees to a bet that dictates he spend the night with a lady of ill repute. Corbett wasn't happy with the result, however: 'The problem wasn't so much to keep him away from Harold Steptoe but something I failed in miserably: to keep Percy away from going too far into what I know about the North.'

Frank Launder and Sidney Gilliat also spotted Corbett's potential as a comedy film star thanks to his fame on television. In 1965 he was cast in the role of the crafty, lovable eponymous spiv in *Joey Boy*, heading a cast that included Stanley Baxter, Bill Fraser and Lance Percival. Set in 1941, it tells the tale of Corbett's Joey Boy and a handful of black-marketeering friends joining the British army. The contrast between the upbeat home-front scenes and the black comedy of the front may not always sit easily, but there is plenty to relish about the film.

With all this film activity for the two *Steptoe* stars, and with Galton and Simpson's involvement not just in *The Bargee* but also in the Peter Sellers vehicle *The Wrong Arm of the Law*, *Steptoe and Son* was happily put on temporary hold.

But still, repeats in October 1964 were gaining very respectable viewing figures of around six million homes. The third series of *Steptoe* had earned Ray Galton and Alan Simpson the runners-up position in the 1964 Writers' Guild Award, an award they had won at the previous two ceremonies. By the end of 1964 they had been justifiably presented with the John Logie Baird Award for Outstanding Contribution to Television.

Galton and Simpson's reputation, thanks to both *Hancock's Half Hour* and *Steptoe and Son*, was secured. The huge appeal of *Steptoe and Son* in Britain in particular had even managed to make an impression in the mecca for entertainment: America. In 1964 the feverish interest in the series in England had convinced an American film producer, Joseph E. Levine, founder of Embassy Pictures, to invest in a pilot episode for the American television network NBC.

However, this initial explosion of American interest in Galton and

Simpson's concept briefly put a strain on the writers' relationship with the BBC. In light of the American pilot, Beryl Vertue, Galton and Simpson's agent, tried to negotiate international terms for the actual 'idea' of *Steptoe and Son*. She had offered the compromise of allowing the BBC first refusal on the American remake, but this didn't appease the corporation. A rather fraught correspondence with R. G. Walford, the Head of Copyright at the BBC, developed.

On 22 May 1964 Walford wrote that 'having done our own series, we might not want the American series for our own programmes, in which case we would not want to make any offer for it'. For Walford and the BBC 'it all boils down to the simple fact that the BBC can and must prevent the American series from being shown commercially in this country'. Vertue responded on 26 May, bleakly believing that Walford's letter 'gives the impression that the BBC are endeavouring to go back on their word, although I find this extremely difficult to believe'. Walford, distressed at this accusation, tried to ease the situation in his final letter on the matter, which expresses the BBC's hope that 'Alan and Ray would agree to write for the BBC 13 *Steptoe and Son* scripts during 1965, giving the BBC United Kingdom rights for the initial performances and for repeats but excluding any overseas uses'. Furthermore, Walford offered the 'usual basic fees' and an offer that the BBC would 'forgo its 10 per cent goodwill share in the proceeds from your American sale'. In addition, the letter hoped that 'the American series could be sold in areas where the English version had already been sold'. This was agreed, 'subject to certain changes of the title, etc'.

The pilot for the American version of *Steptoe and Son*, already well under way by this stage, was to retain the original title but, naturally, not the original cast. Levine employed the character star Aldo Ray as the long-suffering Harold, and for the old man he cast the likeable 1930s B-movie star Lee Tracy. Despite the change of actors, Ray Galton remembers that: 'The final result was very much our show. It was set in Chicago and they even had a horse and cart, which was lovely.'

'Basically, they used one, or more likely two, of our scripts, spliced them together and made the pilot,' recalls Simpson. 'It was quite long, about 35 or 40 minutes. It was pretty good, really; a very faithful adaptation. We were sent a copy from America, but I always remember the completely foreign-sounding delivery of Aldo Ray when he said 'You dirty old man' in this sort of Bronx accent. The line had been completely lifted from our original, and it sounded all wrong to my ears, but both were extremely good in it, especially Lee Tracy. It was such a thrill for us to have this enormous Hollywood star doing our show.'

The pilot was never screened on American television and to this day hasn't seen the light of day. Lee Tracy drifted into semi-retirement and died in 1968. Aldo Ray continued in starring roles in forgettable films until his death in 1991.

The first crack at the American market had failed. But Ray Galton remarks that 'about 80 pilots are made a year and only two get on to the screen. It's amazing anything gets commissioned at all. We found that the big stumbling block to mounting the series for American TV was that *Steptoe and Son* was about unsuccessful people, and sponsors in America like TV series to be about affluent people living in nice houses.' Still, less than 10 years later the format would succeed and lead to a totally new franchise.

The American pilot problem wasn't the only threat to the continuation of *Steptoe and Son*. Few people could have guessed that, at the absolute height of its popularity, the series was very nearly dragged in a completely new direction. The problem can be traced back to the very day that R. G. Walford and Beryl Vertue had begun to iron out their problems with regard to the American rights. In their correspondence Vertue outlined that 'they [Galton and Simpson] have been giving considerable thought to the future of *Steptoe and Son* generally and they do not consider that this series should run for more than a further seven programmes, and that it is better to leave a series "riding high" rather than go on with it until they have run out of ideas'. Walford, corresponding with Tom Sloan about the project, explained that as of 25 June 1964: 'seven *Steptoe and Son* programmes for 1965 ... [would be commissioned] on the understanding that Wilfrid Brambell and Harry H. Corbett will be contracted for these programmes'.

In the meantime plans were afoot for a repeat of the third series, starting on 24 September 1964. But even this was not without controversy. *Steptoe and Son* had now become so famous that even the potential Prime Minister had taken an interest in its broadcast. Harold Wilson, at this time the Leader of the Opposition, contacted the Director-General of the BBC, Sir Hugh Greene, and, it is said, discussed his 'very real worry' about the programme. It was not that he didn't enjoy it. On the contrary, he was naturally delighted with Harold Steptoe's support of the Labour movement and the enduring working-class struggle that sat at the heart of the programme. The problem was the timeslot that *Steptoe and Son* then occupied. On the day of the General Election the show was scheduled for its usual time of 8 o'clock in the evening. For Harold Wilson, this could spell disaster.

Alan Simpson remembers the internal discussions:

> Wilson really did ask the BBC outright to put *Steptoe and Son* back to a later slot. It was ridiculous when you think about it, but in a way it

was a very real backhanded compliment. Wilson's reckoning was that if *Steptoe* was on at its usual time, all the Labour voters wouldn't go out to vote: a cheeky generalization that, that only Labour voters watched it, and a very snobbish attitude when you think about it. But anyway, Wilson thought all the Labour voters would stay at home and watch *Steptoe* and not vote. His idea was for the programme to be on at half past nine, after the polling stations had closed. It is totally true that Labour voters always voted late. They were, as a rule, working people who came home from work, had their tea and then went to vote. Wilson thought they would simply have their tea and watch our show instead, I suppose. All the Tory votes would have been in by then, in Wilson's theory, so he didn't think it was fair. Anyway, the BBC told him to get stuffed – in the nicest possible way, of course – but that's why I think Harold Wilson never liked the BBC from that point on. He gave them hell! I still don't know why he was so put out. He won the election ... mind you, he only got in by four seats. Thanks to Harold and Albert!

Ray Galton was equally put out:

Although I honestly don't think we had any political influence at all, we were keen to voice our thoughts in the programme. It was sort of flattering to be the centre of attention during the run-up to the election, but I felt then and I do feel now that Harold Wilson was guilty of rather downgrading us. I resent his motives concerning the working-class vote. We were loved throughout the land by a cross section of people, from dukes to dustmen, as they say.

The BBC certainly did register its concern at *Steptoe*'s political content, with Billy Cotton Junior writing to Duncan Wood on 16 September 1964: 'Would you please ensure that all the repeats of *Steptoe and Son* are clear of controversial political statements around the election period.' Wilson reputedly told Sir Hugh Greene: 'Thank you very much. That might be worth a dozen seats to me!'

That, however, isn't what Alan Simpson recalls: 'That's just cobblers ... can you imagine the BBC bending over backwards to help a political party? In those days in particular? The people would never have stood for it! No, Wilson won without any help or hindrance from *Steptoe*. Admittedly, we did get very political in the show. But that was our job as writers, to question the government of the time. And at that time that government just happened to be Tory. We had a go at the Labour government when they were in power, don't you worry!'

However, the *Radio Times* indicates that the BBC *did* help Wilson's campaign. On the day of the election, 15 October 1964, *Steptoe* is listed as airing at 9.00 p.m. in contrast to the 8.00 p.m. slots the rest of that series enjoyed.

Galton and Simpson were, though, committed to the Labour cause, as was Harry H. Corbett. Indeed, Corbett addressed Labour Party meetings and canvassed for votes, as Alan Simpson confirms:

> We actually wrote material for him. He went up to Dudley or Wolverhampton or somewhere to speak on behalf of George Wigg at the Labour Party rally. Wigg had been something to do with the secret service during the war, and he was now Harold Wilson's events secretary. He specialized in getting up the nose of MI5! We wrote this monologue in character, with Harold Steptoe talking to the old man on the telephone. It started with Harry answering a call – 'Hello, Dad!' – and went into a long, one-sided conversation obviously reflecting the old man ranting on about the Tories. Harold put the old man's opinions down and tried to convince him to vote Labour.
>
> After the 1964 election, we were invited to a luncheon to be thanked for our contribution to the Labour movement. It was Ray and myself and our wives, Harry and his wife. We were invited to the House of Commons by George Wigg and his secretary, to a dinner with Harold and Mary Wilson. It was seven couples in all, and we were all sitting around waiting for Harold Wilson to turn up. He was in discussions with regard to the declaration of independence in Rhodesia, and he sent a message that he couldn't make it. Mary Wilson freaked out because that meant there would be 13 for dinner, so she went out into the corridor and dragged in a passing Labour MP to join us for the meal. He sat down and had dinner with us and at about half past 11 Harold Wilson turned up. 'I'm sorry I'm late. I've been having discussions with Ian Smith ... Ian Smith, the Prime Minister of Rhodesia ... We've been discussing affairs of state,' and all the usual rubbish. But I couldn't believe it. Here was the Prime Minister name-dropping and trying to impress us!

The lengthy gap in the production of *Steptoe and Son* naturally prompted the actors to accept other work. Each wanted to break away from *Steptoe* and do roles without the other as being recognized as a double act had become a source of mild irritation. During a trip from Dover to Calais to film *San Ferry Ann* with his friend Joan Sims, Brambell had suffered from the unwelcome attentions of an autographer hunter, who greeted him with:

'I recognized you the minute you come on board. I said to the missis,

"That's 'im," I said. She said, "No." I said, "Yes." She said, "Go and ask him," she said.' By this time I was wearing my special face. I was proud. Then he said, 'I know you ... "That's 'arry Corbett," I said.' Joan looked out of the window, and made small noises as though she was going to be seasick. She wasn't. She was simply delighted at me being taken down a peg or four. I explained to the gentleman that I was *not* Harry Corbett, that he had made a mistake. He said, 'Come on, you're 'avin' me on. You *are* Harry Corbett, aren't you? Because you're the image of 'im.' I watched him beat a tail-between-legs retreat back to his battleaxe ... obviously a domestic argument ensued ... within minutes he returned to deliver the ultimate insult. Once more, 'I've just been talking to the missis and she says you're not Harry Corbett after all – you're the other one.'

A quick trip to France wasn't a problem for the *Steptoe and Son* schedule. Brambell's other commitment was, however. On 2 November 1964 it was claimed by Vertue that 'the BBC did not inform the artistes in due time that there was to be a further *Steptoe* series and consequently Wilfred [sic] Brambell has accepted another engagement in America, thus making the production of a series impossible'. Brambell's success with the Beatles in *A Hard Day's Night* had paid handsome dividends. An American audience not only knew who he was but, it was to be supposed, was keen to see him in the flesh. He was offered the lead role opposite Ella Logan in a new Broadway musical, *Kelly*. Brambell accepted.

Also in November, Tom Sloan revealed that he had been trying to 'influence' Galton and Simpson to write a further *Steptoe* series instead of their planned series for Frankie Howerd. But it was a new sketch and stand-up show for Howerd that aired in the *Steptoe* slot from December 1964. The gap in *Steptoe* production had initiated the possibility of collapse. As Sloan explained: 'Wilfrid Brambell felt perfectly entitled to take other engagements rather than wait until the spring of next year, which would be the earliest time that Galton and Simpson could have written another *Steptoe and Son* series. Incidentally, I saw Brambell the other night and, of course, it is within the bounds of possibility that the musical in which he is going to play in America may fold and he could easily be available next year.' Brambell's immediate schedule for *Kelly* was an extensive five-month rehearsal, three weeks at the Schubert Theater, Philadelphia, and then a March 1965 opening at the Broadhurst Theater on Broadway.

Alan Simpson recalls the day when *Steptoe and Son* faced crisis point:

Wilfrid dropped a bombshell, saying that he was going to America for at least two years because he was opening in a big musical on Broadway called *Kelly*. It was heralded as a major Broadway smash, and Wilfrid thought he would be tied up for years. It was written by Jule Styne and it was considered a cast-iron success. So Wilfrid explains to us, 'I won't be around to do any more *Steptoe*s.' Naturally, that wasn't really the news we wanted to hear. We had a smash hit of our own on our hands, and it looked like our programme was over. We did actually seriously consider finishing the series there and then. We would call it a day on a high. Then we thought, hold on a minute. Why should we stop if we don't want to? Ray and I agreed that we could continue without Willie Brambell. In the end, that's what we decided to do. We thought, let's kill the bugger off!

While the writers were considering this upheaval, the BBC schedule for 1965 was due to start with a season of vintage Galton and Simpson. Tom Sloan had floated an idea for *The Galton and Simpson Theatre*, in which 'we rerun all the best *Hancock's Half Hour* programmes and the 20 *Steptoe and Son* programmes'. He had also addressed the casting problem that was facing the production of any new *Steptoe* episodes. He wrote, personally, to Harry H. Corbett, the actor who would be the only link to the earlier programmes. Opening with a congratulatory comment about *Steptoe* 'being elected by the TAM Rating System as the most popular programme', Sloan reassured Corbett about the current situation of the series: 'I am being besieged by press enquiries as to its future.' Sloan had 'discussed this with Ray and Alan and with their agreement' and with the understanding that they were under BBC contract, he was preparing an official press release. The BBC's line would be that Galton and Simpson would continue to write for the corporation. In a reassurance to Corbett, Sloan said that he would further maintain in the press release that it would be 'my hope that a proportion of these will be *Steptoe and Son*'. 'However,' Sloan told Corbett, 'we are all agreed that until we know whether Wilfrid Brambell's musical in the USA is going to be a success or not – and we will not be certain of this fact for approximately a month – we cannot decide definitely that our series this year could feature him. However, I have said that if this musical is successful and he is unavailable to us, it would not be our intention to recast the part of Albert Steptoe but that at the same time his unavailability did not in any way preclude the possibility of us doing a *Steptoe and Son* series this year with yourself and any other element that it suited the scriptwriters to include. In confidence, you will know of the idea I discussed with Ray and Alan and I take your point that if Brambell is unavailable we should not kill him off but simply not have him around for one reason or another during the run of the next series.'

As far as Ray Galton was concerned:

> We had it all worked out. We would start the new series in the ceme-
> tery. The scene would open with a funeral; we would then discover it's
> the funeral of the old man. Then we would cut to Harold, back at
> home, wandering round the house in an emotional daze. The house is
> full of mementoes and photographs and everything reminds him of
> the old man. He would be feeling terribly guilty about the way he had
> treated him and reflect on the last few years – the years we have
> watched them on television, in effect – that he had wasted complain-
> ing and trying to get away from the old man. Suddenly, there would be
> a knock at the door and Harold would open it and find a young boy
> standing there. The boy would look sheepish and say, 'Mr Steptoe? You
> don't know me, but my mum said that if ever I was in trouble I should
> come and see you ... because apparently you're my dad!' An 'Oh, my
> Gawd!' reaction from Harold ... So we were going to do *Steptoe and
> Son* again but a generation down! We had even decided we were going
> to offer the part of the young Steptoe to David Hemmings, who was
> about 22 in those days.

Hemmings had, in fact, already appeared opposite Harry H. Corbett in the
1962 film *Some People*, and by the end of the decade he would be one of the
country's most recognizable and bankable actors, with cult success in *Blow
Out* (1966), *Barbarella* (1967) and *The Charge of the Light Brigade* (1968).
However, he never became part of the *Steptoe* legacy. 'The idea for
Hemmings to join the cast was all being finalized in our minds at least,'
explains Simpson, 'and we were about to start writing when *Kelly* opened on
Broadway and closed the next day. The headline in *Variety* was famously, "Has
anyone here seen *Kelly*?". One week later Wilfrid came flying into London saying: "Here I am ... when are we doing the next *Steptoe*s then?" So although
we knew exactly what we were going to do, we never wrote the alternative version and, as far as I know, David Hemmings has never been aware that he
nearly played the son in *Steptoe and Son: The Next Generation*!'

Reading between the lines of Tom Sloan's letter to Harry H. Corbett, it is
clear that the actor didn't seem keen on the idea of killing the old man off.
Corbett preferred to leave the door open for Brambell's return to the series,
and disliked the notion of severing Brambell's connection with the show
completely.

Once Brambell, with his tail between his legs, was back in Britain, he and
his agent naturally looked forward to forgetting his failure and making money

on a tried and tested success. His *Steptoe* fee, both for new shows and proposed repeats, rose dramatically. 'Joan Reddin has already muttered something about double fees for Brambell,' claimed Tom Sloan on 16 March 1965, 'and I am simply not interested.' Corbett seemed more concerned with the series' billing, but the BBC reasoned that the sequence used in the *Radio Times* for listing Brambell and Corbett was 'both logical and alphabetical. On the screen, depending which character is the first in vision, his name will come up accordingly. The terminal credits on each show will be the reverse of those applied at the beginning.'

On 30 March 1965 Sloan wrote to Duncan Wood describing an arrangement that the BBC deemed fair, namely a fee of £1000 per programme, with a 75 per cent repeat fee, for a possible fourth series: 'If you have any trouble with Brambell's agent over these terms, then be quite clear in stating to her that this is an absolute take it or leave it offer and that if they refuse it we will still feel free to do a series of *Steptoe* programmes without him if it suits our purpose.' Thus, as far as Sloan was concerned, should money become an issue, the original emergency plan to write Albert out of the series would be put into operation. A firm deadline for Brambell's agreement was given as the following day: 'Or we will ask Galton and Simpson, under their contract with us, to write a new series.'

A more threatening tone had been established – but R. G. Walford reiterated that, 'one of the stipulations' for Galton and Simpson's writing new episodes had been the contracting of both Brambell and Corbett: 'This means therefore that if Brambell's agent makes trouble about fees, we cannot ultimately carry out a threat to put on a *Steptoe* series without Brambell.' However, Tom Sloan assured Walford that, according to talks with Galton and Simpson, 'It has almost been agreed that there is a possibility of doing a series of *Steptoe* with or without Wilfrid Brambell'. By 27 April 1965 the waters seemed to be calmer and Brambell looked set to return. A letter from E. K. Wilson to Michael Barber, of Joan Reddin Limited confirmed that 'it is true that Duncan Wood will definitely be producing this series, providing that he is alive and fit at the time of recording. Harry H. Corbett is requesting that the seven programmes to be recorded some time between September 1 and November 14 should be made in consecutive weeks, with no gap in the middle. May I take it that Wilfrid will be happy with the same arrangement?' Brambell certainly was happy with the arrangement. It let him safely back into the series and he could save face after his ill-fated Broadway experience.

Whatever the solution to Brambell's possible absence would have been, it is impossible to guess what effect a new cast member would have had on the longevity of the series. But it is clear that *Steptoe* would have been very, very different if Corbett had been elevated to senior position. He had certainly displayed a great ability to play the 'worried parent' opposite Albert in 'The Stepmother', but he obviously wanted the safety net of Wilfrid Brambell's possible return should the new format fail. 'We hadn't worked out the ins and outs of the script,' admits Alan Simpson, 'but the basic idea was to have the same situation as before, with Harold adopting the same attitude that his father had adopted with him, and Hemmings taking on the dreamy attitude of Harold. It was all pie in the sky, but on reflection it would have been interesting if nothing else.'

Regardless of the advantages and disadvantages of David Hemmings playing 'and son', Brambell's return to England was an extremely timely one.

Chapter 8

Of Meissen Men

When, finally, Brambell's availability was no longer an issue, Galton and Simpson kept their word to deliver more *Steptoe and Son* episodes. It wasn't 13, certainly, but the end of 1965 did bring in a further series of seven programmes. They would be the first new *Steptoe* episodes in 20 months and the last for over four years.

The fourth series of *Steptoe and Son* started on 4 October 1965 and, after the introduction of a second BBC channel in April 1964, the show was 'relaunched' as part of the 'BBC Autumn Plans' on BBC1. After such a long gap, the writers wisely started the new series with a momentous event: Harold's long-awaited wedding. 'With the idea of the old man's funeral gone, we simply kept the location and changed the occasion,' notes Ray Galton. The show's absence from the screen since the end of series three was acknowledged in the *Radio Times* listings, which billed this first episode as 'The Return of *Steptoe and Son*'. Brambell and Corbett were cover stars for the issue.

In the opening episode, 'And Afterwards At ...', the more stereotypical elements of Albert Steptoe's charmless character were already beginning to outweigh the emotional depth of earlier programmes. Although the relationship between father and son is still as fraught as before, Harold is once again threatening to break things up – and this time he's got the girl as far as the altar. The *Steptoe* theme is interrupted with a burst of the wedding march as the title sequence begins, and Harold, proud as Punch on his horse and cart, is the perfect contrast for his sour-faced father. Inside the church Harold goes from jubilation to cow-eyed reverence, but the old man continues to play the wet blanket, disparaging the intended and her family, condemning Harold for leaving the business and callously informing him of all the pitfalls of married life. Still, we soon discover that Harold and his wife-to-be will be staying with the old man and will probably be looking after him until he returns to the very same church in a wooden box.

Mollie Sugden, years before sitcom stardom in *The Liver Birds* and *Are You Being Served?*, is perfectly cast as the distressed mother of Harold's fiancée. Albert hasn't an ounce of sympathy for her weeping ('What's that old boot grizzling about?') and discouragingly mutters: 'Take a good look at her, mate!' Harold isn't convinced that his beloved Melanie will look anything like her mother, and he's relieved to point out that he looks nothing like his father. But this simply allows the old man to cast more doubt on Harold's parentage, in an extension of his diatribe in 'The Stepmother'.

The old man mocks Harold's hopes and aspirations to the bitter end. But he need not have worried. The wedding turns to farce as the bride eventually turns up only to sob profusely and jilt her rag 'n' bone Romeo at the altar. A superbly orchestrated battle of wits develops between Albert and the mother of the bride, while the not so happy couple are pretty much left to their own devices. The episode goes a long way to support the old man's disrespectful opinion of matrimony, for all the men seem henpecked and dominated by their aggressive wives. The women switch from sympathetic chat while trying to comfort Harold, to acidic aggression while struggling with their mild-mannered menfolk. Harold, who had thought this was his last chance at happiness, has already faced the fact that 'I'm not Sean Connery ... I'm Harold Steptoe'. Happy with his lot in life and happy to be getting married, his composure suddenly melts into deep sorrow and self-pity as the truth dawns on him. The old man's attempts to cheer him up by pointing out the futility of marriage recalls our first meeting with the Steptoes in 'The Offer'. Albert is at his best when he is trying to keep his family together and is using his knowledge of harsh reality to console his son for the disappointments life throws at him.

For once, his attempts to drag his son through his latest heartache include a rare display of respect and admiration. Albert's comments on the fact that Harold is never short of female company aren't malicious or bitter, but overflowing with pride. The remark can be traced back to Albert's observation in church that Melanie getting married in white 'is a lie to start with'. This suggestion of Harold's prowess imbues him with an air of power and authority in the eyes of his father. For a moment Harold himself is proud too, but it's a power and authority he clearly doesn't want. Still, Albert's sordid values – at one stage Harold barks 'You horrible little thing!' – is as nothing compared with the scavenging of the extended Steptoe family when they storm Oil Drum Lane. The horde take no notice of Harold's lovelorn depression but are bent on enjoying the 'afterwards at …' party already prepared, fighting amongst themselves to retrieve the wedding presents each has given. Joan Newell, the eponymous stepmother of series two, reappears as one of the Steptoe clan. Interestingly, her attack on her pompous sister suggests a relationship akin to the Steptoe father and son. It's a simple throwaway comment, but when Newell, in the heat of battle, moans that her sister 'left me with mother', it reveals the possibility of a whole history of some long-standing family rift. It is never mentioned again, but it's this intricacy of writing and depth of characterization that make the programmes so rich in detail and credibility.

Within the maelstrom of family feuding the father and son seem relatively united. The old man has already said that his son looks 'very elegant' in his wedding gear, and he means it. The poignancy of Albert and Harold admitting to each other that 'You're the only one I've got' is reinforced by the old man's misty-eyed affection. Harold admits gloomily that he can only see the two of them 'growing old together', but there is a hint of resignation and even acceptance. That's exactly what Albert craves, that is his dream. In the end the show literally gives them a break – but obviously not from each other.

Eventually it is Harold who suggests that Albert goes with him to the seaside for a few days. In effect, the two are sharing a honeymoon and, with the old man packing his bag double quick and Harold warning his father to keep out of the actual wedding bed, this is a refreshingly tranquil conclusion to one of the most traumatic episodes in Harold's fractured love life.

While the episode marked a triumphant return for the nation's favourite rag 'n' bone men, enthusiasm was tempered with words of complaint from a minority of viewers who considered the use of the marriage ceremony to be disrespectful. A handful of responses expressed such views as 'Marriage is a solemn sacrament and to turn it into a joke for this programme is in the worst possible taste,' and 'I'm not a churchgoer, but it seems to me that this went too far'. On 13 October 1965 Galton and Simpson's champion, Frank Muir, drafted a memo on behalf of the BBC: 'I think the only line one can take with these *Steptoe* complaints is to apologize for giving them offence and to assure them that the marriage service was not mucked about with by as much as a word. And perhaps, to point out that truthful comedy like the *Steptoe* series does not "make fun" of the church setting but just uses it as the right and proper background for the conflict between the main characters.' However, the critics were lavishing praise on the series, and review programmes were always eager to use ratings – boosting *Steptoe* clips.

The second episode of the fourth series, 'Crossed Swords', was one of the very few programmes to use the totting profession as the major focal point of the plot. 'The Piano' and 'The Three Feathers' are the only other examples. Alan Simpson told the *Radio Times*: 'We still haven't met any junk merchants, but we've had a lot of nice letters from totters saying they recognize themselves. I gather the trade is more or less how we imagined it except for the prices paid out for scrap. At 5s and 7s 6d, the Steptoes have been overgenerous, with the result that real-life totters, when they've tried to charge for taking stuff away as a service to the public, have had to contend with people citing *Steptoe* prices.' The pair's professional attitudes are, by this time, utterly predictable: when something of apparent worth comes along Harold believes he is the expert, while Albert is quiet, naive and cautious. However, the writers do allow Harold his moment of glory. Corbett lovingly drags a single, boxed item off the cart and searches excitedly for his father (who is trapped in the outdoor toilet). The actual value of the item will be as nothing compared to the glory of impressing and bettering the old man.

This is Harold's moment of glory as he smugly reveals the Meissen porcelain, identified by its hallmark crossed swords and thus providing the programme with its title. Ordering his father's 'bony little chicken claws' off his prized discovery, Corbett brings the interlude to its crescendo only for Brambell to dash his jubilation. The old man's grasping eagerness as the piece is being unwrapped immediately disintegrates, on its appearance, into scorn of the so-called antique. But this isn't ignorance on his part; it comes from a compulsion to undermine his son's triumph. In fact, having tired of the game and ferreted through his huge collection of spectacles, Albert gazes long and hard at the porcelain, makes encouraging noises and finally admits that the piece has interesting qualities.

Once the old man has skilfully avoided heaping deserved praise on his son, the story of the item's purchase can be told. Satisfied with his day's work, Harold settles into a lengthy and detailed description of the old lady he bought it off, with her 'orange hair and big hooter', the 45 cats and 'not a window open'.

The rest of the programme goes for the common denominator, relying on farce and destruction to get laughs. Harold, concerned at his father's growing reputation for thieving stock, complains bitterly that the other traders are calling him 'Steptoe the klepto' behind his back. Although tickled pink by the term, he is genuinely distressed at the disrespect his father attracts. Harold's attempts to control Albert's questionable habits, or at the very least to protect him from polite society at large, are a strong element of their relationship throughout the series. The need to control the old man's pilfering is even more keenly felt when the Steptoes find themselves in a respectable West End antique shop, presided over by none other than Derek Nimmo.

Still to become everybody's favourite comic cleric in *All Gas and Gaiters* and *Oh Brother!*, Nimmo was an inspired choice for the role, expert at assuming the clipped distrust and pompous superiority that the episode required. Opposite the shabby Steptoes, he looks down his nose at the twosome, takes them for dustbin men and suspiciously enquires about the porcelain's provenance.

According to a 1965 interview, Alan Simpson explained: 'We asked for Nimmo because he is a real expert and collector. We knew this because Ray and I are both extremely interested in porcelain and are collectors ourselves in a minor way. Derek is the ideal actor to handle Meissen porcelain with the proper reverence.' Forty years on, Simpson remembers it quite differently: 'That's cobblers! I would never have said that. We couldn't give a monkey's if Derek knew about porcelain or not! There's no need for the actor to know what he's doing ... he's an actor! We certainly wouldn't have known about it before casting. We may have found out about it during rehearsals, but we certainly wouldn't have cast him for that reason. I must have been misquoted. We used Derek because we liked his work, he was very good and we had used him in *The Bargee* with Harry. Derek had played the doctor. He was very good at that pompous sort of authority figure.'

Nimmo's antique dealer appears again at the auction, wordlessly bidding for the same porcelain piece after the greedy Harold has refused his original offer. As the Steptoes, unaware of his presence, both bid on the item to increase the price and somehow end up buying their own antique, the comic confusion and name-calling that results is beautifully orchestrated by director Duncan Wood. The equally predictable fate of the piece – smashed by Albert's overzealous cleaning – is poignant and hilarious.

In the Audience Research Report published on 9 November 1965 *Steptoe* was cited as 'situation comedy at its brilliant best ... 'Crossed Swords' was "one of the best scripts ever" from Ray Galton and Alan Simpson'. Viewers frequently added that, 'In any case one was always sure of plenty of laughs with the combination of scriptwriters and artists'. The show was praised as 'vulgar, perhaps, but in a healthy way', while the 'auction scene was obviously the high spot'.

'Those Magnificent Men and Their Heating Machines' was a chance for Galton and Simpson to take the title of a current cinema hit – *Those Magnificent Men in Their Flying Machines* – and adapt it to their own ends, although the episode in question had nothing whatsoever to do with the film.

When Harold reveals to his father that he has bought radiators and pipes for their own central heating system, Albert reacts with cheerful delight, even pausing to make a moving and heartfelt speech. The tension has been mounting throughout the initial scenes, but as the old man reflects on the harsh things he has said, Brambell lowers his voice and, in a rare moment, Albert admits that he holds 'the highest regard for you, both as a son and as a man'. There's not a hint of irony, although Harry H. Corbett allows Harold a split second of doubt before he takes his father's proffered hand, shakes it and, choking back the tears, thanks the old man. Unfortunately, Harold reveals that he will be installing the system himself and Albert immediately reverts to a tone of humiliating ridicule.

As with many of the early episodes, the writing builds the familiar and repeated conflict between father and son into a spiralling plot line. Harold, returning from work at the start of the programme and bemoaning the fact that Albert has left the gates open, ruminates on his dream of freedom: 'I'll be glad when he's gone!' But on entering the house he finds the old man with his head in the gas oven. He's only cleaning it and not committing suicide but Harold's attachment to his father is clearly revealed. At the close of the episode and after the final row of the night, Albert returns to the kitchen and discovers Harold with his head in the oven. Harold has an equally innocent motive, but Albert jumps to the same wrong conclusion. This circular narrative not only draws the threads of the past together but symbolically illustrates that the life of the Steptoes is equally circular and will never change.

The first 'suicide' incident sees one of Corbett's finest monologues as Harold desperately tries to bring his father round – Albert bangs his head, sizes up the situation and momentarily fakes near-death. Corbett's delivery of Harold enacting the torrent of suspicious questions likely to be asked of him at the inquest makes this an inspired piece of work. A ruthless and subtly hostile note enters as the 'questioner' digs deep and twists Harold's words, while Harold crumbles before the starkly convincing face of distrustful authority that he himself has invented. It's the sort of discussion that's normally played out within the mind, but here it is delivered aloud with such precision and passion that it seems perfectly natural.

Galton and Simpson drop in tantalizing references to both Harold's and his father's childhoods. The roots of Harold's insecurity are buried deep in the traumas caused by Albert's determination to teach his son the realities of life. This even extended to the father 'improving' the boy's school-day drawings, believing this to be in his son's best interest. Albert's pondering on the past may be comically written and acted with breezy disregard, but the gritty realities of the poverty of the time and the domestic violence of the age are unflinchingly evoked. Fondly recalling how his father died, after an overload of whelks, Albert thinks nothing of mentioning the way his mother had been treated by him: 'Locked in the coal hole screaming her head off'. Even when the comedy is at its most obvious, with the house overrun with central heating pipes and the rickety system shaking the building to its foundations, the script takes time to examine the current relationship and chequered pasts of the two characters.

Alan Simpson recalls the problems caused by the heating-system plot line:
> The chief memory about that show was the difficulty that Duncan Wood had in staging it. It was a very complicated system by the time we finished, with pipes all over the set. If we had been filming it, it would have been fine, but doing it in one lump in the studio caused problems. Everything had to work, and Duncan and the set designer had a hell of a job. It had to be working in order to set the house shaking, but it couldn't be too strong or else the entire set would fall down.

While not a two-hander like the best of the early episodes, 'The Siege of Steptoe Street' does revert to the theme of money troubles and domestic dissatisfaction. Business is bad, and the Steptoes face the threat of financial ruin. Despite Harold's liking for exotic aftershaves, it is Albert's secret greed for fine foods that has spelt disaster. The discovery that his father has been treating himself on the sly strikes like a viper in Harold's bosom as he cries 'Grouse! I don't even know what a grouse looks like!' Although he finds humour in the situation, and bemoans the fact that he didn't know they were running 'a miniature Savoy Grill', Harold's sense of betrayal is potent and overpowering. It is this betrayal that results in his determination to keep his head above water and protect the business at all costs.

The show's title is another film reference, tipping its hat to the 1960 *The Siege of Sidney Street*, which recounted the story of a group of anarchists who terrorized London in 1912. In *Steptoe* territory the anarchists become capitalistic bailiffs. Galton and Simpson's playful use of salty language and innuendo continues unabashed, with the biggest laugh coming from a ferocious put-down from Albert. When Harold pompously resolves to keep his finger on the pulse of the situation his father remarks 'You won't find the pulse where you keep your finger!' Brambell's stern expression doesn't falter despite the lengthy audience reaction. But the old man's aggression is tempered by another reference to Harold's less-than-glorious childhood. A disappointing school report that Albert has carefully hidden away from his son for all these years adds a touch of poignancy to the exchange.

Robert Dorning, guest-starring as Mr Stacey the butcher, had been a familiar supporting player opposite Tony Hancock, and here his bombastic persona and bluff manner were perfect for the figure of capitalist authority determined to stop at nothing to get the money he is owed. The old man's pathetic pleas as he grovels before the bailiff are comically counterbalanced by Albert's faked accident. But the pitiful sight of the penniless old man literally begging for his lowly possessions is far from comic, and remains one of Wilfrid Brambell's most touching moments in *Steptoe*. The fact that it's the prelude to a preposterous scam – as Albert succeeds in deterring the bailiffs – doesn't compromise the real emotion behind the performance. Albert is philosophical about accepting what Harold considers 'blood money'. As he puts it: 'Laurence Olivier would have got £500 for that!'

Naturally, for the sake of the series' storylines, the father and son bonding at the end of this episode is hastily shattered for the beginning of 'A Box in Town'. The old man, unseen until the climax of the opening scene, is an ever-present figure in Harold's fraught love life. Yootha Joyce, already a *Steptoe* favourite thanks to her role in 'The Bath', reunites with Harry H. Corbett to stunning effect. The credit sequence, as the light of her cigarette bathes Harold in its glow, is almost film noir in approach. The pre-filmed sequence, shot on 20 September 1965, skilfully captures the relaxed working relationship Joyce and Corbett enjoyed. In many ways the plot is a more subtle and emotive presentation of the themes of the 1974 'And So to Bed' episode to come. The situation – the old man preventing Harold and his girlfriend getting passionate – is the same, but Yootha Joyce's deadpan seriousness on her 'I'm not the open-air type' line is loaded with determination. Harry H. Corbett, clearly at one with his co-star, can ooze with expectation as she ponders on kinky girls; all 'leather and big boots.' Her stark highlighting of Harold's childlike dependence on his father is also breathtakingly effective. In the hands of a lesser actress, the character assassination and sarcastic comments about comics and warm milk would lose their painful quality. The narrative brilliantly falls on the side of the unintentionally snubbed girlfriend for, in mid father and son argument, Harold does indeed pause to pick up his glass of milk. It's a subtle touch, not referred to in the dialogue, but is a moment that bonds the squabbling rag 'n' bone men perfectly. Of course, this particular episode is all about splitting them up again. As the son rants 'I'm Harold Steptoe not Cinderella!' it's time for him to escape the midnight lock-up time and find a place of his own. Wilfrid Brambell's weary, despondent speech of loneliness and despair is peerlessly played. He allows Corbett to step in with a deft touch and highlight that this is the same speech he heard 12 years before. Having rented a tiny boxroom at the top of a house, and typically dubbing it a penthouse, Harold prepares for action. Tellingly, the need for a sock to be darned is the first chore he thinks of for his lady friend, although on reflection he ponders that this can be tackled 'afterward'. Still, getting to first base is easier said than done. While the old man, with his place to himself, entertains a myriad of game old birds, the son struggles through his little black book. Corbett gives a masterclass in 'telephone acting', turning on the charm and small talk, desperately trying to overcome all too-obvious rejections and, finally, muttering 'Stupid bitch!' as the first call on his list proves fruitless. That distinguished character actress Marjorie Rhodes is the old man's final conquest, although the gilt has come off the gingerbread at this stage. Moreover, Harold has returned home in defeat. Interestingly, one of Albert's flings is with an old girl played by Marie Makino, who drapes her boa around him and jives with gusto. The actress had previously appeared in 'Homes Fit for Heroes' and was personally recruited by Duncan Wood. Writing from her Hampstead home on 17 September 1965 she regretted it was 'just a day's work, a walk-on' but graciously explained that, 'for you I will do this and I am so looking forward to being with you in *Steptoe* again. Only wish it was a bit more of Miss Lotterby maybe it is, without words!' Also of note, Annie Leake: who crops up as Harold's forthright landlady near the close of the episode, had previously played Tony Hancock's no-nonsense landlady in 'The Radio Ham' in 1961.

In 'My Old Man's a Tory', it is politics rather than the fairer sex that splits the Steptoes. Typically, the old man supports the Tories while Harold is campaigning for the Labour Party, but despite the petty squabbling their debate embraces important issues and is, reassuringly, for the good of the people. Indeed, it is about true political belief and the naive/switched-on – depending on whose side you are on – power of the individual. For the old man it is mainly about business, as befits his capitalist attitude. He reveals that political affiliation loses customers and, besides, 'Conservative junk is better quality than Labour junk'. While disgusted at this attitude, Harold too plays out the political minefield in terms of the business he knows, ranting: 'All junk is equal!' The British in India, the British out of India, the old image of the Labour powerhouse complete with flat hat and hobnailed boots, the corrupted benefits of being on the council ('It's better than the Masons,' chirps the old man) and even a forthright comment on the Vietnam War: all issues are reflected and discussed via the Oil Drum Lane partnership. At one point Harold is heard to mutter 'I don't think there's a father and son in the country with less rapport than us,' a statement which both sums up the show's success and is belied by the fact that they can have this heated discussion.

Steptoe favourite Damaris Hayman enjoys her role as the overly flirty secretary of the local labour group which is using the Steptoe house as its committee rooms, and even indulges in a wonderful piece of paraphrased Shakespeare when she dubs Harold 'the noblest rag 'n' bone man of them all!'. Another *Steptoe* regular, Dudley Foster, personifies the figure of middle-of-the-road Labour authority who condemns the involvement of local groups in world affairs, and would rather elect university graduates and professional men than the workers who vote for the party. Indeed, Foster seems so involved with the series at this stage that he even gatecrashed production, as Duncan Wood's cheeky memo of 16 September 1965 reveals: 'Since you seem intent on intruding on our location filming sequences I would be grateful if you would do us the honour of appearing in Episode No. 6 personally. Enclosed is the script. The part is that of the Labour Agent Mr Stonelake, which I hope you will like. Naturally you would receive top feature billing for the part if you think likewise. I look forward to seeing you.' Foster gives his usual impeccable performance, quietly spoken, cynical and injecting inadvisable humour into the tense situation with the old man. Corbett works brilliantly opposite him. Harold had relished the chance to don raincoat and pipe in a thinly veiled attempt to emulate his glorious leader, Harold Wilson, but his enthusiasm wanes when Foster's Labour bigwig enters the Steptoe house similarly attired.

Corbett told the *Radio Times* that the new batch of episodes 'takes a swing at all of the old themes without going back over any old ground. There will be a lot of interest in the story that deals with politics as they affect the ordinary man at election times.' A lot of interest indeed, as Alan Simpson explains:

> This was the perfect example of us mocking the Labour movement, rather than the old man's right-wing beliefs. Although old Harold Wilson loved our show, I'm sure he didn't like this one. This was us mocking Harold's socialism. I was, at the time, a member of the Labour Party in Sunbury. In this episode we took the mickey out of the small ward meeting, with the Labour Party representatives crowding into the Steptoe house and producing these pamphlets decrying Tory policy and putting aside a copy to Mao Tse-Tung and a copy to all the Communist world leaders! Anyway, the morning after it was first broadcast I got a phone call from the woman who was the leader of the Labour Party ward that I was a member of. She was furious! She accused me of being a traitor to my class. She snootily said, 'I hope they paid you your 30 pieces of silver on time', and all this. Ridiculous.

We were taking the mickey out of all this earnest, po-faced behaviour, sending silly memorandums to world leaders. The old man was on the sidelines scoffing at them all. The whole situation was bloody stupid, and our job was to show how bloody stupid it was.

Ray Galton continues:

Harold standing for the local council is a reflection of our optimist socialism. Harold is the perfect man for the job, but the Labour Party representative wants a pillar of society. They want someone in a suit, someone to appeal to the Tory voters, in a way. It came true in 1997, didn't it? But that's not socialism. It was these non-socialist tendencies that we were mocking.

Alan Simpson recalls:

Harry Corbett was still very much in with the Labour Party and, as with the 1964 election, he was used as a high-profile supporter during the 1966 election. That time the three of us were invited to Douglas Brayley's yacht. Colonel Brayley was a multimillionaire and ran the Canning Town Glass Works, that was his job. He supported the Labour Party and was thus a friend of George Wigg. We were invited on to this yacht, built in 1898 in Germany. A huge thing it was, and Edward VIII had owned it at one stage. The plates were solid gold and the cutlery was solid silver. It was amazing ... and this was the Labour Party! Just the sort of thing we liked to have a go at! We had another very nice dinner, and Harold Wilson was there from the start that time, still name-dropping rather pathetically! Somebody told us that Brayley later had financial problems. Moreover, he hadn't been a Colonel, but only a Sergeant during the war ... allegedly!

Galton and Simpson ponder that in contrast to socializing with Harry H. Corbett, 'We never socialized with Wilfrid Brambell at all. We never went out to dinner with him or drinks with him. He would come up to the club after recordings for a few but that was about all. We never met him outside. Harry would come up to the office all the time, whether we were doing *Steptoe* or not.'

'Pilgrim's Progress', the very last new *Steptoe and Son* episode for nearly five years, proved an inspired temporary finale awakening distant but undimmed memories of the First World War. Wilfrid Brambell revels in his uniformed entrance and spirited rendition of 'It's a Long Way to Tipperary'. Ken Jones's incidental music adds to the martial flavour of the introduction, merging the *Steptoe* theme with a quick burst of 'Pack Up Your Troubles'. The basic plot echoes the finale of the first series, 'The Holiday', as Harold is now determined to get to St Tropez. At least the old man is keen to travel abroad this time, desperate to see the trench sites of France once more before he dies. Corbett, clearly in one of his regular flights into the fantastical, takes on an upper-class officer's accent barking, 'You can go home now, Tommy'. Harold's observations do not, however, mock the common soldier. They are a cynical comment on his father's pride in the country that saw millions of his contemporaries slaughtered or crippled. Harold defends the poor working classes who laid down their lives for the landed gentry, and reflects on the half-hearted rebellion of the years following the First World War and the futility of nuclear war. Ray Galton believes that 'Harold Steptoe, like Harry Corbett, like Alan and like myself, was a utopian socialist. He couldn't understand why the British soldiers hadn't followed the example of Russia and the rest of Europe and rebelled in 1917. He couldn't understand why we didn't have a revolution in this country in 1926 when the General Strike hit. He just couldn't understand it. And with this bemusement came a frustration with the old man's patriotic pride.' All Harold's dreams, beliefs and needs are channelled into an assault on Albert wearing his old army uniform. 'The old man identified himself with king and country,' comments Alan Simpson. 'It's reflected glory isn't it? He's a Tory because it's a way of gaining status and removing him from his lowly position in life. He was similar to Alf Garnett in that respect.'

It is the old man's pride that is mocked and ridiculed here, not the stance of the old soldier. But the comedy is, suitably, muted and short-lived. Harold's insults are almost immediately withdrawn thanks to the dignity of Albert's response which is one of quiet reflection. However, the lull in laughter is over within moments. Harold, sympathetic and secretly proud of his father's bravery, stops him from donning his uniform for the flight to France, to protect him from the ridicule of others. Eventually, the son does permit his father to wear his medals on the plane, though Harold's observation – 'I thought you sent them back when the Beatles got the MBE' – lightens the moment and highlights Brambell's high-profile association with the group in *A Hard Day's Night*.

That the second half takes place on a plane is established with location shots of the Steptoes filmed at London Airport. Corbett imbues Harold with mischievous delight as he relishes his father's dislike of flying, happily recalling the depressurized aeroplane sequence in *Goldfinger*, and other potential disasters. But the old man gets an easy revenge with a diatribe on spiders and earwigs in Harold's bed at home. Once again, Harold is the little boy, worried about his father's vengeful tendencies and demoralized by the thought of creepy-crawlies.

The encounters on the plane with the American and the Frenchman – a fourth Frank Thornton performance in four series – allow national differences to come to the fore. Alan Gifford, the eternal Yank in British movies, is fiercely proud of America's involvement in the two world wars. Harold tries to calm things down when Albert mutters about the late arrival of the Americans during the First World War, but it is Harold himself who joins the argument when the American talks of the '1941 to 1945 war'. With understated menace, Corbett leans forward and coos: 'The '39 to '45 war!' Whether this unwillingness to forget the ins and outs of conflict is mocked or celebrated is immaterial; Harold's emulation of Albert's patriotic stance shows that his loyalty is to family before all else.

The prop requirements for the episode created problems for props man George Pettican, who had already scoured most of the dental schools in London in search of as many sets of false teeth as he could lay his hands on, and had hired a mound of expensive 'wedding gifts' for 'And Afterwards At ...' only for Harry H. Corbett to toss them out of a window during the denouement. (Pettican positioned a mattress and had to 'hope for the best'.) But 'Pilgrim's Progress' was a real challenge. A total of 250 items, including the complete detail of the interior of an aeroplane, was checked and double-checked before recording: 'rifle, bayonet, pocket watch and chain, cigarette machine, half an ounce of shag, three goldfish, packet of ants' eggs, two passports, grandfather clock, set of bagpipes, human skull ...'

The casting of this last episode was interestingly fraught. *The Navy Lark* star Stephen Murray was originally cited as playing the Frenchman and, indeed, BBC memos have him as a featured member of the cast right up until the recording date. Duncan Wood's assistant had written to him on 30 September 1965: 'Mr Wood is hoping very much that you will ... be able to play the part of the Frenchman for us.' In the end, Frank Thornton landed the role.

'We didn't know that "Pilgrim's Progress" would be the last one because the running order was never finalized, but certainly by that fourth series we felt we had done enough,' remembers Alan Simpson. The public were still besotted with *Steptoe*, but perhaps the cracks were beginning to show. The actors, for ever identified with the characters, were public property and not always separated from the working-class scruffs they played.

Brambell, in the main, accepted this recognition as part of the job. In fact, he rather liked the attention. He happily wrote in a March 1964 edition of *Today* magazine that, 'If you see me in the street, don't hesitate to shout: "You dirty old man!" I know it will be your way of saying that you love me. And I mean "love", not "like".' But by 1965 the pressure had begun to affect even him. He would cringe when relating an episode in a pub concerning a man who trod on his foot: 'Instead of apologizing, he just looked at me and said, "I trod on your foot, didn't I? Step-toe, get it?" I got it!'

Harry H. Corbett had always been a private man, uncomfortable with public adoration. He preferred to avoid the spotlight, donning a hat and glasses in a futile attempt to avoid being recognized. As he reflected in 1972:

> The funny thing is that when I'm stopped in the street people say exactly the same to me as they say to Wilfrid: 'Where's the horse?' There are set phrases to cover up that you are pleased to see someone ... but Harold is not me. Harold only exists on paper; he is nothing more than the changing facets of human beings that impinge on the writers' minds. I don't even know anything about him.

As often as not, though, when relaxed at home during an interview, Corbett would reveal his deep-rooted knowledge of what made the character tick. In an article published in the *Daily Mail* in June 1967, he commented: 'In a way I suppose I'm the fulfilment of Harold's dream. I've got everything Harold longs for and will never have. There is the Marty tragedy. It's all tied up with neurosis. I feel I could run a psychiatrist business, I've learnt so much through living Harold Steptoe.'

The fourth series of *Steptoe and Son* had had success written all over it. Indeed, for the fourth year running Galton and Simpson were honoured by the Writers' Guild Awards. 'You got rosetta stone plaques for coming first, which we did for '62 and '63,' remembers Alan Simpson, 'and a diploma for coming second ... we preferred the plaques! We came second in '64 and '65, so they were obviously getting used to us!'

As early as the delivery of the first few scripts for series four, Tom Sloan had been keen to keep the Steptoes going. He wrote to Galton and Simpson explaining that 'having read the first four *Steptoe* scripts and being quite sure in my own mind that when the series returns in October it will be as well received as ever by the public, I wonder if you have thoughts of doing a further six or seven in the February/March period, instead of racking your brains for another vehicle? I am quite sure myself that this is what the public would most like to see and I also have the feeling that if we declared our intentions *now* to both Harry and Willie, we would find them more than ready to commit themselves to another series.' But Galton and Simpson were, in fact, happy to rack their brains for another vehicle. It was time for a change and there seemed to be no room for *Steptoe and Son* in their plans.

Chapter 9

Radio Times

Writing in 1966, television critic and pop-culture analyst John Russell Taylor commented that 'the best scripts for *Hancock's Half Hour* and *Steptoe and Son* are really one-act plays exploiting the dramatic possibility of the *temps mort* as subtly, one may think in an irreverent moment, as anything from the new French novelists'. He seems to ignore the fact that these were flagships for BBC Light Entertainment, and that social comment and social awareness were always very much secondary to the situation comedy. But the fact that such thoughts were already being expressed was a testament to the speed with which Galton and Simpson's writing had left its mark on British television. It also set their latest achievement in stone. Clearly, the time was right for them to move on to new things. The writers' last concession to *Steptoe* was an agreement to see the 1962 *Christmas Night with the Stars* script in print for the Christmas 1965 issue of the *Radio Times*. This was published as part of the journal's Christmas Crackers feature.

For Alan Simpson the end of 1965 was a natural cut-off point:

We had written four series, which we thought was enough. In our view we had looked at the characters from every angle and simply ran out of things to say about them. Apart from that, the major thought in our heads then was that our career should move on and we should really encompass the cinema ... so Hollywood beckoned!

The cinema was also beckoning to Harry H. Corbett. During January and February 1966 he filmed his starring role as Detective-Sergeant Sidney Bung in what was arguably his best-loved film, *Carry On Screaming!*. Joining the established *Carry On* team for a one-off assignment in the absence of Sid James, Corbett found himself with a seasoned cast of veteran comedy players. Receiving top billing for his performance, Corbett played along with the film-makers' impudent use of *Steptoe* terminology. Notably, Eric Rogers' musical score features a burst of the 'Old Ned' theme as Corbett, in the guise of a werewolf, makes his escape on a horse and cart. However, speaking just over a year after the production of the film, Corbett seemed disillusioned with film work in general:

> It's terrifying working in films. I hate the situation in which I have to work at present. I formed a way of life in acting that requires rehearsal, polishing. I can't give an instant characterization just like that, and that's what I'm required to do.
>
> With *Steptoe*, I'll go in knowing my play – not learning it, but knowing my play, knowing what it's about, knowing what I'm going to do. I'm free. If Wilfrid throws me a line a certain way it'll shake me and I have to reply; this is known as contact. But of course there's not much time for this sort of thing in films. I've either got to go home and work on it all night and take not a blind bit of notice what anybody else is going to say to me on the set – consequently I'm going to be hard, factual, technically brilliant; or else I get into this terrible mess of trying to have the best of both worlds. I get into this terrible mess, waiting to discover what it's about. And by the time I've discovered what it's about, it's over; we've wrapped up.

Corbett had also lost his love of the theatre work that had previously challenged him as an actor. 'We go through phases in life. You don't give up the theatre, the theatre gives you up. At the moment it has basically given me up because it's going through a phase which I admire an awful lot but am not terribly interested in playing in ... The plays I have seen I have felt: splendid, but I don't wish to be in them. It's just that I love the epic in the theatrical sense. There will be a necessity to bring back the epic; but not at the moment.' Even the exhilarating relationship with Joan Littlewood, which continued to some extent during Corbett's initial small-screen stardom, had vanished by 1965. 'I stayed with the Theatre Workshop while still enjoying the fruits of the truth in television – and the money – until even when I was doing *Steptoe* I was going back there, doing shows, doing seasons, and building a building.'

Thus, with the biggest success of both Corbett and Brambell's acting careers and Galton and Simpson's writing careers behind them for all intents and purposes, both actors and writers began to consider the future without the albatross of *Steptoe* around their necks. But, despite the best efforts of the four cornerstones of the series, it was clear that *Steptoe and Son* was not prepared simply to lie down and die. Although almost five years, from the end of 1965 to the beginning of 1970, would pass before the Steptoes' return to television, in the interim the public were far from starved of their favourite rag 'n' bone men.

Pye's records were still selling well, and the BBC still enjoyed healthy viewing figures for repeats: in September 1966 they were attracting audiences of 5.8 million homes. Gale Pedrick had also written a second novelization of scripts for Hodder. Published in 1966, *Steptoe and Son at the Palace* featured an adaptation of the Royal Command Performance sketch, alongside 'The Lead Man Cometh', 'The Musical Evening' (called 'The Keys' in print), 'Steptoe à la Cart' and 'Crossed Swords'. But the most important development by far occurred in 1966, when Corbett and Brambell were recruited to work together on a series of *Steptoe and Son* adaptations for BBC radio. The record albums had proved that soundtrack-only presentations of the programmes not only worked perfectly well but, perhaps more crucially, sold perfectly well too.

In effect, Galton and Simpson returned to their roots. As Alan Simpson says:

> Radio is the great breeding ground for comic writing. You can use your imagination in that medium, and there's no doubt about it, radio does make you use words in a better way. Your audience have simply got nothing else to do but listen to your words. Sometimes the important words are lost on television. On radio, with a good idea and a good cast you are pretty much there. But television can take the edge off a script. Mind you, as far as we were concerned there was very little difference between radio and television. We didn't write any differently for either. To an extent we were always writing radio material for television. It was always talking heads. That's why *Hancock* transferred so well to television and *Steptoe* transferred so well to radio. The two were interchangeable as far as Ray and I were concerned. The scripts are the same: 7500 words for radio, 7500 words for television.

But the transition from television to radio wasn't entirely smooth for *Steptoe and Son*. Although Galton and Simpson would themselves eventually take on the task of adapting their scripts, the radio series was originally the brainchild of Gale Pedrick. Fifteen years previously, he had given the struggling scriptwriters their first big break. The *Steptoe and Son* radio series was first hinted at in a memo from radio executive Roy Rich, dated 16 August 1965. Rich explained that he was 'lunching with Gale Pedrick on Friday this week to discuss the whole question of a radio adaptation of *Steptoe and Son*'. This was, of course, well before the recording and broadcasting of the fourth and 'last' series on television.

By 7 September the radio adaptation had been costed. At £400 per show, the idea seemed appealing and 10 days later Roy Rich wrote to Tom Sloan to explain that 'Gale Pedrick is offering us' the series and 'it goes without saying that we would be v. v. interested'.

But the whole idea was threatened with collapse because the two stars of the series weren't happy with the arrangement. They had not been consulted by Pedrick about the radio proposal, and a memo from the Light Entertainment Booking Manager, Patrick Newman, made it clear that they wouldn't be keen: 'Corbett feels (and he thinks Brambell is with him on this) he wouldn't want to know for at least six months.' This news distressed Roy Rich, and memos went back and forth between him and Sloan for several days. The fact was that both actors had had enough of *Steptoe*. Newman added, 'They would only be interested if a nice free period happened to come along, when both artists are available, and with recordings compressed into a very short period.' Furthermore, Brambell had suggested a fee of £300 per episode. He might be persuaded to consider bringing that price down to £250 but this, as the BBC grumbled, 'we may regard as a firm demand'. With Corbett likely to want an equal amount, the overall budget per show had already been exceeded by at least £100. Pat Newman's memo of 23 September 1965 explained: 'Of course we're all aware of their large television fee these days and I suppose – sad thought – that it could be argued that their worth to Sound Radio today is greater than that of e.g. Sirs Laurence, John, Ralph, Donald, Michael, Alec et al. (and I don't mean Read!). You can chew this over if you wish, but I think it could only be paid over the dead bodies of two Booking Managers (*what* did I hear you say?).'

Tom Sloan, for one, was outraged, confiding to Roy Rich that, in his opinion, 'it is now obvious that Gale Pedrick was flying a very high and very time-wasting kite'. Rich informed Sloan that 'Galton and Simpson are very surprised at this news and are convinced that the two artists' agents have never approached them, as they said they would', but he reluctantly conceded that 'Brambell's fee alone would make the whole project top-heavy and not worth doing'.

Negotiations were grinding to a halt but an optimistic memo from Charles Maxwell, Head of Light Entertainment, Sound, to Gale Pedrick, dated 22 October 1965, shows a change in tone: 'The position as I see it is now that Alan and Ray are keen to keep the door open; that Harry and Wilfrid are not, as was thought, putting difficulties in the way, and that there is still hope that something may be done in the New Year, when all will be comparatively free.'

By that stage the third episode of the fourth television series had been aired and *Steptoe* fever was back with a vengeance. Clearly, the renewed interest had attracted Corbett and Brambell back to the comparatively easy option of rerecording vintage *Steptoe* scripts for radio.

On 22 December 1965 Gale Pedrick was commissioned to adapt two episodes for the proposed radio series, 'which will include at least five minutes of original material'. Ray Galton remembers that:

> Our contribution to the radio shows was very limited at the start. Gale was signed up to radioize the shows. These script adaptations were sent for our approval and Gale had added a prologue that he had written himself. It was Harry talking to himself about his situation in life, with all this 'Oh, my Gawd. How much longer do I have to go on like this?' reflection. Gale was putting all this cockney rhyming slang in without knowing the first thing about it. All these 'Lawks a mercy', 'Gawd love a duck, Dad!' and 'Would you Adam and Eve it?' were creeping in. We had a lot of time for Gale – he gave us our first job at the BBC, after all – but he was of the 'officer class' of public school breeding and he was writing *Steptoe* from the outside looking in. We couldn't blame him. Anyway, rather than adding anything we just cut certain lines out and smoothed the edges. In the end the radio shows were almost word for word what we had done on television. We didn't want to offend Gale because he was a lovely bloke. We altered it very diplomatically.

The New Year reappraisal that Charles Maxwell had hinted at began promptly. The radio show's producer, Bobby Jaye, revealed in a memo of 6 January 1966 that he was off 'to Nottingham in order to discuss with Wilfrid Brambell the projected series due to start recording January 30, as he is unable to be in London before January 29'. Jaye later confirmed that 'the billing [in the *Radio Times*] will be the same as in the television series, i.e. Wilfrid Brambell and Harry H. Corbett in *Steptoe and Son*'.

On 31 January 1966 L. & H. Nathan, theatrical costumiers, were contracted to supply full outfits for the two stars of the radio series. During the preparation for the second radio series, on 10 April 1967, Bobby Jaye justified the added expense of £5 5s: 'The dressing-up of a sound show may sound incongruous, but we found last year that it was a great help to the actors with their characterization, and made a good stage presentation for the very large capacity audience.' So, for a radio series, Corbett donned 'Wellington boots (size $8^{1}/_{2}$), Overcoat, Choker, Cap, Shirt and bow tie (best) 16 neck', while Brambell was kitted out with 'Overcoat, Homburg, Choker, Mittens, Boots'.

In the end the budget for each show was brought down to just £1 less than the £400 originally planned. The fee for Corbett and Brambell was drastically reduced to £105 each per broadcast and, with the scriptwriters' and adaptor's fees, just £26 remained for payment for additional cast. Thus Bobby Jaye was particularly pleased to use the classic two-handers, saving money on each of these shows and putting the difference towards the bigger-cast productions.

With the stars and writers happy to compromise, the originally scheduled series of eight episodes was extended to 13, and Jaye started to build public expectation for the 'return of the Steptoes' in earnest. On 17 May 1966 he wrote to B. Denney at Television Centre in the hope of 'one of your splendid television plugs' before continuing: 'If you require any further information please contact my office and having got that official rubbish off my chest, how are you, you old bastard?' The 'young boys' network' clearly paid dividends. Explaining that he had arranged the adaptations in more or less chronological order, Jaye was delighted that 'after the first announcement on the air earlier this year that the Steptoes were coming back on radio, the reaction was fantastic ... By the first post we had received enough requests for tickets for the first show alone to fill the theatre for the whole of the 13 episodes.'

The first programme of the first series was broadcast on 3 July 1966 and aptly re-created the programme that had started the whole thing. The announcer intoned: 'We now present the first episode in a radio series based on the world-famous BBC comedy success *Steptoe and Son*, with Harry H. Corbett as Harold Steptoe and Wilfrid Brambell as Albert ... and here they are in 'The Offer', the story which introduced us to those remarkable scrap merchants Steptoe and Son ...' The contrast between the radio remake and the television original is fascinating. Of the performances, Brambell's is, obviously, more stable and word-perfect in the radio versions, but the edge of poignancy and helplessness is dimmed. Lacking those skeletal features and misty eyes, the aural presentation cannot hope to compete with the visual. Still, the chemistry between Corbett and Brambell is as potent as ever, and the writing allows the characters to develop at their own pace. Apart from the jettisoning of Albert's frantic singing into his new-found mirror, and a slightly extended piece of dialogue concerning the additions to Harold's wine cellar, there is no difference in the actual script. The major difference is in the audience. In the four years since the *Comedy Playhouse* programme had captured the imagination of the public, the characters of Steptoe and Son had become established in the minds of the nation. Inevitably, the original amazement and shock at a *Comedy Playhouse* focusing on such raw emotions as had been protrayed in 'The Offer' are gone for ever. 'Dirty old man' was now a catchphrase and received a belly laugh of recognition accordingly. Even more telling is the climax. Corbett, 'crying' in the only medium available to him, blubs loudly and openly for the listening public. Without doubt the edge had been taken off the scene's emotional impact. Whereas complete silence greeted the television version, here the audience laugh at the pathos of the ending. They even laugh at Wilfrid Brambell's tear-choked attempts at levity, as he offers to make a cup of tea and tries to comfort his son with upbeat thoughts. This isn't funny; it's tragic. But the scene has become funny simply because the audience are now fully aware that Harold will face countless similar situations and never, ever completely escape the clutches of the old man. Where there was once hope, there is now simply comedy.

Gale Pedrick heralded the radio series in the *Radio Times*: 'Wilfrid Brambell and Harry H. Corbett have brought a freshness and enthusiasm to a medium comparatively new to them ... those familiar unmistakable voices are so expressive.'

The first series of radio adaptations used choice episodes from series one, two and three. The majority were almost complete resurrections of the original scripts, with a little padding required for the series three selections in order to lengthen the original running time from 25 minutes to half an hour. Importantly, every effort was made to recruit the original supporting actors to re-create their television roles. Naturally, this wasn't always possible, and the instances where it wasn't achieved sometimes threw up some interesting recasting. Frank Thornton, for example, was unavailable for the radio broadcasts, and in this first series of radio programmes his roles in three of his television credits were taken by the versatile character actor Ian Burford. Marianne Stone recorded the roles originally taken by Valerie Bell in 'The Bird' and Yootha Joyce in 'The Bath'. Intriguingly, Yootha Joyce herself had been available for the recording of 'The Bonds That Bind Us' and re-created the *femme fatale* originally played by June Whitfield on television.

Happily, four of the finest supporting turns from the television series were re-created for the radio presentations by the original actors. Gwendolyn Watts returned as Monique in 'Steptoe à la Cart', Joan Newell was back for 'The Stepmother' and Colin Gordon again played the understanding doctor in 'The Holiday'. Most welcome of all was Leonard Rossiter, re-creating his dubious Welshman in 'The Lead Man Cometh'. The combination of the original script and the majority of the original cast made these radio programmes an instant hit.

However, as if to prove the old adage that you can't keep a good man (or indeed men) down for long, the Steptoes had already made a brief but fascinating return to BBC television. On 24 July 1966, Harry H. Corbett and Wilfrid Brambell made their small-screen comeback on *The Ken Dodd Show*. Announced by the *Radio Times* cover headline, 'Doddy, the Bluebell Girls and top-line guests – including Steptoe and Son – in the first of eight shows from Blackpool on Sunday', the first episode of the seventh series for the wild-haired comedian from Knotty Ash was produced by *Steptoe*'s Duncan Wood, so the *Steptoe* sketch was in safe hands. The script was especially written for the programme by Ray Galton and Alan Simpson: 'That was a favour for Duncan Wood really, just a quickie with the Steptoes and Ken on Blackpool beach, as I recall. We didn't have anything to do with it other than writing it. The script was put completely in Duncan's hands and left at that.' The sketch featured the Steptoes sunning themselves on Blackpool beach, with Ken Dodd preparing to play golf on the same spot. The actors were ferried to Blackpool for their one-day assignment, performing the sketch from the vicinity of the Opera House.

The final episode of the first radio series was transmitted on 25 September 1966, but a second batch had already been commissioned for the following spring. The reaction of both public and critics was positive in the main. The Audience Research Report detailed that 'the radio adaptation of "The Offer" had "lost little", although several expressed amazement that "one of the weakest" scripts had been chosen as the opener. Some listeners believed that the lack of "facial expressions" dulled the central performances, and one newcomer to *Steptoe* claimed, "I had heard such glowing reports but found it very run of the mill." Still, the majority conceded that although diluted it was "still [a] touching and amusing representation of a successful television series" and that "recollections of the television series ..." enabled them to enjoy this version: "the cocktail cabinet full of bottles containing the dregs of drinks", for example.'

On 12 July 1966, just two days after the broadcast of the second show, 'The Bird', Roy Rich informed producer Bobby Jaye that the board of management had sent 'sincere congratulations' on an inspired radio treatment. They had thought the show 'translated very happily to radio ... the DG himself said that he thought it was, if anything, better than the televised version'. The extremely healthy figures for the third episode, 'Sixty-Five Today', stood at 3.7 million homes.

The radio series was such a clear success that the suggestion was made that it could attract the writers completely back to their roots. On 4 August

1966 Roy Rich wrote to producer Bobby Jaye: 'I am making inquiries, through Gale Pedrick, as to whether Galton and Simpson would consider writing some original scripts for radio. I shouldn't think there is a hope in hell but they can't shoot us for trying!' These new shows were never forthcoming, although Galton and Simpson did eventually take over the adaptation of their original television scripts.

The unexpected resurrection of *Steptoe*, on television with Ken Dodd and in the radio series, was warmly greeted. Undoubtedly, the show's fan base spread across social and age barriers. In December 1966 the headmistress of the Lisburn Convent, County Antrim, sent her local BBC office a painting of a *Steptoe and Son* scene by one of her pupils, 'an ardent admirer of the programme'. The picture was forwarded to producer Duncan Wood, who sent his congratulations and thanks: 'I would be most grateful if you would pass on my thanks to the Headmistress for sending this to me, and ask her to congratulate the pupil concerned on the high standard of the scene depicted.'

In the interim between series one and series two of the radio shows, the BBC transmitted a repeat of the first series. One episode, 'The Bird', was rather awkwardly altered, owing to complaints following its first broadcast. The beginning of the script, featuring Albert reheating old batteries to extend their lives, was considered a threat to safety by the Royal Society for the Prevention of Accidents. The producer, Bobby Jaye, managed to re-edit the offending sequence. Although he was not entirely pleased – 'It leaves a section sounding as if Wilfrid Brambell is making some cakes and perhaps a slight feeling of irritation to some listeners who may remember him putting the batteries in the oven', – the episode was subsequently 'safe' for retransmission.

Meanwhile the actors, given a bit of leave from *Steptoe*, were enjoying themselves in various assignments. Wilfrid Brambell returned to the more abstract, experimental BBC television productions he had excelled in during the 1950s, being cast as the White Rabbit in the inventive and influential adaptation of *Alice in Wonderland* by Jonathan Miller for December 1966. On film he agreed to a cameo as a train guard in the comedy thriller *Where the Bullets Fly* with Tom Adams.

Having long since accepted the fact that his *Steptoe* fame had restricted his career to comedy roles, Harry H. Corbett played the role of Mack, the stage-door manager in Michael Bentine's ambitious 1966 feature film, *The Sandwich Man*. Meanwhile, ITV had headhunted Corbett to star in his own situation comedy. *Mr Aitch* was, in the main, scripted by Dick Clement and Ian La Frenais, but at a moment of crisis Galton and Simpson were drafted in to help.

Alan Simpson remembers that, '*Mr Aitch* was being produced by a friend of ours, Peter Eton. It wasn't going very well, and Peter asked us if we could contribute to it.' Ray Galton continues: 'We were about to go to America, but they bribed us with loads of money so we agreed to do as many as we could before we left. In the event, we wrote four episodes, but only on the proviso that they would be the very last four of the series. The series wasn't very good; it was failing fast, and we wanted to round things off. But apparently our episodes saved the series, and off the back of ours they got an extension to do some more. We gave them a stay of execution – a very brief one, admittedly – but while we were in America they made a few more. At the time it seemed quite important that ours were the last ones, but 30 years later who cares?' Although Corbett was happy to earn beer money from the radio *Steptoe*, he was confident that *Mr Aitch* was a major departure from the rag 'n' bone classic that was dragging his career down towards low comedy.

In *Mr Aitch* he was, apparently, playing a character far closer to himself in social status. With an expensive lifestyle and the status symbol of a chauffeur, played by the lugubrious Norman Chappell, Mr Aitch was a character who seemed to spend most of the time kidding himself.

He had reversed the aspirations of Harold Steptoe, in that he wanted to move away from his boring, moneyed way of life and become a true Londoner, with a streetwise attitude and a 'girl in every port'. But according to Alan Simpson, the actor was kidding himself, in his belief that he was getting away from his most famous creation: 'Harry was Harry. Mr Aitch was a bit more of a flash guy than Harold, but Harry played it just like Steptoe, only a better-dressed Steptoe! I think we suddenly realized that Harry had only one character. He played everything like that.' During the initial run of episodes in January 1967 the show attracted viewing figures of 7.7 million homes, but the ratings dipped and the decision was made not to produce a further series. It seemed that Harold Steptoe was not so easy to throw off.

The recording schedule for the second series of radio *Steptoe* clashed with Corbett's ITV commitments. 'He's tied up with *Mr Aitch*', a BBC memo noted. The situation put a welcome delay (for the actor) on the recording schedule and, with an urgent need for product, introduced a policy of recording two programmes at each session. Thus, the Sunday evening recordings allowed the actors to knock out the series in double-quick time and continue with other, fresh ventures during the working week. The recording of the second series of radio *Steptoe and Son* programmes began on 21 April 1967 and was held at the Camden Theatre between 8 and 10 p.m. The budget had been raised to £425 per programme, but producer Bobby Jaye still had to account for having gone beyond this. In a memo of 8 May he explained that, 'I have used drama rep. whenever possible, and an extraordinary number of "doublings up" and unpaid labour (announcers/scriptwriters etc.), but find myself approximately £6 overspent and facing the final two scripts with a cast which will cost me approximately £70.' With an excess budget of £28 per show for additional cast members, this was a plea for leniency on his overspending. These excessive costs, combined with disappointing listening figures, saw the radio series abandoned until the return of the Television series created renewed interest in the 1970s.

However, when the second series did hit the airwaves from 11 June 1967, the eight episodes were considered to be of a generally high standard. With television series four far enough away in the public's memory, it felt as if there was now another set of original scripts to play with. Indeed, the opener was an adaptation of the series four classic 'The Siege of Steptoe Street', with Robert Dorning re-creating his role as the ruthless butcher Mr Stacey. As in the first radio series, many of the original television guest actors returned to their roles. But in 'The Piano', Roger Avon, who had played the policeman in the television show, was here replaced by the programme's co-writer, Alan Simpson, making a rare return to acting from his own script after a regular run of 'gag' appearances in the early *Hancock's Half Hour* radio programmes. By the time this second series of radio broadcasts came to an end on 30 July 1967 21 of the 27 *Steptoe* television scripts had been adapted.

During the broadcasts the writers were out of the country, as Ray Galton explains:

> We went to America twice in 1967. The first time was in connection with another attempt at doing an American version of *Steptoe*. We were asked to go out there by a company called Screen Gems, which was run by Harry Ackerman and the ex-child-film-star Jackie Cooper. They wanted to do an American version of *Steptoe and Son*, and they had acquired a load of our scripts. We were assigned to adapt them. In the end we just sat around a pool for weeks on end. It was lovely, but we didn't do anything. They were paying us to do nothing because they always seemed too busy to get started. They kept saying, 'Are you all right? ... We'll soon get round to it.' All they had to do was select a script, but one day they obviously had done that. They said, 'OK, we're all yours now. Would you like to do one?' We did it. It took us a day! So we were back round the pool again.

Alan Simpson continues: 'We sent the American adaptation to them and they said, "OK, great. We have to get it copied and sent around to the readers."

ABOVE: Filming 'Homes Fit for Heroes' on location in the grounds of Ham House in December 1963. Almost 10 million homes across the nation tuned in for the episode the following month.

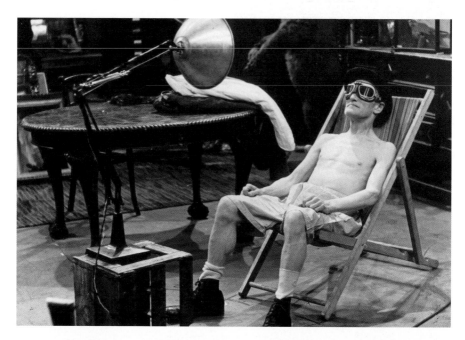

TOP: Albert works on his tan in this scene from 'The Wooden Overcoats' (1964).
ABOVE: A cinematic brief encounter in 'Sunday for Seven Days' (1964). Michael
Brennan plays the audience member disturbed by Albert's thirst-quenching antics.

LEFT: A brazen June Whitfield joins Harry H. Corbett in 'The Bonds that Bind Us' (1964).

BELOW: The first new *Steptoe* episode for 18 months. Karol Hagar joins the cast for a less than 'happy' day for the episode, 'And Afterwards At ...'

RIGHT: The Steptoes
defend their meagre
belongings in 'The Siege
of Steptoe Street' (1965).

BELOW: Yootha Joyce is
reunited with Harry H.
Corbett in her second
Steptoe appearance, 'A
Box in Town' (1965).

TOP: The comic climax to 'A Box in Town'. Marjorie Rhodes accompanies the old man as his disgruntled son looks on.
ABOVE: Harold gets aggressive as he realises 'My Old Man's a Tory' in this politically astute episode from 1965.

TOP: An airborne battle with the Steptoes tackling the Frenchman (Frank Thornton) and the American (Alan Gifford) on points of war in 'Pilgrim's Progress' (1965).

RIGHT: Pride of the regiment – Albert prepares to return to the trenches in 'Pilgrim's Progress'.

ABOVE RIGHT: The *Steptoe* production team gathers for a stunning publicity photograph. Producer/director Duncan wood, dressed in black, consults his clipboard.

ABOVE: Wilfrid Brambell indulges in a laughter-guaranteed leer.

ABOVE: Burnt offering! A television reunion, during a *Steptoe* interlude, for the 1967 *Christmas Night With the Stars*.

ABOVE: Harold endures another depressing yuletide — an ultra-rare still from the
1967 *Christmas Night With the Stars* spectacular.

Meanwhile, we were still round the pool. Another week went by, "Yes, lovely. Now we have to cast it!"'

'That's when their problems started,' recalls Ray Galton. 'In their minds, if it was set in New York people would think they were Jewish. Set in Chicago, Italian. Set in Boston, Irish. They didn't want the poverty element to be associated with any one ethnic group. We said, "Why don't you make them black?" and they said, "Oh, what a great idea … we daren't! We would never get away with it." Thereby hangs a tale of course, because when it did eventually transfer to America, they were black.' Alan Simpson remembers that the casting, in 1967, was exciting:

> It was Hollywood wish-list time again. Mickey Rooney was being discussed for Harold. He had been a suggestion of Jack Benny who had been offered the old man's part. Now Jack really wanted to do it. He had seen our show on his frequent visits to London. But he was practical. He said, 'I'm very old, you know! I'd probably die mid-series!' But he loved the show, he was always ringing up Screen Gems with ideas for the old man. In those days you were talking about 39 episodes a year, though.

In the end, the second stab at an American series failed. As Galton and Simpson recall: 'We came back after eight weeks and nothing was ever done, sadly. But what dream casting. Can you imagine, Jack Benny and Mickey Rooney?'

At the same time as the aborted American venture and the second radio series, BBC Television had screened a repeat season of vintage *Steptoe and Son* episodes. These attracted audiences of 5.5 million homes. The season ran from 7 July through to Christmas Eve 1967. All the episodes, with the exception of the politically dated 'My Old Man's a Tory', were repeated, boosting interest in the new radio adaptations and re-establishing the visual 'feel' of *Steptoe* in the minds of the audience. Great pains were taken to keep topical references up to date. While some of the names of notable people who had since died were retained for the sake of the story – Somerset Maugham was still mentioned in 'The Economist', likewise vintage bandleaders in 'A Musical Evening' – others were removed. A reference to Marilyn Monroe in 'The Economist', originally broadcast weeks before her death, and one to John F. Kennedy in 'Wallah-Wallah Catsmeat' were removed and the Kennedy reference was never reinstated. 'The Bath' which, as the BBC noted, was the 'only occasion in the whole series' (up to that point) to detail an exact date and year, was left intact, as was a reference to Harold Macmillan still being in government in 'Is That Your Horse Outside?'. Only one leading actor had died since the original transmission, Jack Rodney from the poker school in 'Full House', but Duncan Wood explained 'I have cleared this with Bush Bailey'. The print of 'The Offer', with the original *Comedy Playhouse* titles removed, was used as the opening programme in the repeat season. What's more, further negotiations with the principals had been resolved. In the end, Brambell and Corbett received 75 per cent of their original fee of £1000 an episode. Tom Sloan had resisted paying this amount, pointing out that the £1000 fee had been in operation for only the final seven programmes (series four) and thus a payment of £500 for every episode seemed a fair balance. But in a final note on the subject, from the senior booking manager E. K. Wilson, on 21 June 1967, it was confirmed that both actors would receive their £750 per episode as originally requested.

It had been suggested that Duncan Wood should select a *Steptoe* show for the Monte Carlo Festival. At the start of November he chose 'The Bird': 'I know this is one of the earlier ones, but I still think that it has all the essential facets of *Steptoe* in it.' But the notion came to nothing. On the following day, 3 November 1967, Tom Sloan informed Wood that the festival 'rules ... preclude us entering *Steptoe and Son*'. The series had, however, already been sold in 12 countries. As Gale Pedrick wrote: 'They have left a trail of laughter in their wake from Amsterdam to Adelaide.' But even as early as the mid-1960s one country was not content with broadcasting the original episodes, preferring its own adaptation. Holland was the first to adopt and adapt the series, as Alan Simpson remembers: 'The Dutch version was wonderful. The show was called *Stiefbeen En Zoon* over there. It was a huge success and was being made almost parallel with our series. They were direct adaptations of our scripts. As soon as our shows had gone out, we were sending over the scripts for the Dutch translation. Their version was being transmitted about a year or 18 months after our version.' Wilfrid Brambell, a keen traveller, had found himself in Amsterdam at the peak of the show's success:

> I asked the manager of the Amstel Hotel to telephone the studios in Hilversum. As a result of his call, the director of the Dutch *Steptoe* arrived at my hotel together with the Dutch Albert and Harold. Fortunately, the director was bilingual and acted as interpreter all through that splendid drinking evening. Rien van Nunen, who played the dirty old man, was accompanied by his very beautiful wife, who fortunately for me spoke very good English. Later she taught her husband to do so. Rien is a marvellous all-rounder and is equally effective in translated Shakespeare as he is playing my original role. Wearing similar gear, he characterizes Albert superbly, but surprisingly enough

looks more like Harold. I was fêted thereafter by these most hos-
pitable, warm-hearted Dutch people, who even drove me to their studios in Hilversum where, for me alone, they screened two of the Dutch
episodes. It pleased me when I was told that my Dutch counterparts'
series was top favourite in Holland – as was ours in Britain. It was
equally brilliant, but strangely different from the original.

Interestingly, the British episode 'The Wooden Overcoats', which had dealt
with Albert's fear of coffins, had been altered to appease the sensitivity of the
powers that be in Holland: 'Instead of coffins they used waxwork models,'
noted Brambell, 'which were for me much less spooky, but for the Dutch
more digestible.' However, the series came to an abrupt end in Holland, as
Ray Galton remembers: 'The series was huge over there, and all of our
episodes from 1962 through to 1965 were adapted. But after series four, in
around 1967 or 1968, and during our sabbatical from *Steptoe and Son*, their
old man died! The bloody idiot! Some people have no comedy timing!'

The home market repeat series proved a huge success and allowed the
audience plenty of opportunity to reacquaint themselves with the Steptoes
before BBC Television's much-heralded return of the duo. On the very day
after the 'final' programme, 'Pilgrim's Progress', was repeated, television
addicts were treated to a brief but extremely welcome return of *Steptoe and
Son* in another new segment for *Christmas Night with the Stars*. Produced by
Duncan Wood, under the overall production of Stewart Morris, the rehearsals
were set for 14 to 20 November 1967, with the recording taking place on the
final day of rehearsal. Naturally, Ray Galton and Alan Simpson had again
been commissioned to write the script. The new material was the highlight of
the comedy offerings within the 'special programme featuring stars of BBC
light entertainment in 1967'. Other comic contributions came from Roy
Hudd, Kenneth Williams, Harry Worth and the casts of *Till Death Us Do Part*
and *Beggar My Neighbour*. The gala was transmitted on Christmas Day 1967.

That Christmas special really was intended to be the final hurrah for the
Steptoes. All but six of the television shows had been adapted for radio and,
more importantly, the writers were deeply committed to other work, first in
theatre and then in film. Both media would eventually take them back to
America.

For their stage assignments Ray Galton and Alan Simpson were again writing for one of their favourite actors, Frankie Howerd. In November 1966
Howerd opened at the Prince of Wales Theatre in *Way Out In Piccadilly*, a
musical revue written by Galton, Simpson and Eric Sykes which ran for an
astonishing 408 performances. Buoyant with this success, Galton and

Simpson adapted a French farce by René de Obaldia that eventually became *The Wind in the Sassafras Tree*. Opening in Coventry in February 1968, it starred Frankie Howerd and Barbara Windsor. Ray Galton remembers: 'It was a huge success, playing to packed houses every night. Naturally it was decided to take it to the West End but Frankie said, "No, I've done all that. Let's go straight to America." So, that was that. The title was changed to *Rockefeller and the Red Indians* and we played Boston and Washington. Well, the audiences lapped it up. It was a smash hit. Still, with political and artistic problems mounting, the Broadway opening in October 1968 wasn't good. Most of the reviews loved it but the one that mattered, Clive Barnes of the *New York Times* who was a Brit and knew Frankie's work, panned it. That was that!'

'Mind you,' reflects Galton, 'it could have been a lot worse. We heard this terrible story about one show on Broadway that had actually closed in the interval! They played the first act and it was so terrible they said to the audience, "It's not working ... Go home!" At least we ran four days on Broadway!'

Following the success of Galton and Simpson's 1966 comedy thriller *The Spy with the Cold Nose* starring Laurence Harvey, Hollywood also beckoned. 'That was wonderful. Universal asked us to rewrite a film script they had. It was a sort of 18th century James Bond adventure and they wanted Diana Rigg and Michael Caine to star. Because we were English the producer kept asking us, "Do you know Miss Rigg? Do you think she'll do it?" The powers that be at the studio had assessed that the original script would cost $14 million to produce and they wanted us to rewrite in a way that would reduce the budget. Anyway, we worked hard and when they totted up the cost for our version it had gone up to $20 million! Universal only had the budget for one blockbuster that year and we lost out to *Thoroughly Modern Millie*. Still, Hollywood was a great experience, but, as they say, it's very nice to go travelling, but it's oh so nice to come home.'

Chapter 10

The Colour Problem

Back in England the acting career of Harry H. Corbett had gone into something of a slump, as Alan Simpson remembers:

> I did feel very sorry for Harry, because although in a sense we had made him a national and then an international star – or at the very least an internationally recognizable face and character – we did also kind of ruin his career. Even today, people forget what a brilliant, brilliant actor he was. Even watching *Steptoe* they tend not to notice how brilliant he is. To far too many he's just a silly comedy voice, a character actor. But at least I think we managed to give him some good light entertainment work as opposed to some of the stuff he was reduced to doing after *Steptoe* finished. But people also forget what an important actor he was. He wasn't a huge, huge star, but he was singled out in the days before *Steptoe*. But of course practically overnight the straight acting was pretty much dead and buried. Almost as soon as 'The Offer' was broadcast, and certainly after the first series of *Steptoe and Son* had become huge, Harry simply couldn't do the classics any more. You see, that voice of his which became recognized as the 'Steptoe voice' wasn't an act. That's how he actually talked. Harry was a Mancunian and never lost certain elements of his accent. I remember during one rehearsal he said, 'What's that bang-ging?', with that North Country emphasis on the second 'g'. He had a wonderfully unique way of speaking. Before *Steptoe* he had been doing Shakespeare, say *Richard III*, and the critics went potty. How inventive, what an original interpretation of the role. That voice that had been so celebrated and lauded before, was now a joke. After *Steptoe*, audiences

just laughed. His theatrical reputation was in tatters. He decided to dedicate himself to comedy – I mean, he had to. He was forced into playing comedy all the time, and although it made him a good living he wasn't stretched as an actor, which I suspect could have been frustrating for him.

Indeed, despite producer Leonard White casting Corbett in a couple of Donald Churchill-scripted *Armchair Theatre* episodes, 'Hithouse' and 'Second Look', it was comedy that fully took over his career. In June 1966 Corbett starred as Ern Conway in the *Comedy Playhouse* 'Seven-Year Hitch', his first return to the series since the all-important, 'The Offer', in 1962. He grabbed the chance primarily because it was an opportunity to work again with Joan Sims, so soon after enjoying the experience on *Carry On Screaming!*. Importantly, Galton and Simpson had made sure that Corbett was still enjoying the best in comedy writing even in the years between the television *Steptoes*. He played Basil in the third entry of *The Galton & Simpson Comedy* series for London Weekend Television, 'Never Talk to Strangers', in May 1969, with Rosemary Leach. Corbett had also accepted another ITV situation comedy, *The Best Things in Life*, which ran for two series over 1969 and 1970 and co-starred June Whitfield as his fiancée. Corbett played cockney spiv Alfred Wilcox.

Writing in the *Radio Times* in 1970, Russell Miller observed that Corbett's 'is a strange accent, seemingly like none other, with words carefully articulated but strangely blunted somewhere ... it ain't as gorblimey as 'arold's but you know it ain't no one else's neither.' Harold Steptoe had become the actor's albatross.

Wilfrid Brambell's career, meanwhile, continued to attract interesting supporting turns and comedy excursions. In 1969 he followed Corbett's lead and accepted a one-off appearance in a *Carry On* film – *Carry On Again, Doctor*. Brambell's performance, opposite Jim Dale, was completely grounded in *Steptoe* iconography. He accepted a wordless cameo playing the lustful Mr Pullen, a patient who excitedly gropes a blonde nurse before his regular hormone injection. The brief 'dirty old man' appearance was suitably accompanied by a burst of the *Steptoe and Son* theme.

Back on television, producer Rudolph Cartier, who had employed Brambell during the mid-1950s, welcomed the actor back in December 1969. Brambell played the pivotal role of the beggar Saul in Cartier's lavish BBC2 production, *Rembrandt*. On film his roles ranged from horrific to traumatic. He played Master Loach in the classic Vincent Price horror film *Witchfinder General* (1968) and in 1970 Duncan Wood cast him as the manic confidence trickster

Henry Russell in his inheritance comedy *Some Will, Some Won't*. A flashy gag appearance, Brambell's flamboyantly dramatic death from atop Big Ben lends a rollicking start to the bleak fun. He had also seen his *Steptoe* reputation enhance his stage career. He landed top billing playing the multifaceted aged lead role in the musical *Canterbury Tales* at the Phoenix Theatre in London's West End from March 1968. It was directed by Vlado Habunek and the *Daily Sketch* observed that 'Wilfrid Brambell brought off the only show-stopper in years'. Brambell remembered the number:

> Chaucer's Olde English was made less archaic and more understand-able by Professor Nevill Coghill. Richard Hill and John Hawkins had written a marvellous calypso for me to sing and dance. It was decided that two verses would be better than just the one which Nevill had writ-ten, so they telephoned him. He came from his home in Gloucestershire and gave me a typed copy of verse two, asking: 'Is that all right?' I left *Canterbury Tales* by my own free will after six months. I should have done nine, but the management was kind enough to real-ize how exhausted I was. I was followed by several younger and more capable actors, but none played *all* my roles. My enormous role had been divided by five and was no longer a star part. May I boast that my impression was that no single actor of my age still has the stamina to attempt what I tried?

Although *Steptoe* had restricted Harry H. Corbett's career, he was seemingly uninterested in returning to the 'easy' option of re-creating Harold on television. Talking in 1967, he said: 'As far as I can see they've served their time. I think their time has run out.'

But in early 1969 something was rumbling within the BBC. The radio *Steptoe* had proved successful enough, and television repeats were still attracting big audiences. Moreover, Tom Sloan desperately needed the return of an old BBC big gun to wipe out the competition and fully utilize the emerging fresh television technology. The advent of colour in 1968 had opened up new possibil-ities for broadcasters, and although sporting events were natural options for the new system Sloan was keen to experiment with colour in light entertain-ment. If the wacky school of Marty Feldman and *Monty Python's Flying Circus* were to enjoy it, then so too should comedy's established old guard. More important, the BBC was facing its strongest competition ever with the formi-dable comedy output of the new ITV franchise, Thames Television. Frank Muir was in charge of the light entertainment catalogue at Thames and was successfully exercising his common denominator eye for the 'beans on toast' audience. He had already commissioned hits like *Doctor in the House* and *On the Buses*. With Benny Hill decamping from the BBC to Thames in 1969, the situation had reached fever pitch. In Tom Sloan's opinion, the time was right for a resurrection of *Steptoe and Son*.

Alan Simpson reflects on the double-edged sword that was the return of the series:

> None of our films had done any good, to be honest, and Hollywood had been a waste of time. So, like when we parted company with Tony Hancock in 1961, it was Tom Sloan again who said; 'What are you going to do?' This was four years since *Steptoe* had finished on television. Anyway, it was his idea. He said to us: 'Why don't you bring *Steptoe* back?' We hadn't actually thought about it – we weren't really thinking in terms of television any more – but when the idea was put to us we thought: 'Yeah, that's not a bad idea! Why not?' We weren't stupid; we knew which side our bread was buttered. The only problem we really had with it was Tom Sloan's insistence that if it were to come back it would have to be in colour. That worried us a lot. We really thought that colour would ruin *Steptoe*. We thought it would make it look too pretty. The original shows had had this lovely grimy, grainy quality.

Ray Galton agrees: 'We thought that colour might make the home and the yard look too nice and take away the dramatic impact of the greys and the blacks. We were thinking in terms of Ingmar Bergman, with all the shadows and darkness. Still, I think our fears were unfounded.' 'It didn't make a blind bit of difference. In fact, you can see the set better in colour. You could see the filth,' continues Simpson. 'I think we probably wish, in retrospect, that they had all been in colour. They might repeat them a bit more if they were! And in fairness, those four years that we had been away from it had given us a fresher look at the characters. I honestly think that some of the better *Steptoes* were in those later series.'

Ray Galton remembers:

> You really want to know where we were when we decided to bring them back. We were in a Chinese restaurant in Kensington High Street, in February 1969 ... we were eating spare ribs, noodles and bean sprouts with Tom Sloan. With him having planted the notion in our heads, Alan and I had talked it over ourselves beforehand but by the end of the lunch with Tom it was decided we'd do another seven *Steptoes* with an option of six more. All the time *Steptoe* was off, Tom Sloan was always asking when we were going to do another series. If he hadn't been so persistent, I doubt very much if we would have gone to the

BBC and suggested it. No, we certainly wouldn't have suggested it. Tom Sloan, and the number of people who kept saying, 'When are they coming back?' – those are the two things that really decided us. I certainly think the break did us good. There hadn't seemed much more to exploit in terms of the relationship between the two of them when we finished in 1965, so we came back with enthusiasm.

'It was comparatively easy and very enjoyable' remembers Alan Simpson, 'and we certainly wouldn't have done eight series if we hadn't had that break.'

Tom Sloan 'leaked' the exciting news on 11 June 1969 when he wrote: 'I have had discussions with Galton and Simpson with a view to reviving *Steptoe and Son* in 1970, and I am glad to say that in principle this is agreeable to them. It is essential that we first contract the writers before dealing with the artists, as without the scripts we have no show.' An internal memo of 24 June 1969 stated that the BBC 'wants to mount a series of seven *Steptoe and Son* programmes with scripts by Galton and Simpson to be delivered by 31 January 1970 and to be recorded during February or March 1970. This is to be followed by an option for six more programmes to be delivered and recorded later in the year by dates to be mutually agreed.' The scriptwriters' increased fees were fully justified: 'The fact is that their market value, particularly with a property like *Steptoe*, is very high indeed.' Again, however, the writers' agreement had been on the proviso that Wilfrid Brambell and Harry H. Corbett were equally keen on the idea. The BBC approached the two actors with provisional rehearsal and recording dates and was notified that both Brambell and Corbett were keen to return. Galton and Simpson were officially contracted on 1 July 1969.

An internal memo details the payments agreed with Harry H. Corbett: a fee of £1250 per programme. 'There would be an option for a further six programmes at the same fee to be recorded within one year of date of transmission of the last programme in the first series. This fee represents an increase of £250 on the fee paid to the artist for the last *Steptoe and Son* series, which was recorded in 1965. The increase is justified by the lapse of time and by the fact that Corbett has continued to rank as a star since that date, having starred in two ITV series [*Mr Aitch* and *The Best Things in Life*] and in various theatrical shows.' Brambell's deal was similar, although for the first time he was on a lower fee than his co-star, receiving '£1050 for the first seven programmes with an option of six more programmes at a fee of £1250. The justification for increase is the same as for Corbett, though I have managed to keep the demand lower in this case. Brambell's fee for the 1965 series was £1000. In both cases we should have television exclusivity.' Galton and

Simpson, already commissioned by this stage, endeavoured to write the first seven episodes under the provisional title of *The Return of Steptoe and Son*. Alan Simpson remembers that 'the seven new episodes took us about half a year to write ... the times would usually vary. Some episodes would take a couple of days, others three weeks, but that new series was a long old process. It wasn't that it was difficult. Quite the contrary. Both Ray and I felt very refreshed, and we returned to the show with a renewed energy and interest. We widened out the plots, brought in more characters each week for Harold and the old man to interact with and found the scripts both fairly easy and very rewarding.'

When the rag 'n' bone business finally returned to BBC Television in February 1970, the 'return of' prefix had been dropped from the credits. This monumental fifth series of *Steptoe and Son* was, unsurprisingly, eagerly anticipated.

Ron Grainer, the composer of the unforgettable theme tune, and the original incidental-music composer, was offered the assignment for the new episodes. Sadly for him, the dates clashed with a prior engagement. In a letter to Duncan Wood, dated 24 November 1969, Grainer wrote: 'I find that the first date definitely clashes with my next film ... thank you for thinking of me – hope we do work together again.' With the artists now under contract, Brambell's new agent (he had joined Peter Crouch in 1966) was keen to promote his client. On 27 January 1970 he wrote to Duncan Wood: 'I know most of the press people chase after Harry, and I think this is only natural as he is younger and obviously sexier! However, do you think you could have a word with the press office of the BBC and ask them to push as much as possible Wilfrid's way?'

Brambell, as well as Corbett and Galton and Simpson, was interviewed by Gerard Kemp for the *Radio Times* spread launching 'the first new *Steptoe* series since 1965, in colour too', as the cover screamed. He was pedestrianly quizzed on his 'motivations' for Albert Steptoe, and the interview made most reference to the uncomfortable requirements for the actor, noting that he needs four days' growth 'to get the stubble right'. However, it was a rare opportunity for Brambell to reflect on his comic creation and Albert's relationship with Harold: 'He's *very* smart-witted, whereas Harold is comparatively slow. Harold is a bit of a snob. He's insecure too; he wants to get away but can't do it. Something to do with the tyranny of claims. Harold irritates the old man but the old man *needs* him; he does most of the work.' Harry H. Corbett continued that Harold 'doesn't like hard work. He's a great one for taking short cuts. He fancies himself quite a bit, especially when he's driving the cart. He's like Ben Hur when he's up there.' Corbett was also consciously wearing his hair longer for the new programmes in a more fashionable style: 'He's about 75 per cent me,' the actor confided. 'The rest is observation.'

'If the characters were too much changed there would be little point in bringing them back,' Galton and Simpson argued but, clearly, the writers were committed to bringing the show back with a bang, after such a long period in the wilderness. Indeed, the very title of the first episode of the new series, 'A Death in the Family', carried great importance and poignancy. Could the old man, as opposed to the old horse, be heading for the knacker's yard? In the end, of course, it was the ever-loyal Hercules who was put to the sword to begin the new colour programmes on an emotional high. Continuity, however, happily went out of the window. In terms of Harold's age, this episode could quite easily have immediately followed on from his humiliating aeroplane trip to France in 'Pilgrim's Progress'. Speaking in 1970, Ray Galton commented: 'Harold Steptoe is now on the threshold of 40, a man who realizes that he's trapped by his father but who still yearns for the miracle that will take him out of this situation. Harold can be nasty to the old man and the old man can be nasty to *him*. Harold is hanging on for the old man to leave him the business. He can't do anything else.' Alan Simpson continued: 'It's the old umbilical cord, isn't it? One of the reasons Harold stays is that he feels it's the son's duty to look after the father. The old man is more shrewd, more worldly. Harold is completely gullible. The old man has one big fear: fear of being left alone. In a way he's jealous of Harold: age for youth.'

For sure, the lengthy gap between series four and series five, and the brief gap in terms of narrative action, necessitated some hasty rewriting of *Steptoe* mythology, as Alan Simpson remembers: 'Harold aged two years over the space of 14 years on television. He started in 1962 at the age of 37, and by 1974 he was 39, the old man going from 64 to 66 in the same space of time.' Ray Galton remembers that 'it seriously buggered up our histories of the Steptoes. Harry had originally, in our minds, been involved in the Second World War. Now that wouldn't work. Originally, Harold had been the same age as Harry Corbett was. Harold Steptoe was, in the first series, born in 1925. By the time we returned, eight years after we started, Harold had stayed at almost the same age. His involvement in the Second World War would have been unfeasible, so we changed Harold's military background to the Malaya conflict. As for the old man, that was a bit easier. We still kept him in the First World War but just explained that he had lied about his age to enlist. Lot's of people had done that, and we felt that Albert was patriotic and brave and/or stupid enough to do the same'.

The age of the horse, however, certainly set the new episode in stone as contemporary to March 1970, when the show was first broadcast. Hercules was born in August 1930. As the old man proudly remembers: 'Do you realize he was born on the same day as Princess Margaret?' He is certainly very much part of the Steptoe family, as the title suggests. The scene, when tears well up in Wilfrid Brambell's eyes as he recalls wanting to call the horse Margaret Rose if it was a filly, is truly heartbreaking to watch. Clearly, the fact that Harold is, by his own admission, younger than the horse leaves the son firmly in the twilight zone of the early 1960s.

The facts scarcely matter for, whatever the scripted and unscripted ins and outs of the Steptoes, there's no doubting the moving farewell to the third member of the regular cast. It's a pity that the wordless, location material of Harold struggling with the horseless cart after Hercules's death on the Goldhawk Road, and openly sobbing in the street, is met with gales of unsympathetic laughter from the audience viewing this prelude to the studio action. Already the clichés and stereotypes of the 'dirty old man' and the 'hopelessly trapped son' are welded into the audience's consciousness. The height of emotion achieved in the earliest shows could never again be completely replicated thanks, in the main, to the familiarity of the characters and the expectation of an easy laugh. Still, the writing and acting are as flawless as ever and succeed almost audibly in shaming the cackling audience members who refuse to accept that what they are witnessing is tragic not hilarious.

The old man is, suitably, newly introduced as the ultimate in dirty old men. He happily shovels manure, smells the sweet fragrance of his latest load, stuffs his face with a sandwich and wipes the muck off his hands. Brambell's visual tricks are well used, with Albert eating his snack, hurriedly washing his hands before preparing 'faceache's supper' and wiping his hands dry on the net curtains. These are symbols of the filthy old toerag that the previous shows had subtly built up over four series, suddenly reintroduced in full colour. It's clearly business as usual, with Albert continually nattering and complaining as Harold returns home distraught. There's his familiar dig at his son's financial pretensions and political affiliations. The old man proudly boasts of paying for the horse's feed by the sale of its manure, and takes an unsubtle swipe at 'you and your party!' But his full-frontal attack is short-lived. Harold breaks down completely, and the heart-wrenching narrative of Hercules's demise begins in earnest.

Naturally, Harold suffers guilt in silence, as the old man goes into mourning. Corbett's expressive features are used in abundance at the sight of a flashy television advertisement for 'Super Cat' cat food. Although upset by

Hercules's death, Harold can still recover enough to voice disgust at his father's attitude – the old man closes the business for a period of mourning – playing out a mini-enactment of what the firm's sign would have read if Albert had simply lost his son: 'Business as usual, gone to a funeral, back in half an hour.'

But, with the arrival of a new horse – who turns out to be female and gives birth to Hercules the second – and the business back on track, the two rag 'n' bone men prepare for a night out at a 'naughty' foreign film. 'A Death In the Family' plays as if the Steptoes have never been away. In a strange way they never had been.

Reassuringly, the BBC continued to film the location scenes in the same Shepherd's Bush junkyard, which, like the cart, was again hired from the same Notting Hill rag 'n' bone men, Arthur and Chris Arnold. The replacement horse was a female in real life, by the name of Dolly. Arthur Arnold was featured in a 'real Steptoe' article in the *Radio Times* and on the review programme *Late-Night Line-Up*. Despite the promise of the television show's producer that *Steptoe* wouldn't be used as a hook for the item, it clearly was, and this encroachment annoyed producer Duncan Wood. Corbett and Brambell were also less than happy with the treatment they received during the photo shoot for the *Radio Times* cover. The editor, Geoffrey Cannon, had belatedly contacted the *Steptoe* production office with a request for the two actors and 'the dead horse'. This was completely against the grain for all concerned, so much so that Wood circulated a memo saying: 'NO MENTION is to be made of the plot – i.e. the death of the horse. We have managed to avoid this in all press coverage so far and would like to keep it dark until the episode is transmitted.' The caption to the photograph on the *Radio Times* listing page bore the legend: 'Steptoes in mourning – for what?' It was finally agreed that the cover itself would feature 'just the two of them'. The photo session took place on Sunday 4 January 1970. However, the actors were distressed to discover that nobody seemed to know what the shoot was about and, more important, no one from the *Steptoe* production team was present to advise the photographer, Tony Evans. In an exasperated memo Duncan Wood later explained: 'I rang both Harry and Wilf. Each said the other had been very upset.' On reflection, Corbett seemed more perturbed than his co-star. Indeed, he used the situation to twist the knife further into Duncan Wood, requesting to see as many of the new scripts – of which the producer had only two – as possible so as 'to do some proper work on them for once'. While the actors were understandably annoyed at the lack of organization, the coverage proved a useful herald for the new series. Moreover, the *Radio*

Times was extremely loyal to *Steptoe and Son*, running a photograph from the series on the billing page for each week of the six-week run of series five.

The BBC's commitment to a new batch of *Steptoe and Son* episodes clearly paid off. An excited television viewing nation rewarded the new series with some of its highest viewing figures. The first of the fifth series attracted 8.7 million homes and figures for the subsequent episodes rarely dipped below the 8 million mark. The second episode, 'A Winter's Tale', has remained one of Alan Simpson's favourites:

> During the writing of the first new episodes, I remembered when we had written the film *The Spy with a Cold Nose* for Laurence Harvey. He had been starring in 'A Winter's Tale' at the time of filming, and both Ray and myself felt that when we had written this particular episode that title seemed to fit perfectly. The fact that Shakespeare had used it before was just too bad! I really enjoyed the making of that show, and it was back to basics for us. One of our 'famous' two-handers, 'A Death in the Family', had only had two speaking roles – Harold and the old man – but this one didn't even have any extras. The BBC always loved those. They were much cheaper to make, of course, because there were only the two regulars in them. No extra expense for other actors to come in and fill out the supporting roles. We always felt that we could really get down to the characters as well, without anybody else coming in and shifting the emphasis from this very fraught, bickering relationship.

In many ways 'A Winter's Tale' basks in our knowledge of the classic first series episode 'The Holiday'. Albert is, as always, keen to holiday in Bognor, and more crucially determined than ever that his son takes his holiday there as well. Typically, he is overtly distraught when he realizes his son wants to holiday on his own – an ambition that runs throughout the entire history of *Steptoe and Son*. The opening features Harold out on the cart, gazing transfixed at an array of posters advertising exotic holidays. Although clearly recalling 'The Holiday', this time the locations are all Swiss Alps and skiing in France.

Clearly this new series, while keeping Albert and Harold's ages fairly fixed, had moved the Steptoes into a more contemporary way of life. The house is scattered with mod cons – not only a shower but, as witnessed in the previous episode, a television. Ironically, although the 1960s episodes referred to small-screen favourites, from *Z Cars* to *The Avengers*, it wasn't until the first of the 1970s programmes that the Steptoes were seen to actually have a television, never mind watch one. Film references were still irresistible to Galton and Simpson, with Harry H. Corbett relishing a maniacal cameo as he dons a shower cap and attacks Albert in the shower, à la *Psycho*.

Social comment within *Steptoe and Son* was also, reassuringly, still just as rife as before. In this episode Harold is happy to reveal that the Steptoes are on a list for a grant. They are finally considered to be a deprived family. The embrace of fruity language is also shifted up a gear, with Albert lambasting his son with 'you dirty old sod!' when the talk turns to an athletic holiday. Harold's mind is firmly set on the delights of the holiday totty of Austria's Obergurgl which, Alan Simpson recalls, 'sticks in my mind as the most marvellous of names of a place to go on holiday'.

As always, when Harold goes off on one of his fantastic diatribes, his father knows something fishy is afoot. The old, old story, from Albert's ridiculing Harold's skiing ambitions to droning on about being left on his own, allows the actors to build on our preconceptions of both father and son.

The old man continually picks holes in Harold's pathetic collection of mismatched and misshapen skiing gear – 'If you want to look a berk that's up to you!' – but for once Harold refuses to give in. Corbett even repeats 'He's not coming!' to himself with uncontrolled glee all over his face. But as usual, Harold's handiwork – in this case a makeshift ski slope in the yard – causes his final downfall. He breaks his leg and is forced, reluctantly, to allow the old man to shoot off on the holiday he had planned for himself. In the final innuendo-drenched scene Corbett says, 'Go out on the piste first' and Brambell replies, 'I intend to, mate, every bleeding night!' Yet again, it's Albert one, Harold nil.

Again, there's a keen understanding between the two of them in the next episode, 'Any Old Iron?', a script that offers Harold yet another route of escape from rag 'n' bone man, this time to antique-shop respectability if he can only play along with a flamboyantly, blatantly homosexual dealer. Richard Hurndall played the antique dealer with a pompous way of pronouncing his name and exquisite limp-wristed elegance. Here, at the peak of his comedy career, he effortlessly entraps Harold like a fly in a very ornate spider's web. Hurndall was courted for this plum *Steptoe* assignment for many weeks. After several letters from producer Duncan Wood, Hurndall was advised in one of 5 February 1970 that his was 'the part on which the whole plot hangs'. Still, Hurndall's agent, Richard Meyer of Essanay Limited, was quick to try to ensure a special credit for his client. On 25 February 1970 Richard Meyer wrote to Duncan Wood: 'I assume that Richard Hurndall will be billed as "guest star" or something of this sort. This is what will be expected.'

The relationship of Albert and Harold as more like mother and daughter than father and son is brilliantly evoked here. The old man laments the fact that in London men wearing foppish outfits like those Harold now favours can't travel on the bus because the skinheads will get them. Playing the worried mother figure, he offers his son a protective lump of lead piping and even says, 'Ere, put this in yer 'andbag'. The threat to Harold's innocence lies closer to home, with Hurndall's antique dealer playing the polished cad with a suitable touch of the Noel Cowards as he coaxes his wicked way into the confidence of the naive rag 'n' bone man. At his flat, he changes into something 'more comfortable' and dims the lights. Having decided to leave, Harold meets a copper at the door, gives a false name, adopts a false Liverpudlian accent and goes to prove his manhood with Dolly Miller, the spiritual sister of the working man's favourite, Dolly Clackett.

The policeman is played by Roger Avon, who had served the purpose once before in 'The Piano'. But here the authority of the uniform is in question, as Avon's policeman is not simply checking up on the vicinity as part of his beat – he's checking up on his boyfriend. He shares the home of the predatory antique dealer!

The character of Dolly Miller, initially and memorably condemned for being 'as dim as a glow-worm's armpit' by the sophisticated Harold, is played by Valerie Bell. The actress had had the distinction of being *Steptoe and Son's* first guest player as the briefly seen eponymous heroine of 'The Bird' in 1962.

'Any Old Iron?' is both a television document that records changing attitudes to what could and could not be discussed on the medium and a reference point to changing attitudes to sexuality. From our present-day viewpoint, the Steptoes encountering a character who is clearly homosexual loses a lot of the clout it would have had in 1970. With situation comedies such as *Gimme, Gimme, Gimme* and *Ellen* nowadays showcasing the gay community and making a homosexual character the hero or heroine of the humour, the fact that one simply appears is no longer shocking or daring. But the episode was transmitted just three years after homosexuality had become legal. This was indeed a very ambitious half-hour of comedy drama.

'I don't know whether that's true or not,' reasons Ray Galton, 'but I certainly think the BBC may have been rather foolhardy to put it out again a few years back. A certain part of our population thought it was very offensive.' 'Comedy inclusions of gays were, as a rule, very stereotypical in the 1970s,' continues Alan Simpson. 'Ours certainly wasn't, but I think what they objected to was the old man's attitude. It was all this "iron hoof" and "brown hatter" condemnation. But Harry was saying, you know: "Dad, you can't talk like that, you are so prejudiced." Richard Hurndall certainly didn't play the part as a stereotype. He was effeminate, certainly, but he wasn't like John Inman or Larry Grayson or that sort of limp-wristed performance. Still, a couple of people did protest. It was rescreened as one of *The Lost Steptoes*, and a letter was published in one of the newspapers saying it should have stayed lost!' Ray Galton recalls:

> At the time, we thought we were being very even-handed about the whole thing, especially with the hypocrisy of the old man: 'You're no son of mine, having been out all night with him.' Then he finds out he's been out with a girl, so that was all right. Then there was a double twist in that the old man is disgusted at that. 'What sort of a house do you think you've come from?' He was disgusted on both counts, and as usual Harry couldn't win. I think we presented a pretty fair interpretation.

Alan Simpson concludes: 'We didn't get any objections to the show when we first did it. We only got objections when it was repeated 20 years later ... which is interesting!' Interesting, too, that the BBC, clearly unaware of the controversy surrounding the episode, selected the radio version of 'Any Old Iron?' as a 'unique audio birthday card', which could be bought at the BBC Experience Exhibition in the late 1990s.

In direct contrast to 'Any Old Iron?' Harold's clear favouring of the opposite sex was relentlessly thrust home with the following episode, 'Steptoe and Son – and Son!'. Originally broadcast in a 'special' Good Friday slot in 1970, it perfectly illustrated the freedom that the series had given its writers. Ray Galton firmly believes that 'the show had enabled us to use subjects we could never have written about for, say, Tony Hancock or Frankie Howerd or any comedian. Even if a girl was pregnant in a script, she was pregnant with a flat stomach. Nobody showed the reality. In *Steptoe and Son* we could. For once in his miserable life, Harold has seemingly planted some wild oats. As always in *Steptoe*, it's never as simple as that, but the very fact that we could suggest Harold had made a complete stranger pregnant and that he is going to do the right thing and marry her would have been unthinkable 10 years previously. Nowadays anything goes, but in 1970, within a comedy, you just couldn't do what we were doing, but we did it!'

Harold's 'Dear diary' entry relates a swinging party in May 1969 that clearly involved the pregnant girl we see, sheepishly and undemonstratively entering the Steptoes' home. She is played with a gentle understatement by Ann Beach, and the full story is wonderfully constructed. Albert's early rejection of the girl's story is in his son's best interest, but Harold is determined to do the right thing and marry the stranger. From initial shock and denial, the potential increase in the members of the Steptoe clan is gradually warmed to.

Ann Beach, who had found herself free from West End commitments in *Mame* at the time of casting, was offered the *Steptoe* role by producer Duncan Wood. The name for her character, Daphne Tomlin, came from an intriguing source, as Alan Simpson reveals: 'We loved names, and if we were ever stuck for the right one we would often use names taken from the list of members of the Hampton Football Club. We would scan the list for ages and Daphne Tomlin for "Steptoe and Son – and Son!" was one we found that way.'

The use of Harold's diary both as a narrative tool and as a symbol of the lack of privacy in Oil Drum Lane is cleverly woven into the script. Albert is having a crafty look at his son's innermost thoughts and reads about 'that' party, before 'that' girl arrives and he breaks to answer the door and invite her into his home.

Albert's double standards are breathtaking. He refuses to accept that his son is the father of the child, but expresses an amazed 'Cor blimey! No wonder he left her!' when the girl reveals that her ex-boyfriend couldn't be responsible because they didn't consummate their relationship. Harold's dream of a wife and family is, however, all the more potent and welcome when it looks like coming together in a surprise package. Even Albert warms to the idea of becoming a grandfather. The old man hands over £500 as a wedding present (which he had been forced to agree to giving earlier but now gives gladly): 'It's good to see you so happy!' But both Steptoes are aware of the problems that lie ahead, even at the pinnacle of the humour when Harold defends the size of a garment with an exasperated 'Of course it's small. It's for a baby. It's not for Harry Secombe!', tempered with a meek smile.

Needless to say, as Ray Galton noted, all is not as it seems for Harold. No sooner has Albert fallen in love with the idea of an extended family than George the sailor, in the person of Glynn Edwards, crops up admitting that the child is his. At the time Edwards was married to *Steptoe* favourite Yootha Joyce, and would later become nationally adored as George the barman in *Minder*. His role was important, and Edwards was perfectly cast. The scene is played beautifully straight, and Corbett in particular gives a stunning portrayal of a brave face and crumbling collapse of emotions. It's almost too painful to witness at times. Edwards brilliantly avoids playing the stereotypical Jack Tar and brings real power to his performance. His 'I'm proud to know you, Harold' is played with a mixture of admiration and appreciation. Brambell's contribution, as with 'The Offer' and several other episodes, is to lavish fake relief on the situation. He desperately tries to highlight the great escape his son has had, looking on the bright side of a heartbreaking moment. Brambell and the scriptwriters' great gift here is to allow the old man to fail miserably in this ambition. He can't help but show his deep disappointment for both himself and his son. His wordless gaze at his son's crestfallen face is one of the most potent of *Steptoe* moments. As Harold expresses a desire to get steaming drunk, Albert doesn't try to warn him off it with jokes and helpful lies. He meekly mutters 'Harold ... can I come with you?', and the two, as so often, end the episode sharing their pain together.

At the start of this new series it had been established that the Steptoes have a television set. In the fifth episode, 'The Colour Problem', it is revealed that they have had one since 1937. Albert marvels at the promised wonders of colour television while 'suffering' all day watching old black and white films on his old black and white set. 'It's bloody hard work, mate,' he explains as he struggles to use a magnifying glass to bring clarity to the ropy contrast of the ancient television. Harold is in high spirits from the outset. He makes his entrance with a cheerful 'It looks like a junkyard out there!' before condemning the medium of television as a waste of time. Besides, he's got bird-pulling on his mind again. To that end he is eager to pick up a sports car and a bit of Brighton weekend action at the same time. Colour television can wait.

Naturally, the old man has been there and done that, revelling in his erotic and exotic memories of game young girls on the coast: 'Permissive society, they don't know what day it is!' Harold is enraptured by his father's glittering past but, naturally, wants a piece of the action himself before it's too late.

The television depiction of sex and sexual antics was really changing gear by the time these programmes were broadcast at the start of 1970. Not only can Harold pull a stunning young girl who is quite happy to give him what he wants for the weekend, but reference can be made to the local villain, Charlie Miller. Despite being treated like a hero by everybody, including the off-screen vicar, Miller has '15 girls on the game', according to the hapless, law-abiding Harold. Such revelations would have been impossible during the 1960s.

Anthony Sharp, later to become something of a *Steptoe* regular as the semi-streetwise vicar, crops up here for the first time in the series as a concerned and totally unstreetwise doctor who treats Albert in hospital for loss of memory after the old man leaves home and spends the night walking the streets. Ray Galton remembers Sharp as 'another one of those wonderfully reliable people who could come in, sometimes at the last minute, and play authority figures to perfection. There was real energy and belief in Anthony's performance. He was great at the middle-class ineffectual type.' Sharp gets a laugh when he, quite innocently, quotes an old music-hall song: 'He'd be far better off in a home!' Having suggested the idea, the doctor brings out Harold's heartfelt feelings on the subject. Not only is he protective of his father, but he is reluctant to chase his old dream. 'I don't want to live my own life!' he shouts in defiance. With his dirty weekend scuppered, a new television replacing the sports car and the old man delighted ('Oh, look. The weather forecast in colour!'), the die is cast. Harold will never live his own life.

'TB or not TB?' was a real homecoming for the scriptwriters. Naturally, it concentrated on the concern surrounding tuberculosis, the disease that had united Galton and Simpson in 1948. 'It was a good plot, and the only illnesses you could seriously discuss around an X-ray machine were cancer or TB,' reflects Ray Galton. 'As TB had been conquered, it was all right to use it. Lung cancer would have upset a large chunk of the population – you couldn't even say the words – so we wouldn't have tackled that as a subject. TB was more acceptable.'

Alan Simpson continues:

> It wasn't really because we had suffered, although, having said that, it gave us both an insight into the subject and some ammunition when we received one or two complaints at the time. I remember one letter coming in from someone whose distant relation had chronic TB and had been ill for years. This person said, 'How dare you use this for a subject of fun. You don't know the first thing about it!' We took great delight in writing back and saying, 'As it happens, we were both in a sanatorium for three years, so hard luck!'

The episode also provided a harder-hitting treatment of a similar scenario tackled in the old days of television *Hancock's Half Hour*. At one point, Harold is convinced he's dying of TB. The old man, in a terrible panic at the thought of catching it, rushes around like a decontaminating nuclear scientist. The breakfast scene, with a listless Harold in a dressing gown grimly facing his food while Albert protects himself with a handkerchief over his face like a surgeon's mask, is directly lifted from the Tony Hancock and Sid James situation in 'The Cold'. Ray Galton remembers:

> We really liked the idea of the old man putting his mask on and being frightened of catching something. That was good comic value and, on a serious note, a leftover from the early days, our days, of tuberculosis. There was a lot of doubt about the illness, and you really thought it was the ringing of the bell and bring out your dead time when you got it. So in that respect we could bring the serious issues to bear on the comedy. You really would have your own knife and fork, and your own plate, with everything washed up separately. It was a very, very contagious disease.

Albert, having smoked since he left school at the age of eight and a half, is forever coughing his guts up. He pleads with Harold to hang on to his last bit of pleasure and, fearful, is against any suggestion that he should have a medical check-up. For him, medical interference 'don't prevent it; it's looking for it!' He is dismissive of his son's earnest calculations regarding smoking history – 'Who cares?' – and is blissfully happy when completely in the dark about his physical health. It is Harold's insistence and underlying hypochondria that drag Albert down to a mobile X-ray clinic. 'These were everywhere at the time, parked in factories or whatever, and people queuing to be X-rayed,' remembers Ray Galton. 'It just seemed an ideal plot line for the Steptoes.'

When they arrive at the clinic, Harold and Albert waste no time in embarrassing each other. Harold reveals hidden secrets about his father in order to lessen his futile chances of success at chatting up the attractive receptionist, played by Sidonie Bond, while the old man delights in exposing his son's previous X-ray experience 'when the horse kicked you in the cobblers'. Albert goes off on a Frankenstein-inspired tangent about electricity in X-rays and the danger that he could 'turn into a monster'. 'That was a throwback to my youth,' remembers Ray Galton. 'In the afternoons, cinemas would always be half-empty, and I was continually trying to bunk in the exit and not pay my shilling. Some films you were restricted on. I remember once trying every day to see *Frankenstein* and I couldn't get in. You would ask a passing adult – a complete stranger – to accompany you. With any luck he would pay your shilling as well. Anyway, the bloke on the door knew me by now, and I couldn't get past him. I've never seen it ... to this day! I still can't get in! I'm too old!!'

The echo from the writers' past is skilfully merged with Wilfrid Brambell's delicious performance. His absolute relish when he secretly confides, 'She's got TB', grabs the desired reaction from Harold – 'Has she?' – for the gloriously sledgehammering punchline: 'Two Beauties!'

Important in terms of *Steptoe and Son*'s (admittedly shifting) continuity and background, the form-filling scene reveals the Steptoes' full address for the first time – The Mews Cottage, Oil Drum Lane, Shepherd's Bush – as well as both characters' full names: Albert Edward Ladysmith Steptoe and Harold Albert Kitchener Steptoe. Still, after all the bravura and one-upmanship, the cold reality of the aftermath of the medical examination hits home with dramatic clout. Brambell's simple 'Harold, I'm frightened' can make the hairs on the back of your neck stand on end.

When the results arrive in the post they show that Albert's examination has suffered a technical fault and needs to be redone. However, soon it transpires that it's Harold's examination that was faulty and the old man's manner alters accordingly. Selfish at all times, he goes from humble self-pity to skip-ping second childhood with a gleeful 'Where's me fags?' For him a lucky escape means unhealthy business as usual. He is also aggressively unhelp-ful as Harold physically wilts. Corbett behaves, in the words of the old man, like a 'bleeding Victorian poet', effectively injecting a weak cough into his subdued performance. His remorseless self-indulgence as he waxes lyrical – 'I shall miss England in the spring' – is mingled with his political persua-sions, as his will leaves 'a small bequest to the Labour Party'. When he goes to be re-examined he even manages to embrace a trace of the old man, going that little bit too far as he departs the scene with a sense of foreboding: a line about meeting in the morning, 'God willing', is right out of Albert's book of clichés. The return of the totally fit Harold is a scene to treasure: Corbett's behaviour during Albert's reading of the will rejoices in the spirit of Harold returning in full play-acting mode.

However, it wasn't all a bed of roses for Harry H. Corbett. An accident report reveals that during the recording of the episode, on 5 April 1970, he received a deep laceration to his left thumb: as 'part of the action [Corbett was] stick-ing [a] head on to a broken china figure. The action then called for Wilfrid Brambell to nudge Mr Corbett and knock the head off again. This had worked perfectly on rehearsal but during the take Mr Corbett cut his left thumb on the rough edge of the broken china.' Clearly, the cry of 'Is there a doctor in the house?' was answered that night, for the report explains that a member of the studio audience, Dr McManus, assisted by the duty sister at Television Centre, nursed the wound. The actor, a pro to the end, apparently carried on regardless: 'Mr Corbett continued his performance after which he was taken to Hammersmith Hospital for further treatment.'

The final episode in the series, 'Men of Property', turned to a familiar Steptoe and Son hook – father and son waging war through a game. This time it is Monopoly and, naturally, Albert is brilliant at it. Wilfrid Brambell's eager, money-grabbing performance drips with knife-twisting delight in his son's struggling performance, while Harry H. Corbett desperately tries to retain dignity as he checks every 'community chest' his opponent picks up and frus-tratingly determines to pay off his debts as he continually lands on a hotel-enhanced 'Mayfair'. Monopoly, used as an introduction and end to the episode, is a skilful metaphor for the real house-ownership situation of the family business. With their home's 99-year lease coming to a close, the Steptoes are given three months' notice to quit unless they find £750 to buy the place outright. Continuity is retained, with Albert's passionate royalist and Tory beliefs reflected in his condemnation of the government and Harold

Wilson's unfair policies. However, as Harold points out, while Albert is 'a right little Charlie Clore' on the Monopoly board, in real life, he is hopelessly lacking in business sense. Harold's dreams of high finance and important business lunches have the potential to come true when he reveals a successful scam Charlie Miller has been working – finding a new bank manager in the area, applying for a business loan and clearing off with the money. Two sparkling character actors are brought into the mix for this pivotal plot development. Michael Balfour, the glorious cockney spiv of a score of post-war British films, is perfectly flamboyant and streetwise in a very brief cameo as Miller, while *Steptoe* regular Norman Bird landed the role of the supposedly ineffectual, but in fact rather canny, bank manager. The actor had been offered a role in the film *The Raging Moon*, written and directed by his long-time collaborator Bryan Forbes. *Steptoe* producer Duncan Wood agreed to let him take the assignment, juggle his schedule and still be considered as part of the *Steptoe* cast. On 10 March 1970 Bird penned a note thanking Wood for his consideration and concluded: 'I need hardly say how much I like the part!' The role was, indeed, a special one. Rocking the pompous, self-confident persona of Harold Steptoe in full flow, the bank manager is hardly the 'right carrot' that everybody takes him for. Instead, he dangles the carrot of an overdraft and he and his wife enjoy a swanky restaurant dinner at the rag 'n' bone man's expense.

As an effective conclusion to the Steptoes' return season, Wilfrid Brambell and Harry H. Corbett held a select party to celebrate the end of the run in Room B209, in the salubrious basement of Broadcasting House. The totters were back with a vengeance.

Chapter 11

Cuckoos and Criminals

Even as early as the 1970 return to television, Galton and Simpson's scripts were being addressed as much more than just episodes in another situation comedy. A book especially for schools was subsequently published in the autumn of 1971 by the Longman Group. This consisted of four scripts from the third series – 'The Bonds that Bind Us', 'The Lead Man Cometh', 'The Lodger' and 'Homes Fit for Heroes' – edited by David Grant, Head of the English Department at William Forster School in Tottenham, with a specially written introduction by Galton and Simpson themselves. A historically geared sequence of photographs on contemporary rag 'n' bone men in London, taken by Homer W. Sykes, blurred the line between fact and fiction even more. Although a study book for schools, it was, according to Dick Fiddy, writing in *Primetime* magazine in 1983, 'possibly the funniest textbook ever published'.

The second batch of new episodes was broadcast from 2 November 1970 and, once again, was blessed with a *Radio Times* cover. This advertised 'the Steptoes come back fighting ... Harold, Dolly [to give the horse her real name] and Albert in a new series ...' Series six proved an instant success with the public – the opener, 'Robbery with Violence', was watched by 7.6 million households, an estimated peak of 28 million people. It is interesting on many counts, not least as the final television *Steptoe* for familiar guest player Dudley Foster, who returns to Oil Drum Lane, this time as a deadpan, overly tolerant police inspector. The episode also shows the depths of deceit the old man will sink to in order to protect himself from the wrath of his son. The plot line is simple. With Albert having accidentally smashed Harold's collection of porcelain, the old man stages a robbery and claims to have been attacked by six skinheads. This changes over the course of the episode to five skinheads and a Pakistani which, as Dudley Foster's inspector observes, doesn't make the crime any more palatable but at least proves that the 'races can work in harmony'.

Wilfrid Brambell's performance is inspired throughout, from the moment we see him carelessly dusting the house right through to the end credits. He also has a rare opening monologue as he ponders on his son's inflated belief in the worth of his collection, followed by a mad, wide-eyed jumbled narrative when the porcelain is smashed beyond repair. The supposed conversation between father and son is another clever change of track. Usually, it's Corbett who plays these insane flights of fancy, but Brambell takes on the challenge admirably. In reality, Harold is far less suspicious and distrusting than Albert would have supposed and, despite the old man's continual 'You calling me a liar?' in a string of protesting rants, Harold falls for the story hook, line and rolling pin. He even accepts the fact that as the rolling pin – which Albert claims to have fought back with – has gone, then one of the robbers must have taken it for his mother! And even the discovery that his valued property is missing doesn't completely dent Harold's real concern for his father's well-being.

The focal point of the episode is, of course, the arrival of Dudley Foster's law-enforcer, desperately trying to get the story of the crime from the old man while Harold is continually interrupting and confusing the already very confused issue. The show's highlight comes as Albert recalls something that one of the robbers said: 'Ooh, he's kicked me in the goolies!' Brambell's delivery is straight-faced and without a hint of playing up to the audience. He was astute enough to know that Foster's bland reaction to the statement would be enough. Moreover, the writers are happy to inject a choice in-joke into the proceedings. Harold returns home singing a snatch of the title song of Wilfrid Brambell's finest film credit, A Hard Day's Night, while the conclusion, with crime-busting hero Albert Steptoe selling his life story to a newspaper, ushers in a minor supporting turn from Jim McManus, who later played Tony Hancock on stage.

One of the funniest scripts and most inspired of situations was conjured up for 'Come Dancing', with the Steptoes wallowing in ballroom iconography from television's much-loved fixture of sequins and smiles. As if to compensate Harry H. Corbett for the great swathes of silence he suffered in favour of Brambell's pontificating in the previous episode, here it is Harold who starts the programme with an extended monologue on the boredom of the English Sunday. Encapsulating the essence of the famous Hancock's Half Hour, 'A Sunday Afternoon at Home', in about five minutes, Corbett starts in typical Hancockian mood with a depressed: 'Oh, Gawd. What a life!' Harold looks at his wristwatch with a sigh, muttering, 'It's not even time to go to bed yet' and the scene is an inspired mass of peaks and troughs as he desperately tries to amuse himself while the old man sleeps soundly. As Harold imagines what it must have been like at the court of Henry VIII, Corbett uses all his talent for characterization and prop involvement as he plays courtiers and knockabout jesters. He re-enacts the bone-throwing feast from the 1933 Charles Laughton film with a bit of play-acting with the skeleton and finally dips into depression again as he reflects: 'That is the way we should live.' Later in the episode, Harold dismisses all thoughts of housework ('Sod the goldfish bowl!'), and his imagination again starts to kick in, this time with Victorian-melodrama re-enactments of the trial he would face if he did actually murder his father, something he has always, playfully, hinted at: 'I was bored, m'lord. Nothing more, nothing less!'

The final attack on Harold's nerves comes with the cuckoo clock striking the hour. He starts nailing up the door on the clock and wakes his father up. Albert is concerned for his son, but Harold is reluctant to talk about anything and sits back helplessly as the old man runs through what could be dragging him down.

Finally, with Duncan Wood's direction focusing on the kill, Albert sorts it out – it's a bird. He is his usual unsympathetic self as Harold waxes lyrical about his new-found love, Jane, and discloses that he's upset because she's gone dancing – 'Who with? Tarzan?' – and he can't dance. But Albert is able and willing to help his son to find his feet – literally. With the promise that 'You'll make Lionel Blair look like a baby elephant!' the lessons begin. One of *Steptoe*'s landmark encounters – with Tony Melody's petulant milkman – is the pinnacle of the dancing scene. While on his round collecting the milk money, he discovers father and son dancing. He breaks up the fun with 'If you've got your handbag handy...', but his mocking tone soon disappears and he proffers dancing tips to the keen-as-mustard Harold.

Following the departure of the milkman, Albert even reinforces his superior position on the dance floor with misty-eyed memories of auditioning for pantomime as a kid. He proudly reveals Marie Lloyd's comparison of him to Sarah Bernhardt, instantly debased by Harold's observation that 'Sarah Bernhardt had a wooden leg.' Still, when the big night of the dance contest finally arrives and Harold is dressed up for dancing, Brambell and Corbett allow the true affection between father and son to shine. Harold is nervous, sheepish and softly spoken, finding it hard to relinquish completely his long-held habit of whingeing at his father. Brambell seems truly to relish the line 'That's the first thing I've been able to help him in in years' when he is left alone but happy, as his son goes off to make his mark. However, this is *Steptoe* and it is a comedy programme, factors that, in an odd sort of way, intrude into the viewer's desire for the characters to get on and show the love they obviously feel for each other. Unfortunately Harold has been taught the woman's steps and has failed at the dance contest – and the feel-good factor of the episode is instantly wiped out. It is back to square one and the traumatic father and son relationship. The final striking of the cuckoo clock and Harold's destruction of the offending item hammers the final nail in the coffin.

'Two's Company' focuses on the ultimate element to come between the two men: the same woman. Albert's dancing prowess, highlighted in the previous episode, is the starting point of the episode, with Brambell at the Darby and Joan Club waltzing with an uncredited Gilly Flowers (half a decade before she became a permanent resident of *Fawlty Towers*). Perversely, after years of Albert complaining that Harold always leaves him alone during the evening, it is the son who is indoors watching television and waiting for his father to return. Taking on the mantle of a parent with a teenage child, Harold ponders whether he should lock the doors and leave Albert outside for the night. But, like all caring parents, he can't bring himself to be so cruel. He merely waits until his father returns – full of the joys of spring – and intones the immortal 'What time do you call this then?' Fifteen minutes past midnight, and having spent a good bit of time at the house of a new 'friend' in Notting Hill Gate, Albert has walked all the way home safe in the knowledge that the 'kerb crawlers up there aren't looking for old men'.

Albert announces that he is getting married again. He has asked the lady in question that very evening and she has accepted. Harold is crestfallen but not completely taken aback and, rather than being the hurt and wounded son, he continues in his role of father figure. It would seem that he has grown up and accepted that all things must change eventually – even if his life seems, ironically, to have reached its climax when the old man's just restarting.

Whereas in 'The Bird' it was the father who was on show and prepared to meet Harold's girlfriend, here it is Harold who plays host to the nervous Albert and his intended. Both men are suited and booted, and the tense atmosphere, mainly created by Albert's nervousness, is punctured by Harold's friendly jibes. Then, as always in *Steptoe*, the dramatic bombshell: the woman in question was Harold's girlfriend 20 years earlier in the days before he was stationed in Malaya. Galton and Simpson skilfully explain why this realization hadn't dawned earlier, with swift and believable reasons that fit perfectly with the characters. Obviously Mrs Goodlace has been married – to a Tory twit whom Harold happily condemns until he finds out he died, suddenly, three years previously and, equally suddenly, remembers that 'he had some very good points'. What is less easily explained is why Daphne did not recognize the Steptoe name when first she met Albert – and the reason for this reflects Harold's long-standing shame at his roots and his romantic flights of fancy to escape his rag 'n' bone reality. He spent his dashing, younger days calling himself Harry Faversham! It was a comic pseudonym for the son that was later recycled for the film *Steptoe and Son Ride Again*.

Once Harold and Daphne are alone, as the old man books a taxi to whisk them off for their evening meal, the romance is immediately rekindled. Daphne says she has always loved Harold but didn't get any of his letters when he was abroad. Daphne's mother, who never liked the young Steptoe, had clearly destroyed them. But now, with their romance awakened after all these years, Harold faces the nightmare of having to break the news gently to his father. The reaction of Albert to Harold's revelation that he and Daphne were lovers is a joyously bemused one: 'But she's only been here 10 minutes!' As the penny drops, the episode reaches emotional breaking point.

Daphne's role is blessed with a sterling performance by the British film legend Jean Kent. Alan Simpson was delighted to work with a star of her magnitude:

> One of the lovely things about writing was that we could write for actors and actresses we had always admired, and, of course, the lovely Jean Kent was one of them. We were absolutely delighted when she agreed to play Mrs Goodlace in 'Two's Company', and she was wonderful in it. I'm also pleased to say she was delightful company, very professional and without a hint of airs and graces, having come from those great British films on to our little show. She was, in fact, living in Malta at the time and had flown over especially on the strength of our script, which I was very honoured about.

Kent's contribution to the episode is immense and, paradoxically, at its most potent when she has no dialogue. With the shocking news about Harold and Daphne out in the open, the father and son discuss their options. Harold is for all three living together, with him and Daphne as man and wife, but the old man can't face the thought of living with them while he's still deeply in love with his son's other half. He ponders moving to his sister's in Stoke, always a useful plot device, or moving into an old people's home, another useful hook, but Harold is determined that the family should not be split up: 'This is our home!' Jean Kent, looking on during this discussion, leaves the scene, with a note explaining that father and son would be better alone. Marriage to either of them wouldn't have worked because they are already

married. Both Harold and Albert are completely nonplussed by this last statement, and Corbett brilliantly milks the phrase as he ruminates on her mean-
ing. It is, of course, clear to the audience. Harold and Albert are 'married' to
each other and nothing can come between their 'relationship', a close bond
which is fully illustrated by the two leaving for a restaurant and Harold playing the wife as he fusses over Albert's tie.

'Tea For Two', the next episode, was a belated return to the world of politics
for *Steptoe and Son*. It was also a timely reflection of the shift in power since
Harold Wilson had been hot under the collar about *Steptoe* affecting Labour's
chances in 1964. Now Wilson was history – in June 1970 the Conservatives
had stormed into power with Edward Heath at their helm. Indeed, the old
man forcibly makes the point when he tells his son he'll 'be as sick as Harold
Wilson was when the furniture van turned up'. Alan Simpson recalls: 'We
wanted to make one of our rare, full-on forays into the political scene. It was
a natural source of argument for our two characters, with Harold being a raving left-wing socialist and the old man being the complete opposite. He's a
right-wing fascist Tory swine!'

The division in political persuasion is as deep and stringent as the generation gap. Harold is adamantly true to his working-class roots. Albert considers himself management and even condemns the ever-worsening class of
Tory voter, dismayed as he is at the council estate scruffs who are lining up
to support Ted Heath's policies. Ray Galton remembers: 'We gave all the out-
and-out comic put-down lines to the old man because he always got huge
laughs when undermining Harry. And there's something extremely funny, for
us, in a working-class Londoner fighting passionately for the tradition of the
ruling classes. Our good friend Johnny Speight explored that idea with Alf
Garnett, of course.' Indeed, while Harold's dreams of a Jerusalem and power-
to-the-people Utopia are idealistic and revolutionary in the Russian sense of
the word, Albert's true-blue attitudes tend to have the distinct ring of,
however unpalatable, truth about them. Certainly, despite Harold's strong
commitment to the ethnic minorities who are quickly becoming the ethnic
majorities in the area, Albert effortlessly exposes the British worker's negative
respect for his 'coloured brother'. Harold thinks he is treating the Indian population as equals when he explains that he likes curry and admires their cricket team, whereas it is Albert who, as he succinctly puts it, 'talks to them ...
not talks about them'. Thus, the writers can smile at the old man's commitment to a system designed to keep him and his fellows and their income level
exactly where they are, while giving him a certain degree of humanity.

Still, typically, the Steptoes' relationship is never cut and dried. Harold is indignant at his father's 'playing fields of Eton' terminology and, thus, tries to vent the anger that the younger generation had concerning the supposed flippant attitude of their parents. For Harold, the modern labour movement is of vital impotance: 'This isn't a game of cricket ... our future's at stake!' And while the writers were injecting a bit of political comment into the show, why not go the full hog and embrace a bit of religious controversy as well? Albert is outraged and wide-eyed when Harold matter-of-factly explains that Jesus Christ was a socialist. The old man mutters that just because he shared 'the loaves and Lillian Gish with the five thousand' means nothing at all.

As Alan Simpson says: 'We knew we had to have some momentous focal point for all this disagreement, so we came up with what would be Harold's worst nightmare: the thought of the leader of the Tory Party coming to have tea with the old man during a by-election, in the house where Harold, the secretary of the local Labour Party, lived. It was too good to avoid. We were also keen to emphasize that the leaders of parties, of whichever political leaning, were happy to exploit their party faithful for a photograph opportunity. So here we would have those in power, Edward Heath on this occasion, on a walkabout tour looking at the deprived inner suburbs. The fact that he is going to see Albert brings out the disgust of "comrade" Harold.' The beauty of the episode is Brambell's almost forelock-tugging grovelling at the feet of the Conservative Party. He is clearly a scruffy oik in the eyes of the landed gentry who represent both the local Tories and the Prime Minister himself, but the working-class member supporting the Conservatives is seen as an ideal front-page headline grabber. It's the painful naivety and eagerness of Albert's faithful Tory foot soldier that really adds poignancy to the episode. He is being used and gently abused by the beliefs he holds dear.

Having only hinted at, and otherwise skilfully avoided, the immigration situation in the Britain of the late 1960s and early 1970s in 'The Colour Problem', Galton and Simpson profess that 'Without Prejudice', while again not tackling the issue head-on, 'was a social comment script as far as it goes'. With redevelopment diverting foundation-shaking traffic past the rag 'n' bone yard and the leaking roof showering the living room with rain water, the future at Shepherd's Bush looks grim. Once the old man has stopped enjoying the fun by singing 'raindrops keep falling on me Barnet Fair', in homage to Paul Newman's bicycle ride in *Butch Cassidy and the Sundance Kid* from the previous year, the show moves on to a series of thinly veiled comments on the racial divide. As Alan Simpson recalls: 'They get out of this terrible house and down to some lush part of outer London ... Esher or somewhere, although I doubt the Steptoes could have afforded the price there. Even in 1970.'

In effect, the Steptoes represent the working class moving on and moving out of the slum areas of London and coming up against the middle class, who consider them a threat to the quality of their neighbourhood. Across the country in 1970 millions of immigrants were facing the same cold-shoulder treatment. Ray Galton reveals: 'The episode was based on a story we saw in the paper concerning an incident in Croydon. A group of residents in this middle-class road had got together to buy this house in order to stop a black family moving in.' The connection between the Steptoes and the immigrants, or the class minority and the ethnic minority, is slight and subtle but still very, very potent. Harold, as he fights the losing battle against the rain-sodden house, mumbles to himself: 'Honestly, those underdeveloped nations, they don't know what they're missing!' When the threatened residents of the area where the Steptoes are buying a property storm into Oil Drum Lane and desperately try to make it worth their while to retract the offer, it is all middle-England values to the fore.

The major points of reference are reassuringly familiar, with the jargon-packed gentility of the estate agent's tour. Alan Simpson recalls: 'Gerald Flood played the estate agent and he was brilliant, a very good actor. In *Steptoe* he balances Harry and Willie perfectly.' Albert is obsessed with death: he wonders where you keep the dead bodies before a funeral in these new houses without back parlours. As well as with patriotism: when he finds out the estate agent's firm was founded in 1942, he rants: 'Why weren't you in the army? Spiv, were yer?' And alcohol: he's not interested in the golf club and churches nearby but simply asks, 'Where's the nearest boozer?' Harold is, of course, very interested in the golf club, still convinced that all the best deals are struck while playing the game.

The episode also allows an early reference to the close proximity of the Steptoes to BBC Television Centre. Harold, keen for a quick sale on the house, is happy in the knowledge that, 'We could flog it to one of those poofy producers'. Clearly, the old man's attitude from 'Any Old Iron?' is rubbing off on him. Albert is far more practical, bemoaning the fact that despite the BBC being only down the road, they 'still get a rotten picture'. It is only fitting, therefore, that the following episode, 'Pot Black', should be the second of the series to be based around a popular BBC television programme, the other being 'Come Dancing'. As Ray Galton remembers:

> 'Pot Black' was a natural title simply because it was about snooker, and if we could use a title that was familiar to television viewers all well and good. We would just sit around thinking of good subjects for Harold and the old man, and usually chatting about everything else but. I

remember growing up as a kid and I always fancied having a house big enough to have a full-size snooker table in one day. Most people had to make do with a quarter-size table, if that. All that business with the cues through the window was a reflection of the space restriction in the normal home. That was the one beauty of the rag 'n' bone yard. You could bring in anything, be it false teeth, coffins or a snooker table, to move the plot along. Why would they have that? It's not a normal house so literally anything could go.

Alan Simpson continues that 'Ray had a friend called Johnnie Spooner who was always trying to get us to buy a table; a huge, really heavy old billiard table from some club that had been pulled down. So we pooled the ideas. A full-size table would be a good status symbol for Harry and a chance for him to finally beat the old man. The table doesn't fit, the old man is better than Harry and, bingo, you've got another show.'

Again, Galton and Simpson pull out the stops to display Albert in definitive 'dirty old man' mode while Harold is out of the house. At the start of this particular episode Albert is boozing from a beer bottle, using the empty bottle as a pastry rolling pin and finally using an old set of false teeth to pattern the crust of his home-made steak and kidney pie.

For Harold, this working-class hell is going to be improved, even slightly, by his latest purchase: a full-size billiard table, bought from the Temperance Hall which was set for demolition. Albert is distressed at the closure of the 'working man's playing fields of Ealing' and even more distressed at Harold's intention of taking over the entire living room with his billiard equipment. With fantasy images of country houses, oceans of port and good conversation, gleaned from a myriad of old films, Harold dreams of playing snooker in his own home and, more important, finally beating his father at something … anything. Of course, the junk from the living room has to go somewhere, and that place is Albert's bedroom. Harold helpfully suggests that he sleep in the cupboard under the stairs. The comment refers back to series two in 1963 when, to accommodate Harold's new bath, the old man is forced into this same cupboard. Only a viewer with a very long and very good memory would appreciate the line: 'You been there before. Very comfortable, you said it was!'

A hilariously simple and beautifully executed half-hour of comedy, this is a rare *Steptoe and Son* episode in that it relies heavily on visual humour and wordless, facial reaction shots from the two leads. As Ray Galton says:

It's a perfect example of the father and son conflict. We used games a lot as opening scenes. We used indoor games: Scrabble in 'Men of Letters', Monopoly in 'Men of Property', chess, cards, whatever. Just as an opener for the episode. We used outdoor games: badminton in 'Loathe Story', Harry's skiing pursuits in 'A Winter's Tale'. 'Pot Black' was a bit of indoors and a bit of outdoors. The use of games was a good device to pit the two against each other, and this episode simply extended that opening scene to the whole half-hour. Harry would always lose and always invest in all the gear, while the old man didn't bother ... and beat him at everything!

The restricted size of the living room hampers Harold's play, with the table almost filling the room. This results in shots being played through the window and up in the air or with snooker cues broken in anger. With a frustrated 'This is bloody ridiculous', Harold takes action. The table is moved outside into the yard, and Corbett's performance moves into truly breathtaking top gear. He's like a butterfly emerging from a chrysalis, feeling his cue in his hand, preparing for a scintillating match and joyfully muttering 'Oh cream' as he feels the baize under his fingers. Albert has already condemned him as 'potty', and Harold gets worse as the episode goes on. Determined to beat his father, he can hardly stand up to play his shots as the time passes, it is three in the morning and rain storms down on to the table. Dennis Wilson's imaginative musical score heightens the effect with a cheeky resurrection of 'Raindrops Keep Falling on My Head' which the old man had sung in 'Without Prejudice'. Finally, Albert gives in and lets Harold win. The old man could beat his son blindfolded, as his trick shots in the close-of-show credits demonstrate, but this episode allows Harold at least a moment of glory.

As Alan Simpson recalls: 'The following episode, 'The Three Feathers', was an example of where we used the background of the business as the subject matter. Usually, we tried to avoid completely any rag 'n' bone trading forming the entire basis of a plot. It was usually Harold's problem with the latest girl-friend or the problem he was having with the old man. But here, we used Harold's ambitions in the antique business to do him up like a kipper!'

Indeed, in 'The Three Feathers' the writers show Harold in a playfully cruel mood from the beginning, as he laughs uproariously at the old man's predicament: stuck in a yoga position he can't get out of. In the meantime, Harold revels in his big break in obtaining a nineteenth-century commode bearing the three feathers of the Prince of Wales. Unfortunately, unlike the geniune antique he locates in the 1960s episode, 'Crossed Swords', this find is nothing more than a catalyst for a confidence trick. Harold's taunting of his father comes back to haunt him as the plot thickens.

If the conclusion of the episode – as Albert reveals an intricate con that Harold has fallen for – is to be believed, the old man knows the score from the beginning. It is likely that he is simply keeping quiet to teach his big-headed offspring a lesson. For Albert is dubious about Harold's immoral business practices as his son bounces one offer for the commode off a better one and sinks himself deeper and deeper into debt as the battle of wits continues. Before long the con is complete and Harold has been well and truly turned over by the tricksters who sold him the commode in the first place. As the old man heartlessly comments: 'You've been sucked in, mate, and blown out in bubbles!'

Worse is to come for Harold in 'Cuckoo in the Nest', the last episode of series six, originally broadcast on 21 December 1970. Continuing their obsession with competitive games, the programme starts with an intense chess match with the Steptoes using various bits of cutlery to double for the pieces. Albert's misunderstanding of which are and which aren't his pieces ruins the flow of the game as Harold moans: 'That's cocked up my Sicilian defence!'

The cuckoo in the nest of the title is brilliantly played by the big and beefy actor Kenneth J. Warren. He had starred as the thieving miller, with Wilfrid Brambell, in the original 1968 production of *Canterbury Tales* at the Phoenix Theatre and was still appearing in the run, long after Brambell's exit, at the time of the *Steptoe* broadcast. Landing the featured role of Arthur, the old man's homecoming and illegitimate elder son, Warren storms into the Shepherd's Bush scene with a seemingly non-stop tirade of Australian slang. His over-the-top performance is joyfully littered with quotable one-liners. He complains that he has brought some Fosters from home because the beer in England is 'flatter than a witch's tit'. He reveals that his 'mouth was as dry as a kangaroo's jockstrap' and, before relieving himself, says he needs to 'point Percy at the porcelain'. Immediately on the cadge for money, and pleading that he'll cash his copious traveller's cheques, he enters the house and leaves the cab driver waiting for his fare. Outraged at the cost – £5 10s – Arthur isn't interested in the cabby's moans that he turned the clock off when he arrived: 'You must have turned the bastard on when I left Melbourne!' Harold, of course, is drafted in, and reluctantly pays the fare. The contrast between lowly man of culture and loud-mouthed man of ignorance is blissfully played by Corbett and Warren. Tension is bubbling under the surface from the outset, but nothing the Aussie newcomer can do seems to upset the old man. 'We made him come from Australia to give the 25-years-away plot a needed credibility, but we thoroughly enjoyed all those Oz phrases,' reflects Ray Galton. 'Maybe we should have cast Bill Kerr.'

While Kenneth J. Warren is indulged with all the hilarious one-liners and bone-idle loafing, Corbett is blessed with the cream of Galton and Simpson's sympathetic writing. Jealous, bitter and disgusted with his treatment, he bemoans his father's loose morals ('You've sired more offsprings than an Aberdeen Angus, you have!') and reflects on his poor education and wasted youth ('I could have been a doctor … or a bandleader or something!'). The acting is inspired, and Brambell's mild interjections show real control of the partnership. The old man, after a torrent of innermost thoughts, seems not to have paid attention to his son as he mutters: 'I didn't know you wanted to be a bandleader!' Harold doesn't falter and carries on regardless. He complains about the fact that his musical ability was ignored, save being taught how to whistle, and that the final discovery of a piano on the round whose lid bashed his fingers every time he tried to play it was 'aversion therapy' before there was such a buzzword.

With every, albeit miserable, thing that Harold has worked at over the years about to be split with a total stranger, echoes of 'The Offer' are rekindled and the son once more threatens to leave home. This time he does so. Of course, once Harold is out of the way, much to the pleasure of the new kid on the block, Albert's treatment of his elder son changes. The Australian is a lazy good-for-nothing who fleeces the old man for money and sells the horse and cart. Albert, facing up to his error of judgement, manfully swallows his pride, tracks Harold down to his bedsit and begs him to come home. Harold, naturally, presents a feel-good picture of his new surroundings, condemns his lowly digs as merely temporary accommodation and boasts of how well his new business, Harold Steptoe and Co., is doing. However, as in the earlier episode, 'The Lodger', the old man has been checking up on his son's progress and knows full well that business is anything but booming. But the fact that he has the upper hand in his own mind does not change the real fact that he needs his son back in the business. Albert goes along with Harold's ridiculous notion of a business merger and doesn't mock his high-flying boardroom terminology. He is, however, more than confident that his son will not be returning to the lodging house. Unknown to Harold, the old man pays off his back rent. Endearingly, there is a sense of reality within the fiction: during the closing credits a passer-by goes to get into his car, looks up, spots the camera and hastily backs out of shot.

The series ends with Albert and Harold back together again, walking home and spotting the recently sold Delilah in the street. The entire series could have come to a natural end with the two of them giving chase, but thankfully, with ratings through the roof, there was more, much more, in store for the Steptoes.

Chapter 12

The Desperate (Half) Hour

Kenneth J. Warren would have the opportunity of re-creating his most memorable television performance when 'Cuckoo in the Nest' was immediately adapted for the third radio series of *Steptoe and Son*. He was delighted to reprise his love-loathe relationship with Harry H. Corbett's Harold Steptoe when the show was recorded just over two months after the television version, on St Valentine's Day 1971.

The series was broadcast from 21 March 1971 and gave over its eight-week run to adaptations of the new colour television episodes from 1970. Suitably enough, the first of the radio series, again produced by Bobby Jaye, was a remake of 'A Death in the Family'. It was almost identical to the television version apart from making the horse a tad older at the time of his death to fit the timescale of the broadcast.

Galton and Simpson themselves were now rewriting their original television scripts for the pleasure of listeners: 'It wasn't a very hard job at all,' says Alan Simpson. 'We took over mainly because Ray had heard some of the previous episodes. He said to me: "I really think we should do this ourselves from now on." All you had to do was take out the pauses and that was that!' For 'A Death in the Family', an extra speaking part was written, that of the policeman who witnesses the collapse of Hercules in Goldhawk Road. Alan Simpson himself played this historical part. Gwendolyn Watts, who had so excelled in the earlier episode, 'Steptoe à la Cart', was recruited to play the expectant mother in 'Steptoe and Son – and Son!', with that (latterly) distinguished actor of *Pie in the Sky*, *Gormenghast* and *Harry Potter* fame, Richard Griffiths, as her husband-to-be, George the sailor. The name of the female lead was changed from Daphne Tomlin to Beryl Tomlin, for the simple reason that the adaptation of this episode, from series five, was in the same radio run, and was recorded on the same day – 26 January 1971 – as an adaptation of the series six show 'Two's Company', which also featured a Daphne – Daphne Goodlace. With Jean Kent unavailable, Galton and Simpson had the luck to employ June Whitfield, who had already left her mark on television's *Steptoe and Son*, for the radio version. The actress was delighted to be reunited with the team and gave her customary impeccable performance: 'Galton and Simpson's scripts were always a joy, and Harry H. Corbett and Wilfrid Brambell were great to work with, though it did come as a bit of a shock when Wilfrid took his teeth out for authentic effect.'

The final programme, broadcast on 9 May 1971, saw a reappraisal of the opening episode from series six, 'Robbery with Violence', and welcomed back *Steptoe* regular Dudley Foster to reprise his role of the police inspector. Sadly, it was his last contribution to the series: the actor commited suicide in January 1973 at the age of 47.

Following a successful television repeat season from October 1971, a further series of eight *Steptoe and Son* radio adaptations was broadcast from 30 January 1972, although only three scripts were selected from the new batch of television episodes. Richard Hurndall returned as the homosexual antique dealer in 'Any Old Iron?', Anthony Sharp reprised his medical performance for 'The Colour Problem', and the con-artist plot, 'The Three Feathers', was also adapted for sound only. The remaining five shows, naturally, returned to the vintage days of *Steptoe* and were largely recast. Only Yootha Joyce, reprising her role as Mavis in 'A Box in Town', returned to record her performance for the radio. One of the best of the series, 'And Afterwards At ...', cast a hand-picked gallery of cockney character stars, chief among whom were Galton and Simpson favourites Patricia Hayes and Pat Coombs. The adaptation allowed for further character development and additional material for the central characters. For example, Corbett is heard to sing a snatch of the song 'I Will' which wasn't included in the original television script.

The fourth radio series came to an end on 19 March 1972, by which time a new series of television episodes had already started on BBC1. After a break of 14 months Brambell and Corbett had returned to BBC Television Centre on 13 February 1972 to begin recording the seventh series. The entire seven-episode run still remains the absolute pinnacle of *Steptoe and Son*. After 10 years, on and off, the partnership was as funny as ever, if not funnier. 'That's very nice to know,' says Ray Galton. 'It's odd, because the last series of *Hancock* is considered the best. Maybe we should have only done tail-end series. Rather than end early, we should have started late!' Duncan Wood, who had been elevated to the position of Head of TV Comedy, still kept a parental eye on the series advising John Howard Davies, who had pioneered *Monty Python's Flying Circus* and had taken over the production of *Steptoe and Son*, on its structure.

Just a week and a day after recording, the first episode, 'Men of Letters', was broadcast on BBC1 on 21 February 1972. By the following week the viewing figures had rocketed to eight million homes. That first episode was the culmination of several ongoing trends throughout the series. Naturally, there is tension between father and son, something which had always been intensified by Albert and Harold competing with each other in one way or another. Here the script starts with a fairly frivolous competition playing Scrabble, which eventually evolves into a frantic battle to see which one will write an article on 100 years of totting for the parish magazine. A circular plot is again employed. Albert's dirty-minded word power in Scrabble is utilized in his magazine contribution: a dirty crossword puzzle that gets the publication impounded by the police before anybody can read Harold's painstaking article. The central theme of the plot was inspired by the contemporary controversy over *Oz* magazine, which had been prosecuted because of questions of taste and decency. Harold even draws the parallel in his final rant, as he moans that 'his' magazine is changing hands for twice as much as a 'school's edition of *Oz*!'

The Scrabble game at the start of the episode is one of the best self-contained battles between Steptoe and Son ever written. Although they had re-enacted vintage scripts for radio as little as a month before, there is a real freshness and energy in the performances of Harry H. Corbett and Wilfrid Brambell. Their rivalry is intense, and made even more so by the old man's seemingly effortless skill in always beating his son. Harold is bursting with fraught indignation at being beaten by a string of disgusting words from his father. The script, of course, can't really relate the dirtiest of these words. Indeed, the language they used had been toned down a little since episodes in 1970: at one point Harold complains that Albert gets on his 'threepenny bits', although that is in front of the vicar. The actual, hasty shot of the Scrabble board illustrates the old man's winning run of words, from 'nipple' to 'spunk', but the dirtiest one within the dialogue is 'bum'. And despite Albert's screamed 'My bum's not dirty', this is as rude as it gets for the rest of the episode. Wilfrid Brambell was appalled at the reaction of Mary Whitehouse and the Clean-Up Television Campaign: 'We don't leer at the lens and say: "Now I'm going to say something filthy – *bum*!" That would be offensive to me. But the way Harold and his father talk to each other is part and parcel of the lives of the characters, and it is therefore important.'

The Scrabble is a battle of wordplay which Harold's play-the-game-fairly mentality can't win. Even though he is keen to denounce the tactics of the old man and mock his spelling of 'crum', his joy is short-lived. Albert's spelling may not be tip-top, but that 'crum', 'that you get in bed after eating biscuits', perfectly becomes 'crumpet', 'which you also get in bed'. The old man, always with an answer and not actually cheating for once, wins hands down. What's more, when the vicar arrives with a request for contributions to the parish magazine, it is Harold and not his father who unwittingly puts his foot in it. Albert, with age on his side, can get away with murder, complaining about the housing problem and receiving nods of gentle agreement from the man of God. His toast – 'Gawd bless yer and the devil miss yer!' – isn't meant to be rude and isn't taken to be. But Harold, quickly destroying the evidence of their offensive game, declines the vicar's invitation to join his wife and him for a foursome at Scrabble. Desperate not to expose the poor woman to his father's wordplay, Harold refuses and claims that the couple would be too good for them. 'You'd crucify us!' he laughs before suddenly realizing what he's said.

The vicar, played with the perfect amount of reverence and spiritual well-being by Anthony Sharp, proves a worthy, albeit unwitting, referee. The old man, devious and happy to humiliate his son in front of their visitor, questions Harold's ability to write the rag 'n' bone history for the magazine. Like a spoilt child, he challenges him to spell 'chrysanthemum', the name of Charlie Harris's horse, and relishes his son's struggling discomfort. Anthony Sharp's performance here, without dialogue, captures the real embarrassment of an 'outsider' trapped in this very personal infighting, as he looks uneasy and uncomfortable while the son tries to impress with his hopeless spelling.

Writing the article is a chance for Harold to explore his creative side. He goes for it fully, adopting a shirt-and-tie dress code, donning his 'editor's visor' and pontificating on the pain that great writing causes the great writer. The old man's crossword, filth 'from one across to 38 down', rains on Harold's modest literary parade but, undaunted, he continues with his artistic efforts and aspirations to fame.

'A Star is Born', the next episode, is, of course, a reference to the original Janet Gaynor and Fredric March film about Hollywood struggle. Harold is besotted with amateur dramatics, which could lead to a starry career making films all over the world: 'Sean Connery's the same age as me, and I've got more hair than he has!' The script, while retaining all the angst-ridden comic energy of the familiar banter, succeeds in reaching an even more personal level, thanks to the dialogue reflecting the pains and career moves of the two actors. Brambell is the wonderful stick-in-the-mud, undermining his son's stage-bound dreams with a combination of hilarious put-down and, ultimately, humiliation. Harold's far-fetched desire to star alongside the cinema's great beauties is mocked by Albert's: 'Irene Handl's more your mark, mate!' But again, a string of comic observations is merely a mask for the old man's concern over his son's totally unattainable ambitions.

Albert's preconception about actors, particularly amateurs, is refreshingly upheld by the appearance of the cast of this latest production. Trevor Bannister plays the flamboyant producer of the acting group, just before he went on to record the pilot for his biggest comedy success, *Are You Being Served?*, in which he played Mr Lucas for seven series until 1979. Bannister has affectionate memories of his time on *Steptoe and Son*: 'I always regarded the series as one of the few *true* situation comedies. Harry and Wilfrid were of course exceptional in their characterization. The writing of Galton and Simpson was some of the best on TV. It was a very happy show to work on. Harry was a very generous actor to work with. I feel very privileged to have been a small part of it. Such quality is sadly missed on TV today.'

The other am. dram. actors, ranging from haughty and 'darling'-laden Betty Huntley-Wright to the stunning blonde bimbo of ex-nude-model and *Carry On* glamour girl Margaret Nolan, fit the types perfectly. Corbett, adorning Harold's struggling wannabe actor with knowledge of the highs and lows of the profession, gives arguably his best *Steptoe* performance ever. Harold defends the world of acting as a great escape from poverty and uncertainty – 'You don't need A-levels to become an actor!' – and knowingly comments that 'rep. is the finest training you can have'. His recital of Marlon Brando's 'Charlie ... I could have been a contender' speech from *On the Waterfront*, for his audition, is a brilliant parody. 'Harry loved doing that speech,' remembers Ray Galton. 'It was amazing for an actor as good as Harry to act acting badly. He was having the time of his life, and doing Marlon Brando ... boy! I have a feeling that Harry christened the Steptoes' goldfish "Charlie" because of his love for *On the Waterfront*.'

The following episode, 'Oh, What a Beautiful Mourning', neatly settled in as a companion piece to the 1965 programme, 'And Afterwards At ...'. Both focused on the extended family of the Steptoes – at Harold's disastrous non-wedding in the earlier show, and here at the funeral of Albert's eldest brother and Harold's long-absent godfather, George. The connection is made by recruiting some of the original supporting cast. Both Mollie

Sugden and Rita Webb made return visits, albeit to play different characters from previously, while George A. Cooper re-created his cheerfully dominant turn as Uncle Arthur. Ray Galton and Alan Simpson, always at their best writing about one of life's inevitables, create a spirited, dark slab of humour. Indeed, Harold's nonplussed observation that 'They drop like flies and breed like rabbits!' explains why there never seem to be fewer members of the family, no matter how many funerals Harold and the old man are expected to attend.

The old man is as bad as the rest of the Steptoes. Despite a showing of out-and-out grief at his brother's death, Albert's only concern is what he can get out of the old swine who has dearly departed. Moaning about the money he lent his brother years before, crying profusely before leaving the house – in case any of the neighbours are watching – and complaining that the deceased was 'as tight as a gnat's chuff!', his overriding feelings of self-preservation and self-improvement permeate the episode.

During the initial conversation between father and son the history of the Steptoes is beautifully detailed, bringing previously unheard-of characters to life and setting the scene for the bleak bun-fight to come.

Harold spends his entire time at the funeral dismissing and dissecting the feverish greed of his family, but he himself is happy to select the prize item – a porcelain figurine – and plans to partake of a bit of interfamily sexual pursuit with his distant cousin – an idea which, although his father warns him that the girl 'could be any of ours', still seems to be on the cards as the episode comes to a close.

'At home with Harry and Wilf', an interview feature in the *Radio Times* which heralded the start of the 1972 series, quoted Corbett with regard to the sexual development of his character:

> The naivety he displayed 10 years ago is no longer quite valid ... take women, for example. I mean, in 10 years he's got to have pulled some birds, hasn't he? So he can be more knowledgeable about sex, more able to discuss it. He can now say: 'Father, making love with the lights on is not considered a sexual deviation these days.' Well, that can't come out of the lips of a man who has supposedly never made love to a woman.

The final gag: George, knowing what sort of family he is from, has sold his possessions before his death and arranged for them to be removed during the funeral service, leaving the family an empty house. Harold is happy to lead the younger members of the family in a joyful reflection on George: 'The only Steptoe I ever knew with a sense of humour.' Refreshingly, although when Harold and Albert lag behind in the empty house the old man reveals the figurine under his hat, the Steptoes we have known and loved for over a decade are shown in their best light. Family relationships, friendship and the understanding of death as a game of 'who goes first' is brought to a stunning conclusion when Albert joins his son in a toast to the departed member of the family. Brambell's energetic, affectionate salute to George – 'Better luck next time' – is right and natural.

Truth and credibility were, however, the last things on the scriptwriters' minds in the next episode, 'Live Now, PAYE Later', whose major comic gimmick saw Albert in a fraud that involved his dearly departed wife, and Harry H. Corbett masquerading as Harold's sister. Men in drag would have seemed almost unthinkable in *Steptoe and Son* when the series had started a decade earlier, but here the farce is rooted in financial necessity. The situation is heightened with the casting of Colin Gordon as the figure of authority, Mr Greenwood from the Inland Revenue. Gordon's performance – his first return to the series since playing the doctor in the radio adaptation of 'The Holiday' in 1966 – allows Brambell and Corbett to indulge themselves in over-the-top behaviour. For the old man, memories of the First World War trenches, and for Harold, at the show's close, dressing up as Muriel, his own 'sister' who is mourning the recent loss of 'her' mother. Gordon, getting drunker and drunker at the first meeting and, unwittingly, planting the seed for Albert's impersonation of his dead wife, starts as the faceless figure of authority and ends up a raving mad, sex-crazed beast as he chases the dragged-up Harold around the living room. Colin Gordon brings off a brilliantly farcical performance just months before his death at the age of 61.

The plot line casts Gordon as the ogre-in-waiting – the old man has claimed a married man's allowance on his income tax returns for the 33 years his wife has been dead. Plying the tax man with whisky, the Steptoes energetically drop in 'Cheers' whenever the conversation turns towards the 'wife' mentioned on the form. At one point a 'drunken' Gordon actually 'Cheers' the gathering himself as if to signpost the fact that he knows he's being had and is quite happy to go along with it. The favourable outcome is that the wife should have been receiving a pension for the last six years, a backdated amount that adds up to over £1100. Cue Albert in silly hat and wig, to receive the cheque, which startles Harold: 'You look like Old Mother Riley!' Brambell doesn't camp it up but acts in drag with convincing refinement. The wardrobe and make-up sheet records the drag requirements of a 'greying wig – if poss. a little on the blue rinse side. Little bit of rouge & lipstick.' The act is an inspired one, albeit incongruous in the great scheme of things, and so committed is Brambell the actor that, when he drops a piece of paper on the floor by mistake he ad-libs a muttered 'Ooh!' still in female character.

Brambell was initially unhappy about the entire 'drag' storyline. Duncan Wood, *Steptoe*'s original producer, now Head of TV Comedy, penned a hand-written note to the new producer, John Howard Davies, explaining:

> Wilfrid has expressed reservations to me over the 'drag' bits. *Personally* I think the whole thing is very funny. It's not one of those scripts seeking 'truth'; it's just a romp. I'm sure that – treated on that level – it will go like a bomb. There's not much depth in the piece – in fact, I accept that it is a bit in Dick Emery territory. But it's very funny. Try to get them to see it in this light and go in and enjoy it. I think page 52 could be treated a bit more subtly for Harry. There's a lot to be got out of his total incredulity at Albert's suggestion that he – Harry – does Muriel!

Ray Galton comments: 'It was a natural situation, really. You've been lying to the authorities, you have to produce a dead wife from somewhere ... what else can you do? It wasn't a case of us thinking, Oh, wouldn't it be funny if they were in drag. It worked within the situation. Harry hated the idea of dressing up as a woman, as a matter of fact. As for Willie, he looked better than he did normally!'

Peter Madden turns in an excellent cameo as Norman, the ex-Fraud-Squad detective who chats up the female Albert and even suggests that they watch the cinema matinée presentation of *What Are You Doing after the Orgy?* Madden's lusty, suggestive acting adds great weight to Brambell's flamboyant performance as Mrs Gertrude Mary Steptoe.

Despite being almost totally out of character, this is a deliciously funny *Steptoe* episode. While it may lack the subtle nuances of the very best shows in this very best series, the determination of Harold to demean himself to the point of *Some Like It Hot* humiliation, merely to save his father's skin, is testament to the fact that, even when the writers indulged themselves, the fundamental truthfulness of the characters was clearly visible between the farce.

The following episode, 'Loathe Story', was recorded just the day before 'Live Now, PAYE Later' was broadcast. Again, as with the previous programme, it may not be in the same league as the start and end episodes of this seventh series, but the writing is still rich in invention. It also consciously deepens the angst that Harold feels for his on-going home-based life. 'Loathe Story', a punning and unsubtle variation on the novel and film *Love Story*, uses a plot device to reheat an old element of the programme – Harold's oft-repeated attempt to welcome a new girlfriend into the off-putting Oil Drum Lane environment.

The plot is established with Harold warming up for his tennis club by playing a less-than-friendly game of badminton with Albert in the junkyard. Typically Harold wears tennis gear and sips gently at Robinson's barley water, while the old man gulps cider and wears his usual tattered clothes. Harold, losing royally, goes to bed and suffers a nightmare that gallops through a cat-alogue of games and sports. The long and the short of it is that Harold, sleep-walking, attempts to murder his sleeping father with a meat cleaver.

The continual defeat at the hands of his father, the continual defeat of his efforts at bettering himself with a higher class of people and the continual defeat of his attempts to marry and move away are hinted at again. They are all evidence of his depressed, frustrated state. Raymond Huntley gives an exquisite performance as a laid-back psychiatrist. Obsessed with big breasts and leading the conversation down that avenue at every junction, he offends Harold by enquiring whether he is married. He then asks whether he is a homosexual and Harold reverts to violent tendencies. With the psychiatrist concealing shots of topless models in his drawers, reflecting on the size of Harold's mother's breasts during breastfeeding ('We couldn't afford proper milk!') and, ultimately, doodling a naked woman as Harold waffles on about his childhood, Huntley's detached and clinical performance is a master class in scene-stealing.

The obsessional shrink was originally accompanied by his wife, played by Damaris Hayman, fresh from *Dr Who: The Daemons* and familiar to *Steptoe* watchers as the cinema cashier in 'Sunday for Seven Days' and the Party secretary in 'My Old Man's a Tory'. However, her sequence was finally cut from the broadcast programme. Producer John Howard Davies personally wrote her a note on 15 March 1972: 'My dear Damaris, I am sorry to have to tell you that I have had to cut you out of *Steptoe*, not for any reason other than the fact that we overran rather too much, and I thought I ought to tell you before you sat down to see it next Monday evening. I am very sorry about this and hope you will forgive me. I shall try to make it up to you in the future.' The actress was, nevertheless, justifiably paid in full for her work on the show.

With the psychiatrist continually wiping his nice clean couch where his patient's dirty feet have spread mud and happily discussing his own fan-tasies, much to Harold's embarrassment, the teamwork between Huntley and Corbett is easily the most effective element in the programme.

An early flashback sequence, with Brambell playing himself as a 36-year-old and Philip Bruce as the young Harold waiting, on the horse and cart, for his father to finish drinking in the Skinner's Arms, was filmed on location using the Latimer Arms, Latimer Street, for the pub exterior scene. Brambell's wardrobe report details the youthful transformation: 'In the style of the times, rounded edge collar, bowler hat. Good pair of teeth. Quite smartly dressed. Dark hair. Ronald Colman moustache.'

A lengthier flashback sequence showing Albert's unpleasant treatment of Harold's posh girlfriend, played by Joanna Lumley, while well scripted repeats elements of the 1960s shows 'The Bird' and 'The Bath'. The situation – that the rag 'n' bone business is beneath Harold's intended – had been a sub-plot in many episodes, while certain gags – food being a waste of time, 'One burp and you're empty!' – are repeated from earlier programmes. Certainly there is a sense that we have been here before.

Duncan Wood was slightly uneasy about the programme, in particular the breast-obsessed psychiatrist. Writing to John Howard Davies on 31 January 1972, he explained: 'I think one has to be a bit careful here in that unless the part is played at a pretty high level, it could become a bit distasteful.' The casting of Raymond Huntley was a solution, of course. Moreover the brutal 'pay-off' ending, with Harold attacking his father with a knife when he hears that Albert has joined the tennis club, was also causing Wood concern. He suggested that Davies 'film the closing sequence of Albert playing tennis with "the bird" and Harry lying back on the psychiatrist couch, which would bring the story to a satisfying conclusion'. Although locations were scouted for the tennis court and the Hammersmith Park tennis courts behind TV Centre were selected, the sequence featuring Jill Hope as the tennis-playing blonde was abandoned and the original scripted attack on the old man was retained.

Even though the quality of this episode had dipped slightly below their own extremely high standards, Galton and Simpson were safe in the knowledge that the best were yet to come. Indeed, the final two programmes of series seven can rightfully be considered the best episodes of all. And number six of the season was a return to basics: Albert and Harold bickering once more about their sordid environment and the close proximity in which they live. 'Divided We Stand' draws heavily on the style and feel of 'The Offer'.

The idea of separating their property into two separate units by building a wall had been suggested by Harold as long ago as 1964, in 'Steptoe à la Cart', but here, nearly 10 years later, it finally came to fruition.

With Albert reluctant to splash out on new decoration for the family home, Harold is pushed over the edge in his quest to escape the filth he has to live in. The old man's love of 'chocolate paint ... dark green and chocolate, them's the colours, mate' goes against all the aesthetic delicacies of Harold's *Homes-and-Gardens*-inspired colour schemes. Albert's condemnation of his son's high ambitions ('that's Blenheim Palace!') falls on deaf ears, but the old man is determined to squash Harold's lofty aspirations.

Harold's discovery of Albert's missing false teeth, which disappeared when a land mine exploded down the road in 1941, provides the straw that breaks the camel's back. The old man, eyes sparkling with delight, hastily puts them back in, complains his gums have shrunk and sits back with a look of utter disappointment. Harold hangs his head in shame, while Harry H. Corbett the actor tries to control his giggles at the sight – providing the viewer with an interesting contrast.

After 10 years of threatening, Harold finally decides that this is the moment: one of them has to leave. Naturally, he thinks his father should go, but Albert refuses. Apartheid is the way forward, and Harold goes ahead with the separate development of Steptoe and Son. 'The border has been sealed,' he says, delightedly showing Albert around the new environment. Checkpoint Charlie, requiring a penny from Harold for access to the stairs and a penny from Albert for access to the kitchen, presents a further bone of contention before the experiment has even started.

The visual comedy in this episode is a delight, with one audience member clearly tickled pink at the sight of Albert's hat gliding gracefully along the top of the partition wall (the cry of 'His hat!' is heard amongst the laughter). Corbett tossing a book and shouting 'and take that bleeding hat off' adds to the humour, thanks to the actor's accurate aim.

Within their finely balanced relationship, Harold's peaceful isolation has hardly started before Albert's loneliness hits home. He longs to come into his son's part of the house for a game of cards. The father is clearly in need of company, while the son is happy to be left alone.

Suitably, the great divide is never greater than when the two are struggling to watch television, each with half the screen on his side of the dividing wall. This cultural war is wonderfully executed, even down to retaining continuity from the arrival of the new colour set in 'The Colour Problem', with who gets the bigger half of the 21-inch screen being hotly contested. Everything is wonderfully contrasted. Harold wants the ballet, Albert wants *Blood of the Ripper*, Harold consults the *Radio Times*, Albert flicks through his newspaper television page. But all things being equal, both men are basically the same. When Albert joyfully shouts during the ballet that 'Her drawers have just dropped off!' Harold dutifully sticks his head directly next to the television screen to get a better look.

But the gentleman's agreement has gone by the wayside, and Albert has broken the television-watching arrangement. Cue one of the cleverest and most oft-quoted *Steptoe* exchanges as Harold, calmly and rationally, says:

'I've got the law of contract on my side'; and the old man, craning just that bit closer for maximum effect, mutters gleefully, 'I have the knobs on my side'. The scene is a perfect piece of comedy acting and writing. The compromise of football, Harold's childish unplugging of the set and the even more childish act of flushing the toilet as the old man sits on it, all reach a comic climax as the two go to their beds. They sleep through a kitchen fire and end up next to each other in hospital.

Wilfrid Brambell was amazed at the public's regard for the duo:

> It's amazing that people have such affection for the old man. He's an evil old dog – he wins because he kicks lower than anyone else, but people still have a sneaking regard for him. I can only suppose that the love-hate relationship between Albert and Harold is something which echoes in people's subconscious. The relationship is the central core of the series, and perhaps because Harry and I as actors have dug deeper into the characters than pure comedians might have done, they have become more real. Certainly the ones I have enjoyed most have been the duologues between Harry and myself.

The high quality of 'Divided We Stand' is all the more amazing in that David Croft, sitcom supremo of *Dad's Army*, was drafted in to produce and direct this episode as a one-off assignment. Alan Simpson recalls: 'Our director on that series, John Howard Davies, had suddenly caught a cold so he couldn't do it. That's why we brought David Croft in for that one and only episode, and very good he was too. It was the old 'Those Magnificent Men and Their Heating Machines' problem. 'Divided We Stand' was a very complicated set-up with all those partitions.' The majority watching the episode probably thought that it couldn't be bettered, unless, of course, any of them had been a part of the audience for the previous evening's recording of the last episode of the series, 'The Desperate Hours'.

The episode was based on the 1955 film of the same name which had starred Humphrey Bogart and Fredric March. Ray Galton explains:

> We had used film titles before, of course. 'A Star Is Born' in that same series. And previously we had used film plots as a starting point for our own ends. We had even been doing that as long ago as the days with *Hancock's Half Hour*. 'Twelve Angry Men' was an early example. 'The Desperate Hours' was another. A couple of convicts come in and threaten this group of people in their own home, so we used that as the theme and built Harold and the old man into the structure. We were using a dramatic plot for comedy or, to put it simply, we nicked the idea!

Alan Simpson believes: 'It's either plagiarism or homage, depending on whose side you are on. Anyway, call it what you will, it saved us thinking up a story that week!'

Apart from a wordless prison officer and a couple of detached voices on the radio – performed by rock disc jockey Tommy Vance and Corbett Woodall, newsreader on *The Goodies* – this is a closely knit piece. Father and son are pitted against two desperate criminals whose ages, 38 and 64, neatly parallel the ages of Steptoe and Son themselves. 'The names in *Steptoe* were very important, and the names of the convicts particularly so,' recalls Alan Simpson. 'For the convicts in 'The Desperate Hours' we used a couple of friends of ours, who would often get in our scripts, Johnnie Spooner and Frank Ferris. The names seemed right for convicts, somehow. After all, it was Johnnie who was always trying to flog us that snooker table that had helped spark off the 'Pot Black' episode.'

For Frank Ferris, the older of the two convicts and the parallel to Albert Steptoe, the writers remembered a distinguished character actor by the name of J. G. Devlin. Suitably, as he was to contrast Brambell's performance, Devlin was an Irish actor and familiar to Brambell from his days with the Abbey Theatre. Devlin and Brambell gelled immediately, lilting into Irish attitude and understanding. Moreover, the early sequences, when the threat from the convicts is still very real, benefit from Devlin's semi-controlled fiery temperament. The actor had also appeared in one of the original series of *Comedy Playhouse*, the same series that had spawned *Steptoe and Son* itself. He had appeared with Dick Emery and Patrick Cargill in 'The Reunion', under the direction of original *Steptoe* producer Duncan Wood It was the fifth programme in the series and the one immediately following the transmission of 'The Offer', the *Steptoe* pilot. Iondeed, Devlin was second choice for the role of Albert Steptoe if Wilfrid Brambell had been reluctant or unavailable.

For the younger convict, John Spooner, the casting net offered a previous *Steptoe and Son* guest, Leonard Rossiter. Having excelled as the outsider in 'The Lead Man Cometh' in 1964, Rossiter was just a year from making his own mark on gritty situation comedy with the role of landlord Rigsby in *Rising Damp*. Ray Galton recalls: 'We didn't cast Leonard for "The Lead Man Cometh"; that would have been Duncan Wood. We didn't really know much about him at that stage. He wasn't a star at the time, but he played the part brilliantly. We did become admirers of him later. I saw him in *The Resistible Rise of Arturo Ui* in the late sixties and he was absolutely marvellous. He had certainly become a force to be reckoned with by the time we did "The Desperate Hours".'

Alan Simpson agrees: 'When Leonard Rossiter came on board for 'The Desperate Hours', Harry raised his game completely. Leonard came in for the first day of rehearsal and played his part perfectly straight, and it was brilliant. Harry realized immediately that he had got a fight on his hands. It was amazing to watch. It just unfolded before your very eyes. It was like witnessing two stags in the glen coming together. For my money, it's the best performance Harry ever gave.' Ray Galton concurs: 'Harry was getting very lazy. I thought he had coasted through a few of that series, to be honest. It's not surprising. I mean, after 10 years of playing the same part, he was getting stylized. I think he was probably getting bored and a bit frustrated by that stage. It wasn't a challenge any more.'

'He had certainly picked up little coat pegs along the way,' continues Simpson, 'little tricks of the trade that he knew would assure him a laugh. And if anything, the old man was even worse. Willie realized quite early on that he could get a laugh by doing the leer before saying the line. When in doubt or desperation, do the leer and you get a laugh! It became very easy for both of them. They had both examined these characters so deeply that they could play them on autopilot and still get reasonable results. However, Harry in particular wasn't about to let "his show" get pinched from under his nose. It was clear from the very first day of rehearsal that this was going to be a good episode ... that's probably why we, or the powers that be, wanted to put it at the end of the series so it wouldn't be lost in the shuffle. Leave the punters wanting more, as they say.'

Although Rossiter was getting paid a fifth of what the two regulars were earning, his agent, David Bradley, was keen to catapult him to the forefront of the episode. At the time, Rossiter was starring in *The Caretaker* at the Mermaid Theatre, and thus, with good reason, Bradley wrote to John Howard Davies on 15 March 1972 requesting that 'his name will be in the same size as Wilfred's [sic] and Harry's and that Devlin's name will be separated from Leonard: by a "with" or an "and" or whatever. I am sorry you think I have been making rather a fuss about this, but I think perhaps you have slightly misunderstood Leonard's standing in the profession at this time.'

Although Galton and Simpson were restricted by the half-hour format, and had to not only introduce the two desperate criminals but also melt the tense situation and end with the four 'inmates' of Oil Drum Lane becoming friendly and parting on equal terms, they still managed to build the tension within the relationship between father and son.

With a single electric fire shared between them, a pawned television and a radio that is continually on the blink, playing cards is the last pleasure left to

the Steptoes. Their camaraderie is forced, however. Albert's cooing pleas-
antries and gratitude to Harold for staying in and keeping him company elicit
the reply: 'I can't afford to go out!' Food is also in short supply. Harold fan-
tasizes that the old man has turned into a chicken, as the only grub he himself has had all day is half a carrot, 'and I had to fight to get that out of the
horse's mouth'. Cigarettes, the only calming influence on Harold's nerves,
are also non-existent. Even his father's proffered dog-ends are the dog-ends
of previous dog-ends: 'There hasn't been a proper fag since Christmas!'

But life at Oil Drum Lane is about to become even more unpleasant. If an
Englishman's home is his castle, the outsiders are just about to be unwittingly welcomed inside.

With the radio miraculously working for a moment and Albert thinking the
voice of the announcer is Harold mucking about, the outside world of broadcast news invades the home of the two rag 'n' bone men. The news reveals
that two dangerous convicts have escaped from Wormwood Scrubs. Harold,
play-acting as always, fires an imaginary rifle at the radio while Albert reflects
on a cause for concern: living in the area of a prison that can't keep its prisoners inside. After struggling in the darkness and discovering that his pfennigs fit the electricity meter slot, Harold's delight is cut short by the sight of
his father clasped by an iron-bar-wielding Leonard Rossiter and flanked by a
ferret-like J. G. Devlin. Harold splutters: 'What are you doing here?', momentarily unable to take it in, for this is real danger invading the Steptoes' world.

Leonard Rossiter, menacingly taking charge, is not a comic character at all.
That sneer, that thump of metal on wooden table, that threatening tone are
all very real and terrifying. There's a real sense of fear, although the humour
is still very much in play. With a threat to mess up the face of 'pretty boy here',
the younger escaped convict puts his cards on the table and makes his
demands.

But the central joke of the situation – the fact that the 'free men' are far
worse off than the two who have recently absconded from Her Majesty's
prison – is hard-hitting indeed. Rossiter, demanding the keys to the Steptoes'
car, won't accept that they don't own one and that the outbuilding is not a
garage but a stable: 'What, you mean an 'orse?' Devlin, exposing the timid little man beneath, pipes up 'We can't make a getaway on a horse, Johnnie',
while Harold comments: 'Dick Turpin did!' The genius at work here allows
the comedy to intermingle with the very serious storyline. Rossiter simply lets
the humour waft over him. Harold's joke is caught by the audience but is dismissed by the other characters. Rossiter isn't in the mood for a laugh: he's
'not mucking about'. But his guard is already beginning to come down. When

he demands all the money in the house Harold is forced to empty his pockets. Rossiter, brilliantly working off this embarrassed tension, slows down the performance and ponders.

This is the moment when the Corbett-Rossiter fight is at its peak. Rossiter pushes the miserable three and a half pence on the table with the end of his iron bar – the convict's dream is evaporating.

It's when Rossiter sits down and relates the bungled escape from prison that the humour of his situation creeps in. The puffing of the cigarette, the relaxing of the posture: his defences are coming down. The older convict getting his 'bleeding trousers caught on the barbed wire' evokes the similarities between the young convict saddled with an old companion and the young rag 'n' bone dealer saddled with an old father. Rossiter sums it all up when he says, 'You're better off on your own I reckon!'

Over the course of the episode the groundwork is established, and the four feel relaxed enough to argue without threats. Rossiter reflects on his best-laid plans 'all gone for a toss'. J. G. Devlin pleads exhaustion after just 500 yards on the run and begs to stay the night with the Steptoes.

The moments of heightened argument between the four of them are simply a double-strength two-hander, played out to perfection by the four actors. The youngsters are further bonded by the lack of scope and freedom their elders have imposed: Harold reflects on wanting to be a doctor, while Johnnie reveals that he was a law-abiding bank clerk before he met the old codger. The older convict greets Albert's ridicule of Harold's professional aspirations with cackling, shared hilarity. The younger one sides completely, for the first time, with Harold, defending his ambitions and laughing loud and long when Harold ponders the joys of euthanasia.

The debate reaches an emotional peak when Albert screams about the agonies of old age that await both Harold and Johnnie, delighting in the thought that they will know what it's like to be old one day. Harold's determination never to be a liability like his father, and his spat-out condemnation that if that's the case 'I don't want to grow that old', is, strangely, even more poignant when viewing this episode in retrospect. In the event, of course, neither Corbett nor Rossiter would get that old. Brambell and Devlin would outlive them both. When a police siren is heard, Harold's earnest plea to Johnnie to abandon the old man and make a getaway, and Albert's call that they should stick together, bring the episode to an emotional climax. Corbett arguably transcends anything he ever did on the show with his simple pleading with Johnnie not to take the old man with him. His pained 'Don't ... don't!' is heartbreaking, even more so in that you can tell Harold knows he has already lost the argument. What persuades Rossiter to take the older man with him is not the old convict's fake heart problem that prompts Harold's moan of: 'Oh, Gawd! Not that one!', but Albert's cutting: 'I thought there was supposed to be honour amongst thieves!' Rossiter looks from the old man to Harold and finally mumbles his thoughts to his new friend: 'Well, what can you do?' 'I know how you feel,' Harold mutters; and you know he does.

Each of the old men, congratulating themselves in the corner, reflects that their 'young companion' isn't all that bad after all, and as Rossiter and Corbett prepare to disengage there's one final moment. Rossiter, minding his manners and saying, 'Well, thanks for everything,' allows Corbett the last laugh: 'It wasn't much, was it?' The convicts leave in the darkness to go back to jail and father and son are alone. Albert, cheered by the thought that he and Harold have agreed to keep in touch with the convicts, is delighted with the outcome. His 'I'm glad they stayed together' allows Corbett to close this most vibrant of episodes with a steely acceptance of his own fate: 'Yeah ... I expect you are!' The venom contained in that phrase is almost tangible, as Harold's lifetime 'sentence' starts again. With the prisoners on their way back to prison, the Shepherd's Bush two continue their poverty-bound sentence together. Harry H. Corbett gives Harold grace, depth and hidden defeat in the final line: 'Oh well, better go and lock the cage up!' It is a beautifully played moment and a flawless conclusion to a flawless piece of writing and acting.

It is nigh impossible to select the all-time finest *Steptoe and Son*, but this programme comes closer than most. It certainly sums up what makes *Steptoe* such a towering achievement. This is fly-on-the-wall sitcom, and everything rings true.

In a way this would have been the ideal final episode. Instead, Galton and Simpson grabbed the chance to spread the wings of their characters further. The rag 'n' bone anti-heroes were about to be launched as film stars.

Chapter 13

Hoo-Ray For Cricklewood ... and Hollywood!

The trend for transforming British television programmes into films was long established. During the 1950s TV programmes were the staple diet of the fledgling Hammer Films, which adapted cult comedy and science-fiction classics for the big screen. TV situation comedy got the treatment in 1959 when *I Only Arsked!* utilized as its title Bernard Bresslaw's legendary catch-phrase from the ITV success *The Army Game*.

But it wasn't until the early 1970s that a glut of film spin-offs rolled off the production lines. Originally, television viewers had been attracted to the spin-offs because they could see a longer and more expensive production of a familiar story in full colour. But by the 1970s colour television was all the rage, and people were staying away from cinemas in their droves. The solution that British film-makers, in the main, came up with was to give them exactly what they were watching at home, but on a bigger screen. All of these feature-length productions of popular sitcoms retained the essence of what had made them great television. *Up Pompeii, Dad's Army, On the Buses* and *Bless This House* were all part of the first flush of production from 1969 through to 1972, and it seemed only reasonable that the BBC's biggest comedy success, *Steptoe and Son*, should go down the same route.

So in 1971 Ray Galton and Alan Simpson were tempted to write a feature-length adventure for the rag 'n' bone business. As Alan Simpson says:

It was a natural extension of the television series, really. Mind you, the first suggestion had been for us to do a stage show in Blackpool. We turned that down straight away: no, thank you, that might work for *'Allo, 'Allo* and *Dad's Army* but not our show. Our work of art as mere seaside entertainment! How dare they try and exploit our dramatic prose! We had that sort of pretentious thought then! But a film was a very agreeable idea. We had been writing films, on and off, for over 10 years and we loved the movies. So, in order to make films with Frankie Howerd and also the *Steptoe* film we formed our own production company. It was, naturally, called Associated London Films, and we were ready for business.

The result, simply entitled *Steptoe and Son*, was released in April 1972 and proved a commercial blockbuster: 'It was the biggest box-office sensation of the time,' reveals Alan Simpson. 'It broke 84 box-office records throughout the country.' Moreover, the script won Galton and Simpson the 1972 Writers' Guild Award for Best Screenplay.

Harry H. Corbett for one had been vocal in his opinion that *Steptoe and Son* wouldn't work on the big screen. Talking in 1963, when rumours of a *Steptoe* film had begun circulating, he was quick to point out that *The Bargee*, his feature film collaboration with writers Galton and Simpson, was nothing to do with the rag 'n' bone comedy. He was defending and celebrating his departure from the familiar character of Harold Steptoe when he assured people that it was 'not *Steptoe*; it wouldn't translate from television'.

Many critics agreed with Corbett's earlier opinion when the *Steptoe and Son* film first hit the screens, but there is no question that both Harry H. Corbett and Wilfrid Brambell were expert film actors as well as expert television actors. They had a longer, more relaxed shooting schedule and the option to redo scenes that hadn't worked first time around, but apart from that added luxury, nothing much had changed. Certainly, the on-screen chemistry of Corbett and Brambell was as effective as ever. 'I think they were both excellent in the films,' asserts Ray Galton. 'It's not easy to retain what you've done on television and make it the same but bigger for the cinema screen. Harry and Willie did it perfectly and, of course, we were lucky that both had been experienced in film acting for a long, long time. Willie had worked with Carol Reed, for heaven's sake!'

The opening credits of *Steptoe and Son* reintroduce the main characters and establish a sequence that takes place three years after the major events of the film. The old man is moaning 'Well, that marriage didn't last long did it?', as the two wander away from the divorce court, and Harold's ex-wife, in extreme long shot, walks off in the other direction. The stirring 'oompah' version of the familiar *Steptoe* theme was arranged by Roy Budd and Jack Fishman, who had been instrumental in the Pye recording deals for *Steptoe*. The score makes a smooth segue into a spiralling barrel-organ arrangement as a London traffic warden surveys a row of cars and stops at the ragged Steptoe cart. Ray Galton and Alan Simpson give themselves a self-deprecating on-screen mention as scriptwriters, as the shot focuses on an extreme close-up of the word 'Litter' written above a waste bin. The script is anything but 'lit-ter', of course, although many elements were reworked and rearranged from the television series.

Simpson reflects on the difference between writing for television and cinema:

> We knew the characters backwards for *Steptoe and Son*, of course, but it's not the construction of the characters that's the problem. The tricky part of writing films is the construction of the plot. It's particu-larly difficult on a comedy film. Our major problem had always been that we overwrote on everything. The terrible thing about overwriting a film screenplay is when you get to the cuts. You have to edit your beau-tifully constructed scenes, and we would often have almost three hours of material for an hour-and-forty-minute film. You can't cut the plot, so you have to cut the incidental comedy bits, the bits your story can do without. Unfortunately with the *Steptoe* film, those were often the best bits of writing and gave the characters more of their familiar edge. In the end we had a very tight screenplay and nobody had any room to move. All the jokes are timed to the split second and you lose that spontaneity we had on television. Mind you it can't have hurt that much because I can't for the life of me remember what we took out of the *Steptoe* film.

'I can hardly remember what we left in!' reflects Ray Galton.

The seeds of disaster in Harold's marriage are sown, of course, by the inter-vention and continual complaining of the old man. Harold is fighting a los-ing battle against Albert's unshakeable opinion that his son is 'too good for her'. Interviewed on location at St John's Church, Ladbroke Grove, for the February 1972 issue of *Film Review*, Corbett reflected on the marriage:

> That's something that never happened on telly, though I've had one or two narrow escapes with some right little darlings. In the film we final-ly get Harold to the altar, but his married bliss doesn't last long. But you can't capture the sheer horror of marriage on film! Weddings are still in fashion, you know. It's the mums who like to see white wed-dings. You've only got to stand outside a church any Saturday to see that. We've been shooting this wedding scene all day. It takes longer than the real thing, although you have more time to rehearse and get everything just right. I'm playing this wedding dead straight. It isn't really funny, you know. It's rather pathetic, the whole thing. Tragic even. I think a lot of blokes will be able to sympathize with how Harold felt.

The young lady in question is played by Carolyn Seymour, who had been critically acclaimed for her role in *Take Three Girls*. She encounters Harold at a football-club stag night, where she performs a striptease. The dirty old man, hearing the mention of strippers, is keen to join his son at the bash, of course, and the preparation for the evening draws heavily on memories of television's 'The Bath'. Here, it is Harold, and not his father, who sits in surprising comfort in a tin bath in the front room, while Albert awkwardly carries out his ablutions at the kitchen sink. The old man's skinny, grotesque form, his soap-sudded exit from the sink, and his hasty grabbing of a packet of 'Flash' to cover his privates when a neighbour appears, take his 'dirtiness' to new levels.

Later in the evening, the dirtiness of his mind plumbs new depths, with his wizened contempt at Harold's boast that he's chatted up one of the strippers, in fact his wife-to-be. Albert isn't impressed: 'Geezers with money, that's what they want ... or girls!' The prurient disgust of the final thought is sneered out of the side of Brambell's mouth with clear relish. But the girl is a cracker: the old man practically bites through his glasses as she performs her routine. Indeed, the striptease sequence is probably the funniest part of the film as Harold, typically shy and sheepish, struggles with the young lady's bra, and Albert climbs on to his seat and bellows, 'Get 'em off!' with complete abandon. But Albert is determined to ruin Harold's evening, joining him in the bar afterwards as he awaits his date and gleefully muttering: 'She's blown you out!' But the football club interlude ends with real promise for the son and an unpleasant surprise for the old man, who unwittingly chats up a drag artiste in full costume. His cocky 'I might be late meself, mate!' boast gives Harold a truly bright moment, a precursor to a night of passionate and philosophical conversation with a beautiful woman.

Even Albert admits that 'She's better than the usual scrubbers' Harold attracts, but the old man is outraged when marriage is mentioned: 'You bloody fool ... they're not for marrying, they're for looking at!' Elements of all Harold's failed romances are brought to mind, from 'The Bird' in 1962 to 'Loathe Story' in 1972 but it's the 1965 episode, 'And Afterwards At ...', which is most obviously plundered, for the wedding sequence. Albert gives the marriage six months and approves of the apt hymn 'Fight the Good Fight', delighting in the lateness of the bride-to-be. When she finally arrives Albert's train of thought is momentarily silenced, before the wedding march starts and he grimaces, 'It's a wonder she's not taking her clothes off!' The wider freedom afforded to a feature film made in the more permissive 1970s was reflected in the publicity blurb on the film's poster. Presented as old man

Steptoe dialogue, it read: 'You'd think if the berk's going to get tied up with a stripper, he'd do it on the telly – not on the big screen where everybody can see it – dirty little devil.'

'The Holiday' and every other episode that suggested Harold was off to a foreign clime without his father are invoked during the honeymoon sequences. The newlyweds, dressed for the Spanish heat, arrive at their hotel closely followed by a wheezing Albert in his usual heavy gear. What's more, he's complaining that they should have gone to Bognor because this place is 'too hot'. During the uncharacteristic Continental honeymoon the really tragic elements of the Steptoes' relationship come to the fore. Naturally, Albert is determined to ruin this defining moment in his son's life, dragging his feet while finishing his lobster supper and desperately trying to detect sexual activity in his son's room. He finally (and for once unintentionally) brings Harold's dreams of married bliss to an abrupt end, thanks to a sudden attack of food poisoning from a dubious lobster. Terrified of dying on foreign soil, Albert whispers: 'Take me home. I'm frightened!' He clings on to his son in tears, and later the two men fly home to England taking the last two seats on the plane and leaving Harold's wife in Spain.

As the foreign doctors had predicted the old man is soon up and about, distressing Harold further by reflecting that his son's wife is 'on the nest with old oily!', a reference to the comic she used to work with, who clearly wanted to tend her in her moment of loneliness. But when Harold receives a 'Dear John' letter, the old man takes no comfort in it. His face falls and his heart goes out to his son.

Harold's heartbreak is compounded when he learns that he is about to become a father. In a reworking of 'Steptoe and Son – and Son!' his wife is pregnant and Harold is willing to do the right thing. 'I want that kid. I've never had one before!' he says. He also wants his wife back, and there is an emotionally charged showdown between unfaithful wife, cuckolded husband and outraged father. Albert is adamant, and his vindictive, unmoving attitude is brilliantly brought to life as Brambell lowers his eyelids and firms up his voice. The wife gives a final ultimatum: either Harold leaves the old man or their marriage is over. But Harold cannot leave his father. Jokes, pleading and downright offensive behaviour can't cover up the truth of the wife's final comment on her husband: 'You're a prisoner!'

He is a prisoner, and the bonds of family are tied around him more tightly when, with a nod to religious iconography, he discovers a baby abandoned in the stable. The Steptoes naturally jump to the conclusion that the baby is Harold's. Fed through an adapted beer bottle and a finger off one of Harold's old gloves, the baby boy is clearly set to follow in the family business. But Harold, determined to give his son the best education, adopts a Harold-Wilson-like posture, with pipe clenched between his teeth, as he maps out the road to wealth and prosperity for his pride and joy. The father and son can't decide on a suitable name, with Albert's liking for a film star ('Dirk Steptoe ... Kirk Steptoe ...') being dismissed with Harold's: 'And when the kids round here find out, Berk Steptoe!' But *Steptoe* being *Steptoe*, nothing remains pleasant for long. The sentimental scenes of father and son bathing the baby are roughly juxtaposed with their blind panic when he is retrieved by his mother and Harold tracking down his estranged stripper wife. As he enters another club and sits through another routine, the dramatic climactic scene is painfully realistic and difficult to watch. Harold is attacked and humiliated by a gang of leering, drunken rugby players. Severely beaten up, he ultimately discovers that his wife's baby wasn't his after all. The abandoned child wasn't left by his wife and, besides, his wife's baby is black and female, fathered by a striptease pianist we had seen in action in an earlier scene.

The philosophical Harold reflects on losing two babies, neither of which were his, on the same day, rounding off the film where we, the audience, came in. In an attempt to end on a comic high point, the Steptoes resurrect memories of the 1963 Royal Variety Performance and coast down the Mall. Giving a two-fingered salute to the vehicle behind them, they cheekily doff their hats when they recognize the royal standard and smile as Prince Philip, or at least an extra wearing a naval officer's uniform, replies in kind. The scene can't quite lighten the heart-wrenching narrative that preceded it, but that's probably just as well: this is a funny film but, like the best of the television shows, its uncompromising realism makes it great. However, while the audience flocked to the cinema, the *Monthly Film Bulletin* believed that the big screen 'spoilt the intimacy of the scene and coarsened the characterizations', while the 'comic possibilities of the wedding are ... wasted in an endless joke about horse manure'. In summing up, the *MFB* commented that the film was 'lively enough entertainment [but] no match for the best *Steptoe* episodes of 1962.'

If only for the supporting cast, the film should be remembered as a classic of 1970s British comedy. There's a turn as a slightly drunk chauffeur from Victor Maddern, familiar from such classics as *I'm All Right, Jack* and *Carry On Cleo*. Arthur Howard, late of the Jimmy Edwards series *Whacko!*, crops up as the benevolent vicar. Patsy Smart, later remembered as the fragile neighbour in *Terry and June*, plays the neighbour who reacts with shocked disbelief at Albert's early exposure of himself. Fred Griffiths gives a typically enjoyable cameo as the football club barman, and Mike Reid appears as the fruity comic compère at the striptease show.

The film was directed by Cliff Owen, who had been in the industry since the age of 18, in 1937, and had directed two big-screen ventures for Eric Morecambe and Ernie Wise (*That Riviera Touch* and *The Magnificent Two*).

As Alan Simpson remembers:

> There was no question of using our television director. John Howard Davies had no experience in films, apart from being in them when he was a kid. Duncan Wood, who had directed *The Bargee*, was now a television executive, so he had left directing behind him. Aida Young was the producer on the film and she suggested Cliff Owen. We both got on with Cliff very well and he had directed our screenplay of *The Wrong Arm of the Law* in the early 1960s, so we knew how he worked. Mind you, Willie Brambell wasn't happy about Cliff. The old man would get very uppity with Cliff Owen. He thought he was a slob and an awful bully. Admittedly, Cliff would shout a lot and Willie didn't like that; he was a gentleman actor.

'I think it was probably because Cliff found it easier to relate to Harry,' reflects Ray Galton. 'Both Alan and I found it easier to relate to Harry as well. It wasn't so much an age thing, although that probably played a part. It's just that Harry shared our cultural touchstones. Willie never went out of his way to engage us in conversation. He was a pro, he learnt the lines and did the job. That's fine. He was always pleasant company and fun on set, but there was no attempt to draw us into his life or his circle. Things were always on a purely professional level. Maybe on the film, with a longer, more intensive time together, that surfaced more than usual.'

The American publication *The Motion Picture Guide* didn't seem to understand the structure of the *Steptoe and Son* film or, indeed, the original television series at all. In a review of the film they expressed the opinion that 'the TV stars don't work well on the screen and the writing is bad throughout'.

This was ironic, as the *Steptoe and Son* format had just been voted a smash hit on America's CBS. From January 1972 it had been appearing in the States as *Sanford and Son*.

Television producer Norman Lear had taken up the relinquished rights to produce an American version of *Steptoe and Son* in 1971. His previous hit show, *All in the Family*, had itself been based on another classic BBC situation comedy, Johnny Speight's *Till Death Us Do Part*, and had provided America with its own Alf Garnett in Archie Bunker. Lear was now on the lookout for a vehicle with which to repeat the winning formula. He considered the eternal bickering in *Steptoe and Son* to be easily convertible to an American setting. But an untransmitted pilot programme starring Barnard Hughes and Paul Sorvino was considered a failure by all concerned. Luckily, Lear persevered and hit on the novel idea of reworking the original scripts to fit a black father and son's junk business at 9114 South Central, Los Angeles, just as Galton and Simpson had suggested to Screen Gems in 1967. Lear calculated correctly that by keying into already existing racial tension the show would be able to provide a satirical commentary on American society of the day. Respected stand-up comedian Redd Foxx was cast as the wily, 65-year-old head of the family, Fred G. Sanford, while Demond Wilson played his 34-year-old son, Lamont Sanford. The original Galton and Simpson scripts were fully developed for the American version, although the nature of television in the US dictated that *Sanford and Son* and its various spin-offs would outstrip *Steptoe and Son* in sheer number of episodes many times over.

Although *Sanford and Son* was never transmitted on British television, viewers familiar with the banter of *Steptoe and Son* would easily recognize the situation. The father's history was even more colourful than Albert Steptoe's, with a career in vaudeville rescuing him from the poverty-stricken childhood he had endured in Georgia. A widower for 23 years, Fred Sanford, like his British counterpart, indulged himself with countless heart attacks whenever he didn't get his own way. He has 15 before the end of the first episode! His long speeches to his dearly departed wife – Elizabeth in the American shows – soon became audience-pleasers and Foxx made a catchphrase out of his lament: 'I'm coming, Elizabeth, I'm coming. This is the big one!' In his more aggressive moments, Foxx could turn his ageing parent into a threatening fighter, clenching his fist in the face of authority and muttering: 'How would you like one across your lips?' Young Lamont feels a relentless yearning to move away from the junk business and get into the antique trade but, as Harold has for Albert, he has a genuine affection and love for the old man.

Although the relationship between father and son was a familiar element from the British series, *Sanford and Son* brought in a regular supporting cast that would infringe on the centrality of the two leads. Ray Galton remembers:

> Our contribution to *Sanford and Son* was very limited. We just gave our permission for them to use our scripts and characters in the adaptation. The first series was something like 14 programmes, 11 of which were based on our shows. After that it was turned into a gang show and we had nothing to do with it. They brought in aunties, friends, next-door neighbours ... but it was still our idea, just!

From the show's first transmission, on 14 January 1972, *Sanford and Son* became an instant hit, regularly making the top 10 in television rankings during its original run and enjoying extended repeat seasons ever since.

Galton and Simpson had wisely retrieved both the US and European rights to *Steptoe and Son* after signing up for the colour resurrection of the series in 1969. And in the early 1970s one of the best-loved and most successful *Steptoe* hybrids had hit Swedish television. 'It would have started in about 1971,' remembers Alan Simpson, 'and it was called *Albert Och Herbert.*'

'We didn't want to redub the originals, and they wanted their own version, so everybody was happy,' recalls Ray Galton. 'And unlike the American series, this and all the other foreign shows were tremendously faithful to our original scripts. They just translated what we had written, and the one for Sweden was probably the best.' In the end, *Albert Och Herbert* ran until the early 1990s.

With *Steptoe* being adapted internationally, and given the huge popularity of the television series and the box-office success of the first film, it wasn't surprising that Ray Galton and Alan Simpson were commissioned to write the screenplay for a second feature-length film. They came up with a less emotionally charged but much funnier follow-up. Brambell was certainly happier in his role after the change of director from Cliff Owen to an Australian, Peter Sykes. 'Willie was much happier with Peter, and the entire film was a pleasure from start to finish,' recalls Ray Galton. Again, perfectly in tune with the television series, as before, *Steptoe and Son Ride Again* can claim to be one of the funniest British films of the 1970s.

The production was another Associated London Films offering. It was filmed at Lee International Studios in west London, as the previous one had been, and as before, the Steptoes' house and yard were built from scratch by the production team, next door to the studios, and demolished after filming was completed.

From the moment the familiar horse and cart appear on screen and an early-bird Albert tries to shoot the chicken in his neighbour's yard, this is definitive *Steptoe*. He blasts away with his toy rifle, eventually destroying Harold's bed, and prepares his son's sandwiches, complete with fag ash and cheese pushed through the mangle, while giving the horse's bottom a cursory wipe. Harold is so disturbed that he wanders into a flight of fancy concerning Albert's day of toil in the garden: the old man is, in fact, raking over the manure as Harold drives off to work.

The plot focuses once again on the Steptoes' financial insecurity, and borrows slightly from both 'The Siege of Steptoe Street' and 'The Desperate Hours'. The image of a carrot half-shared with the horse is taken from the latter show, and from the former comes a mounting pile of bills which the Steptoes can't hope to pay. The earlier episode is also subtly evoked when Harold wearily instructs 'And no secret eating before I get home!' – the discovery that his father had concealed a supply of chocolate biscuits had been the final insult that broke Harold's spirit and ushered in the bailiffs in the television 'siege'.

The vandalized inner-city landscape and bleak location filming perfectly contrast with the bittersweet comic script and establish the Steptoes within the harsh Britain of the early 1970s. A Britain where high-rise flats, which Harold energetically has to clamber to because the lifts are broken, are covered in graffiti. This sour picture of contemporary London is juxtaposed with scenes from the totting past that was fast crumbling at the time of filming. The decline of tradition is one of the central themes of the last part of the film, and locations like Southall market, the White City stadium and the backstreets of Shepherd's Bush perfectly capture the end-of-an-era sentiment of the screenplay.

The black humour that permeates the film is ushered in early, with the first of two outstanding guest performances coming from the blonde bombshell, Diana Dors. Clearly making a play for young Harold, Dors draws on 30 years of movie vampery for her few minutes of screen time. She brilliantly provokes pained, flattered and horrified reactions from Corbett as she desperately tries to force her dead husband's clothes, and herself, on to the rag 'n' bone man. When she claims that her husband used to beat her, Corbett's struggling, pinned-down whimper, 'The swine!', hilariously sets the scene for the revealing of the actual body: dead since yesterday and hardly cold while his widow tries to seduce stray men. Corbett's repulsion at the thought, his sharp intake of breath and desperate scramble to ditch the rags and get out, all are perfectly performed. The disappointed Dors, alone and frustrated and lighting a cigarette, mutters, 'What are you bleeding grinning at?' to her 'dear departed' and, to an extent, us the audience.

It's no laughing matter for Harold either, for he drops off to sleep, drives the horse and cart into an open-backed removal van and ends up in York. On his return, the delicious meal of stolen chicken that Albert has prepared and devoured is long gone: 'A Bombay shitehawk would have left more on it than that!' Worse than Harold's empty stomach, the horse is lame. Here, Galton and Simpson take a step back in time, for the horse is none other than Hercules. In terms of chronology that would mean that the events featured in Ride Again actually precede the events in the first Steptoe film. What's more, while making several script references to 'A Death in the Family', the television episode that killed off Hercules, the film allows the writers to rewrite a happy ending for the faithful old horse. Harold, untypically, is moved by the thought of Hercules ending up as pet food, and the beast is pensioned off to a rest home for old horses, looking forward to cheerful gallivanting with a filly. According to an affectionate Harold: 'He'll be dead in a week.' At the very end of the film, the Steptoes are back in business with a new filly whom we must assume to be Delilah.

However, Hercules the Second is the name given not to the filly's foal, as in the television show, but to a greyhound that a drunken Harold has bought from local spiv and hard man, Frankie Barrow. The diminutive Henry Woolf with his distinctive voice and menacing manner, is flanked continually by at least a couple of hulking henchmen, and he can say and do as he likes. Harold, with £140 owing on the dog, is caught in his trap.

With a script more attuned to the old two-hander conversation of the television series, the Corbett-Brambell scenes are given more room for the traditional *Steptoe* bickering than in the first film. As Harold, nursing the hangover to end all hangovers, tries to explain the good fortune and money-in-the-bank reality of owning a greyhound, he reveals that the dog's 'descended from Mick the Miller'. 'I don't care if he's descended from Max Miller!' replies the old man with a cruel twist of the lip. Of course, Albert seems to be right. The trial race for the greyhound is a disaster. The dog stays in the trap, the Steptoes wander home dejectedly, Albert bitterly points out that if someone tries to sell Harold a talking parrot, 'You better look for a tape recorder stuffed up its Khyber' and, more seriously, Frankie Barrow, 'the Godfather of Shepherd's Bush', is on the warpath for his money.

But it doesn't take a genius to work out that Hercules the Second is short-sighted. The scenes of greyhound training are spirited and enjoyable, but the high point comes at the very start of this thread of plot. Albert lovingly tries the dog with glasses from his huge collection while Harold, to test the dog's sight, suddenly sticks a stuffed lion's head on a pole over the top of the sofa. Visually hilarious, and endearing when the dog finally spots the offending creature, the scene reveals the innocent side of Harold's character. This innocence is starkly contrasted with his street-trader instincts, displayed as the contents of the Steptoe home are sold off to the public. To raise enough money to gamble on the greyhound's first major race, Harold, with a real gift of the gab, flogs anything and everything. References to television episodes crop up, notably as a gentleman wanders off with a set of skiing gear, clearly left over from 'A Winter's Tale'. The scene even includes a reference to Harold's pet goldfish, Charlie.

But the dog's affection for its owners is too great and, spotting Albert in the crowd, rather than finishing the race it runs into the old man's arms. A more drastic plan for a fast buck is needed, and the old man reveals that he has a life insurance policy which makes him 'worth more dead than alive'. The established tension and black humour of the film give credibility to Corbett's mad act as he looks through the glass of the door with an air of detached intent. But it is not murder that is on his mind; rather it is an untypical plan to defraud the insurance company.

Enter celebrated Irish character star, Milo O'Shea, who excels as a bespectacled, drunken medical man, Dr Popplewell. O'Shea mumbles on the phone with pompous grandeur, confirming Harold's hopes that he's 'as pissed as a fart'. With the help of a shop-window dummy (whose torso is snugly fitted around the old man), copious amounts of the hard stuff and the doctor's natural short-sightedness, the plan is working. A genuine death certificate for the very much alive Albert Steptoe will get the insurance money and save the day. The scene could have been over in moments, but Corbett and O'Shea milk the situation for all it's worth. It remains one of the funniest self-contained vignettes in the Galton and Simpson canon.

After Popplewell's departure, the black humour is taken up a notch with the appearance at the window of the dummy's head, mournfully demanding its body back. Albert is terrified, and even the dog hides under the bed, but of course it turns out to be Harold mucking about.

The film momentarily creates the impression that the old man really has suffered from heart failure, as the scene cuts to Albert in his coffin and Harold regretfully wandering in with the coffin lid under his arm. Thankfully, it's just Albert trying out the coffin for comfort. With the morbid spell broken and Harold's hasty whistle, cheerful optimism returns.

The funeral itself is an epic of situation comedy. Harold, who has been informed that the insurance policy had been signed over to an 18-year-old bird his 'dirty old man' father was knocking about with during the son's military stay in Malaya, faces the fact that he won't get the money, and sets about trying to resurrect his father.

The final, brilliantly orchestrated graveyard farce, filmed on location at Kensal Green Cemetery, brings the film's black humour to its natural conclusion. A slumbering, coffin-encased Albert wakes up thanks to the greyhound shovelling earth on to the top of his coffin. Harold, who has been knocked out cold by an opening lorry door on his way to the funeral, rushes from intensive care into the scene, complete with white bedwear. He promptly crashes into a nearby crypt. The emergence of the old man, with the mourners looking down into the hole and the audience enjoying both their and Albert's point of view, starts a hilarious chain reaction, culminating in a mournful Harold emerging from the crypt and terrifying the already spooked-out vicar, played by Geoffrey Bayldon. With all the threads tied together, and Frank Thornton's insurance man revealing that Albert's girlfriend forfeited the money when she married, the Steptoes are allowed to cash in and get out. Part of the resultant £876 goes on a new horse ... a filly.

Thus, in the end, we pick up the television series where this alternative version of 'A Death in the Family' left off. Harold has been fleeced again – he spends the rest of the money on a part share in a racehorse owned by 'H. M. Queen'. Albert takes in the royal connection and, as with the previous film, *Steptoe and Son Ride Again* comes to a royal conclusion. The horse, pulling the cart, clip-clops down the furlong within the royal parade. Albert merrily turns on the regal wave, while Harold lifts the dog's head up for perfect posture.

The film is blessed with familiar faces from everybody's favourite Welshman in *Please, Sir!*, Richard Davies, to blouse-stretching Grazina Frame, fresh from *Up Pompeii* who cheekily offers to 'try it on' during Harold's junkyard jumble sale. But it's the gallery of eccentric totting types invading Albert's 'funeral' and turning it into a drunken party that provides the film with a backbone of glorious character actors. Neil McCarthy, after a lifetime of playing screen heavies, excels as the kind and caring Lennie and rationally explains: 'If we have one more drink we're all gonna fall down the bleeding hole with him, ain't we?' Bill Maynard is the increasingly drunken and forthright George, who allows his sorrow to be replaced by a desire to get drunk as quickly as possible. Sam Kydd adds his prolific clout to the graveyard humour while George Tovey perfectly bridges the film *Steptoe* with television *Steptoe*. He had appeared as one of the kindly totters in 'Wallah-Wallah Catsmeat' in 1963, played a wedding guest in 'And Afterwards At ...' in 1965 and cropped up shifting the snooker table in the 1970 episode 'Pot Black'. Another familiar *Steptoe* face is Yootha Joyce who, again, reacts brilliantly opposite Harry H. Corbett and joins Olga Lowe and Joyce Hamson as the totting wives.

When the film was released in August 1973 the critics condemned it for not staying faithful to its television roots. Indeed, the *Monthly Film Bulletin* believed that the film 'retains the trappings but none of the subtlety or intimacy of the original television series'. It also contended that Ray Galton and Alan Simpson had moved completely away from the bittersweet pathos of the series in favour of barrel-scraping belly laughs, with realism 'sacrificed to the demands of the basic British screen comedy with its emphasis on lavatories, booze, breasts and (curiously enough) the hilarity of death'. Still, the *MFB* did praise the film's director, Peter Sykes. The journal was 'pleased' to note that he 'at least tried to direct the whole enterprise as a film rather than as a blown-up *Comedy Playhouse*' and hinted at some 'forbidden' enjoyment of the ghoulish climax, admitting that the funeral sequence 'almost comes off'.

For Brambell and Corbett, their *Steptoe* film careers came to a halt after the blaze of publicity for their second adventure. Although a far superior film, the sequel failed to match the runaway box-office success of the first effort. 'We had all been delighted with the reaction to the first film, obviously,' remembers Alan Simpson, 'and we thought the second film was a foregone conclusion. I always thought the second film was better than the first. But it died on its feet. It didn't even get the cost of its production back.'

'We speculate on whether the title was a mistake,' continues Galton. 'People may have thought it was a reshowing of the first *Steptoe and Son* film, again!'

'These days you can call it *Steptoe and Son II* so there would be no problem,' chuckles Alan Simpson. 'It's not so much of a catchy title, I'll grant you, but we more than likely would have made a third film if the second one had done as well as the first. The only thing I can think of was that everybody who had flocked to see the first film didn't like it so they didn't bother to go and see the second one.'

Chapter 14

Tinsel and Tantrums

Six adaptations for radio were recorded, two a night in the space of a working week, in September 1973. Scheduled for broadcast the following summer, the series picked up from where the television one had left off by recruiting Leonard Rossiter to re-create his convict role from 'The Desperate Hours'. J. G. Devlin proved unavailable so his part was recast, with Paddy Joyce stepping into the role. The result is disappointing in comparison with the television original, and Rossiter in particular seems to be sleepwalking through the episode.

Trevor Bannister, Norman Bird and Anthony Sharp also reprised their original roles in radio versions of 'A Star is Born', 'Men of Property' and 'Men of Letters'. However, these productions were eclipsed by the news that, for the first time since April 1972, Brambell and Corbett were returning for a brand-new television *Steptoe and Son*. During the 1960s they had recorded a couple of filmed inserts for *Christmas Night with the Stars*, but this comeback was the first extended *Steptoe* Christmas episode, broadcast on Christmas Eve 1973. It was produced by Graeme Muir who had overseen the 1962 *Christmas Night with the Stars* which had featured a brief *Steptoe* segment.

The first full-length Christmas special had its beginnings on 25 July 1973, when Ray Galton and Alan Simpson were commissioned to pen an extended-length *Steptoe and Son* episode for that year's seasonal schedule. It wasn't attached to a series budget but conceived as a stand-alone 'highlight'. With a designated running time of 45 minutes, the finished script was to be delivered no later than 29 October 1973. In fact, it was completed before that date, with rehearsals starting in earnest at the North Kensington Community Centre on Tuesday 20 October and concluding on Sunday 2 November 1973.

Harry H. Corbett had been the first of the acting duo to return to his role, filming the opening location material of Harold parking his horse and cart at a meter the day before rehearsals began. Corbett was also in preparation for pantomime and, following the *Steptoe* recording on 3 and 4 December, he immediately went into rehearsals for his starring role in *Robinson Crusoe* at the Prince's Theatre, Aldershot.

Despite the rather large cast of supporting actors the programme is, fundamentally, a two-hander with interventions from the outside world beginning and ending the piece. Frank Thornton, following his recent excursion into the world of *Steptoe* at the cinema, returned for his sixth and final credit with the rag 'n' bone comedy. His impeccable performance as the snobbish travel agent provides the perfect contrast with Harold's scruffy, hopeful holidaymaker. The opening scene, with Corbett at centre stage, explores class distinction in Britain as a refined couple at the travel agency change their plans once it becomes clear that Harold is travelling to the same destination and the same hotel. Galton and Simpson also satirize working-class aspirations, with Harold condemning the bad construction of Spanish hotels and adopting the British-abroad attitude of expecting to show the foreigners how to enjoy Christmas. His overkeen attempt to make friends with a better class of people is, clearly, doomed from the outset.

The closing sequence, with Harold's holiday cancelled and the money blown on a lavish spread of Christmas fare, ushers in another set of supporting actors – this time as characters of the Steptoes' own class. But this potentially riotous party is curtailed, thanks to both father and son catching chickenpox. Harold cannot win. Whether it's fun overseas or excess at home, circumstances or Albert ruin it.

The bulk of the episode simply allows Brambell and Corbett to do what they do best, but before the bickering in Oil Drum Lane Brambell is given ample opportunity to play to the crowd, with a delightful monologue on Christmases past. Beginning with a satirical rendition of 'I'm Dreaming of a White Christmas' as he sticks paper chains together, Albert clearly relishes the festivities, hanging up wrapping paper in the outside toilet and giving the skeleton a paper hat and a cigar 'There you are, John Gregson!' He addresses his memories of festive seasons good and bad to a ramshackle Christmas-tree fairy, reflecting on Harold's first Christmas, the first after his mother's death ('I'd bought her Christmas present already!') and this, the first Common Market one: 'We remember the bad old days ... bleeding sight better than they are now!' Most importantly, the fairy allows Albert to set up the fulcrum of the plot, confiding that he couldn't spend Christmas on his own, 'not at my age'. At that moment Harold returns home and, with his holiday plans, threatens to make Albert do just that.

The show then breaks into two segments. First, Harold reasons with his father, complains about the 'soul-destroying' Christmases of the past and reveals that he has secured the old man a place at the Christmas dinner at the old people's home. A delightful reference back to the previous series sees Harold explain that the vicar is happy, despite the fact that 'He ain't forgotten the crossword puzzle' that Albert compiled (in 'Men of Letters'). But Albert is having none of it. He's proud of his son, and refuses to give the community ammunition to knock Harold for leaving his father at Christmas. He's prepared for a quiet time reflecting at his wife's grave and watching television. Guilt on Harold's part, a feeble collapse on Albert's and the unsubtle introduction of a bottle of pills that allows the old man to reveal a 'secret' illness seal the fate of the Steptoes' Christmas. Harold is staying at home.

The next segment sees Harold relentlessly jolly and festive. His genial entrance, bearing a sack of poultry, is still, however, contrasted with Albert's miserable demeanour. Harold's plan for a huge party takes care of the entire festive season even though Albert 'doesn't like having the house full of people'. The rag 'n' bone lifestyle, disgusting to the polished Harold, finally triumphs when he agrees to use a china 'po' for a punchbowl. The guest list for the party even allows a *Steptoe* in-joke: Among the named guests are Chris and Arthur, the real rag 'n' boning Arnolds who had provided the horse and cart for the series since the beginning.

This first major Christmas with the Steptoes is a masterpiece. Certainly, no other television special would be able to comment on seductive ATS girls, possible Nazi sympathies during the war, illness, horse manure and the crime of dragging religion into Christmas. Harold's commercial awareness, as he sniffs the air and moans, 'Ah! Bisto!', is brought sharply into perspective as the sick Albert comes close to emulating Jesus Christ and spending Christmas in the stable. As the two chickenpox-struck bickerers settle down to their feast, the credits roll.

The Audience Reaction Report was decidedly merry. 'So often "specials" fall a bit flat,' observed one viewer, 'but this was excellent. [I] missed a lot of the dialogue through laughing.' Another commented that, 'One feels so at home with the Steptoes, setting and costumes are taken for granted, I could tell you exactly where the skeleton stands', while another simply remarked: 'This down to earth stuff appeals to me; it is *life*.'

The fifth radio series received a belated first run from 26 May through to 30 June 1974, and by then the eighth series of television episodes was already well under way. Ray Galton recalls the deadlines: 'The thing is, if we were given, say, five months before a deadline for a series, we would take five months to write it. We would talk about everything but the series, until we had to knuckle down and write it.'

'We would always write one episode at a time,' recalls Alan Simpson, 'but we would keep a sheet of paper handy. Any half-ideas, we would write them on this piece of paper. We would keep this piece of paper for series after series, so on series three we might have used a half-idea from series one and a half-idea from series two and stuck them together. You would never know the difference. We always started a new show by going through the list of ideas. Something from the previous year might have sparked us off this time round. On two or three occasions we did resurrect old ideas. Admittedly, by the start of series eight I think that piece of paper had been exhausted. To an extent we found it hard work. We were in serious danger of repeating ourselves. There literally was nothing left to go on.'

On 31 August 1974 Wilfrid Brambell and Harry H. Corbett were back at Television Centre to record the first episode of the eighth and final series of *Steptoe and Son*, their fees still £1250 per programme. The series was greeted with high expectations and excitement by critics and fans alike. Indeed, the first episode, broadcast on 4 September 1974, attracted laudable viewing figures of 7.8 million homes. But these figures were not sustained and, by October, the show had lost a million of its original audience. The *Radio Times* had also lost interest. No photographs or features accompanied the series. Attitudes had clearly changed. Although the scripts still had much of the brilliance they had always displayed, the plots were, if anything, more intricate, and distracted from the basic relationship of father and son. The performances, while showing flashes of inspiration, were more caricatured and sloppy, and even the design, always an important facet of the *Steptoe* experience, seemed lacklustre.

Ray Galton admits:

There was a certain tension creeping in. Harry started getting a little irritated. The four of us, and the producer, would usually go down the pub for our lunch hour, and Willie would probably have one gin and tonic too many. So Harry eventually made a point of not coming with us. He started bringing in his own sandwiches and would sit in the studio. When we were leaving, he'd say, 'Oh, I'll wait here until you come back, shall I? I'll go over the script while you're out!'

Alan Simpson continues:

Eventually, Harry wouldn't say anything at all. When we came back from lunch, Harry would be sitting there with his empty sandwich box and the script open on his lap. He would be going over the lines, making annotations on the script. In other words, it was to say: 'Look, I've been working while the old man's been boozing!' That would get up Willie's nose, and he'd probably have one gin and tonic too many the next lunchtime just to spite Harry. As a result, rehearsals would stop at about 3 o'clock, half past three, simply because Harry was getting annoyed. He'd say, 'It's not much use carrying on, really, is it?' The old man's nose would be throbbing away there and he'd be fluffing his lines. Harry would never cause a big scene. It was never unpleasant. He would just come over to us or the producer and say, 'Shall we call it a day?' He was very professional about it. There were never any punch-ups on set, you understand. It was just Harry getting a little bit irritated, that's all, and it was always like friends in the playground, always muttering behind each other's back. Harry would say to me, 'Look, he's drunk again!' and raise his eyebrows as if to say, the things I have to put up with! Mind you, it wasn't always Willie's fault.

Ray Galton agrees:

Harry had, quite early on, I think, taken it on himself to explain to Willie what the show was about. Of course, Willie knew. He was a professional actor. But we would see the two of them in a corner running over a scene, and Willie would look rather nonplussed at some of the stuff Harry was coming out with.

'There was a different attitude,' thinks Alan Simpson. 'Harry was always exploring the part and experimenting with different ways of doing it, while Wilfrid was the old school of acting. He would learn the lines, decide how to do them and do them exactly the same way every time. Then suddenly he would be confronted with Harry, who would try something new every time they went through it. The old-fashioned actor against the method actor. It was a contrast that worked wonderfully well for the show, but the cracks were certainly beginning to show. I think Harry was sometimes under the impression that it was his show. It wasn't!'

Although the four central writing and acting talents were still gelling, something was undoubtedly missing. The sitting-room décor was less grotty and cluttered than before. The attention to detail was less evident and even the familiar Steptoe and Son sign, usually painstakingly painted on the gate of the location and removed after filming, was replaced by a hastily written placard, hung for easy removal. The opening episode of the new series was the most disappointing start to any of the television runs.

In 'Back in Fashion' the old themes and opinions on society, government, the British way of life and the generation gap are hinted at but fail to take off into something more significant as they had in previous shows. It is a typical episode that explores the way Harold eternally comes off second best to his father, but if 'Live Now, PAYE Later' had suffered from being too farcical to be believable, this programme is both atypical and rather depressing. The basic plot sees the junkyard become the backdrop for a *Vogue* fashion shoot, with Harold delighted that six models are about to drape themselves over the rags and old tyres. It's all about the contrast of beauty and muck. Harold manages to get £40 of the £60 the old man charges the photographer's agent, and everything seems set for them to ogle to their hearts' content. The fashion photographer, played by Roy Holder, is the perfect contrast to Harold and Albert, having experienced the squalor of London slums but risen above it. He's got away from the lifestyle while retaining affection for it. But apart from Brambell's spirited 'Get your hair cut!', there is little of the old working-class pride of Shepherd's Bush. Any there is soon gives way to the greedy desire for a few seconds of fame and the company of females. The old man, of course, is as keen to see the models as the next man, but Harold goes over the top, donning a smoking jacket, dark glasses and an air of sophistication. The misunderstanding that Harold is blind arises and the stunning Madeline Smith, leading a clutch of seductive models, shows kindness and considera-tion which are lapped up by Harold – but which are quickly curtailed when the truth is revealed. But Harold hasn't been trying to fool the girls; he's just been enjoying the attention he thinks his 'stylish' outfit has attracted. Naturally, his chances are gone from that moment on and, as he continually finds himself in compromising positions with the girls, he reaches his lowest ebb. His father condemns his efforts at fashion as being 'about as trendy as a Russian motor car'. Likewise, Harold's old-fashioned courtesy means he's pained and distressed when the photographer urges the girls to 'think of Oliver Reed' to make their poses sexier. Humiliated, jeered at by his father, shunned by the models and mocked by the amazed fashion people, Harold the dreamer is shown up as an embarrassing loser.

The old Harold is hinted at, though. Early in the episode, Corbett clearly rel-ishes a mock ITN-newsreader interlude, shuffling his mound of newspapers with diligent energy. The battle over politics still rages, but has less satirical bite, as Harold bemoans the state of the country and the promise of revolu-tion: 'Two years ... that's what I give it, two years'. The reflection on the repeat of 'two years' is the high point of Corbett's performance, and he milks the moment for all it's worth. The old man's characteristic rant about the state of the nation – 'crimewaves ... long hair ... drugs ... strikes' – is merely a list of complaints and does not really address the issues as an earlier episode might have. Albert's determined explanation that when you've been through a war 'you can hear a worm start a new hole' is hilarious, but this return to the classic two-hander dialogue is, sadly, not typical.

The conclusion, with the old man dressed up as a 1920s gangster, lording it over the fashion shoot and becoming a star of *Vogue*, is beyond realism, while Corbett's overplayed anger at the fact that he has been shown up again comes across as more pantomime than truly pathetic.

Thankfully, the lacklustre return was short-lived. Although some episodes in this last series were rather less focused and hard-hitting than others, and the plots were occasionally far-fetched and the characterization could drag, the writers and the acting partnership of Brambell and Corbett were back to their usual standard in others. The performances were, undoubtedly, much larger than life for the most part, but the basic clichés of *Steptoe and Son* stem for the most part from this series and, as a result, it remains what the majority of viewers remember as 'classic' *Steptoe*. Indeed, television impressionist Mike Yarwood successfully incorporated *Steptoe* into his act, and Brambell and Corbett were so taken with Yarwood's tribute that they were invited to one of the studio recordings for his show, *Look – Mike Yarwood*. 'We weren't invited!' reflects Ray Galton with mock outrage.

The second new episode, 'And So to Bed', includes elements of the first official *Steptoe and Son*, 'The Bird', as well as 'A Box in Town'. Thus, despite 10 years of increasing permissiveness in British society, and 10 years of almost constant *Steptoe* activity, the episode shows up the fact that, for Harold, life has hardly changed at all. His latest catch is Marcia, a tarty piece whom he met when she dropped the letter 'E' on his head as she changed the name of the film at the local cinema, replacing *Naughty Knickers* and *Lash of Lust* with *Herbie Rides Again*. The two are desperate for a little privacy at Oil Drum Lane, but the combination of the old man's eavesdropping and a bug-infested bed means Harold's lustful intentions come to naught. He is a little concerned that the young lady (played by Lynn Farleigh) is married and that her husband is in prison for GBH, but his urges still get the better of him.

The two main actors are clearly playing by numbers at this stage, but it's still entertaining to watch – Brambell placing his teeth in a glass of water and happily drinking from the same glass, while Corbett overdoes things delightfully with his romantic treatment of the girl, who just wants to get on with it. But there is real feeling in the two-hander conversation the next morning. The old man may mock his son's failed love life, cheerfully observing that 'She was out of here faster than a bishop at a brothel raid', but he sympathizes with Harold's keenness to settle down. Corbett says 'I was entitled to a result last night' with the perfect fusion of regret and frustrated animal instinct.

Harold decides to invest in a new bed for his future encounters, and Angus Mackay, effete and supercilious as the salesman in the furniture shop, immediately assumes that the rag 'n' bone men have come to the wrong place, and informs them that the betting shop is next door. The misunderstanding brings out Harold's pride in his position as an 'antique dealer' with enough money to buy what he wants, and also a steadfastly heterosexual stance. As a foppish Mackay tries to ascertain the best bed to fit the atmosphere of Harold's room, he eventually gets that tiny bit too close to body contact. 'Is the room aggressively masculine?' he asks earnestly. 'Yes, it is,' replies Harold, 'and so am I!' The old man's conclusion as they leave – 'He's a poof!' – for once doesn't attract his son's usual defence of the 'victim' of his preconceptions. Brambell's down-to-earth reaction – 'Where do you put the Edgar Allan?' – to a bed that goes right down to the floor is vintage *Steptoe*, and there's even a touch of parental affection, missing from the previous episode, when Harold falls in love with a newfangled waterbed and begs: ''Ere, give it a shove, Dad!' However, the old man unwittingly ruins Harold's big night of passion with Marcia when he tries to cut the wire for a new plug to heat the water and plunges his knife into the mattress, splitting it. The passionate couple are left dripping wet. Brambell's manic, 'Oh, cobblers', is great comedy and proof, if it were needed, that *Steptoe*, after a shaky start, was back on form.

The third episode, 'Porn Yesterday', is the gem of the Steptoes' final hurrah. The show features the discovery of an old What the Butler Saw machine which contains Albert's guilty secret from the 1920s, namely his vintage career in near-the-knuckle flip movies. The writing flows naturally, and the fraught relationship between the two men bristles with renewed life.

Harold is disgruntled as the old man's life of luxury – beer, book and ice cream – is contrasted with his own meagre refreshments of 'a corned beef sandwich and a drink from the horse's bucket'. His casual, deflated line on his early return home – 'Because I'm knackered, and it's hot today!' – is beautifully delivered by Corbett, whose vocal inflection sounds totally in tune with the character's frustrated, flattened feeling.

Continuity is well served by the welcome reappearance of Anthony Sharp's vicar. The role was created for the series seven opener, 'Men of Letters', and Sharp is excellent throughout 'Porn Yesterday', caustically clearing his throat as his less-than-sheltered wife revels in memories of their days as missionaries.

The appearance of these local dignitaries presents ample opportunity for embarrassment, as the old man appears in nothing but a tiny towel and Harold tries painfully hard for an air of sophisticated grandeur, offering a glass of sherry and assuring them that 'It's very good; it's the one Orson Welles drinks.' The What the Butler Saw machine attracts the eye of the vicar, who's on the scrounge for items for his charity fête. His appreciation of this vintage type of innocent smut is well rounded and, eventually, quite fruity. Harold, meanwhile, decries the material as disgusting porn and desperately tries to keep a film drum featuring Albert out of the vicar's hands. The narrative comes to a farcical and, rare in this particular series of *Steptoe*, totally believable conclusion.

The performances of Corbett and, in particular, Brambell make this episode a joy. Brambell's 'dirty old man' persona is skilfully used from the outset, his eagerness mounting as Harold reveals and sets up the old What the Butler Saw attraction. His lustful memories of the films he once enjoyed are balanced by frustration with the corrupt modern world. Instructed by Harold that the machine takes only old pennies he mutters, 'Oh, Gawd', and condemns the decimalization of sterling, as most of the country had recently been doing. Harold, searching for an old penny and finding one featuring Edward VII, takes pleasure in the wistful thought that the monarch probably knew the model in the attraction and smiles as he pushes the coin in the slot: 'Well, go on, have another look at her!' Corbett plays this with a masterly lightness of touch.

Hogging the machine while mocking its contents, Harold enjoys his father's ever-mounting frustration as the old man tries to get a look-in. But a major change in Albert occurs when Harold gets to the third and final film, unhappily moaning that it's from the wrong period – a 1920s effort with a lady in a bath. Gone is Albert's earlier rampant fervour, and we see in its place a downtrodden, battle-scarred veteran of the poverty of 1920s Britain. The transition is quite extraordinary, with extra weight given to the already emotional script as the old man remembers the need and want of the age. His attitude to smut also changes as he listlessly condemns the whole thing as 'disgusting', remarks that the so-called producers were 'exploiting innocent people' and reflects, all too clearly close to home, on the lengths to which the poor would go in order to be famous, rich and able to provide for their families: 'Everything we had was in pawn!' The audience almost cheer with relief when Harold comes back with the inevitable: 'So were you!'

Previously in the episode, before the penny has dropped, Harold has observed that the trouserless milkman hero of the film looks like Albert. It *is*

Albert, of course, and 'You dirty old man' was never said with such reso-nance. It's a prelude to Harold's truly disgusted explosion at the fact that his father is 'a male Linda Lovelace' (the star of the current box-office-breaking pornographic fest, *Deep Throat*). Albert's matter-of-fact observation that Marlon Brando (*Last Tango in Paris*) and Oliver Reed (*Women in Love*), have both 'shown their bums' also gives the programme a cinematic knowledge typical of Galton and Simpson.

The truth, as so often happens, is revealed to Harold far too quickly as Albert's distant memories of making the film flood back – the police raiding the studio and impounding the film, and the fact that Harold's mother knew about it, 'Course she did: that was her sister in the bath!'. He adds that the sister 'died of pneumonia two weeks later'.

Harold's selfishness is brought to the fore as, disgusted by Albert's past, he doesn't seem interested in the family troubles that forced his father into the film. He is only concerned about what people, important people, will make of the revelations – he could be blackballed at the golf club. He takes to his favourite chair and mopes: 'Once again you've ruined my chances to better myself!' The scene reaches its climax when Harold, treating the old man like a dog in front of its own mess, forces him to watch the disgusting film in the machine. Silenced and tearful, the old man turns away, but his tears are not of shame but of regret for bygone times, pleasant memories, his own youth: 'It's funny seeing what you looked like all those years ago.' Harold's appreci-ation of the fact that everybody gets old – 'It'll happen to me one day' – is touching. Albert's regret turns to excitement as Harold reveals that the flip film has a cast list, 'Milkman – Albert Steptoe', but his happiness is crushed by Harold's refusal to let him keep one of the images as a souvenir. Harold is adamant that they must all be destroyed, but tries to make his father real-ize that this is for the best. In a moment that never seems false, cloying or hypocritical, he actually plants a gentle kiss on the old man's forehead. It is without doubt the most touching moment between the two.

Thankfully, the plot returns to the all-important machine and the elevation of Albert to temporary film-star status. The machine is in place at the fête and with a newly discovered film, *A Night in a Turkish Harem*, is doing great busi-ness. Harold goes berserk, the film gets broken and the crowd rush to grab a photograph and an autograph from the old man. Before the rush there's a beautiful moment as Albert happily snatches a picture for himself and pock-ets it. The vicar shows his commercial instincts and bellows, 'Autographs one shilling each', before looking at one of the pictures, registering amazement and distress, and bellowing, 'Autographs two shillings each!'

Although the fourth episode, 'The Seven Steptoerai', is an example of the series at its most self-indulgent, the emotional heart of *Steptoe* is retained within this action-packed tribute to Bruce Lee. Akira Kurosawa's 1954 masterpiece, *The Seven Samurai*, formed the basis for the plot. The funniest moment is the brief dialogue between Harold and Albert as the son desperately tries to remember the name of the film. The father makes unhelpful suggestions, citing the plot of the James Mason film, *The Seventh Veil* – 'Francesca, you'll never play the joanna again!' – and coming up with 'the seven ...', '... year itch' and '... dwarfs! ...' before Harold finally gets it.

In this episode the threat to the Steptoes' health and their business comes in the form of a resurrection of an old favourite from the past. The villain is none other than diminutive Frankie Barrow, as played by Henry Woolf, a character seen before only in the film *Steptoe and Son Ride Again*. Galton and Simpson's continual merging of film and television plot lines is a delight, and unique in situation comedy: 'We liked the idea of bridging the film with the new series. Different medium but same situation, it sort of dragged the films into the "canon" of the television series.' Clearly, judging by the narrative, Frankie has been in prison since the big-screen adventure, but Harold's ominous 'welcome' to the tinpot gangster relies totally on viewers' knowledge of their previous business arrangements. As in the film, Woolf's performance combines real menace with gentle touches. His protection racket, masquerading as an insurance firm, cleans out the Steptoes and looks set to ruin their lives.

The violence and the heartbreaking destruction of the Steptoes' property fill the episode with a grim sense of despair and suppressed anger. And, as in the previous episode, there is a moment of love between father and son. With Harold having been beaten up for asking too many questions, Albert spontaneously kisses his son's injured arm better, and the two hold hands and reluctantly walk to the table to sign Frankie's insurance agreement. There is never an instant when this scene seems out of place or syrupy. Corbett and Brambell play it absolutely straight, and the result is serious and convincing.

Although Brambell enjoys himself hugely with his kung fu movements at the start, the collapse into slow-motion kung fu as the old-age pensioners – the Steptoes' own samurai, rounded up by Albert – finish off the Barrow boys drags at times, and takes the series to new levels of incredibility. But there's a lovely scene of the ancient revellers celebrating victory at the close.

'Upstairs, Downstairs, Upstairs, Downstairs' is in many ways the definitive *Steptoe* episode. It contains all the clichés that everybody, from Mike Yarwood to Alistair McGowan, have plundered for larger-than-life impersonations.

The plot is simplicity itself. Albert is suffering from a back injury, so the doctor orders complete rest and Harold must do everything around the house, with the old man showing his vindictive, aggressive and self-pitying streaks by turns. The exaggerated acting of Corbett and Brambell – in stark contrast to vintage episodes – adds a new dash of vigour and comic expression to the basic two-hander narrative.

Alan Simpson recalls: 'In a funny sort of way, although we returned to that old, familiar two-hander style for the episode, the 12 years had taken us full circle and almost back to a time before *Steptoe* had broken down all the barriers it did break down.' Ray Galton continues: 'It was Tom Sloan who had been instrumental in us getting away with more realistic language. But I remember on 'Upstairs, Downstairs, Upstairs, Downstairs', Duncan Wood – the then Head of Light Entertainment for BBC Television – was up in arms at one scene. The old man is confined to bed and wants to go to the lavatory. Harold asks him, "What is it, a number one or number two?", and Duncan refused to allow it. I mean, every kid in the world has been asked that by his mother. It was madness!'

The orgy of clichés begins as Harold literally counts down to the old man's screamed 'Harold ...'. Brambell, bellowing his son's name throughout the episode, had never relied so heavily on this annoying, obvious trick, but from this moment on anybody could simply scream 'Harold!' and the old man's character would unmistakably be evoked.

Typically, Harold's reaction to his impending slavery is bleak, bleak humour, as he tries to convince his father firstly, that he, Albert, is dying, and then, that he himself is going to leave him to his illness for a holiday in Cornwall. Corbett's freewheeling, carnivalesque performance during the Cornwall play-acting ('Your son Harold has been took by a man-eating pilchard') is made all the more powerful and funny in the light of his immediate change of pace for the following scene. In a flash he is a dutiful, loving son, breezily but reassuringly running through the advice the doctor has left, comforting his father, rearranging his pillow and, with a loving smile, simply saying: 'We'll manage. We always do'. It's a wonderful, heartbreaking performance, and an outstanding *Steptoe* moment, comically contrasted as it is with Brambell's immediate breaking of his promise not to be 'a burden'.

Of course, Harold is run ragged by the demands his father makes on him, but the really important moment features the old man talking to a friend on the telephone. All the mod cons, including the TV, have been moved to his bedside but despite an early burst of affection and 'You're a good boy, Harold', the effect of this gesture soon wears off. By the time of the phone

call Albert is condemning Harold with 'Oh, he's useless!', and is undervalu-
ing his son's help, unable to admit the true extent of his reliance on Harold.
Brambell's understanding of what makes Albert tick had clearly reached a
pinnacle. The chemistry between the two principals was also still working
well. The revelation that the old man is hiding the fact that his back has finally healed allows Corbett a knowing burst of 'What Kind of Fool Am I?' Harold
creeps around the house, mimes a well-placed kick up the backside and
watches from his hiding place in the kitchen cupboard as Albert creeps downstairs, fumbles, drops a sweet he is pinching from Harold and bends down
to pick it up. The by-play with the sweets is continued during the closing credits, after the son has given his father a blanket bath with surgical spirit as
Corbett idly throws the confectionery towards Brambell's mouth. Brambell
reacts immediately, grudgingly trying to catch the sweets as he bathes his
unmentionables, burnt with the surgical spirit, in the kitchen sink.

The very last programme of the regular series, 'Seance in a Wet Rag and
Bone Yard', boasts a subtle, hilarious and poignant script, returning as it
does to the subjects of spooks, suspense and scary images. The programme,
first transmitted on 10 October 1974, provides Corbett with a wonderful
opportunity to combine his, by now accepted, over-the-top turn with a naive,
childlike fear of the unknown and a deep, character-shaping longing to talk to
his late mother. Beginning the episode with smouldering socks, burnt by rest-
ing his feet on the electric fire, Harold is showing off his enjoyment of his
classical music collection, even though it has obviously sent him to sleep. He
cheerfully shouts, 'That's it, Mahler, baby!', as the music touches his cultur-
ally aspirational soul and releases an inept torrent of praise. He is clearly in
a musical mood – there's a George Formby impersonation to come, with
Corbett using the spinning head of the ever-present skeleton to emphasize
his performance on the air-ukulele.

The old man, out after midnight in the rain, returns miserable, wet and frustrated. He complains about the rubbish his son listens to and the fact that
it's prevented him hearing his knock on the door. An earlier episode from the
series is touched on, greeted with a warm response by the audience, as
Harold notes: 'It ain't your kung fu night!' The source material, the 1962
Richard Attenborough film *Seance on a Wet Afternoon*, is brought into play
with Albert's reluctant revelation that he's been to a spiritualist meeting.
Revelling in his contact with the dead, Albert reveals: 'I spoke to Dan Leno
tonight and Henry VIII.' The opportunity for one of Harold's comic flights of
fancy is too great to miss, and he imagines that the musical-hall legend and
the much-married monarch have teamed up as a double act: 'Who was that

lady I saw you with last night?' 'That was no lady, that was my fourth wife!' He skilfully uses *Henry Hall's Guest Night* as the basis for Henry VIII's gala mix of comedy and song, but behind the mockery and trickery Harold is painfully aware of the con artists who use old people's gullibility for financial gain. To him a medium's just 'some old bird doing a Mike Yarwood', but the old man is convinced. He's even spoken to Gandhi, who has assured him that Harold will be all right. Harold is affronted. Not only has he never met the humanitarian but: 'I *am* all right. I don't need Gandhi to tell me!'

Harold is sick of this celebrity farce, commenting that the seance resembles the green room of the *Parkinson* show. He questions why famous figures should want to talk to the likes of his father, but the old man isn't put off, reflecting: 'Why does anyone want to talk to Parkinson?' Albert is totally convinced and, as it happens, he's also in love with an old lady who visits the spiritualist. Harold's attitude shifts, revealing quite touching thoughts on mortality: 'Every tombstone, "rest in peace" – why can't they leave 'em alone?' Still, he's not so philosophical that he can't ridicule and ruin the old man's makeshift Ouija board exercise. While Harold pushes the glass, suggests that it is Hitler that he and his father have contacted and offers 'Ask him who won the war' as an opening gambit, Brambell's steadfast performance shows Albert's true conviction. His shocked, 'It's Hitler!' is masterfully delivered, while his fear of the spirit world is displayed in his soft, underplayed reply, 'It might upset him', to Harold's frivolous question.

The showdown comes when the seance party turns up at Oil Drum Lane. Gilly Flower is part of the old-time spirit-hunting team, but a wonderful star turn by Patricia Routledge as the medium, Madame Fontana, steals this particular scene with a flourish of sentimentality and flamboyantly overdone spirit voices. 'She was a very famous revue lady before she became famous on television,' recalls Alan Simpson. 'She was a West End rival to Maggie Smith at one stage. We caught her before the public knew her widely, but she was a catch for our show and perfect for all those impressions and play-acting.'

Harold remains his sceptical self, both with regards to supernatural pursuits and to the proposed marriage of his father to Dorothy Duddy, played with gusto by Gwen Nelson. His comic asides are peppered throughout the serious business. When Routledge contacts Mrs Duddy's late husband, the widow is immediately convinced by the familiar banter Routledge employs: 'He always called me Dotty!' 'He wasn't a bad judge!' notes Harold with relish.

But Corbett's performance touches true greatness when the jokes are curtailed and Routledge starts singing sweet and simple refrains as Harold's long-dead mother. His reaction is complete denial. Corbett's stony-faced expression hints at Harold's inner turmoil. He doesn't want to play along with the charade, and he is angry that this phoney medium is using his mother's name and personality for her own ends. But deep inside he longs to believe that the experience is real and that he can finally talk to his mother properly. His manner doesn't change for the rest of the episode, even as Routledge goes into a wonderful mishmash of characterizations, rounding off with a rousing rendition of 'I'm Henry VIII I Am'. Brambell's almost climactic line, 'It's stopped raining', signals, as it does in Richard Attenborough's film, the end of the mysterious goings-on. Still Corbett retains his impression of bemused indignation. On his own and quietly looking at his mother's portrait, he mutters 'It would have been nice to have a chat with you, Mum' with such wistfulness that the ghostly 'Goodnight, Harold' from his mother's spirit is funny while achingly poignant. As he does in the Steptoes' other ghostly brush with the unknown in 'The Wooden Overcoats', Harold reverts to terrified child, screaming, 'Dad, can I sleep in your bed, Dad?', as he exits stage right.

'It was our only foray into the supernatural, other than taking the mickey out of it,' remembers Ray Galton, 'and that bit right at the end was us trying to suggest that there may well be life after death after all. But did she really speak to Harry or is she in his imagination? I think we cheated a bit. We were trying to get the best of both worlds.'

Chapter 15

The Last Hurrah!

Despite the effectiveness of the majority of the series eight episodes, Audience Research Reports noted that many viewers 'found the series increasingly disappointing nowadays' – hardly surprising in light of the fact that 'Back in Fashion' was the episode that was reviewed as 'indicative' of the entire series, which it patently was not. However, although the reaction may have hastened the demise of the series, early plans had been made to leave this run, at least, with a seasonal bang. In a letter of 30 August 1974 James Gilbert advised Douglas Argent and John Moore that: 'Originally we commissioned a series of seven shows of 30 minutes each. What I would now like to do is keep a series of six and turn the seventh commissioned script into the Christmas special, extending it by 15 minutes.' Galton and Simpson simply adapted the already planned final episode and delivered the result at the start of October. Rehearsals for the special were held from 16 October at the Latimer Mission, and the finished programme was first transmitted on Boxing Day 1974. It was the last television episode of *Steptoe and Son*. Suitably, it was a special in every sense of the word.

In essence, the programme takes off from where the 1973 Christmas episode finished, with Harold returning home to find the old man happily decorating the house with tatty Christmas streamers. His rapturous 'Veritable fairyland!' reaction pleases Albert before his face drops and he mutters: 'Are you taking the Arthur Bliss?' Despite his clear distaste for a festive season spent at home, Harold makes some effort to join the seasonal mood. He warbles extracts from Disney favourites *Pinocchio* ('When You Wish Upon a Star') and *Snow White and the Seven Dwarfs* ('Heigh-Ho'), before Albert's anger erupts. With a furious, 'Oh, sod yer then', the old man grabs a stick and pulls the feeble decorations to bits. The moment is both aggressive and poignant, with everything from the Christmas tree fairy to the skeleton in its party hat emphasizing the destruction of Albert's humble but loving efforts. His distress at Harold's uninterest is played out in furious overreaction, but his 'That's me finished; that's my Christmas over' promises four days of boredom and rowing.

Harold blames the television programmes that are aired every festive season for stuffing Christmas 'down yer cakehole'. He lists the expected 'treats' in store, from 'Z Cars with holly stuck in their helmets' through to a special *Coronation Street* with 'a party at the Rovers Return'. The old man's misty-eyed appreciation of 'all those stars giving up their Christmases to entertain' the nation lets Harold deliver the bemused revelation: 'All those Christmas shows are recorded in October.' As was this one!

Within the programme, *Steptoe* clichés and conventions are resurrected one final time. Once and for all, Harold is planning a holiday abroad. Although he is happy to allow his father to join him, he is adamantly not going to Bognor. Knowing the rules of the game backwards by now, he comments 'You can have as many heart attacks as you like' as he considers his destination and heaves the weighty 'swear box' – a dog-shaped charity collection box – over to his father. Charging Albert for a couple of exclamations of 'bleeding', Harold pats the dog's head and mutters 'Thank you ... ruff, ruff ... thank you' as the old man reluctantly drops in his coins. Corbett dives into a huge mound of travel brochures and indulges himself with a Groucho Marx moment as he points out: 'You can have your turkey in the Canaries or your canary in the Turkeys ...' Rejecting Britain because of its half past ten closing time for everything, Harold delights in the thought of going to Acapulco ('That's where Frank Sinatra goes'), or big-game hunting in Kenya; Albert jokes that he could 'do that up in my bed'. With a cheery laugh and an affectionate poke at his son, Brambell clearly relishes the moment. But the old man is still dismissing foreign travel. France is 'horrible! ... full of holes and mud', while Holland is hardly conducive to skiing, being 'as flat as a witch's tit'. Even Denmark, with its live sex shows, can't tempt the 'dirty old man' ('not over Christmas'). Albert's joyful realization that he's being fooled is one of the most heart-warming moments in the programme. But the warmth is extremely short-lived. When his father longs for somewhere 'clean and respectable', Harold suggests: 'How about four days in a launderette in Cheltenham?'

They finally settle on Switzerland, but this raises another problem. Albert has lost his passport and he claims that he doesn't know where his birth certificate, which he needs to get a new one, is. Finally, he reluctantly remembers that it is in the cupboard under the stairs. This holds bleak memories for Harold, memories of air raids and darkness. As the old man protests about entering it, squeaking, 'It's dark, Harold', you can feel the hairs on the back of Harold's neck rise with 'Yeah, it was during the war as well'. In the cupboard there are secrets – leftovers of Christmases past in the shape of several Quality Street tins – and, for Harold, memories of his happier childhood ('Ooh, my number nine bus!').

The scene captures perfectly a close family forced to investigate and re-examine its collective past, and Brambell and Corbett shine as the son dons his old school cap and beams with innocence and affection. Brambell, bursting with pride, is speechless as Harold displays a childlike desire to be loved and respected. The motto, translated from the Latin – 'Know Thy Place and Be Grateful' – sums up the ethos of Harold Steptoe, and Harold knows it. For a moment he does know his place. And he knows he will never fully get out of it. But then the socially aware rebel within him sends up the whole concept, as he mutters 'What a con trick' and plonks his school cap on the head of the swear box.

But the major peaks are reserved for the climax. The truth about Albert's birth certificate is revealed. He doesn't want to find it because it specifies his father as 'unknown'. Harold is tickled pink, while Albert is wounded. His tearful breaking down on the line 'You've got a father' is perhaps Brambell's acting pinnacle in the final series. But the humour surfaces again with the revelation that the framed photograph of Harold's 'grandfather' is, in fact, Gladstone. When Harold indulges himself with a fantasy of aristocratic blood, his father dampens his aspirations by remembering that his mother was very upset 'when the muffin man died'. But with this one vital piece of information out in the open, Albert's misery seems to be lifted. His pleasure in the truth being known is tangible. The wish that maybe the two might get to 'know each other better' signals a possible new beginning for the pair.

However, with the belated discovery that Harold's passport is out of date, Albert makes the seasonal journey abroad alone. Director Douglas Argent heightens the emotional tension as Harold is left on the station platform at Victoria trying to put a brave face on the situation. But the sting in the tail is, at long last, in the son's favour. The old man has fallen for a scam, and Harold's depressed wander away from camera turns into a joyful skip as he jumps into a sports car next to a flashy blonde, plants a kiss and cheerfully bellows: 'Bognor, here we come!'

For Galton and Simpson, the few days of freedom was the most upbeat way in which Harold could depart the scene. 'When we had written the series that was to become the last one, we didn't realize it was going to be the last one!' explains Alan Simpson. 'There was always a chance that the BBC might want some more. But, to be honest, the atmosphere during the making of the eighth series, although not tension-packed, was different. You could tell that Harry and Willie were getting a bit fed up with it. We would see Harry a lot, both during the production of a series and not. He would come for lunch and, although he never slagged the old man off, the irritation was clear in his voice. During the making of the eighth series Harry had made it clear that he didn't want to do any more. He just couldn't go on.'

'It wasn't as bad as grumpy old men,' jokes Ray Galton, 'but something was turning sour. Don't forget, they had worked together a lot and over a long period of time. They were also firmly paired in the public's eye. That's quite a strain for anybody. Besides, they lasted a lot longer than most marriages these days! Apart from the Harry and Willie situation, we had also got to the stage where we couldn't think of any more plot lines. Our cup of ideas had been drained. More to the point, that sheet of half-ideas had been used up. We had written nearly 60 half-hours, the films ... life was too short to drag it down to arguments and half-hearted plot ideas.'

On the evening of the last studio recording, cast and crew were treated to a slap-up party by the stars of the show. On the invitation were the words: 'Jazz band, buffet & booze: Wilfrid and Harry would like to invite you to their party after the show on Sunday 27 October.' Held at the Lucifer Room of the Western Hotel, the invitation told guests to 'feel free to bring one of the following: 1) husband 2) wife 3) girlfriend 4) boyfriend 5) mistress 6) carthorse'. This was the wrap-up party for *Steptoe and Son*. The series would never reappear. Instead, it would pass into the status of a classic, enjoying a cult following and frequent repeats.

But for the actors who had created the roles life from then on would always be qualified by the label 'ex-*Steptoe* actor'. Almost immediately after finishing the last television episode, Brambell and Corbett went into rehearsals for an all-star pantomime, *Cinderella*, playing the broker's men, Badger and Ben, alongside Twiggy, Nicky Henson, Roy Kinnear and Hugh Paddick. The production opened at the Casino Theatre, London, on Wednesday 18 December 1974. During this run, Brambell and Corbett recorded a guest appearance for the Radio Two soap opera *Waggoners Walk*. The programme, broadcast on 21 January 1975, featured the actors backstage at the theatre.

Brambell seemed to wear the *Steptoe* label with more acceptance than Corbett. Even as early as 1970, with colour *Steptoe* about to be launched,

Corbett was irritable about the notion of typecasting and was defensive when the subject cropped up, as it increasingly did: 'You've been reading too many show business interviews,' he would reply. 'I haven't found it troubled me.' But it had and it would.

Brambell seemed to relish the memories of his best-loved part. Writing fondly in 1976, he commented:

> There must be an enormous number of cranky, selfish but nonetheless much-loved grandfathers in existence. This is my only explanation for the fact that I am so constantly approached by babes who seem to like me – or Albert Steptoe. Four little fans recently surrounded me outside my own hall door and requested 'Mr Brambell' to do Steptoe for them. I declined and explained to them that I got paid for doing it. They formed a rugby scrum and when it broke had made a collection. The 'mouthpiece' then pressed four old pennies into my hand and said: 'Well, do it now then!' I accepted my fee and to the amazement of passers-by gave my requested performance.

Chapter 16

Atlantic Discontent

Steptoe on BBC Television may have come to an end, but across the Atlantic the American fraternity of *Sanford and Son* was still riding the crest of a wave. Whitman Mayo, who played Grady, even got his own short-lived, eponymous spin-off series. Back in England, the final radio adaptations were recorded over the November and December of 1975 and recruited Wilfrid Brambell and Harry H. Corbett for a sixth series round-up of the 'best of the rest' of the remaining television episodes. Quite understandably, most of these were selected from the choicest episodes of series seven and eight, with the programmes being broadcast from 8 February 1976. The series was kick-started with 'Loathe Story'. Raymond Huntley proved unavailable, so the breast-obsessed, focal character of the psychiatrist was recast and offered to Graham Stark, the comedy actor and sometime director who had predicted 'The Offer' would start something big just over 14 years earlier. Other guest stars gladly returned to re-create their television roles for radio, with George A. Cooper back as Uncle Arthur in 'Oh, What a Beautiful Mourning' and Anthony Sharp making a welcome reappearance as the good-natured vicar in 'Porn Yesterday'. For the final show of the series, broadcast on 28 March 1976, Patricia Routledge upped the radio supporting-role ante once more, with her flamboyant return to Madam Fontana in 'Seance in a Wet Rag and Bone Yard'.

As before, the radio versions were almost exactly the same as the television programmes, with one notable exception. Clearly dissatisfied with the conclusion of the series eight show 'And So to Bed', the scriptwriters got the old man to split the waterbed not with a knife but by burning a hole in it. A newly scripted telephone conversation with an old woman trying to sell the firm six empty jam jars removes Albert from the scene and signals the disaster with a much more powerful, and feasible, soldering iron. As if to add further clout to this improvement to the logic of the plot, the name of Harold's girl-friend was changed from Marcia to Merrissa. Michael Burlington's interpre-tation of the bed salesman was also far more camp than Angus Mackay's television original.

Perhaps most interesting of all was the radio version of the kung fu classic 'The Seven Steptoerai'. That it was attempted at all was amazing, as it was a very visually orientated episode. At least three of the television originals not adapted for the radio series were left out purely because of their reliance on visual humour: 'Those Magnificent Men and Their Heating Machines', the snooker-heavy action of 'Pot Black' and the 1972 classic 'Divided We Stand'. The series eight opener, 'Back in Fashion', and the 1973 Christmas special also failed to make the transition. 'The Seven Steptoerai', thankfully, wel-comed back actor Henry Woolf, the originator of the Shepherd's Bush Godfather, while his two dunderheaded heavies were played for their first and only time together in the series – by Alan Simpson and Ray Galton. 'Alan would be in them occasionally,' recalls Galton.

'Only,' continues Simpson, 'when the producer couldn't afford a real actor!' Ray Galton says: 'For "The Seven Steptoerai" I was cast as well. We both loved Henry Woolf's performance, and it was fun to ham our way through!'

There was certainly something like sixth sense in the air in 1976, for not only were the writers recruited into the cast for the penultimate episode of the last radio series, but after many years of performances on stage, film and, most famously of course, television, Harry H. Corbett was awarded the Order of the British Empire in 1976. That same year, Wilfrid Brambell gave his prolific acting career a sense of closure by publishing his autobiography, *All Above Board*.

The *Steptoe* legacy at the BBC was coming to a rapid close. On 30 November 1976 Brambell and Corbett were recalled to the recording theatre for one final assignment, a one-off Christmas special, for radio. Fittingly, it was an adaptation of the last television episode, the 1974 Christmas special, which would release Harold for a few days of freedom from his father. The show was first transmitted on Christmas Day 1976 as part of a two-and-a-half-hour comic celebration, *David Jacobs' Crackers*, on Radio 4. A nation bade a fond farewell to the world's best-loved rag 'n' bone men. But that was far, far from the end of the story.

Whatever form or name they may have adopted, the essence of *Steptoe and Son* was still delighting television audiences in America. By 1976, with several of the familiar supporting cast departed from *Sanford and Son*, a clutch of new faces was drafted in to add some fresh life and some solid love interest for 'and son'. Marlene Clark played the divorcee Janet Lawson, with a young son, Roger (Edward Crawford) in tow. Raymond Allen was the third new regular cast member to debut in the 1976 episodes, playing Woody Anderson and marrying the regular character Aunt Esther, played by LaWanda Page. The final programme of the series, broadcast on Friday 2 September 1977, ended with the eventual engagement of Lamont Sanford to his beloved Janet. But the marriage, planned for the opening of the next season, never took place. The ratings were still impressive, but Redd Foxx, a stand-up comedian at heart who simply 'acted a bit', had made a firm commitment to a variety series for ABC and informed NBC that he would be unavailable for further *Sanford and Son* episodes. Cracks had already started to form in the working relationship with Demond Wilson in any case. He was mooted to be hastily elevated to solo star status with Foxx's departure.

However, as with the similar situation when Harry H. Corbett was almost left standing with Wilfrid Brambell's potential success on Broadway in 1965, the jettisoning of Sanford senior from the series never came about. Demond Wilson reasoned that, with Foxx gone, he was the major star attraction for the on-going series and started a dispute over an increased fee. NBC were not willing to discuss the issue and decided to abandon the proposal to continue with the series. Instead, Wilson defected to NBC's rival, CBS, and landed another situation-comedy role. He was cast as wife-deserting husband Raymond Ellis in *Baby, I'm Back*. The plot involved the Ellis character, seven years on from his desertion, trying to recapture the old days on hearing of his wife's sudden death. Hardly the stuff of rib-tickling hilarity, the show debuted at the end of January 1978 and by the 12 August of that year had reached the end of its shelf life.

However, NBC were still keen to continue the *Sanford* franchise for as long as possible. To that end they put another spin-off series into motion. Now, with both Foxx and Wilson out of the show, a glut of the best-loved supporting characters were recruited for a follow-up series called *The Sanford Arms*. Woody Anderson (Raymond Allen), Budda Hoover (Don Bexley) and Aunt Esther (LaWanda Page) helped to make the scenery familiar and appealing, and Quincy Jones, who had composed the unforgettable *Sanford and Son* theme, returned to score the new series. The fresh narrative had the old neighbourhood joined by Phil Wheeler (played by Theodore Wilson), a widower looking after two children, Angie and Nat. With the original Sanford and Son having apparently moved out of the area to Arizona, Wheeler had made a down payment on their entire property, encompassing the house, the junk-yard and an all-important boarding house which became the focal point of the series. In charge of the business interest was Esther, who collected the monthly mortage payments and looked after Budda, who was now employed as bellboy and maintenance man for the Sanford Arms hotel. Despite the inventiveness of the notion, the series failed to interest *Sanford and Son*'s many followers. The show debuted on NBC on Friday 16 September 1977, just a fortnight after the last episode of *Sanford and Son* finally aired, but came to a close less than a month later, on 14 October 1977.

And still, American audiences hadn't had enough of the ageing rogue and his ambitious son. Repeats were enjoying constantly impressive ratings and, in a last-ditch attempt to resurrect the glories of the mid-1970s, NBC announced yet another spin-off series. The original 'son' Demond Wilson was still blackballed by the corporation after his bitter rows over increased payments, but the producers thought they had pulled off the ultimate coup when it became clear that Redd Foxx was willing to return to his role of Fred Sanford.

Thus, with the original star back in place, the title was simply shortened to *Sanford* and appeared on screen on NBC on Saturday 15 March 1980. With his son written out of the action – Lamont had, it seems, gone to work on an Alaskan pipeline – Fred Sanford was saddled with two new incompetent work colleagues. A friend of the Lamont Sanford character, Rollo Larson (as played by Nathaniel Taylor) had been a constant fixture in the original *Sanford and Son* episodes. The new character, Cal Pettie (played by Dennis Burkley), was an overweight white Southerner who invested $2000 to stake a claim in the less than extensive 'Sanford Empire'. It was all back to junkyard basics and socially aware comedy, while Fred enjoyed an incongruous relationship with a new girlfriend: a wealthy Beverly Hills widow by the name of Eve Lewis (Marguerite Ray). Much comic mileage was gleaned from the amazed reaction to the relationship from her daughter Cissy (Suzanne Stone), her brother Winston (Percy Rodriguez) and her forthright and mouthy maid, Clara (Cathy Cooper). The introduction of these new, moneyed characters was contrasted with an echo from the past in the shape of Fred's house guest: Cliff Anderson, Aunt Esther's college student offspring, played by Clinton Derricks-Carroll. But, unfortunately for NBC, even with the original star back in harness the old magic couldn't be recaptured. After just three, extremely untypical and extremely short seasons, the final *Sanford* show was broadcast on 10 July 1981. And with it came the rather too long-drawn-out close to the entire *Sanford* franchise.

Its place in American popular culture is, of course, assured, and so desperate were the attempts to spin off a winning series from the original that
the NBC gallery of *Sanford* stars was given the definitive, backhanded compliment when, in May 1997, it was mocked in *The Simpsons Spin-Off
Showcase*. An audience rejoiced when the much-missed Phil Hartman, as
acting legend Troy McClure, introduced the fun with: 'Spin-off – is there any
word more thrilling to the human soul? Hi! I'm Troy McClure! You may
remember me from such TV spin-offs as "Son of *Sanford and Son*" and
"After Mannix". Fantastic.

Neither Wilfrid Brambell nor Harry H. Corbett had quite given up on the
Steptoe trail. For a 1977 Australian cabaret run, the scriptwriters wrote the
actors a special stage presentation that delighted fans of the series. Ray
Galton recalls:

> *Steptoe and Son* was regularly on television over there and the records
> had been released on an Australian label, so *Steptoe* was big news.
> Alan and I wrote a cabaret act for Harry and Willie. We never went to
> rehearsals. We just wrote the script and they rehearsed it out there. It
> was about 50 minutes, a cabaret revue-type piece for the club circuit.
> We wrote a linking storyline explaining why Steptoe and Son were out
> in Australia. There were a couple of sketches, cockney knees-up songs
> ... that sort of thing. It went extremely well. In fact, they went back for
> a second tour in 1978, and maybe a third. They certainly toured
> England with an adapted version shortly afterwards. By this time Harry
> had clearly got over his irritations with Willie, because he was direct-
> ing and organizing the whole thing. I suppose needs must – the cof-
> fers were running short – but he seemed to really enjoy doing it. They
> also featured in a 1978 World Cup radio programme, *Good Luck
> Scotland*, driving up the motorway arguing as usual.

This successful resurrection of the Steptoes in the late 1970s led to their last
television appearance in October 1980. Alan Simpson explains:

> There was never any discussion about bringing them back in another
> series. Maybe Harry would have been up for it by that stage, I don't
> know. But Ray and I certainly wrote an advert for them. I had pretty
> much retired by that stage, and Ray was working with Johnny Speight.
> So it was me, with a bit more time on my hands, who went down when
> Harry and Willie filmed it in Maida Vale. It was for Kenco coffee. The
> company spent their entire budget for the year in order to reunite Ray
> and me and Harry and Willie for just one 60-second commercial. It
> was a typical *Steptoe* scene, drinking this coffee, and the company

would either screen the entire thing or cut it down to 15-second bursts. That way they could get their money's worth, I suppose. I don't know what it did to the sales, but I've still got my free coffee percolator and complimentary packet of coffee to this day!

Brambell's stage career hit a real peak in the 1970s, with the actor relishing the character he was born to play: Scrooge in *A Christmas Carol*, in both the musical and occasionally the dramatic version. His run broke the record set 'by the Royal Shakespeare Company in their own theatre in Stratford-upon-Avon'. Ebenezer Scrooge had long been a role Brambell was desperate to play. With the essence of old man Steptoe intact, he could break out into joyous rapture as Dickens' miserable old miser sees the true beauty of Christmas. 'I only wish that I could take out a patent and play Scrooge every Christmas right through to my bath chair days, because whilst I hate sentimentality, I love sentiment,' Brambell wrote in 1976.

Brambell had also capitalized on his *Steptoe* clout in other stage work, including flamboyant, grotesque fun as one of the ugly sisters in *Cinderella*, the cantankerous old stationmaster in Arnold Ridley's *The Ghost Train*, the cunning judge in Agatha Christie's *Ten Little Niggers* and a 15-week regional tour in 1973 with the murder mystery, *The Killer*, with Geoffrey Davies and Imogen Hassell. On television, he was still much in demand, notably giving a touching performance in the 1978 *All Creatures Great and Small* episode 'A Dog's Life'. And still he basked in situation comedy, memorably cast as a lift attendant in the 1979 episode of John Sullivan's *Citizen Smith*, (prophetically entitled 'Only Fools and Horses'), a guest appearance that was pure Albert Steptoe. Brambell cropped up later that same year in the Christmas Day special of Ted Rogers's quiz game *3-2-1*.

Harry H. Corbett's film career had hit the bottom by the mid-1970s, but he was still managing to give well-rounded and often hilarious performances in some notorious sex comedies of the day. In fact, his contribution added real lustre to the genre, his first dalliance coming with an excellent parody of Prime Minister Harold Wilson in the Leigh Lawson romp *Percy's Progress* in 1974. His dogged detective opposite Christopher Mitchell in *What's Up, Superdoc?* (1978) is a fine comic characterization, and arguably his finest sex comedy turn had come as the energetic eccentric head of the family in *The Adventures of a Private Eye* (1977). At times his roles were reduced to mere cameos, as with the Fiona Richmond biopic *Hardcore*, which featured him in just one scene. Corbett's finest film of the period, however, was something completely different: the wonderfully bleak and bizarre middle-earth world of Terry Gilliam's *Jabberwocky* (1976), with Michael Palin, Max Wall and John Le

Mesurier. Corbett's glorious, eye-rolling, lusty performance as the squire is a *tour de force*. Romping into the action late in the film, his larger-than-life character is a masterpiece.

He continued to accept stage assignments, usually restricted to summer-season comedies and Christmas-season pantomimes, while television credits included such diverse fare as *The Basil Brush Show* broadcast on 26 May 1979, and *Shoestring*: 'Nine Tenths of the Law', on 4 November 1979. Corbett also grabbed the opportunity of working with Eric Sykes in the 1979 television remake of *The Plank*, playing a randy lorry driver in a scene with Charles Hawtrey and 'Loathe Story' guest star Joanna Lumley.

As the American franchise was spinning out of control and into obscurity in the early 1980s, back in England the original Steptoe and Son were trudging through the final years of their careers. It was only a matter of months since the characters had finally been put to rest, on commercial television in the autumn of 1980, and the image of the Steptoes was one of the most indelible of popular icons. 'You dirty old man', in that familiar Harry H. Corbett voice, could still be rolled out by every fifth-rate comic and get a laugh. But Corbett wasn't bitter. He was, after all, still working and still loved by millions.

Situation comedy was perceived as his natural home, and in 1979 he had joined the Roy Clarke-scripted BBC series *Potter*, starring Arthur Lowe. Harry was a semi-regular cast member playing Harry Tooms. Corbett's final sitcom role, as the eponymous newsagent Grundy, first appeared on 14 July 1980. The transmission of the series had been postponed for some six months because a strike at ITV and Corbett's ill health – he had suffered a heart attack at the end of 1979 – meant filming had been delayed. The role of Grundy, written with perception by Ken Hoare, was perfect for Corbett. He was the head of a one-parent family, bemoaning the loosening morals of females and the state of Britain, a situation that pitched him up against a frantically lusty Beryl (played by Lynda Baron) and his teenage daughter Sharon (Julie Dawn Cole). Sadly, the series didn't gel with the public and lasted just one series of six episodes.

Later in 1980 Corbett made his last feature film, the motor-track thriller *Silver Dream Racer* with David Essex. He had also been reunited with Galton and Simpson for the television spectacular *Comedy Tonight* and rounded the year off with a majestic guest star turn in *The Dick Emery Christmas Special*: *For Whom the Death Bells Toll*, on 27 December. Corbett would also appear in a comedy-heavy *Tales of the Unexpected*: 'The Moles' in 1981.

Wilfrid Brambell was still accepting the occasional film and television assignment, joining other veterans like Harry Fowler and Sam Kydd in the

Children's Film Foundation presentation *High Rise Donkey* in 1980.

At the start of 1982, the 20th anniversary of *Steptoe and Son* was marked by the publication of the original half-hour, 'The Offer', in the compendium of British comedy, *No More Curried Eggs for Me*. Ironically, Harry H. Corbett's final television appearance, as a guest on *Give Us a Clue*, was broadcast on 5 January 1982, 20 years to the day since 'The Offer' was first aired. On 21 March 1982 he suffered a second heart attack and died, in Hastings, Sussex, at the age of just 57. After all those wonderfully scripted reflections on the death of his father and his reaction to being alone, the son died first – on the day before Brambell's 70th birthday. Live on *Nationwide* Brambell broke down in tears at the death of his 'son'. In tribute to this most modest and emotive of actors the BBC screened the classic episode 'Divided We Stand'. He had once pondered that 'The only morality I have finished up with, in this business, is the morality of keeping my word'. It serves as a fitting epitaph.

Wilfrid Brambell continued to make brief film appearances, playing old Robert Tucker in the Terence Davies trilogy and, in his last, posthumously released film role, a grumpy, decidedly Albert-Steptoe-style porter in the mythical fantasy *The Sword of Valiant*. He died at his London home on 18 January 1985, finally succumbing to cancer at the age of 72. He had written: 'I have enjoyed every moment of living. My wish to everyone is that each may be as lucky in life as I have been.' Again, his fine, diverse career was all but forgotten as the nation mourned the passing of the 'dirty old man' and reflected on the reunion of two comedy actors who had become almost a married couple in the eyes of the public.

Steptoe and Son, of course, would keep the names and talents of Brambell and Corbett alive. If anything, their deaths within three years of each other elevated the series to cult status and misty-eyed nostalgia. This wasn't just hilarious, poignant and brilliantly observed television; it was a constant reminder of two of the most extraordinary actors ever to walk through the doors of Television Centre.

The development of the BBC's commercial arm, BBC Worldwide, and the huge demand for *Steptoe* episodes opened the floodgates in the late 1980s. Now, happy fans could wallow in Shepherd's Bush hilarity at the flick of a button. The classic colour episodes of *Steptoe and Son*, particularly those from series seven and eight, were being devoured on BBC video. Alan Simpson remembers another big underestimation by the writers: 'Like we were very wrong about *Steptoe* coming back in colour in 1970, we were very wrong about putting the shows out on video. Both of us felt at the time that no one would go out and pay money for a programme they had already seen on television. It just didn't compute with us at all. Why would anybody want to buy a television programme? How wrong could we be?'

Ray Galton was outraged:

> I said at the time, you are repeating these programmes on television again. Who on earth is going to go out and buy the tapes having just, that moment, finished watching the programme on television? It seemed ridiculous to me. But, of course, we were completely wrong. We actually insisted that the tapes go out before the repeats began. Once the repeats began, of course, the sales went through the roof. The BBC clearly knew this fledgling market.

Amazingly, the reputation of *Steptoe and Son* was pretty much restricted to just a handful of episodes. The only surviving programmes in the archives that were considered repeatable were those in colour. This selection amounted to a mere 15 programmes: the entire series seven and series eight, and two episodes from series six. That, plus the Christmas specials and the two films, was all of *Steptoe* that could be repackaged and repeated for many years.

Still, an old audience with memories of the show, and a brand-new audience falling under the spell of *Steptoe and Son* devoured these episodes constantly. A 1988 season gleaned the show its biggest repeat audience-figures ever, with the highest-rated programme, 'Oh, What a Beautiful Mourning', pulling in an amazing 18 million viewers. That same year, Alan Simpson introduced a very, very late repeat for 'Come Dancing' as part of the May 1988 *Comic Relief* evening.

Chapter 17

Junked

As undoubted classics of television the *Steptoe and Son* episodes cited as touchstones of greatness in situation comedy, were not only suitable time-fillers in repeat seasons but also a valuable commodity for the BBC. Sadly, the BBC archives were far from complete.

A memo from Tom Sloan dated 15 November 1962 reads: 'An interesting problem was raised today ... if the one and only series of *Steptoe and Son* should be retained for further repeat purposes. Obviously, since we have repeated it once, it is unlikely that you would wish to do so within the reasonable future, but thinking ahead to the problems of the second channel, etc., I wonder if we would not be wise to transfer some of the cream of our output to film and store it away for possible use in two or three years' time at renegotiated rates?' The very notion that old programmes could one day seriously reach a sell-by date was commonplace right up until the early 1980s. Great swathes of vintage black and white and, indeed, colour shows were systematically piled up as part of a mass junking programme. As Ray Galton notes: 'It was simply a question of storage. The BBC just couldn't justify keeping all these tapes. There just wasn't enough room. And, of course, in those days nobody, and I mean nobody, within the BBC seriously thought there would be a market for old television. In 1964, say, the thought of a series made just two years earlier being really worth keeping was beyond belief. The thought that in 40 years' time that series would still be enjoying repeats and major video and even DVD sales was just not in the equation.' Alan Simpson agrees: 'The BBC would select one or two episodes of a series for preservation in the archive. But it was purely for archival reasons. No one thought there would be any commercial value in these programmes at all.'

TOP: Albert casts a disparaging eye over his son's makeshift ski slope ...
ABOVE: ... as Harold gets in some practice before his holiday in the snow in
'A Winter's Tale' (1970).

TOP: Wilfrid Brambell and Harry H. Corbett relax and share a joke on location in Shepherd's Bush for the 1970 revival of *Steptoe and Son*.

LEFT: Steptoe and Son ... and horse. A promotional shot for the new series of colour episodes in 1970.

ABOVE: The Steptoes try to come to terms with 'A Death in the Family', the first of the colour episodes (1970).

ABOVE: Harold discovers the remains of his prized porcelain collection in 'Robbery with Violence' (1970).

RIGHT: Frank Thornton, *Steptoe*'s most frequent guest star, chalks up his final appearance in the 1973 Christmas Special.

ABOVE: Harry H. Corbett and Wilfrid Brambell pose for contrasting 'Christmas at Home' publicity shots for the 1973 *Steptoe and Son* seasonal special.

ABOVE: A shared moment of comic high jinks during the closing festivities of the 1973 Christmas Special.

TOP: The eighth and final series of *Steptoe and Son* gets underway with a typical junkyard debate in the 1974 episode 'Back in Fashion' ...

ABOVE: ... which closes with Albert posing with gangster's moll, Madeleine Smith.

TOP: Harold is very taken by the luxury waterbed that the salesman (Angus Mackay) promotes in 'And So to Bed' (1974).

ABOVE: Harry H. Corbett and Wilfrid Brambell take direction seriously during a break in recording the final series of *Steptoe and Son* in 1974.

This was at the time of a great surge of interest in snooker, thanks to *Pot Black* and those fetching waistcoats of Ray Reardon. Such was the interest in the sport that the decision was made to wipe the tapes holding some of the BBC's most important programmes of the 1960s and 1970s and to rerecord snooker on the newly available tapes. Ironically, John Spencer and Graham Miles playing snooker in *Pot Black* could conceivably have been recorded over Wilfrid Brambell and Harry H. Corbett playing snooker in 'Pot Black', for the classic series six battle of wits on the green baize was one of the many *Steptoe and Son* casualties. The Beatles on *Juke Box Jury* and the original BBC coverage of the moon landing with specially commissioned music from Pink Floyd, plus some episodes of *Hancock's Half Hour*, *Till Death Us Do Part* and *Dad's Army*, were all, quite extraordinarily, wiped without a second thought. As Alan Simpson wryly observes: 'Today they keep everything – even the weather reports!' Even now, over 100 vintage episodes of William Hartnell's and Patrick Troughton's *Dr Who* are thought to no longer exist. Thankfully, *Steptoe and Son* now enjoys a complete representation – albeit in slightly sub-standard format – within the BBC archive.

The story of how the missing programmes were discovered is a worthy totting exercise indeed.

With strong interest in old programmes gaining momentum in the video age of the late 1980s, the BBC sent out a request to television stations across the world, desperately hoping that tapes lent or copied for foreign stations had survived. Some irreplaceable television, sometimes the only copy in the world, was discovered, including several of the 1960s *Steptoe and Son* episodes.

However, the most amazing gaps in the *Steptoe* vault came from the first two series of colour programmes broadcast in 1970. For whatever reason, these were considered dispensable and junked. The master tapes of 13 of the 15 episodes were thought to have been lost for ever. Only two episodes, the oft-repeated 'Come Dancing' and 'Cuckoo in the Nest', were retained as examples of the series.

Miraculously, Ray Galton held video copies of some of these 'lost' episodes. He recalls:

> In 1970 we recorded them on a then very sophisticated, revolutionary video system, and now a very antiquated, steam-driven format, for our own personal use. In fact, we recorded them because we could never get copies of our stuff from the BBC, and something in the back of our minds thought we'd better make a record of them just in case the BBC lost them ... which was very, very unlikely – or so we thought. But that,

as you know, is exactly what the BBC did. They lost one-and-a-half series. Fortunately, in my basement, gathering dust, were those old tapes recorded all those years before. They were certainly not up to BBC standard because they were not meant for reshowing, they were recorded for our personal archives, to watch on a little portable machine. Mind you, they still stand up, just about, to today's require- ments, and I think we're extremely lucky that we've got them in any for- mat. After I discovered these tapes in the basement we gave them to the British Film Institute people, who could restore them to the best quality possible.

The restoration called on dedicated television historians at the British Film Institute (BFI). Dick Fiddy, the author of *Missing, Believed Wiped* and a long-standing television historian attached to the British Film Institute, acquired the tapes and, most important of all, the machine on which they were record-ed for the National Film Archive. Without the ancient recording equipment the tapes themselves would have been useless. They simply could not have been transferred to a workable format for the archivists to restore the prints.

The tapes had been recorded on a Sony half-inch reel-to-reel format – in essence the very first domestic standard video format – and as a pioneering piece of kit the recorder had its immediate drawbacks. It was designed pri-marily for use by broadcasters within an office environment and the tapes could be played back only in black and white. With the influx of Beta and, more crucially, VHS in Britain's homes from the mid-1970s, this vintage product quickly went out of favour.

Of the missing programmes, Galton's material initially yielded eight precious half-hours from the 1970s. And so began the painstaking work of transferring the programmes from the old reel-to-reel format to a viewable screening copy on contemporary machinery. The National Film Archive's consultant, Brian Jenkinson, laboured long and hard on the programmes. The process involved a time-consuming and often frustrating system of physically coaxing the frag-ile tape through the player in short, workable sections. The quality had suf-fered an expected high level of deterioration and, in tandem with the original, obsolete equipment being used in the loop, the shows were often assembled bit by bit. They were reassembled into complete, viewable programmes much later. Naturally, the final version of the completed 'missing' episodes is of poor quality, but poor-quality black and white prints of missing colour *Steptoe and Son* episodes are far, far more desirable than nothing at all. As Ray Galton says: 'The main thing is that they're there. They hadn't been wiped after all. We are just thankful that we have some record of them.'

The final restoration process was celebrated in 1991 when three of the res-urrected episodes – 'A Winter's Tale', 'Steptoe and Son – and Son!' and 'Pot Black' – were presented at the National Film Theatre. The snooker pro-gramme, a classic episode in itself, was perhaps the worst affected by the grainy black and white copy. Sometimes the quality is so bad you can't see who's potting what, and in a game where the colour of the ball is vital the edge is naturally taken off Harold's humiliating defeat. But, no matter: the comedy sparkled through in spades, and the NFT audience were delighted with the results. Galton and Simpson were interviewed on stage by fellow comedy-writer Laurence Marks and discussed the lengthy effort made to recover these missing treasures. Later, Galton remembered the evening with great fondess: 'There they were, up on the big screen – a format they were, of course, not made for. But I'm pleased to say the audience reacted to them magnificently. They laughed in the right places, made all the right noises afterwards and seemed to thoroughly enjoy them.'

BBC Video was quick to appreciate the importance of the recently recovered programmes and wisely capitalized on the commercial appeal in 1992 by releasing two volumes of the black and white copies. Galton and Simpson were even commissioned by the BBC to record an introductory link for the tapes. Sales were high enough for terrestrial television to make the bold move of rescreening the black and white programmes on BBC2. In an autumn 1993 season called *The Lost Steptoes* the grainy, precious images were repeated for the first time in nearly 25 years, with a credit announcing: 'The BBC wishes to acknowledge the help of the BFI and the Steptoe and Son Appreciation Society in obtaining this archive programme for transmission.' Nobody seemed to worry about the quality of the picture; it was the quality of the actual programme that mattered. One could even forgive the cheeky con-tinuity announcer, gleefully and shamefacedly muttering: 'We didn't actually lose these comedy classics; we just couldn't remember where we put them!'

The original black and white episodes of the 1960s had also started to filter through on to home video, and with the successful repeats of *The Lost Steptoes* these early programmes were, once again, considered suitable enough to rebroadcast. Less high profile certainly, but still gaining respectable audiences, 'The Offer' was justifiably showcased in BBC2's mam-moth *A Day in the Sixties* theme afternoon and evening, while other vintage gems appeared in the schedules all over BBC2. An extensive repeat season from November 1994 to June 1995 kept interest in *Steptoe* high.

By 1995 all but two *Steptoe and Son* episodes – the last one from the 1960s and one from the 1970s – were safely lodged in the vaults. And in that same year the 1960s programme, 'A Box in Town', was recovered. Just a few months later an even more amazing discovery was made. In November 1995 the final missing *Steptoe and Son*, 'Men of Property', was found in the very last place anybody would have thought to look for it: on one of Ray Galton's original videotapes, first presented to the BFI in 1991. Neil Ingoe of the *Steptoe and Son* Society suggested that Brian Jenkinson of the BFI check the Ray Galton videotapes. He scrolled through the tape that was indexed as a copy of 'Men of Letters' and found it was, in fact, 'Men of Property'. Again, it was a colour episode only retained in black and white, but it completed the entire series, although several remnants of the *Steptoe and Son* guest appearances are still missing in action.

Interest in *Steptoe and Son* is still as keen as ever. Under licence from the BBC Lledo issued a Vintage Comedy Classics Collection range of model vehicles in 1993 featuring a *Steptoe* horse and cart complete with waving 'Harold'. *The Totting Times*, the official newsletter of the Steptoe and Son Appreciation Society, is published quarterly, with gossip, interviews, news and reviews for the show's many fans across the world. Indeed, Portugal started to produce its first series of *Steptoe* episodes in autumn 1995, with titles adapted from 'Divided We Stand', 'Full House', 'Seance in a Wet Rag and Bone Yard', 'And So to Bed', 'Upstairs, Downstairs, Upstairs, Downstairs', 'The Desperate Hours', 'Steptoe and Son – and Son!' and 'Two's Company'. The show was called *Camilo Y Filho* but proved a short-lived success, as Alan Simpson remembers:

> The Portuguese version took our scripts and adapted them very faithfully. They produced one series of about 20 programmes but, amazingly, the two actors had a punch-up and fell out. They simply refused to work with each other. It was the biggest programme in the country, but they just wouldn't work together, so that was that! It makes Harry and Willie's mild irritation after 13 years seem small fry really, doesn't it? Our guys were professional through and through.

In Holland, at around the same time, the hugely successful *Stiefbeen En Zoon* was earmarked for a revival. As Ray Galton recalls:

> There was talk about doing the second batch. The original old man had died in the late 1960s and stopped the run, but now, years later, the actor who had played the son now had a son who was also an actor. The idea was for the original son to take over playing the old man and his real son to play his son on the show. It would have been a wonderful idea, but the production company got cold feet and didn't make them. There had been a film and stage version of the Dutch show, though.

In Britain the influence of, and affection for, *Steptoe and Son* continues unabated. The show and its central characters continually feature in the 'Top 10' of that or the 'Best 100' of the other. In a millennium *Radio Times* poll the series was voted Best Sitcom of the 1950s/60s, and the teaming of father and son was named Best Sitcom Double Act. Most reassuringly of all was the 1999 'situations vacant' Internet poll which asked comedy writers to vote for their number-one situation comedy. British writers taking part named *Steptoe and Son* as their number one, while U.S. writers placed their own *Sanford and Son* at number two. Ray Galton was delighted: 'This result is quite fantastic, and I'm choked because it's been voted for by my peers.'

In March 2000 Ray Galton and Alan Simpson proudly picked up OBEs for their services to comedy drama. Just over a year later, on 25 March 2001, Galton, Simpson, long-time admirer Paul Merton and Susannah Corbett, the actress daughter of Harry, attended the unveiling of a special Comic Heritage plaque to Wilfrid Brambell and Harry H. Corbett within BBC Television Centre.

The richest tribute of all came from impressionist Alistair McGowan who, on his *Big Impression* series, skilfully re-created the colourfully cluttered Steptoe living room. His *Steptoe and Son*-structured take on *EastEnders* character Dot Cotton and her wayward son Nick was inspired by the fact that June Brown's caricatured performance in the BBC soap opera was, in McGowan's mind, always just a curled lip and an elongated complaint away from becoming Albert Steptoe. In a combination of the two characterizations McGowan created a mini, recurring masterpiece. But it is his Nick Cotton who with no pretence at all of doing the original, wallows completely in Harold Steptoeisms. It is a quite remarkable feat as he embraces bizarre dream-world interludes, and notably takes a 'puff, puff, puff' on his cigarette at one point. The studio décor is perfect too, with the grizzly bear looking identical to the original. Indeed, this isn't beyond possibility. The original prop has been on display in a Cornish pub, Mr Potter's Museum of Curiosities at the Jamaica Inn, Bolventor. Its label reads: 'A large display on the right features animals that were once part of the stock of Gerrard Hire Ltd of London. They lent specimens to film and TV companies. The grizzly bear was seen every week on TV in *Steptoe and Son* as a prominent feature in their chaotic living room.'

The iconography of *Steptoe* is now part of our language. Talking to the *Radio Times* in 2002 comedian Arthur Smith, commenting that his home was in Balham, said, 'Kensington is Harold Pinter, Balham is Harold Steptoe', while the oft-used phrase, 'It looks like Steptoes' yard in here', has passed through the generations.

Even the incongruity of a remake of *The Likely Lads* with Ant and Dec pro-
voked the ample wit of Radio 2's Terry Wogan to ponder: 'What next? *The
Liver Birds* with Atomic Kitten ... *Steptoe and Son* starring Ainsley Harriott and
Dale Winton?'

The interest in the programme still remains hot internationally, as Ray
Galton reflects:

> We've recently completed a special-length episode of the Hancock
> show, *Fleksnes*, which rounds that show off after 30 years. We've
> brought in the young actor from the old Swedish *Steptoe*, *Albert Och
> Herbert*, to play the long-lost, illegitimate brother of the Hancock char-
> acter who turns up after 25 years. That seems fairly apt to us and com-
> bines the two shows very nicely. Romania film their first series of their
> own version of *Steptoe* in the Autumn and are looking to use their
> series for other language versions for adjacent countries. *Steptoe* has
> been under option in France, Australasia and the Far East, so fingers
> crossed for those. Just recently there has been interest expressed from
> India. John Antrobus and myself have written a *Steptoe* stage play. The
> working title is *Steptoe and Son: The Wasted Years*, and this play is
> under option for a United Kingdom production. It is a speculative fan-
> tasy of what may have happened to Albert and Harold in later life, after
> the television series finished. There has even been talk of a film version
> of *Sanford and Son* starring Richard Pryor and Eddie Murphy.'.

But what of the original and the best? 'Well,' reveals Alan Simpson, 'it has
been suggested that we resurrect the old scripts with other people. But the
original programmes still stand up very well after several repeats, so we both
feel that is enough.' However, to mark the 40th anniversary of the programme at the start of 2002, Galton and Simpson broke a 20-year silence in
their writing partnership by penning a special *Steptoe and Son* sketch for the
fan club magazine, *The Rag 'n' Bone*. As Ray Galton says:

> We were asked to contribute something about the anniversary, and
> rather than just thinking about what we had written and giving our
> memories of the first show, we thought we'd write something new.
> That, for us, was the best way to celebrate the series, with a brand-new
> sketch. We just took the view of what age would they be now. Harry
> was keeping the old man alive on an intensive-care machine that he
> got from a hospital that had closed down, and he himself was now old.
> He was 77, and the old man was 104. We have them arguing, just like
> the start of 'The Offer', and Harold reveals that the house, now in a
> desirable area, is worth two million pounds ... or, at least, the land is.

He's just bundling up the old man to move from the house when the demolition people move in. We killed them off at the end. They get hit by one of those big balls on a chain that comes through the door as the house comes tumbling down. It would have to be done with computerized film if we ever made it. All of it would, in fact!

The sign of a great drama is when the audience are so completely immersed in the story that they totally forget that they are watching actors delivering painstakingly scripted lines from the mind of another. If that's the case, *Steptoe and Son* is as near perfect drama as situation comedy has ever come.

The series continues to impress, inform and inspire. And, for ever modest, Ray Galton and Alan Simpson have one simple closing thought on the programme: 'Let us not lose sight of the fact that the primary purpose of a television comedy series is to entertain. We hope we have been able to do this with *Steptoe and Son*.'

Appendix

The Complete *Steptoe and Son*:
Episode Guide, Films, Videos, Audios, DVDs, Books, Societies

TELEVISION

Comedy Playhouse

The Offer

Recorded 4 January 1962, broadcast 5 January 1962, Friday, 8.45–9.15 p.m., BBC
Television, in black and white

Starring Wilfrid Brambell and Harry H. Corbett

Written by Alan Simpson and Ray Galton

At the Shepherd's Bush rag 'n' bone business of Steptoe and Son, tempers flare as
Albert castigates Harold for his disappointing load of junk. Picking the best items
for himself – a mattress, a plate, a barometer and a mirror – the father continues to
frustrate the 'above his station' aspirations of his son's feeble wine cellar. Moreover,
the old man has consumed some of Harold's precious gin supply. It is the straw
that breaks the camel's back. Revealing that he's been offered a new job, and tor-
mented with his lot in life, the son finally decides to leave the family concern.

Produced by Duncan Wood Designed by Malcolm Goulding Production assistant
Syd Lotterby Secretary Elizabeth Cranston Incidental music Ron Grainer Assistant
floor manager Joan Duncan Floor assistant Ben Rea Costume supervisor Jane
Roberts Make-up supervisor Jean Lord Lighting supervisor Jimmy Richardson
Sound supervisor Len Shorey Grams operator Bert Power Vision mixer Steve Turner

Series One

7 June–12 July 1962, Thursday 8.45–9.15 p.m., BBC Television, in black and white
Starring Harry H. Corbett as Harold and Wilfrid Brambell as Albert
Written by Alan Simpson and Ray Galton

The Offer

A repeat of the *Comedy Playhouse* episode, broadcast 7 June 1962

The Bird

Recorded 16 May 1962, broadcast 14 June 1962
With Valerie Bell as Roxanne

Having finished work for the day, Harold hides a secret from the old man: he's got a date with a bird ... a refined young lady from the local factory. Suited and booted, shaved and wearing a new shirt, he leaves the old man to his evening indoors watching *Perry Mason* on the box. Having lost the battle but not the war, Albert suggests Harold invite the bird round for a fish 'n' chip supper. He pulls out all the stops to make it an evening to remember, but the bird is over an hour late and Harold goes berserk, pondering his fate of a life without women. But the old man has put the clock back an hour!

Produced by Duncan Wood Designed by Roger Andrews Production assistant Syd Lotterby Secretary Elizabeth Cranston Incidental music Ron Grainer Assistant floor manager Joan Duncan Floor assistant Ken Howard Costume supervisor Maureen Copley Make-up supervisor Lilias Munro Lighting supervisor Jimmy Richardson Sound supervisor Norman Greaves Grams operator Mark Howell Vision mixer Steve Turner

The Piano

Recorded 6 June 1962, broadcast 21 June 1962
With Brian Oulton as the Man and Roger Avon as the Policeman

Harold's rag 'n' bone round is interrupted by a posh chap calling him from the top floor of a luxury block of flats. Suspicious of the man's ultra-fussy ways and envious of his attractive, bird-pulling apartment, Harold finally gets round to looking at the object he wants removed – a grand piano. Successfully fleecing the chap of a fiver to take the valuable piece away, Harold departs to fetch his father. With elaborate tales of the trenches of the First World War and a pathetic display of exhaustion, the old man manages to get the chap's sympathy and a sip or two of brandy. Then they spend an entire day trying to squeeze the piano through the doorway. A policeman warns the Steptoes that their horse and cart is parked outside without a light and must be moved. Harold gives up the job as a bad lot, and the totters leave the owner and the policeman struggling to shift the instrument back.

Produced by Duncan Wood Designed by Roger Andrews Production assistant Syd Lotterby Secretary Elizabeth Cranston Incidental music Ron Grainer Assistant floor manager Joan Duncan Floor assistant Ken Howard Costume supervisor Maureen Copley Make-up supervisor Lilias Munro Lighting supervisor Jimmy Richardson Sound supervisor Norman Greaves Grams operator Mark Howell Vision mixer Steve Turner

The Economist

Recorded 30 May 1962, broadcast 28 June 1962

With Frank Thornton as the Man

Harold is at home trying to improve his business sense by reading a book on capitalism while the old man happily sorts through, and irons, a bundle of old clothes picked up on the round. Distressed at the business's financial situation, Harold initially suggests setting fire to the house and contents in order to claim the insurance. But the jokey suggestion turns sour when Albert reveals the insurance is only worth £200. Harold decides to bulk-buy to improve their cash flow. Haggling with a white-coated boffin, he manages to secure 4000 mismatched dentures for £40. Albert is disgusted at the sight and refuses to allow them in the house. Harold places an advert in the *Times*, and practises golf in the yard while he waits for customers. However, interest isn't forthcoming and soon he is offering the whole lot at the knockdown price of £10. Still with no sale, Harold refuses to give in and invests £10 in 400 gas masks, suggesting free teeth with every purchase.

Produced by Duncan Wood Designed by Roger Andrews Production assistant Syd Lotterby Secretary Elizabeth Cranston Incidental music Ron Grainer Assistant floor manager Joan Duncan Floor assistant Ken Howard Costume supervisor Maureen Muggeridge Make-up supervisor Lilias Munro Lighting supervisor Bob Wright Sound supervisor Norman Greaves Grams operator Mark Howell Vision mixer Steve Turner

The Diploma

Recorded 23 May 1962, broadcast 5 July 1962

With Trevor Maskell as the Announcer

While out on his round Harold is engrossed in a book, *How To Be a Television Engineer*. Wet and dejected after an unsuccessful day's totting in the rain, he leaves the business and concentrates on his new career in television repair. But first he must study for his diploma and he desperately tries to block out his father's inane chatter about the shoddy quality of the junk off the cart. Albert struggles to find a pair of spectacles before he realises that he can read Harold's book without them. He condemns the diploma as a rip-off and vows to take over the totting round. After another hard day both Harold's complicated television repair work and Albert's feeble attempt at totting prove worthless, but each try to fool the other that he's been successful. Finally, the old man insists on Harold testing the television he has constructed. The set fails to work but a bit of readjustment by Albert succeeds in getting a picture and he relishes his new hobby. Harold, meanwhile, faces a lifetime on the horse and cart.

Produced by Duncan Wood Designed by Roger Andrews Production assistant Syd Lotterby Secretary Elizabeth Cranston Incidental music Ron Grainer Assistant floor manager Joan Duncan Floor assistant Ken Howard Costume supervisor Maureen Muggeridge Make-up supervisor Lilias Munro Lighting supervisor Jimmy Richardson Sound supervisor Norman Greaves Grams operator Mark Howell Vision mixer Steve Turner

The Holiday

Recorded 13 June 1962, broadcast 12 July 1962

With Colin Gordon as the Doctor Uncredited: Rowena Bragg and Monica Van Zyl as the Girls and Charles Bird as the Rock Seller

Harold's vivid imagination is captured by a tempting poster advertising for foreign holidays, and his dreams of sun and sex convince him to holiday abroad and – for the first time – on his own. The old man, devastated by the news, reflects on the fun to be had together at Mrs Clifton's boarding house in Bognor and finally retires, poorly, to bed. While Harold is finally making up his mind about his foreign destination and practising his pearl-fishing technique, Albert has a seizure and, with a little help from an upturned bedside cabinet, collapses with a thump. The doctor is summoned, and the old man is ordered to have complete rest. But there is a depressing proviso: not only is Harold advised that leaving his father for a fortnight would be a bad idea but his grudging decision to take him to St Tropez is also frowned upon. Harold and the old man end up in Bognor as usual, and Albert seems to have made an amazingly speedy recovery!

Produced by Duncan Wood Designed by Roger Andrews Film cameraman Tony Leggo Film editor Geoff Botterill Production assistant Bob Gilbreath Secretary Elizabeth Cranston Incidental music Ron Grainer Assistant floor manager Joan Duncan Floor assistant Ken Howard Costume supervisor Maureen Muggeridge Make-up supervisor Lilias Munro Lighting supervisor Jimmy Richardson Sound supervisor Norman Greaves Grams operator Mark Howell Vision mixer Steve Turner

Series Two

3 January–14 February 1963, Thursday, 7.55–8.25pm, BBC Television, in black and white

Starring Wilfrid Brambell as Albert and Harry H. Corbett as Harold

Written by Alan Simpson and Ray Galton

Wallah-Wallah Catsmeat

Recorded 20 December 1962, broadcast 3 January 1963

With John Laurie as the Vet, Leslie Dwyer as Lionel Sturgess, George Betton as Charlie and George Tovey as the rag 'n' bone man Uncredited: Herbie Nelson, Stan Simmons, Charles Bird and George Crowther as other rag 'n' bone men

It's the middle of winter, Harold's been offered 25 quid by the catsmeat man for Hercules the horse and all's right with the world. The threat of flogging an undead horse is a joke to distress Albert, but Harold is struck with guilt when he discovers that Hercules is sick and can't work. Impending debts and no money to pay them leads to Harold considering a three-way suicide pact – him, his father and the horse – before salvation is found in the community spirit of the Shepherd's Bush totters. Each rival firm picks up extra rags 'n' bones for the Steptoes to aid them while the horse is unwell. The goodwill gesture is far too tempting for Harold and Albert to relinquish. They pay the friendly totters what they themselves have paid for the scrap and sell it at a profit. While the vet may give the horse the all-clear to return to work, the Steptoes keep quiet, ply him with Scotch and sit back waiting for the business to roll in.

Produced by Duncan Wood Designed by Roger Andrews Production assistant Bob
Gilbreath Secretary Elizabeth Cranston Incidental music Ron Grainer Assistant floor
manager Alison Dalgleish Floor assistant David Hine Costume supervisor Jane
Roberts Make-up supervisor Shirley Rowlands Lighting supervisor Jimmy Richardson
Sound supervisor Norman Greaves Grams operator Buster Cole Vision mixer
Steve Turner

The Bath

Recorded 13 December 1962, broadcast 10 January 1963

With Yootha Joyce as Delia and Marjie Lawrence as Martine

Harold's latest girlfriend is due to come round to the family home for pre-bingo
cocktails, but Albert is relishing a soak in his tin bath in front of the fire in the living
room and enjoying his dinner at the same time. Even worse, he refuses to get out
before he's finished his meal, mislaying several pickled onions in the soapy water
along the way. With Albert hurriedly sent off to bed, Harold's young lady enters the
shabby quarters, chokes on horse liniment-contaminated whisky and collapses into
the bath – which Harold has shoddily concealed with a blanket. Determined to
impress his next girlfriend, and in an attempt to improve his social peace of mind,
Harold buys a proper bath and goes DIY, converting the old man's bedroom into a
bathroom. Relegated to the cupboard under the stairs, Albert complains as Harold
throws himself into his building work. With the job done, Harold returns with
another girlfriend, but the new bath has fallen through the rotting floorboards and
the old man is bathing, again in the living room, much to the distress of the girl
and the anger of Harold.

Produced by Duncan Wood Designed by Roger Andrews Production assistant Bob
Gilbreath Secretary Elizabeth Cranston Incidental music Ron Grainer Assistant floor
manager Joan Duncan Floor assistant David Hine Costume supervisor Jane Roberts
Make-up supervisor Shirley Rowlands Lighting supervisor Jimmy Richardson Sound
supervisor Norman Greaves Grams operator George Cassidy Vision mixer
Steve Turner

The Stepmother

Recorded 3 January 1963, broadcast 17 January 1963

With Joan Newell as Emma Marshall

Albert returns home to the junkyard with a lady admirer in tow while Harold, having
had a hard day on the cart, is patiently waiting for his long-overdue dinner. Amid
the ensuing argument, Harold again threatens to leave home, allowing Albert to
reveal his good news: he's getting married again. Harold, distressed at this mis-
treatment of the memory of his mother, is having none of it, but the old man's
mind is made up. He's retiring to a cottage in Cornwall and giving his son the freedom to get the bachelor flat he's always wanted. At least Harold is treated a bit better, enjoying a steak and kidney pudding for dinner after another hard day's work.
But the dinner has been cooked by Albert's intended second wife. A further argument erupts, and Mrs Marshall, seeing the old man in his true colours, departs,
leaving a reflective Albert and a cheerfully optimistic Harold. Better off on their
own, the two tuck into the meal.

Produced by Duncan Wood Designed by Roger Andrews Production assistant Bob

Gilbreath Secretary Elizabeth Cranston Incidental music Ron Grainer Assistant floor manager Joan Duncan Floor assistant David Hine Costume supervisor Jane Roberts Make-up supervisor Shirley Rowlands Lighting supervisor Jimmy Richardson Sound supervisor Norman Greaves Grams operator Buster Cole Vision mixer Steve Turner

Sixty-Five Today

Recorded 10 January 1963, broadcast 24 January 1963

With Frank Thornton as the Barman, Richard Caldicot as the Man in Restaurant, Michael Bird as the Man in Bar, Anthony Chinn as the Head Waiter, Peter Ching as the Second Waiter, Myo Toon as the Third Waiter and Aman Tokyo as the Wine Waiter Uncredited: William Raynor, Walter Swash, Frank Littlewood and Michael Earl as the Men in Bar, Paddy Kent as the Girl in Bar, Joyce Donaldson as the Old Vic Barmaid, Victor Harrington, Carol Tennent, Dick Downes, Dorothy Nichols, Ian Gray and Evelyn Lewis as the Couples in Bar, John Cabot, David Charlesworth, Brian Goodman, Michael Kayne, Vi Dix, Helga Wallrow, Jeanette Rossini and Lyn Turner as the Theatre Audience, Rose Howlett as the Old Vic Dowager, Charles Gilbert, Brenda Skilton and June Sellars as the Customers with Man in Restaurant and Eamonn O'Callaghan, Richard Cuthbert, Joan Mane, Rita Tate and Maeve Leslie as the other Restaurant Customers

It's Albert's birthday, but Harold pretends to forget it in order to wind him up. Inspecting the new additions to his library of the classics, he finally gives in and gives the old man his present – a pair of pigskin gloves – and his birthday card, which his father treasures. As an extra surprise, Harold has arranged an evening out in the West End. Unfortunately, Albert's ideal night out – a few pints of bitter down the Skinners Arms, a trip to the Windmill Theatre and a plate of egg and chips – is replaced by Harold's sophisticated choice of a cocktail lounge, *Richard III* at the Old Vic and a slap-up Chinese meal. The old man does nothing but complain for the entire evening and, fed up with the humiliation, Harold pays the restaurant bill, leaves his food and stomps off on his own. The old man is left to get the underground back home and, while searching through his pockets for some change, unknowingly drops his gloves and loses them.

Produced by Duncan Wood Designed by Roger Andrews Production assistant Bob Gilbreath Secretary Elizabeth Cranston Incidental music Ron Grainer Assistant floor managers Joan Duncan and John Newman Floor assistant David Hine Costume supervisor Jane Roberts Make-up supervisor Shirley Rowlands Lighting supervisor Jimmy Richardson Sound supervisor Norman Greaves Grams operator Buster Cole Vision mixer Steve Turner

A Musical Evening

Recorded 17 January 1963, broadcast 31 January 1963

Harold is delighted on his return home, for he's picked up some old 78rpm gramophone records which he's keen to add to his classical musical collection. He excitedly plans a musical soirée, but his highbrow tastes don't appeal to the old man, who prefers to mend his shoes noisily while the music is playing. A battle of wits ensues which ends in Albert's hammer being tossed through the window and prized records being smashed. Finally, Albert locks Harold's record cupboard and throws the key in the junkyard. It suddenly dawns on both of them that the set of keys also opens the stable, the safe and the gates to the yard, so a frantic search begins. At 1 o'clock in the morning the old man locates the keys within the horn of another old gramophone which he insists on keeping. Otherwise he will drop the keys down the drain. Blackmailed, Harold reluctantly agrees, and a battle between Tchaikovsky and the twist erupts. Harold throws the old man's gramophone out in the yard but, locked out of the house, he can do nothing about Albert playing ragtime on his own machine.

Produced by Duncan Wood Designed by Roger Andrews Film cameraman Tony Leggo Film editor Geoff Botterill Production assistant Bob Gilbreath Secretary Elizabeth Cranston Incidental music Ron Grainer Assistant floor manager Joan Duncan Floor assistant David Hine Costume supervisor Jane Roberts Make-up supervisor Shirley Rowlands Lighting supervisor Jimmy Richardson Sound supervisor Norman Greaves Grams operator Buster Cole Vision mixer Steve Turner

Full House

Recorded 24 January 1963, broadcast 7 February 1963

With Dudley Foster as Martin, Jack Rodney as Rex and Anthony Sagar as George

When Harold returns home Albert quickly stops sleeping and starts sweeping. Loaded down with fine wine and cheese, Harold is planning an evening of cards with a group of friends. The old man is outraged and begins quoting chapter and verse about the sin of gambling and Harold's mother's hatred of cards. Suspicious that these so-called friends are going to fleece Harold of all his money, Albert stays and watches the game. As he thought, his son is completely fleeced. Sending him off to the pub for a jug of bitter, Albert suggests a quick hand while the guests are waiting for Harold to come back. He has a stack of £50 and his own, 'unopened' pack of cards and the three players gladly accept the offer. On Harold's return, the three friends are departing, having been cleaned out by the old man's marked deck of cards and special spectacles. Albert gives his son his lost £30, and the Steptoes start another game of cards, but this time for just a halfpenny a hand and with the old man happily denied his 'lucky' glasses!

Produced by Duncan Wood Designed by Roger Andrews Production assistant Bob Gilbreath Secretary Elizabeth Cranston Incidental music Ron Grainer Assistant floor manager Joan Duncan Floor assistant David Hine Costume supervisor Jane Roberts Make-up supervisor Shirley Rowlands Lighting supervisor Jimmy Richardson Sound supervisor Norman Greaves Grams operator Buster Cole Vision mixer Steve Turner

Is That Your Horse Outside?

Recorded 4 February 1963, broadcast 14 February 1963

With Patricia Haines as Dorothea, Richard Shaw as the Coalman and Jo Rowbottom as the Waitress

Out on his rounds in a posh area of London, Harold helps to carry a rich lady's parcels into her home. While he is enjoying a glass of whisky as a reward, she suggests that he return the following morning at nine. With this clear promise, Harold is up with the lark and into his best suit for the morning round. Albert, test-running a bicycle he has been mending, follows his son's horse and cart and tracks him down to the posh house. Sitting in a café and observing the scene, he passes seven hours before Harold finally emerges. Racing back on the bike to be home before his son, he advises him on the facts of life and recalls his many fleeting encounters with posh birds in the old days. Harold is adamant that this is real love and selects some books to discuss with the lady the following day. When he arrives, he discovers the coalman is the new flavour of the day and departs, tossing his prized books at his father en route.

Produced by Duncan Wood Designed by Roger Andrews Film cameraman Tony Leggo Film editor Geoff Botterill Production assistant Bob Gilbreath Secretary Elizabeth Cranston Incidental music Ron Grainer Assistant floor manager Joan Duncan Floor assistant David Hine Costume supervisor Jane Roberts Make-up supervisor Shirley Rowlands Lighting supervisor Jimmy Richardson Sound supervisor Norman Greaves Grams operator Buster Cole Vision mixer Steve Turner

Series Three

7 January–18 February 1964, Tuesday 8–8.25 p.m., BBC Television, in black and white

Starring Harry H. Corbett as Harold and Wilfrid Brambell as Albert

Written by Alan Simpson and Ray Galton

Homes Fit for Heroes

Recorded 12 December 1963, broadcast 7 January 1964

With Peggy Thorpe-Bates as the Matron, Marie Makino as Old Lady Uncredited: Gladys Dawson, Jean Doree, Doris Hall, Evelyn Lund, Molly Veness, Yvette Yorke, Lawrence Archer, Philip Becker, Howell Davies, George Loudow, David Olive and George Ricarde as the Old People's Home Residents

On a pleasant Sunday trip out on the cart, Harold waxes lyrical about the beautiful country and the even more beautiful stately home they are passing. Albert is freezing cold and would prefer to be at home watching an old film on the TV, but his son's ulterior motive is soon made clear when the stately home is revealed to be Chartwell House, an old people's home. Terrified and angry, the old man refuses to discuss the possibility of ending up there and grabs the reins to make a speedy getaway. Back at Oil Drum Lane, Harold explains that he's signed up for a two-year sailing trip around the world on a sloop with four other blokes and five birds. Planning to sell the business, he moves Albert into the home. The old man warns the matron that he's a troublemaker, but after an emotional parting with his son he is reflective and lonely in his little room. Harold receives a letter from the trip organizer explaining that he is too old to join them and reluctantly takes Albert home.

Produced by Duncan Wood Designed by Lionel Radford Film cameraman John McGlashan Film editor Peter Pierce Secretary Elizabeth Cranston Incidental music Norman Percival Assistant floor manager Cynthia Harris Floor assistant Bill Wilson Costume supervisor Susan Wheal Make-up supervisor Jill Summers Lighting supervisor Jimmy Richardson Sound supervisor Norman Greaves Grams operator Buster Cole Vision mixer Granville Jenkins

The Wooden Overcoats

Recorded 19 December 1963, broadcast 14 January 1964

While Albert is trying to get a tan from a sunlamp fitted with an ordinary 60-watt bulb, Harold returns home keen to unload his day's stock – a cartful of coffins. The ultrasuperstitious old man refuses to have them in the house, but Harold is adamant and has to face a torrent of talk about omens, witchcraft and devils from his father, who threatens to leave the house if the coffins aren't removed. Harold insists they stay, so Albert heads off for a night's sleep in the stable. Once alone with the coffins, Harold's imagination starts to play tricks on him: he sees danger in every shadow and, at one in the morning, eventually makes for the relative comfort of the stables. Insisting that he's merely there to look after Albert, he soon reveals his childlike nervousness with pleas for his father to stay awake until he falls asleep.

Produced by Duncan Wood Designed by Martin Johnson Secretary Elizabeth Cranston Floor manager Gordon Pert Incidental music Norman Percival Assistant floor manager Cynthia Harris Floor assistant Bill Wilson Costume supervisor Susan Wheal Make-up supervisor Jill Summers Lighting supervisor Jimmy Richardson Sound supervisor Norman Greaves Grams operator Buster Cole Vision mixer Granville Jenkins

The Lead Man Cometh

Recorded 2 January 1964, broadcast 21 January 1964

With Leonard Rossiter as Welsh Hughie and Billy Maxam as the Policeman

The business is doing badly and the Steptoes are having to break into their savings to keep their heads above water. Then a Welsh stranger appears and offers them a ton of lead for 10 quid. The old man, suspicious of the stranger, is convinced the lead is stolen property, but Harold, excited at a 500 per cent profit on his investment, happily believes the man's story that the lead is from a chapel earmarked for demolition. Harold buys the lead, and Albert is distressed that the rag 'n' bone business is being dragged into criminal dealings. But before Harold can decide on the best outlet for getting rid of the lead, a policeman enters the yard. The Steptoes pretend to be out, and the copper drops a police notice through the door advising traders that lead thieves are in operation. Father and son load the lead on to the cart and dump it in the canal. The two men return to a rain-sodden home: the lead having been stolen from their own roof!

Produced by Duncan Wood Designed by Lionel Radford Secretary Elizabeth Cranston Floor manager Gordon Pert Incidental music Norman Percival Assistant floor manager Cynthia Harris Floor assistant Bill Wilson Costume supervisor Susan Wheal Make-up supervisor Jill Summers Lighting supervisor Jimmy Richardson Sound supervisor Norman Greaves Grams operator Buster Cole Vision mixer Granville Jenkins

Steptoe à la Cart

Recorded 9 Janaury 1964, broadcast 28 January 1964

With Gwendolyn Watts as Monique Fouberge, Frank Thornton as the Butler and Lala Lloyd as the Woman at the Door

Harold has managed to gain access to a private block of flats and is working his way through the occupants. He meets an attractive French au pair girl and strikes up an awkward, pidgin English conversation with her. With the relationship going well, he decides to learn French and brings out a 'speak French' gramophone record. Desperate to impress, he invites the girl back to meet Albert after insisting that he be on his best behaviour. Draping English and French flags in the living room, Albert makes an effort but when he discovers that Harold has described him as 'old misery guts' he reveals he can speak fluent French and shows up his son's lack of knowledge. Even worse, during the conversation it becomes clear that Albert is in fact the girl's grandfather, having been billeted with her grandmother for six months during the Great War. Harold, who has gained a niece but lost a girlfriend, reluctantly joins in the celebration.

Produced by Duncan Wood French Lesson recorded by Pierre Le Seve Designed by Martin Johnson Secretary Elizabeth Cranston Incidental music Norman Percival Floor manager Gordon Pert Assistant floor manager Cynthia Harris Floor assistant Bill Wilson Costume supervisor Susan Wheal Make-up supervisor Jill Summers Lighting supervisor Jimmy Richardson Sound supervisor Norman Greaves Grams operator Buster Cole Vision mixer Granville Jenkins

Sunday For Seven Days

Recorded 16 January 1964, broadcast 4 February 1964

With Michael Brennan as the Audience Member Who Threatens Albert, Michael Stainton as the Audience Member Who Threatens the Audience Member Who Threatens Albert, Mark Singleton as the Cinema Manager, Damaris Hayman as the Cashier of Cinema Screening Fellini, George Betton as the Cinema Audience Member Next to the Audience Member Who Threatens Albert, Alec Bregonzi as the Protective Boyfriend, Billy Maxam as the Commissionaire, Betty Cardno as the Cashier of Cinema Screening *Nudes of 1964*, Kathleen Heath as Woman Next to Albert and Katie Cashfield as the Usherette Uncredited: Margaret Reed as the Protected Girlfriend, William Raynor as the 'Sssh!' man, Tim Buckland as the Other Disgruntled Man, Joyce Donaldson, Leopold Siromba and Peter Thompson as the Rest of the Cinema Audience. Tracy Alexander, Joanne Hawtrey, Bella Emberg, Enid Cleaver, Avril Wheatley, Rosemary Reeves, Claire Mayne, Joy Burnett, Gladys Bacon, Stella Marris, Patricia Scofield, Geraldine Hart, Dorothy Watson, Daryl Stuart, John Murch, Bryn Stewart, Denis Venton, Robert Manning, George Ricarde, Ian McGuigan, John Lynn, Billy John and John Cowan as the Queue for Fellini's *8½*. Daryll Richards, Frank Wheatley, Fred Taylor, Lance George, Fred Maxted, Bert Simms, Charles Gilbert, Roy Denton, Yasha Adams, David Brewster, David Bond, Brian Bate, Dean Webb and Barry Stevens as the Queue for *Nudes of 1964*

It's a big night out, and Harold and Albert are getting ready for an evening at the pictures. Typically, Albert's seen most of the films already but the two still disagree about their choice – Harold wants the culture of Fellini's *8½*, the old man wants the busty eye-candy of *Nudes of 1964*. Harold wins, but his father is determined to wreck the evening, continually talking and complaining, and loudly consuming his orange drink. A fight breaks out in the cinema and when Harold is accused by a protective boyfriend of trying to touch up his date the management throws him out and Albert is dragged along too. The old man reluctantly pays for a seat to see *Nudes of 1964* next door, and after several seconds of consideration Harold pays for a more expensive seat in a different part of the same cinema.

Produced by Duncan Wood Designed by Roger Andrews Secretary Elizabeth Cranston Incidental music Norman Percival Floor manager Gordon Pert Assistant floor manager Cynthia Harris Floor assistant Bill Wilson Costume supervisor Susan Wheal Make-up supervisor Jill Summers Lighting supervisor Jimmy Richardson

Sound supervisor Norman Greaves Grams operator Buster Cole Vision mixer Granville Jenkins

The Bonds That Bind Us

Recorded 23 January 1964, broadcast 11 February 1964

With June Whitfield as Madge Uncredited: Frank Littlewood, Philip Howard and Tony Lambden as the Tailors, Alistair McFarlane as the Barber, Sheila Dunn as the Manicurist, Walter Swash as the Dentist and Sally Corday as the Receptionist

Harold is rather pleased with himself. He's working on his bodybuilding exercises, and the day's totting has yielded a collection of torture instruments. Albert, meanwhile, is keen to check his premium bonds. His son's ridicule quickly turns to excitement when the old man wins £1000, but as Harold sold his share the previous year to afford tennis club membership, Albert gets the lot and heads off for a few nights in the West End. Returning briefly with an electric razor for Harold, the old man introduces his fiancée, Madge, a 27-year-old blonde he's picked up in a Soho club. He's bought a ring and has plans for a Monte Carlo holiday, but Harold steps in to break up the engagement. Wrapping Albert up in a straitjacket he has just bought, and applying shaving foam to his mouth, he pretends the old man has gone mad and stolen the money. When the police are mentioned, Madge reveals her gold-digging scam and makes a speedy getaway. Albert, pondering his escape, shows he's not so foolish after all. The ring Madge has returned to him was a paste imitation.

Produced by Duncan Wood Designed by Roger Andrews Secretary Elizabeth Cranston Incidental music Norman Percival Floor manager Gordon Pert Assistant floor manager Cynthia Harris Floor assistant Bill Wilson Costume supervisor Susan Wheal Make-up supervisor Jill Summers Lighting supervisor Jimmy Richardson Sound supervisor Norman Greaves Grams operator Buster Cole Vision mixer Granville Jenkins

The Lodger

Recorded 30 January 1964, broadcast 18 February 1964

Uncredited: Walter Swash as the Shopkeeper

Harold has his nose deep in George Bernard Shaw's political theory while Albert desperately tries to work out how to pay the ever-mounting pile of bills. The only solution is to get a lodger. Harold threatens to move out if his wage-earning credibility is questioned. Still, the old man is determined and places an advertisement in the local sweet-shop window. Harold, having followed Albert, removes the card and tears it up. But his father sees him do this. Harold works harder than ever in an attempt to impress Albert, but his dignity is once again questioned when the old man reveals that he saw Harold take the card. The son moves out. One week later he returns. With Albert having had no luck in securing a lodger, and Harold stuck in a dead-end job as a sandwich-board man for an Indian restaurant, the two are reunited under the same roof.

Produced by Duncan Wood Designed by Roger Andrews Secretary Elizabeth Cranston Incidental music Norman Percival Floor manager Gordon Pert Assistant floor manager Cynthia Harris Floor assistant Bill Wilson Costume supervisor Susan Wheal Make-up supervisor Jill Summers Lighting supervisor Jimmy Richardson

Sound supervisor Norman Greaves Grams operator Buster Cole Vision mixer
Granville Jenkins

Series Four

4 October–15 November 1965, Monday 7.30–8 p.m., BBC1, in black and white
Starring Wilfrid Brambell as Albert and Harry H. Corbett as Harold
Written by Alan Simpson and Ray Galton

And Afterwards At...

Recorded 12 September 1965, broadcast 4 October 1965

With George A. Cooper as Uncle Arthur, Rose Hill as Auntie May, Joan Newell as Aunt
Ethel, Mollie Sugden as Melanie's Mother, Robert Webber as the Vicar, Karol Hagar as
Melanie, Rita Webb as Auntie Freda, Gretchen Franklin as Aunt Daphne, Fred Hugh as
First Man, Leslie Sarony as Melanie's Father, George Tovey as Second Man, George
Hirste as Uncle Ted, Betty Cardno as First Woman, Margaret Flint as Second Woman,
Gerald Rowland as the Telegraph Boy, James Bulloch as Uncle Herbert, and Tony
Lambden Uncredited: Denise Peck, Nicola Ashwood and Marie Phillips as the
Bridesmaids, Michael Earl as the Usher, Patrick Martin as the Nephew, Lois Hyett as
the Niece, Frank Littlewood as the Church Warden, and Bill Hahn, Peter Thompson,
Lionel Wheeler, Lance George, Len Russell, Eddie Davis, Sally Russell, Margot Abbott,
Doreen Ubells, Lyn Turner and Pat Macdermot as the Wedding Guests

It's Harold's wedding day and, despite continuous undermining comments from
Albert, he is determined to enjoy himself. But his intended, Melanie, jilts him at the
altar and he returns to Oil Drum Lane in deep humiliation. Albert is delighted and
optimistic. Harold just wants to get drunk and wallow in self-pity. But there's very
little chance of that. The Steptoe clan, sensing free drinks and the chance of getting
their wedding presents back, storm into the house with thinly veiled sympathy and
family-tie tension. As a free-for-all for the wedding gifts breaks out, both Harold and
Albert erupt with anger, tossing presents out of the window and forcing the family
out of the house. With a honeymoon suite booked and a few days by the sea paid
for, Harold suggests the old man might like to join him. Albert hurriedly packs his
bags.

Produced by Duncan Wood Designed by Roger Andrews Secretary Elizabeth
Cranston Incidental music Ken Jones Production assistant Gordon Pert Assistant
floor manager Tony James Floor assistant Trevor Beckett Costume supervisor
Michael Robbie Make-up supervisor Sandra Hurll Lighting supervisor Jimmy
Richardson Sound supervisor Brian Hiles Grams operator Denis Heape
Vision mixer Bob Hallman

Crossed Swords

Recorded 19 September 1965, broadcast 11 October 1965

With Derek Nimmo as the Antique Shop Assistant, Basil Dignam as the Second
Auctioneer, Mark Singleton as the First Auctioneer, Ralph Nossek as the Fourth
Bidder, Tim Buckland as the Spoons Purchaser, Philip Howard as the Third Bidder,
William Raynor as the First Bidder, Frank Littlewood as the Second Bidder and Peter
Thompson as the Porter Uncredited: Michael Earl as the Bidder at Auction and
Corrine Burford, Jessica Davey, Joy Burnett, Dorothy Watson, Nancy Adams, Sydney

King, Jack Niles, Lauderdale Beckett, David Raynor, Richard Neller, Anthony Mayne, Peter Rocca and Colin Vancao as the Crowd at Auction

Albert, trapped in the outside toilet all afternoon, amuses himself by reading the toilet paper cut from scraps of newspaper. Harold returns, removes the fallen junk that is jamming the toilet door and excitedly prepares to reveal his special find of the day. Bought for a fiver from an old dear in Notting Hill, the valuable piece of porcelain bears the distintive crossed swords hallmark of Meissen. The Steptoes take the piece to a West End antique expert to have it valued, but Harold refuses the £250 the assistant offers him, much to his father's chagrin, and takes the piece to auction. He hopes to boost the bidding and gives the auctioneer the wink, while Albert eventually buys it for 550 guineas by mistake. Saddled with the commission fee, Harold disappointedly goes to bed but returns to the living room when he hears the sound of breaking china. Albert, having decided to give the Meissen piece a wash, has dropped it and smashed it. The old man runs back to the toilet and tries to defend himself against Harold's maniacally wielded sword.

Produced by Duncan Wood Designed by Roger Andrews Secretary Elizabeth Cranston Incidental music Ken Jones Production assistant Gordon Pert Assistant floor manager Tony James Floor assistant Trevor Beckett Costume supervisor Michael Robbie Make-up supervisor Ureli Fry Lighting supervisor Jimmy Richardson Sound supervisor Brian Hiles Grams operator Pat Heigham Vision mixer Bob Hallman

Those Magnificent Men and Their Heating Machines

Recorded 26 September 1965, broadcast 18 October 1965

Albert is cleaning the gas oven, but when Harold wanders in the old man bangs his head and collapses. Believing he's trying to commit suicide, Harold desperately tries to revive him until Albert stops playing dead and wakes up. Harold has a surprise for the old man: a complete set of radiators and pipes for their very own central heating system. Albert is delighted but outraged when Harold is determined to install the system himself. With exposed pipes, blocked doorways and a complicated way of heating the old man's brass bed, the system is seemingly doomed to disaster. Sure enough, when Harold switches it on, the radiators jump, bang and eventually leak, the ceiling caves in and the two men sit in the rubble. The old man goes to bed in a huff but returns to find his son checking out the gas oven. He jumps to the same suicide conclusion that Harold had done previously.

Produced by Duncan Wood Designed by Roger Andrews Secretary Elizabeth Cranston Incidental music Ken Jones Production assistant Gordon Pert Assistant floor manager Tony James Floor assistant Trevor Beckett Costume supervisor Michael Robbie Make-up supervisor Janet Nethercott Lighting supervisor Jimmy Richardson Sound supervisor Norman Greaves Grams operator Denis Heape Vision mixer Bob Hallman

The Siege of Steptoe Street

Recorded 3 October 1965, broadcast 25 October 1965

With Robert Dorning as Mr Stacey the Butcher, Lane Meddick as the First Summons Server, Edwin Brown as the First Bailiff, Bill Maxam as the Second Bailiff, Charles Bird as the Third Summons Server and Stan Simmons as the Second Summons Server

The bills are mounting up again in the Steptoe residence. While totting up the expenses, Harold notices that the butcher and fishmonger have been providing grouse, salmon and other luxuries that he has never eaten. The old man has seemingly been living off the fat of the land while Harold has been 'treated' to sausage meat and a pig's trotter. Legal proceedings are in the offing and a bailiff tries, unsuccessfully, to deliver a summons. It's a siege situation at the Steptoes' house, and with a small crowd gathering in the junkyard Harold tries to convince them that his father has gone insane. He makes the old man shout out in French and don a Napoleon costume to convince them! Having agreed to survive on the only food in the house – snails and asparagus tips – Harold is outraged to discover that Albert has concealed a secret supply of chocolate biscuits all for himself. He lets the bailiffs in, but the old man feigns a fall and manages to secure £250 from the butcher to keep quiet about the accident. Harold is appalled but soon comes round to the idea of a midnight feast at a Chinese restaurant.

Produced by Duncan Wood Designed by Roger Andrews Secretary Elizabeth Cranston Incidental music Ken Jones Production assistant Gordon Pert Assistant floor manager Tony James Floor assistant Trevor Beckett Costume supervisor Michael Robbie Make-up supervisor Sandra Hurll Lighting supervisor Jimmy Richardson Sound supervisor Norman Greaves Grams operator Laurie Taylor Vision mixer Bob Hallman

A Box in Town

Recorded 10 October 1965, broadcast 1 November 1965

With Yootha Joyce as Avis, Freda Bamford as Mrs Blackett, Annie Leake as Harold's Landlady, Philip Howard as the Estate Agent and Marjorie Rhodes, Kathleen Heath, Audrey Binham, Hilda Barry, Marie Makino, Eileen Matthews and Ann Jay as the Women

After watching *Dr. No* at the cinema Harold and his new girlfriend, Avis, stumble back to Oil Drum Lane in search of a cosy spot to snuggle up in. But the old man is still awake and Harold refuses to enter the house. Much to the young lady's chagrin, he attempts to set up a romantic scene with a battered screen, a dirty sofa and a blanket off the horse. But the old man appears and gives him two minutes to get rid of the girl and get inside. Harold dutifully obeys, but vows to get a place of his own. Despite his father's reaction, he rents a boxroom at the top of a house and flicks through his address book to find the first lucky lady to christen it. However, his old flames are either not interested or married so he spends his first night of freedom watching television. Albert, meanwhile, is having a swinging time with a non-stop string of even older old flames. Harold finally manages to get Avis up to his room, but before anything can happen his landlady appears and throws her out. Harold is given his marching orders and returns home, much to Albert's relief. The old man is exhausted after all his entertaining and just wants to go to bed. Both father and son frantically tear up their little black books and settle back to a life of perfect disharmony.

Produced by Duncan Wood Designed by Roger Andrews Secretary Elizabeth Cranston Incidental music Ken Jones Production assistant Gordon Pert Assistant floor manager Tony James Floor assistant Trevor Beckett Costume supervisor Michael Robbie Make-up supervisor Elizabeth Armstrong Lighting supervisor Jimmy Richardson Sound supervisor Norman Greaves Grams operator Pat Heigham Vision mixer Bob Hallman

My Old Man's a Tory

Recorded 17 October 1965, broadcast 8 November 1965

With Dudley Foster as Mr Stonelake, Damaris Hayman as Karen Frobisher, Howard Douglas as Arthur Biggs, Evelyn Lund as Miss Bronley and Peter Thompson as the Young Man

Harold is out on his rounds proudly displaying his 'Vote Labour' posters while the old man is at home parading his Conservative paraphernalia. Back in the yard each starts destroying the other's political displays and Harold even tries to attack his father with a big stick. But reason prevails and the battle of strength turns into a battle of words. Harold celebrates the National Health Service, which has kept his father going since 1948, and then condemns his beloved party for, in effect, keeping the old man alive. Albert then condemns his son for doing nothing but chatting about putting the country to rights. But the son has the ultimate bombshell to drop: the house is to be used as the committee rooms for the local Labour group. Soon it is full of Harold's comrades as well as an important figure from the Labour Head Office. Harold, complete in Harold Wilson get-up, desperately tries to impress them in the hope of being elected to the Local Council. However, although the group supports him, the Labour agent nominates university-educated Jeremy Stewart, who should attract the new, middle-class voters in the area. Harold, crest-fallen, continues to support the cause, resigns his nomination and vows allegiance to the new candidate. His outraged father condemns the situation, breaks up the meeting and starts another political one-to-one with his son.

Produced by Duncan Wood Designed by Roger Andrews Secretary Elizabeth Cranston Incidental music Ken Jones Production assistant Gordon Pert Assistant floor manager Tony James Floor assistant Trevor Beckett Costume supervisor Michael Robbie Make-up supervisor Sandra Hurll Lighting supervisor Jimmy Richardson Sound supervisor Norman Greaves Grams operator Pat Heigham Vision mixer Bob Hallman

Pilgrim's Progress

Recorded 24 October 1965, broadcast 15 November 1965

With Alan Gifford as the American, Frank Thornton as the Frenchman, Sidonie Bond as the Air Hostess, Frederick Schiller as the German, Catharina Ferraz as the Frenchman's Wife and Tim Buckland as the Voice-Over on the Tannoy Uncredited: Ernest Blyth, Keith Ashley, Gordon Lang, Maurice Quick, Greville Steele, John Moore, Aubert Hill, Bill Hahn, Kim Burney, Vicki Shields, Esme Davey, Rosamund Hall and Iris Darbyshire as the Plane Passengers and Richard Graham-Clarke as the Motorcycle Driver

Albert is trying on his old First World War army uniform in preparation for a return trip to no-man's-land in France. Harold is annoyed. His familiar but futile attempt to take his annual holiday in St Tropez is put back another year in order to allow his father one more look at the 'trenches' before he dies. Having been persuaded not to wear his uniform on the plane, Albert takes his seat. Immediately, he shows his fear of flying. After reassuring him, Harold delightedly compounds the problem by explaining what would happen if things *were* to go wrong. However, the old man soon forgets his troubles when an American passenger comments on his war medals and a Frenchman defends the honour of his country against his xenophobic comments. A punch-up erupts en route and the Steptoes, arrested and deported, return home to Oil Drum Lane. With his passport stamped 'undesirable alien', Harold's St Tropez plans are curtailed, but Albert digs out his old Arabian gear and plans a trip to another one of his wartime locations.

Produced by Duncan Wood Designed by Roger Andrews Secretary Elizabeth Cranston Incidental music Ken Jones Production assistant Gordon Pert Assistant floor manager Tony James Floor assistant Trevor Beckett Costume supervisor Michael Robbie Make-up supervisor Elizabeth Armstrong Lighting supervisor Jimmy Richardson Sound supervisor Norman Greaves Grams operator Laurie Taylor Senior cameraman Stanley Appel Vision mixer Bob Hallman

Series Five

6 March–17 April 1970, Friday 7.55–8.25 p.m., BBC1, in colour

Starring Harry H. Corbett as Harold and Wilfrid Brambell as Albert

Written by Ray Galton and Alan Simpson

A Death in the Family

Recorded 15 February 1970, broadcast 6 March 1970

Uncredited: Patrick Milner as the Policeman, Arthur Arnold as the Horse Dealer, Mark Marharha and Wayne Thistleto as the Urchins, Vi Ward, Elizabeth Broome, Kathleen Heath, Barbara Shackleton as Passers-By, Arthur Zan and George Day as the Abattoir Men and Charles Young as the Voice

No sooner do we welcome back Harold – totting on Hercules – and Albert – picking up horse manure for a profit – than we lose the third regular member of the cast, the poor old horse. Having reached the grand old age of 39, it succumbs to a heart attack on the Goldhawk Road and is loaded up for the knacker's yard. Harold is distressed, but the old man is heartbroken, reflecting on the loss of the best friend he has ever had and closing the business for a period of mourning. Harold, having bought a new horse which he has decided to call Samson, can't shake the old man out of his depression. Even the offer of breakfast in bed, and the chance to see the promisingly dirty film *I Am Curious – Yellow*, can't raise him from his bed. Just before heading off to work Harold discovers that Samson is poorly and begs his father's help. Albert 'cures' the new horse, who has just given birth to Hercules the Second, and it is renamed Delilah. The Steptoes, back in harness, make plans for the cinema trip.

Produced by Duncan Wood Designed by Roger Liminton Incidental music Dennis Wilson Musical link and conductor Ronnie Hazlehurst Theme music Ron Grainer Production assistant Gordon Pert Producer's assistant Liz Cranston Assistant floor manager John Kilby Floor assistant John Pollock Costume supervisor Marjorie Lewis Make-up supervisor Sylvia James Lighting supervisor Jimmy Richardson Sound supervisor Mike McCarthy Film cameraman Max Samett Film editor Bob Rymer Grams operator Mike Barclay Vision mixer Mike Catherwood

A Winter's Tale

Recorded 22 February 1970, broadcast 13 March 1970

It's time again for the Steptoes' annual holiday and, as usual, Albert wants to go to

Bognor with his son. Harold, however, has plans for a fortnight's skiing and pulling 'brown crumpet' on the piste in Obergurgl, Austria. Having picked up various bits of ill-fitting and mismatching skiing equipment on his round, He is happily preparing himself for his first holiday alone. Harold suggests that the old man stay with his sister in Stoke-on-Trent. Building a makeshift ski slope in the yard, he climbs up the ladder, puts on his skis and makes his first descent: right into the house and into disaster. His leg broken, he's forced to sit with his leg in a plaster cast as the old man triumphantly enters in full skiing gear. Off on holiday in his son's place, Albert suggests Harold stay with his aunt in Stoke-on-Trent.

Produced by Duncan Wood Designed by Austin Ruddy Ski stunt double Wally Schulberg Incidental music Dennis Wilson From an original theme by Ron Grainer Production assistant Gordon Pert Producer's assistant Liz Cranston Assistant floor manager John Kilby Floor assistant John Pollock Costume supervisor Marjorie Lewis Make-up supervisor Sylvia James Lighting supervisor Ritchie Richardson Sound supervisor Michael McCarthy Film cameraman Max Samett Film editor Bob Rymer Grams operator Mike Barclay Vision mixer Mike Catherwood

Any Old Iron?

Recorded 8 March 1970, broadcast 20 March 1970

With Richard Hurndall as Timothy Stanhope, Valerie Bell as Dolly Miller and Roger Avon as Edgar the Policeman

When a sophisticated gentleman antique dealer, Timothy Stanhope, comes into the junkyard on the lookout for some rarities, he seems uninterested until Harold appears. Stanhope takes a shine to him immediately, and a friendship based on the appreciation of the finer things in life is struck up. The old man doesn't trust the dealer and instantly brands him a poof. Stanhope returns with gifts and invitations to the Bolshoi Ballet, and Harold eagerly agrees to spend more time with him despite Albert's distrustful pleading. Eventually Harold, dressed up to the nines, plans to go round to Timmy's flat for dinner to discuss plans the dealer has for investing in Harold's own antique shop. Once the meal draws to a close, Stanhope changes into his dressing gown, dims the lights and makes an advance on Harold. With nerves mounting, the arrival of a policeman – Stanhope's partner – frightens Harold out of the house and into the arms of 'sure-thing' Dolly Miller for the night. The old man is outraged, first at the thought of Harold having been with Timothy, and then at the loose morals at being with Dolly Miller.

Produced by Duncan Wood Designed by Austin Ruddy Incidental music Dennis Wilson, from an original theme by Ron Grainer Production assistant Gordon Pert Producer's assistant Liz Cranston Assistant floor manager John Kilby Floor assistant John Pollock Costume supervisor Marjorie Lewis Make-up supervisor Sylvia James Lighting supervisor Ritchie Richardson Sound supervisor Michael McCarthy Film cameraman Max Samett Film editor Bob Rymer Grams operator John Lloyd Vision mixer Mike Catherwood

Steptoe and Son – and Son!

Recorded 15 March 1970, broadcast 27 March 1970

With Ann Beach as Daphne Tomlin and Glynn Edwards as George

Harold's flirting with a girl on his round comes to naught, but the old man is disturbed at home by a young unmarried woman, eight months pregnant, who claims that the father of her unborn child is none other than his son. Being the dutiful father, he denies all knowledge, but the girl is persistent and as soon as Harold arrives home the diary is consulted and checked for likely clues to the coupling. A party during the previous May is singled out and, although both Harold and the girl can't remember doing anything, Harold faces up to his responsibility and agrees to marry her. Albert is outraged at first, but a kiss and a promise from the girl that if the child's a boy it will be named after him brings him round to the idea. Besides, Harold's happiness and the thought of being a grandfather cheer him up. However, having bought a load of baby clothes, the girl returns to the yard with George, a sailor, who was also at the party and admits the baby is his. The two decide to get married, leaving Harold and Albert heartbroken and determined to go out and get drunk.

Produced by Duncan Wood Designed by Roger Liminton Incidental music Dennis Wilson, from an original theme by Ron Grainer Production assistant Gordon Pert Producer's assistant Liz Cranston Assistant floor manager John Kilby Floor assistant John Pollock Costume supervisor Marjorie Lewis Make-up supervisor Sylvia James Lighting supervisor Ritchie Richardson Sound supervisor Michael McCarthy Film cameraman Max Samett Film editor Bob Rymer Grams operator John Lloyd Vision mixer Mike Catherwood

The Colour Problem

Recorded 22 March 1970, broadcast 3 April 1970

With Anthony Sharp as the Doctor, Geoffrey Adams as the Policeman and Carmel Cryan as Murial Duddy

Returning from his round, Harold finds the old man watching a vintage horror film on television. Albert complains that the only thing he really wants in life is a colour set, but Harold has decided to treat himself to a sports car in order to woo and win the latest potential dolly bird. The two argue and the old man mentions notorious local villain Charlie Miller's generosity towards his father, and leaves the house. Having bought his car the following day, Harold is visited by the police who tell him that Albert is in hospital after spending the night walking the streets. The doctor informs Harold that his father is suffering from loss of memory. Only a colour tele-vision and fond memories of Hercules the horse seem to be coming through. A proposed weekend of debauchery is cancelled, Harold returns his car and buys a colour set for the old man's homecoming. When Albert sees the set, his memory miraculously comes back and, although Harold crossly dismantles the aerial, the television flickers, continues to work and the two sit back and watch.

Produced by Duncan Wood Designed by Austin Ruddy Incidental music Dennis Wilson, from an original theme by Ron Grainer Production assistant Gordon Pert Producer's assistant Liz Cranston Assistant floor manager John Kilby Floor assistant John Pollock Costume supervisor Marjorie Lewis Make-up supervisor Sylvia James Lighting supervisor Ritchie Richardson Sound supervisor Michael McCarthy Film cameramen Len Newson and Stewart Farnell Film editor Bob Rymer Grams operator John Lloyd Vision mixer Mike Catherwood

TB Or Not TB?

Recorded 5 April 1970, broadcast 10 April 1970

With Sidonie Bond as the Receptionist and Lala Lloyd as the Nurse

Harold passes a mobile X-ray unit on his round and returning home finds his father choking on his cigarette. Working out that Albert has smoked the equivalent of 45 miles in his time, Harold insists that the old man join him the following morning for a routine X-ray. Although Albert tries to escape outside the unit, he soons starts chatting up the attractive receptionist. The X-rays seem to go without a hitch, but Albert is terrified of what his will show. When the results arrive in the post, he makes Harold open his first. His son is fine, but the old man's letter reveals a technical fault in his test. He jumps to the conclusion that he has TB but soon cheers up when he notices the results have been put in the wrong envelopes. It is Harold who has to be checked again. Facing death with self-pity, Harold makes his will over to Albert and prepares for the TB sanatorium. Harold returns from his re-examination to find Albert reading the will. Fit and well, Harold is back, but in an attempt to decontaminate the house Albert has burnt his son's bed and clothes.

Produced by Duncan Wood Designed by Roger Liminton Incidental music Dennis Wilson, from an original theme by Ron Grainer Production assistant Gordon Pert Producer's assistant Liz Cranston Assistant floor manager John Kilby Costume supervisor Marjorie Lewis Make-up supervisor Sylvia James Lighting supervisor Ritchie Richardson Sound supervisor Michael McCarthy Film cameraman Max Samett Film editor Bob Rymer Grams operator John Lloyd Vision mixer Mike Catherwood

Men of Property

Recorded 29 March 1970, broadcast 17 April 1970

With Norman Bird as Mr Wood the Bank Manager, Hilda Fenemore as Mrs Wood, Michael Balfour as Charlie Miller, Jan Rossini as Miss Merry, Michael Earl as the Bank Clerk, Peter J. Elliott as the First Waiter, Peter Thompson as the Wine Waiter, Michael Stainton as the Cigar Waiter, Stella Kemball and Ernest Arnley as the Couple at the Next Table, Tim Buckland as the Maître d'Hôtel and Walter Swash, Victor Harrington, Peggy Scrimshaw and Kathleen Cattermole as the Customers

Harold and Albert are playing Monopoly and the old man, as usual, is easily beating his son. When the postman knocks at the door Albert can't resist cheating, but the news puts the game into perspective. Unbeknown to Harold, the Mews Cottage doesn't belong to the Steptoes. It is held on a 99-year lease – a lease that expires in three months' time. As long-standing tenants, the Steptoes have the opportunity to buy the property at the very reasonable price of £750, but even that amount is beyond them. Harold has heard about a naive bank manager in the area who could be persuaded to give them a bank account and overdraft for the amount. Scammaster Charlie Miller has already succeeded and, smartly dressed, the Steptoes try their luck. But the bank manager is no fool. He suggests, however, that the deal could be done after a social gathering of manager and client and suggests a swanky restaurant where he and his wife enjoy an expensive meal at Harold's expense. But at least he is promised his overdraft. However, the gaming tables are a tempting after-dinner diversion. The old man loses big time and Harold is forced to write out a cheque for almost the entire overdraft. Up to their eyes in debt, father and son sit down to another game of Monopoly.

Produced by Duncan Wood Designed by Roger Liminton Incidental music Dennis
Wilson, from an original theme by Ron Grainer Production assistant Gordon Pert
Producer's assistant Liz Cranston Assistant floor manager John Kilby Floor assistant
John Pollock Costume supervisor Marjorie Lewis Make-up supervisor Sylvia James
Lighting supervisor Ritchie Richardson Sound supervisor Michael McCarthy
Grams operator John Lloyd

Series Six

2 November–21 December 1970, Monday 9.20–9.50 p.m., BBC1, in colour

Starring Wilfrid Brambell as Albert and Harry H. Corbett as Harold

Written by Ray Galton and Alan Simpson

Robbery with Violence

Recorded 18 October 1970, broadcast 2 November 1970

With Dudley Foster as the Inspector, Edward Evans as the Doctor, Graham Ashley and
Michael Stainton as the Policemen and James McManus as the Reporter

Albert is hoovering the house when he accidentally knocks over the display cabinet
containing Harold's 'valuable' collection of porcelain. Frantically trying to think of
an excuse, the old man decides to pretend the place has been burgled. Knocking
over the furniture and knocking himself on the head with a poker, he sets the scene
for his son's return home. Harold believes Albert's story of his desperate attempt to
stop the criminals, and a doctor and the police are called. The police inspector
takes down the details of the robbery and fingerprints the Steptoes but no clues are
found. Albert meanwhile is considered a local hero and is awarded a medal for
bravery. Just before the old man returns home Harold finds the broken pieces of his
porcelain in an old gas stove in the yard and realizes the old man's story was a lie.
Harold pretends to have been attacked by the same gang. Albert decides to let him
keep the 'stolen' £150 rather than be exposed as a liar but a local reporter arrives,
offers the old man £250 for his life story and the rogue is back on top.

Produced by Duncan Wood Designed by David Chandler Incidental music Dennis
Wilson Theme music Ron Grainer Production assistant Gordon Pert Producer's
assistant Liz Cranston Assistant floor manager John Kilby Floor assistant John Van
Duyken Costume supervisor Mary Jones Make-up supervisor Anne Ailes Lighting
supervisor Ritchie Richardson Sound supervisor Michael McCarthy Film cameraman
James Balfour Film editor Bob Rymer Grams operator Dave Thompson Vision mixer
Mike Catherwood

Come Dancing

Recorded 25 October 1970, broadcast 9 November 1970

With Tony Melody as the Milkman

It's a boring Sunday afternoon, and Harold drifts into a fantasy about Henry VIII as
Albert sleeps on the sofa. Harold's nerves are on edge and even the cuckoo clock is
plaguing him. The old man finally discovers that his son has 'bird' trouble again
and all because the girl is obsessed with championship ballroom dancing. Harold,
who has told her he is a world-class dancer, can't dance a step so the old man
offers to teach him. Before long the two are waltzing around the house. The follow-

ing morning they are disturbed by the milkman. After ridicule and feminine insinuations, the milkman chips in with some helpful dancing tips. He departs with a flea
in his ear when Albert warns him off. Finally, it's the night of the dance contest and
Harold, in dress suit and slicked-back hair, departs. He returns home early with neither the 'bird' nor the winning cup – the old man had taught him the woman's steps.

Produced by Duncan Wood Designed by Austin Ruddy Dancing sequences arranged
by Harry Smith Hampshire and Doreen Casey Incidental music Dennis Wilson
Theme music Ron Grainer Production assistant Gordon Pert Producer's assistant Liz
Cranston Assistant floor manager John Kilby Floor assistant John Van Duyken
Costume supervisor Mary Jones   Make-up supervisor Anne Ailes Lighting supervisor
Ritchie Richardson Sound supervisor Michael McCarthy Senior cameraman Peter
Ware Grams operator Dave Thompson Vision mixer Mike Catherwood

Two's Company

Recorded 1 November 1970, broadcast 16 November 1970

With Jean Kent as Daphne Goodlace and Clinton Morris as the Taxi Driver Uncredited:
Gilly Flower as Albert's Dance Partner

Albert is out dancing at the Darby and Joan Club while Harold patiently waits up at
home. The old man comes back at quarter past midnight with a cheerful announcement: he's met someone at the club and he's asked her to marry him. Harold gives
the wedding his blessing and prepares to meet the lady in question the following
night. The lady, Daphne Goodlace, turns out to be a 42-year-old widow who works
at the club, part-time. She is also Harold's ex-lover from 20 years earlier. The flame
still burns for both of them. Harold explains that she can't marry his father; he
wants to marry her himself. Albert is devastated when the news is broken to him
and intends to leave the house. As father and son discuss what they should do,
Daphne quietly leaves a note and walks away from the situation. She explains in the
note that things wouldn't have worked out for a marriage with either Harold or
Albert because they are married already. As the two prepare to use the restaurant
reservation Albert has booked for his engagement celebration party, Harold fusses
with the tie of his 'date'.

Produced by Duncan Wood Designed by David Chandler Incidental music Dennis
Wilson Theme music Ron Grainer Production assistant Gordon Pert Producer's
assistant Liz Cranston Assistant floor manager John Kilby Floor assistant John Van
Duyken Costume supervisor Mary Jones Make-up supervisor Anne Ailes Lighting
supervisor Ritchie Richardson Sound supervisor Michael McCarthy Senior
cameraman Peter Ware Film cameraman James Balfour Film editor Bob Rymer
Grams operator Dave Thompson Vision mixer Mike Catherwood

Tea For Two

Recorded 8 November 1970, broadcast 23 November 1970

With Geoffrey Chater as Peregrine de Burville and Robert Raglan as Mr Cadwell

The Shepherd's Bush by-election has drawn the battle lines between Harold's support for Labour and Albert's for the Tories. Both are hard at work canvassing for
their respective party, but the old man swaps the pile of envelopes and lets Harold
deliver the Tory leaflets. Albert is contacted by Tory Central Office and informed that
the Prime Minister, Edward Heath, is actively supporting the local candidate. It is

arranged that Heath will take tea with Albert for a photograph opportunity. Harold is outraged and plans to ruin the momentous day. He dons a 'Vote Labour' dressing gown and threatens to parade stark naked once the cameras start clicking. However, Heath is detained and a Tory representative informs Harold that the visit is cancelled. Not missing a trick, Harold extracts a promise of a refund for the money Albert has lashed out on food. However, a whitewash-filled bucket set up by Harold as a booby trap in the outside toilet does its worst to the Tory, and the Steptoes try to comfort him in their home.

Produced by Duncan Wood Designed by Austin Ruddy Incidental music Dennis Wilson Theme music Ron Grainer Production assistant Gordon Pert Producer's assistant Liz Cranston Assistant floor manager John Kilby Floor assistant John Van Duyken Costume supervisor Mary Jones Make-up supervisor Anne Ailes Lighting supervisor Ritchie Richardson Sound supervisor Michael McCarthy Senior cameraman Peter Ware Film cameraman James Balfour Film editor Bob Rymer Grams operator Dave Thompson Vision mixer Mike Catherwood

Without Prejudice

Recorded 15 November 1970, broadcast 30 November 1970

With Gerald Flood as Mr Ferris the Estate Agent, Norman Bird as Mr Drizen and Ernest Arnley, Tim Buckland, Philip Howard and Victor Harrington as the Neighbours

What with the new motorway, the heavy traffic and the already crumbling house, Harold is desperate to move from Oil Drum Lane. The old man isn't, of course. He was born in the house and thought he would die in it. But with the promise of a garden and a load of gnomes around his pond, he relents and Harold sorts out an estate agent. When he drives the horse and cart to a select, leafy suburb, the residents of Highview Avenue are horrified at the thought of the rag 'n' bone business moving in. The estate agent relishes their reaction and pushes through the sale. Back in Shepherd's Bush, members of the Residents' Association of Highview Avenue come to make the Steptoes a cash offer – not to move themselves and their junk business into their area. Harold is outraged at this blatant class discrimination, but Albert pushes the financial reward up to £850 and greedily accepts on behalf of the firm. In order to afford to renovate their old home, the Steptoes view another select property in a scam to repeat this profitable reaction to their attempt to move to the suburbs.

Produced by Duncan Wood Designed by David Chandler Incidental music Dennis Wilson Theme music Ron Grainer Production assistant Gordon Pert Producer's assistant Liz Cranston Assistant floor manager John Kilby Floor assistant John Van Duyken Costume supervisor Mary Jones Make-up supervisor Anne Ailes Lighting supervisor Ritchie Richardson Sound supervisor Michael McCarthy Senior cameraman Peter Ware Film cameraman James Balfour Film editor Bob Rymer Grams operator Dave Thompson Vision mixer Mike Catherwood

Pot Black

Recorded 22 November 1970, broadcast 7 December 1970

With George Tovey, Alf Mangan, Pat Milner and Bert Rogers as the Delivery Men

With the closure of the Temperance Hall Harold, who has spent two nights a week for the last year playing table number 8, has bought snooker's 'lock, stock and barrel' for £25. Once the full-size table has been delivered and installed, it takes up the entire living room and in order to play Harold has to open the window, play shots from outside and generally compromise his game. Although he claims not to have played for 40 years, Albert takes up Harold's challenge to a match and sails into the lead, thanks to cheating and the extra points he picks up for his son's foul shots. Harold is determined to beat him, however long it may take, and, having had the table moved outside for more room, he drags the match out until past three in the morning. The game even continues through a thunderstorm. Finally, Harold wins and revels in the title of 'champ'. The old man secretly goes out and displays his true skill with a string of trick shots.

Produced by Duncan Wood Designed by Austin Ruddy Snooker sequences by Sydney Lee Incidental music Dennis Wilson Theme music Ron Grainer Production assistant Gordon Pert Producer's assistant Liz Cranston Assistant floor manager John Kilby Floor assistant John Van Duyken Costume supervisor Mary Jones Make-up supervisor Anne Ailes Lighting supervisor Ritchie Richardson Sound supervisor Michael McCarthy Senior cameraman Peter Ware Film cameraman Max Samett Film editor Bob Rymer Grams operator Dave Thompson Vision mixer Mike Catherwood

The Three Feathers

Recorded 29 November 1970, broadcast 14 December 1970

With John Arnatt as Mr Copeland and John Bailey as Mr De Vere

While the old man is stuck in a painful yoga position, Harold returns home in a cheerful mood. He's picked up a bargain, an early nineteenth-century commode bearing the Prince of Wales' crest of three feathers. Having paid £7 10s for it, Harold reckons it's worth at least £200. Albert is outraged that the Steptoe firm is ripping customers off, and the husband of the woman Harold bought it from soon comes to buy it back. He offers £150, which Harold accepts. Later, an antique dealer who buys for the Italian market calls, spots the commode and offers £600. Harold agrees again. Having bought the original owner out, Harold waits expectantly for the return of the Continental dealer. He never comes. Albert, who has taken a back seat throughout, explains that the whole thing has been a con, from the moment the woman sold the commode. What's more, the original £150 cheque has bounced and the commode, still in Harold's possession, is a contemporary copy worth £7 10s. Harold removes the 'po' from the commode with the intention of smashing it over the head of the teacher of his antiques appreciation course.

Produced by Duncan Wood Designed by David Chandler Incidental music Dennis Wilson Theme music Ron Grainer Production assistant Gordon Pert Producer's assistant Liz Cranston Assistant floor manager John Kilby Floor assistant John Van Duyken Costume supervisor Mary Jones Make-up supervisor Anne Ailes Lighting supervisor Ritchie Richardson Sound supervisor Michael McCarthy Senior camera-man Peter Ware Grams operator Dave Thompson Vision mixer Mike Catherwood

Cuckoo in the Nest

Recorded 6 December 1970, broadcast 21 December 1970

With Kenneth J. Warren as Arthur and Edwin Brown as the Taxi Driver

Harold and Albert are playing a makeshift game of chess, using the salt cellar, the pepper pot and an egg cup among their pieces, when a knock comes at the door.

Harold answers it and in barges a bald-headed Australian who claims to be Arthur, Albert's long-lost, illegitimate elder son. The old man is delighted to see him again, but Harold is immediately on the defensive. Arthur settles in and accepts the proffered chance to become a partner in the business. According to Harold, Arthur is a lazy conman, and he tells the old man to choose between them. When Albert protests that he can't, Harold moves out and leaves Arthur to face his father's sharp tongue. With his handcart, Harold tries to build a new business while Arthur takes the Steptoes' horse and cart, sells them and does a bunk. Albert tracks Harold down to his lowly bedsit, offers to merge the two new companies and takes him home, paying his back rent as he leaves. Walking back, the two spot their old horse and cart and give chase down the street.

Produced by Duncan Wood Designed by Austin Ruddy Incidental music Dennis Wilson Theme music Ron Grainer Production assistant Gordon Pert Producer's assistant Liz Cranston Assistant floor manager John Kilby Floor assistant John Van Duyken Costume supervisor Mary Jones Make-up supervisor Anne Ailes Lighting supervisor Ritchie Richardson Sound supervisor Michael McCarthy Senior cameraman Peter Ware Film cameraman Max Samett Film editor Bob Rymer Grams operator Dave Thompson Vision mixer Mike Catherwood

Series Seven

21 February–3 April 1972, Monday, BBC1, in colour

Starring Harry H. Corbett as Harold and Wilfrid Brambell as Albert

Written by Ray Galton and Alan Simpson

Men of Letters

Recorded 13 February 1972, broadcast 21 February 1972, 9.25–9.55 p.m.

With Anthony Sharp as the Vicar Uncredited: Bill Maxam as the Voice of Charlie Harris

Harold and Albert are playing Scrabble and the old man is continually using rude words to win, much to his son's chagrin. A knock at the door ushers in the vicar, who isn't after a contribution to the fund as usual but is enquiring whether one of the Steptoes would like to write an article celebrating the rag 'n' bone businesses in the area for the centenary edition of the parish magazine. Harold and Albert fight about who should write it but the solution is reached by the vicar's toss of a coin. Harold wins, but the vicar insists that Albert can contribute something else to the publication. Harold labours for seven days on his article, even interviewing his initially reluctant father. The vicar is very pleased with the result, but the community doesn't get the chance to read it. On the morning of publication, the magazine is impounded by the police for breaking the Obscene Publications Act and the vicar is arrested for peddling indecent literature. The old man had compiled a crossword for the magazine, and the clues and answers reflect his command of rude words, as used in the Scrabble match.

Produced by John Howard Davies Designed by Roger Liminton Incidental music Dennis Wilson From an original theme by Ron Grainer Production assistant Gordon Pert Producer's assistant Heather Gilder Assistant floor manager Simon Betts Floor assistant Tony Newman Costume supervisor Susan Wheal Make-up supervisor Penny Delamar Lighting supervisor Ritchie Richardson Sound supervisor Michael McCarthy Grams operator Dave Thompson Vision mixer Mike Catherwood

A Star is Born

Recorded 20 February 1972, broadcast 28 February 1972, 9.25–9.55 p.m.

With Trevor Bannister as Rupert Faines Muir, Margaret Nolan as Nemone Wagstaff, Betty Huntley-Wright as Deirdre, John Quayle as the Drama Critic, Cy Town as Timmy and John Anderson as the Autograph Hunter Uncredited: Charles Gaynor as Jeremy, Neville Symonds as Manvile and Reggie Dodd, John Mayne, Frank Lester, Miome Sandford and Pat Dooley as the Crowd in the Dressing Room

While Albert is out picking up a curry for lunch, Harold is busy in the junkyard collecting props for the local amateur dramatic society's new production. Not only is he helping behind the scenes, but this time he has been cast in a leading role and for him the bright lights of film stardom surely beckon. The producer and cast convene at Oil Drum Lane for a read-through of the play, *Guilt: The White Man's Burden*, and Harold is enjoying the experience, nestled close to the blonde and buxom leading lady Nemone Wagstaff. However, one cast member has been inconvenienced and the producer, Rupert Faines Muir, casts the old man, much to Harold's anger. Albert is, of course, brilliant and steals the show on the opening night. Harold's performance is a disaster and, as his father holds court at the aftershow party, he wanders back home to drown his sorrows.

Produced by John Howard Davies Designed by Roger Liminton Incidental music Dennis Wilson, from an original theme by Ron Grainer Production assistant Gordon Pert Producer's assistant Heather Gilder Assistant floor manager Simon Betts Floor assistant Tony Newman Costume supervisor Susan Wheal Make-up supervisor Penny Delamar Lighting supervisor Ritchie Richardson Sound supervisor Michael McCarthy Film cameraman Stewart A. Farnell Film editor Bob Rymer Grams operator Dave Thompson Vision mixer Mike Catherwood

Oh, What a Beautiful Mourning

Recorded 27 February 1972, broadcast 6 March 1972, 9.20–9.50 p.m.

With George A. Cooper as Uncle Arthur, Mollie Sugden as Auntie Minnie, Rita Webb as Potty Aida, Yvonne Antrobus as Caroline, Bartlett Mullins as the Old Man, Tommy Godfrey as Uncle Nobby, Queenie Watts as Joyce, Stella Moray as Elsie, Margaret Flint as Jessie, Simon Cord as Jeffrey and Gilly Flower as Alice Uncredited: Jack Hewitt as the Petrol Station Attendant, Alan Troy and Patrick Travis as the Pallbearers, May Warden, Len Saunders, Iris Fry and Johnnie Clamp as the Mourners

Albert's eldest brother George has died at the age of 93 and the thought of yet another Steptoe funeral depresses Harold. But his father insists they both turn out, mainly because of the share out of personal property and money that always happens after someone has been buried. Clad in their black suits and bowler hats, Harold and Albert face the family who, even before the funeral, are already fighting for the best items. Harold notes that a small porcelain figurine on the mantelpiece is the only worthwhile piece, but everybody else seems to think the same. When the family returns from the funeral they find that the house has been completely stripped bare. But it's not burglars; it's the terms of the will. George has arranged for all his possessions to be sold and the money given to charity. Albert, canny to the last, has the last laugh. He hid the figurine under his hat before they left for the cemetery.

Produced by John Howard Davies Designed by Roger Liminton Incidental music

Dennis Wilson, from an original theme by Ron Grainer Production assistant Gordon
Pert Producer's assistant Heather Gilder Assistant floor manager Simon Betts Floor
assistant Tony Newman Costume supervisor Susan Wheal Make-up supervisor
Penny Delamar Lighting supervisor Ritchie Richardson Sound supervisor Michael
McCarthy Film cameraman Stewart A. Farnell Film editor Bob Rymer Grams
operator Dave Thompson Vision mixer Mike Catherwood

Live Now, PAYE Later

Recorded 5 March 1972, broadcast 13 March 1972, 9.20–9.50 p.m.

With Colin Gordon as Mr Greenwood, Edwin Apps as the Man from the Ministry,
Peter Madden as Norman and Carole Roberts as the Girl in Bra and Panties
Uncredited: Jack Hewitt as the Garage Attendant, Bobby Beaumont as the Post Office
Clerk, Varley Thomas, Gertrude Kaye, Vi Ward and Francis Batsoni as the Post Office
Queue, Sam Manseray as the Bus Conductor, Chalmers Peddie as the Lavatory
Attendant, Pip and Mike Mungaven as the Young Couple in the Cinema and George
Lowdell, Jack Sharp, Alan Cope, George Boon, Mary Masters, Florence Allsworth and
Jean Cambell-Ballas as the Darby and Joan Dancers

With Albert accidentally locked in a wardrobe, and Harold hastily giving some collected 'rags' back to a scantily clad dolly bird, the two are in severely contrasting
moods when they meet back at home. Both are, however, quickly reunited in a joint
struggle against the Inland Revenue. Albert has been claiming a marriage allowance
since his wife died 33 years earlier and a taxman, Mr Greenwood, arrives to question him. After he and Harold get Greenwood drunk, the situation doesn't seem so
bleak. Indeed, it seems that 'Mrs Steptoe' is entitled to six years' back pension
money. Albert, dressed in woman's clothing to receive the cheque and sign on for
'her' pension, is approached by an ex-Fraud-Squad detective who takes 'her' to the
cinema and a dance. Harold hits on the idea of killing off his 'mother'. He dictates
a letter from his father explaining to the Inland Revenue that she has suddenly died.
But the death duties reveal that Albert has also created a 'sister' for Harold, to save
income tax payments. 'Her' signature is required for the forms and Harold is forced
to drag up, ultimately being hotly pursued by Mr Greenwood.

Produced by John Howard Davies Designed by Roger Liminton Incidental music
Dennis Wilson, from an original theme by Ron Grainer Production assistant Gordon
Pert Producer's assistant Heather Gilder Assistant floor manager Simon Betts Floor
assistant Tony Newman Costume supervisor Susan Wheal Make-up supervisor
Penny Delamar Lighting supervisor Ritchie Richardson Sound supervisor Michael
McCarthy Film cameraman Stewart A. Farnell Film editor Bob Rymer Grams
operator Dave Thompson Vision mixer Mike Catherwood

Loathe Story

Recorded 13 March 1972, broadcast 20 March 1972, 9.20–9.50 p.m.

With Raymond Huntley as the Psychiatrist, Georgina Cookson as Mrs Kennington-
Stroud, Joanna Lumley as Bunty Kennington-Stroud Uncredited: Philip Bruce as Young
Harold Steptoe, Elwyn Francis, Johnnie Watson, Francis Batsoni and Leslie Glenroy as
the Young Albert's Drunken Mates

Harold's frustration at losing a game of badminton with his father in the junkyard
leads to a dream of always losing to the old man. The dream leads to sleepwalking,

and Harold tries to chop Albert's head off with a meat cleaver. Terrified, he goes to see a psychiatrist and pours out his hatred of his father, reflecting on a childhood spent on the horse and cart waiting for his drunken father to emerge from the Skinners Arms. He also recalls a more recent interlude when he invited his posh girlfriend and her mother to tea. Albert, as scruffy and common as usual, caused a scene, and the two guests, who became infested with fleas, rushed off. The psychiatrist is unperturbed by what he hears and reflects that Harold's behaviour is a subconscious wish fulfilment that is quite common with a married couple in a confined space. He prescribes a course of tranquillizers. Although the news that his father is about to rent out his room doesn't completely set him back, when Albert tells Harold that he's joined his tennis club and is playing the young lady Harold had his eye on, the son grabs a knife and goes berserk again.

Produced by John Howard Davies Designed by Roger Liminton Incidental music Dennis Wilson, from an original theme by Ron Grainer Production assistant Gordon Pert Producer's assistant Heather Gilder Assistant floor manager Simon Betts Floor assistant Tony Newman Costume supervisor Susan Wheal Make-up supervisor Penny Delamar Lighting supervisor Ritchie Richardson Sound supervisor Michael McCarthy Grams operator Dave Thompson Vision mixer Mike Catherwood

Divided We Stand

Recorded 19 March 1972, broadcast 27 March 1972, 9.20–9.50 p.m.

Uncredited: Paul Lindley and Reginald Dodd as the Hospital Patients, Roberta Symes-Schotzma and Emma Stephenson as the Nurses and Keith Ashley as the Doctor

Harold is trying to make his father decide on new wallpaper and carpets for the Mews Cottage, Oil Drum Lane. But Albert is completely uninterested and refuses to co-operate. As far as he's concerned, the decorating that Harold's late mother did in 1918 is perfectly acceptable. Harold, finally frustrated beyond endurance by the filth in the house, decides to split the property into two self-contained flats. A pay turnstile allows him access to upstairs and the old man access to the kitchen, but as far as he's concerned that's it. The two can live entirely separate lives outside business hours. Albert is lonely almost immediately and wants to play cards, but Harold is happy just reading his book. Problems arise when the two want to watch television, with half the screen on either side of the partition wall. Albert complains that he hasn't got his fair share, and after pushing the entire set into the old man's quarters Harold unplugs it and forces the old man to go to bed. A rag Albert has left above the oven catches fire and, having been rescued by the fire brigade, father and son end up in the same hospital ward, in beds next to each other.

Produced by David Croft Designed by Roger Liminton Incidental music Dennis Wilson, from an original theme by Ron Grainer Production assistant Gordon Pert Producer's assistant Kay Johnson Assistant floor manager Simon Betts Floor assistant Tony Newman Costume supervisor Susan Wheal Make-up supervisor Penny Delamar Lighting supervisor Ritchie Richardson Sound supervisor Michael McCarthy Grams operator Dave Thompson Vision mixer Mike Catherwood

The Desperate Hours

Recorded 26 March 1972, broadcast 3 April 1972, 9.35–10.05 p.m.

With guest star Leonard Rossiter as John Spooner and J. G. Devlin as Frank Ferris,

Corbett Woodall as the Newsreader and Tommy Vance as the Announcer Uncredited:
Michael Earl as the Prison Warder

Harold and Albert struggle to keep warm as they play cards in a freezing house.
With no cigarettes, no money and no decent food, life seems very miserable indeed.
The television set is pawned, they are running short of shillings for the electricity
meter and the radio comes on and goes off of its own accord. A radio newsflash
warns people in the local area that a couple of dangerous convicts have escaped
from Wormwood Scrubs. While Harold struggles in the dark to feed pfennigs into
the meter there is a knock at the door and Albert goes to open it. When the lights
come on again they reveal him ushering in the two convicts in question. But the
Steptoes have no car, no money and no food, and the criminals seem to have been
better off inside. Soon, a bond develops between the young convict and Harold and
the old convict and Albert. While the four of them argue, a police siren is heard,
and the younger convict decides to break away alone. After much pressure from the
elders, he agrees to stick with his partner and give themselves up. Agreeing to visit
them inside the prison, the Steptoes prepare for bed and Harold locks up his own
prison: the house he shares with Albert.

Produced by John Howard Davies Designed by Roger Liminton Incidental music
Dennis Wilson, from an original theme by Ron Grainer Production assistants Gordon
Pert and John Adams Producer's assistant Heather Gilder Assistant floor manager
Simon Betts Floor assistant John Bishop Costume supervisor Susan Wheal Make-up
supervisor Rhian Davies Lighting supervisor Ritchie Richardson Sound supervisor
Michael McCarthy Grams operator Dave Thompson Vision mixer Mike Catherwood

Christmas Special

Recorded 3 and 4 December 1973, broadcast Monday 24 December 1973,
9.30–10.15 p.m., BBC1, in colour

Starring Wilfrid Brambell as Albert and Harry H. Corbett as Harold

Written by Ray Galton and Alan Simpson

With Frank Thornton as the Travel Agent, Arnold Diamond and Mary Barclay as the
Snobbish Couple in the Travel Agency, Peter Hughes, Valerie Bell, Jenny Cox, Peter
Thornton, Sue Walker and Shirley Hafey as the Party Guests Uncredited: Laurel
Brown, Peter Hughes, Frank Lester, Doug Lester and John Lord

Having booked a 10-day Christmas holiday in Majorca, Harold faces the trip alone
when his girlfriend dumps him. In the travel agency he meets up with a posh couple planning to stay in the same hotel. As soon as they discover that Harold is also
staying there, they change their plans to a trip to Bournemouth. Albert happily puts
up the Christmas decorations and is full of festive cheer until Harold breaks the
news about his holiday. Harold, nursing a pricked posterior – he sat on a wreath of
holly in the outside toilet – explains his need to escape from the typical Oil Drum
Lane Christmas. Albert gives Harold his present – three handkerchiefs and a pair of
Y-fronts – early but refuses to go to the old people's home for Christmas lunch as
Harold has arranged. Accidentally on purpose, the old man drops his bottle of pills,
reveals his 'secret' illness and finally gets his own way. Harold reluctantly agrees to
stay at home but blows his holiday money on a slap-up Christmas party. However,
just before the guests arrive Albert and Harold discover they are suffering from
chickenpox. Father and son are left, as usual, on their own for Christmas, pulling a
cracker and sampling the potent punch from a china 'po'.

Produced by Graeme Muir Designed by David Chandler Incidental music Dennis
Wilson, from an original theme by Ron Grainer Production assistants George Clarke
and John Hughes Producer's assistant Liz Cranston Assistant floor manager Frank
Mullen Floor assistant Laurence Vulliamy Film cameraman James Balfour Film
editor Ray Millichope Costume supervisor Rupert Jarvis Make-up supervisor Joan
Barrett Lighting supervisor Ritchie Richardson Sound supervisor John Lloyd
Grams operator Mike Felton Vision mixer Joan Duncan

Series Eight

4 September–10 October 1974, BBC1, in colour

Starring Wilfrid Brambell as Albert and Harry H. Corbett as Harold

Written by Ray Galton and Alan Simpson

Back in Fashion

Recorded 31 August 1974, broadcast Wednesday 4 September 1974, 9.30–10 p.m.

With Madeline Smith as Carol, Roy Holder as Bernie the Photographer, Peter Birrel as
the Agent, Michael Earl as the Policeman and Ava Cadell, Christine Donna, Sally
Farmiloe, Claire Russell and Hazel Wilson as the Models

Harold has been in trouble with the law after a bundle of rags he tossed over the
balcony of a high-rise block of flats hit a policeman on the head. Returning home,
he expresses distaste at his father's fashion sense and cleans up a fake antique
table. The old man hears two men in the yard and, on investigation, discovers that
they want to use the location as a backdrop for a shoot for a fashion magazine.
Harold is very keen on the idea, especially as six young girls are the models and,
with a £60 fee, the old man agrees. Harold dons dark glasses and smoking jacket
the following morning, but Carol, one of the models, mistakenly thinks he is blind.
When she discovers the truth, she immediately brands him a peeping Tom. The
fashion shoot, with the girls as 1920s flappers, goes badly, and Harold suggests
that a male model might be the answer. Just as the photographer reluctantly agrees
to use Harold, Albert appears in his Al Capone suit, complete with a machine gun
in a violin case. Albert is a sensation and the photographs appear in *Vogue*, much
to the annoyance of his son, who tears a page out of the magazine and sticks it on
the paper-holder in the outside lavatory.

Produced by Douglas Argent Designed by Paul Allen Incidental music Dennis
Wilson, from an original theme by Ron Grainer Production assistant Mike Crisp
Producer's assistant Liz Cranston Assistant floor manager Paul Jackson Floor
assistant Clive Swan Costume supervisor Dorinda Rea Make-up supervisor Kezia de
Winne Senior cameraman Peter Ware Film cameraman John Tiley Stills
photographer John Jefford Lighting supervisor Ritchie Richardson Sound supervisor
Jack Sudic Grams operator Ian Tomlin Vision mixer Bill Morton

And So to Bed

Recorded 7 September 1974, broadcast Wednesday 11 September 1974,
9.25–9.55 p.m.

With Lynn Farleigh as Marcia Wiggley and Angus Mackay as the Salesman

Having finally got a smashing bird back home, Harold waits for his father to stop cobbling old boots in bed to get the girl in question into his bedroom. Marcia is unimpressed, and before the couple can get passionate Albert is listening outside the door. The discovery of a bedbug sees the girl leave hastily, and Harold, having spent the night on the sofa, vows to buy himself a brand-new bed. The salesman in the furniture shop believes the rag 'n' bone men have come into it mistaking it for the betting shop next door. He changes his tune when he realizes Harold has money to spend. After much debate, the salesman persuades Harold to buy a waterbed, which is delivered and installed in his bedroom. Harold discovers that the electric plug hasn't been attached and that as a result he can't heat the water in the bed. He is late for his rag 'n' bone round, and the old man offers to find a plug and prepare the bed for Harold's return. However, frustrated with cutting the wire, Albert plunges his knife into the water-filled mattress and splits it. He barricades himself in his room and a drunken Harold returns home with an equally drunken Marcia. The couple immediately decamp to the bedroom and collapse on to the sopping-wet bed.

Produced by Douglas Argent Designed by Paul Allen Incidental music Dennis Wilson, from an original theme by Ron Grainer Production assistant Mike Crisp Producer's assistant Liz Cranston Assistant floor manager Paul Jackson Floor assistant Clive Swan Costume supervisor Dorinda Rea Make-up supervisor Kezia de Winne Film cameraman John Tiley Lighting supervisor Ritchie Richardson Sound supervisor Jack Sudic Grams operator Ian Tomlin Visual effects Dave Havard Vision mixer Bill Morton

Porn Yesterday

Recorded 14 September 1974, broadcast Wednesday 18 September 1974, 9.25–9.55 p.m.

With Anthony Sharp as the Vicar, Dorothy Frere as the Vicar's Wife Mrs Charles Cakebread, Joyce Windsor as Woman at Fête and Harry Fielder as Man at Fête Uncredited: Vi Kane, Mary Maxted, Joan Ware, Nina Talbot Rice, Yvonne Rubins, Anna Von Karenina, Lily Ritter Grayson, Christine Davies, Suzanne Fleuret, Anna Fellowes, Sarah Hamilton, Michele Barrie, Madeline Simpson, Kleshna Handel, Pat Symons, Daphne Lea, Marjorie Paington, Nicholas Kane, David Brooks, Anthony Holloway, Francis Alwyn, Keith Chamberlain, Richard Orme, David Rolfe, Gerald Fox, Andrew Crofts and Roy Caesar as the Crowd at Fête, Ray Burdis, Mario Renzullo, Peter Newby, Linda Robson, June Page and Kim Taylforth as the Teenagers

A heatwave has hit Shepherd's Bush, and as Harold struggles on the horse and cart Albert lies back with a beer, an ice cream and a good book. Returning home early, Harold reveals his prized item of the day, an old What the Butler Saw machine. The old man can't wait to have a look at it, but Harold hogs the vintage erotica and delights in the corny, harmless smut. However, after two early reels, the third film is a 1920s effort featuring a milkman with no trousers. It transpires that Albert is the star of the film. Harold is disgusted and vows to destroy the evidence. But the vicar, on the lookout for items for his fête, sees the machine and persuades a reluctant Harold to donate it. Harold removes the film drum that shows Albert, but on the day of the fête the machine is doing a roaring trade. The Scouts have found another film drum at the site where Harold picked up the machine. It's another of Albert's starring roles. Harold grabs the offending reel and tries to make a run for it, but the crowd stop him, the reel is broken and Albert happily signs photographs for his 'fans'.

Produced by Douglas Argent Designed by Paul Allen Incidental music Dennis
Wilson, from an original theme by Ron Grainer Production assistant Mike Crisp
Producer's assistant Liz Cranston Assistant floor manager Paul Jackson Floor
assistant Clive Swan Costume supervisor Dorinda Rea Make-up supervisor Kezia de
Winne Film cameraman John Tiley Lighting supervisor Ritchie Richardson Sound
supervisor Jack Sudic Grams operator Ian Tomlin Vision mixer Bill Morton

The Seven Steptoerai

Recorded 21 September 1974, broadcast Wednesday 25 September 1974,
9.25–9.55 p.m.

With Henry Woolf as Frankie Barrow, Billy Horrigan, Dougie Robinson, Marc Boyle,
Tim Condron and Vic Armstrong as the Heavies, Bill Weston, Stuart Fell, Paddy Ryan,
Tony Smart, Aubrey Danvers-Walker, Ernest Jennings and David J. Graham as the
Seven Steptoerai

Albert returns from a double bill of kung fu films as Harold unveils his latest 'find',
a huge oriental vase. He is convinced it is an antique, but Albert spots 'Made in
Britain'. The origin of the piece doesn't matter, however, for local gangster Frankie
Barrow turns up with his heavies and smashes it. He is offering an insurance policy
to the Steptoes, a protection against his boys smashing up the house, the contents
and the owners. Paying the first instalment, £15 for a week, the Steptoes face a
bleak future. Harold remembers a film, *The Seven Samurai*, which reflects their situation, and the old man rounds up his own band of fighters – his fellow old-age-pen-
sioner kung fu cinema-goers. Albert has refused to pay the next week's money and
Frankie and the boys arrive to do maximum damage. But the old man and his gang
soon exercise their martial arts and see them off.

Produced by Douglas Argent Designed by Paul Allen Incidental music Dennis
Wilson, from an original theme by Ron Grainer Fight arranged by Bill Weston and
directed by Mike Crisp Production assistant Mike Crisp Producer's assistant Liz
Cranston Assistant floor manager Paul Jackson Floor assistant Carol Scott Costume
supervisor Dorinda Rea Make-up supervisor Kezia de Winne Film cameramen Colin
Deehan and Ken Westbury Film editor Howard Waters Lighting supervisor Ritchie
Richardson Sound supervisor Jack Sudic Grams operator Ian Tomlin Visual effects
Dave Havard Vision mixer Bill Morton

Upstairs, Downstairs, Upstairs, Downstairs

Recorded 28 September 1974, broadcast Thursday 3 October 1974, 9.35–10.05 p.m.

With Robert James as the Doctor

The old man, suffering from a bad back, is confined to bed. Harold takes on the
unenviable task of looking after his every need, while still struggling to keep the
business afloat. Although Albert promises not to be a burden, almost immediately
he is screaming for his son with a never-ending list of errands and demands. While
attempting to get out of bed to turn up the sound on his television set, his back
clicks back into place and he feels fine. But he decides to keep his son working for
as long as possible. Harold returns home with a little luxury of his own, a bag of
liquorice allsorts, and decides to wash down the sweets with a beer. But the fridge
is empty and two empty lager tins in the bin alert his suspicions. Albert shouts
down from his room and concludes that Harold is out. With the son hiding in the

kitchen cupboard, the old man creeps downstairs and creeps back upstairs. Harold pretends to 'return home' and proceeds to give his father a blanket bath. With surgical spirit burning his privates, the old man jumps out of bed, 'cured'!

Produced by Douglas Argent Designed by Paul Allen Incidental music Dennis Wilson, from an original theme by Ron Grainer Production assistant Mike Crisp Producer's assistant Liz Cranston Assistant floor manager Paul Jackson Floor assistant Carol Scott Costume supervisor Dorinda Rea Make-up supervisor Kezia de Winne Lighting supervisor Ritchie Richardson Sound supervisor Jack Sudic Grams operator Ian Tomlin Vision mixer Bill Morton

Seance in a Wet Rag and Bone Yard

Recorded 5 October 1974, broadcast Thursday 10 October 1974, 9.30–10 p.m.

With Patricia Routledge as Madame Fontana, Gwen Nelson as Dorothy Duddy, and Gilly Flower and David J. Graham as Mr and Mrs Sheldon

Having treated himself to a classical music evening at home alone, Harold has fallen asleep and, with some relief, missed the George Formby film on late-night television. Albert returns home after midnight and eventually reveals he has spent the evening at a spiritualist meeting with his latest flame, Dorothy. Harold mocks the parade of the dearly departed great and good that his father has apparently been chatting with, and makes a mockery of Albert's makeshift Ouija-board session. Believing that his father is about to be conned, he is against the seance group convening at the Steptoes' house for their next meeting. Harold sends up the evening but is distressed when the flamboyant medium, Madame Fontana, conjures up the spirit of his long-dead mother. Thankfully, the scam is quickly revealed. Dorothy is in fact the mother of Madame Fontana, and has used the fake advice of the 'spirits' to advise an apparently very wealthy Albert to marry again. The group disperse, but just before going to bed Harold hears the voice of his mother wishing him goodnight. He races up the stairs begging to sleep in his father's bed for the night.

Produced by Douglas Argent Designed by Paul Allen Incidental music Dennis Wilson, from an original theme by Ron Grainer Production assistant Mike Crisp Producer's assistant Penny Thompson Assistant floor manager Paul Jackson Floor assistant Carol Scott Costume supervisor Dorinda Rea Make-up supervisor Kezia de Winne Lighting supervisor Ritchie Richardson Sound supervisor Jack Sudic Grams operator Ian Tomlin Vision mixer Mike Turner

Christmas Special

Recorded 26 and 27 October 1974, broadcast Thursday 26 December 1974, 9.05–9.45 p.m., BBC1, in colour

Starring Harry H. Corbett as Harold and Wilfrid Brambell as Albert

Written by Ray Galton and Alan Simpson

With Leon Eagles as the Immigration Officer Uncredited: Steve Ismay and Ian Elliot as the Customs Officers, Helen Baine and Stefani Thornton as the Dolly Birds, Jeremy Rand and Tricia Clarke as the Young Couple, Anthony Holloway as the Traveller, Claire Russell as Harold's Girlfriend

Once again, Harold is determined to spend Christmas abroad. He's even prepared to compromise and take Albert with him. Working through a mountain of holiday brochures, the old man continually puts obstacles in the way of all destinations. If they have to go away for Christmas, Albert wants to go to Bognor.

Finally, they both agree on a Christmas holiday in Switzerland, but still Albert causes problems. He explains that he can't find his passport. He needs his birth certificate to apply for a replacement one, but he can't remember where that is either. Eventually, the old man 'remembers' it's in the cupboard under the stairs. His reluctance in finding it is revealed when it reveals that Albert's father was unknown. Harold is delighted that after all these years of thinking it, written evidence proves him right! Albert is relieved that the truth is finally out, and Harold takes his father's photograph for the new passport. Arriving at the railway station, Harold is informed that his passport is out of date. Albert boards the train alone and leaves his son to his own devices for Christmas. But Harold is delighted. He jumps into a sports car with an attractive blonde and zooms off to Bognor for Christmas. Harold is free at last – at least for a few days.

Produced by Douglas Argent Designed by Paul Allen Incidental music Dennis Wilson, from an original theme by Ron Grainer Production assistant Mike Crisp Producer's assistant Penny Thompson Assistant floor manager Paul Jackson Floor assistant Clive Swan Costume supervisor Dorinda Rea Make-up supervisor Kezia de Winne Lighting supervisor Ritchie Richardson Sound supervisor Jack Sudic Film cameraman Elmer Cossey Assistant cameraman John Adderley Film ops Mike Barnard and Roy Osborne Film editor Richard Seel Grips Stan Swetman Assistant grips Norman Johnston Sound recordist Ron Blight British Rail contact Gary Smith Grams operator Liam Donnelly Vision mixer John Gorman

TV GUEST APPEARANCES

Christmas Night With the Stars

Recorded 13 December 1962, broadcast Tuesday 25 December 1962, 7.15–8.50 p.m., BBC Television, in black and white

Steptoe and Son segment starring Wilfrid Brambell as Albert and Harry H. Corbett as Harold

Written by Alan Simpson and Ray Galton

Directed by Duncan Wood

Continuity script by John Law and Eamonn Andrews Edited by Richard Barclay Produced by Graeme Muir and Ronald Marsh

Royal Variety Show

Recorded 4 November 1963, broadcast Sunday 10 November 1963, ITV, in black and white

Starring Harry H. Corbett as Harold and Wilfrid Brambell as Albert

Written by Alan Simpson and Ray Galton

Also featuring Marlene Dietrich, Flanders and Swann, Buddy Greene, Los Paraguayos, Susan Maughan, Pinky and Perky, Harry Secombe, Tommy Steele and the Beatles.

Night of 100 Stars
Broadcast Friday 25 December 1964, ITV, in black and white

The Ken Dodd Show
Broadcast live Sunday 24 July 1966, 8.15–9 p.m., BBC1, in black and white

Ken Dodd introduces his special guest stars Steptoe and Son alias Wilfrid Brambell and Harry H. Corbett, with Salena Jones, Graham Stark and the world-famous Bluebell Girls, also featuring Roger Stevenson and his Diddy Men, the Shepherd Singers and the Augmented Northern Dance Orchestra conducted by Bernard Herrman.

Written by Eddie Braben and Ken Dodd *Steptoe and Son* written by Ray Galton and Alan Simpson The Bluebell Girls choreography by Kenneth Lawson Produced by Duncan Wood

Christmas Night with the Stars
Recorded 20 November 1967, broadcast Monday 25 December 1967, 6.40–8.40pm BBC1

Starring Harry H. Corbett as Harold and Wilfrid Brambell as Albert

Written by Alan Simpson and Ray Galton

Also featuring Cilla Black, Billy Cotton, Val Doonican, Lulu, David Nixon, Beryl Reid with Avril Elgar, Susan Shaw, Kenneth Williams, *Till Death Us Do Part, Beggar My Neighbour, The Illustrated Weekly Hudd* and Harry Worth.

Introduced by Rolf Harris with the Boys and Girls' Choreography by Douglas Squires Orchestration by Ronnie Hazlehurst, Alan Roper and Dennis Wilson Directed by Alyn Ainsworth Continuity script by David Cumming Designed by Victor Meredith Produced by Stewart Morris

RADIO

Series One
3 July–25 September 1966, Sunday 7–7.30 p.m., the Light Programme, repeated the following Monday, 10–10.30 p.m.

Starring Wilfrid Brambell as Albert and Harry H. Corbett as Harold

Written by Alan Simpson and Ray Galton, adapted for radio by Gale Pedrick Produced by Bobby Jaye

The Offer
Recorded 6 February 1966, broadcast 3 July 1966

The Bird
Recorded 12 March 1966, broadcast 10 July 1966, with Marianne Stone as Roxanne

Sixty-Five Today

Recorded 27 February 1966, broadcast 17 July 1966, with Ian Burford as the Man in Bar and David Charlesworth as the Waiter

The Stepmother

Recorded 13 February 1966, broadcast 24 July 1966, with Joan Newell as Emma Marshall

The Economist

Recorded 20 February 1966, broadcast 31 July 1966, with Ian Burford as the Man

Wallah-Wallah Catsmeat

Recorded 12 March 1966, broadcast 7 August 1966, with Eric Woodburn as the Vet, Leslie Dwyer as Lionel Sturgess and Peter Hawkins as Charlie

The Diploma

Recorded 6 March 1966, broadcast 14 August 1966

Steptoe à la Cart

(credited as Steptoe à la Carte)
Recorded 6 February 1966, broadcast 21 August 1966, with Gwendolyn Watts as Monique Fouberge and Ian Burford as the Butler

The Holiday

Recorded 13 February 1966, broadcast 28 August 1966, with Colin Gordon as the Doctor

The Bath

Recorded 6 March 1966, broadcast 4 September 1966, with Marianne Stone as Delia

The Lead Man Cometh

Recorded 27 February 1966, broadcast 11 September 1966, with Leonard Rossiter as Welsh Hughie

A Musical Evening

Recorded 12 March 1966, broadcast 18 September 1966

The Bonds That Bind Us

Recorded 20 February 1966, broadcast 25 September 1966, with Yootha Joyce as Madge and Ian Burford

Series Two

11 June–30 July 1967, Sunday 2–2.30 p.m., the Light Programme, repeated the following Monday 8.15–8.45 p.m.

Starring Harry H. Corbett as Harold and Wilfrid Brambell as Albert

Written by Alan Simpson and Ray Galton, adapted for radio by Gale Pedrick
Produced by Bobby Jaye

The Siege of Steptoe Street

Recorded 23 April 1967, broadcast 11 June 1967, with Robert Dorning as Mr Stacey the Butcher, Michael McClain as the Summons Server and Alan Dudley as the Bailiff

Pilgrim's Progress

Recorded 23 April 1967, broadcast 18 June 1967, with Leon Thau as the Frenchman, Norman Mitchell as the American, Alan Dudley as the German and Wendy Hall as the Air Hostess

The Wooden Overcoats

Recorded 30 April 1967, broadcast 25 June 1967

Sunday for Seven Days

Recorded 30 April 1967, broadcast 2 July 1967, with Marianne Stone as the Cashier of the cinema screening Fellini's 8½, Beth Boyd as the Cashier at the cinema screening *Nudes of 1967* and Peter Hawkins and Nigel Clayton as the Men in Cinema

The Piano

Recorded 7 May 1967, broadcast 9 July 1967, featuring Brian Oulton as the Man and, uncredited, Alan Simpson as the Policeman

My Old Man's a Tory

Recorded 7 May 1967, broadcast 16 July 1967, with Dudley Foster as Mr Stonelake and Beth Boyd as Karen Frobisher

Homes Fit for Heroes

Recorded 30 April 1967, broadcast 23 July 1967, with Olwen Brooks as the Matron and Marie Makino as Miss Lotterby

Crossed Swords

Recorded 14 May 1967, broadcast 30 July 1967, with Derek Nimmo as the Antique Shop Assistant, Michael McClain as the Auctioneer and John Curle as the Announcer

Series Three

21 March–9 May 1971, Sunday 2–2.30 p.m., Radio 2, repeated the following Monday 6.15–6.45 p.m., Radio 4

Starring Wilfrid Brambell as Albert and Harry H. Corbett as Harold

Written and adapted for radio by Ray Galton and Alan Simpson Produced by Bobby Jaye

A Death in the Family

Recorded 14 February 1971, broadcast 21 March 1971, with, uncredited, Alan Simpson as the Policeman

Two's Company

Recorded 26 January 1971, broadcast 28 March 1971, with June Whitfield as Daphne Goodlace

Tea for Two

Recorded 31 January 1971, broadcast 4 April 1971, with John Rye as Peregrine de Burville and Edward Kelsey as Mr Cadwell

TB or not TB?

Recorded 31 January 1971, broadcast 11 April 1971, with Margot Boyd as the Nurse and Jo Manning Wilson as the Receptionist

Without Prejudice

Recorded 13 February 1971, broadcast 18 April 1971, with Garard Green as Mr Drizen, Edward Kelsey as the Estate Agent and Trevor Martin as the Neighbour

Cuckoo in the Nest

Recorded 14 February 1971, broadcast 25 April 1971, with Kenneth J. Warren as Arthur and David Brierly as the Taxi Driver Lennie Jenkins

Steptoe and Son – and Son!

Recorded 26 January 1971, broadcast 2 May 1971, with Gwendolyn Watts as Beryl Tomlin and Richard Griffiths as George

Robbery with Violence

Recorded 13 February 1971, broadcast 9 May 1971, with Dudley Foster as the Inspector, Edward Kelsey and Garard Green as the Policemen and Trevor Martin as the Reporter

Series Four

30 January–19 March 1972, Sunday 2–2.30 p.m., Radio 2, repeated the following Monday 8–8.30 p.m.

Starring Harry H. Corbett as Harold and Wilfrid Brambell as Albert

Written and adapted for radio by Ray Galton and Alan Simpson. Produced by Bobby Jaye

Full House

Recorded 7 January 1972, broadcast 30 January 1972, with Martin Friend, Douglas Blackwell and Michael Kilgarriff as the Card Players

Is That Your Horse Outside?

Recorded 10 January 1972, broadcast 6 February 1972, with Jo Manning Wilson as Dorothea and John Samson as the Coalman

The Lodger

Recorded 30 January 1972, broadcast 13 February 1972, with William Eedle as the Shopkeeper

A Box in Town

Recorded 14 January 1972, broadcast 20 February 1972, with Yootha Joyce as Avis, Katherine Parr as Mrs Blackett and Sheila Grant as Harold's Landlady

The Three Feathers

Recorded 7 January 1972, broadcast 27 February 1972, with Douglas Blackwell as Mr Copeland and Leslie Heritage as Mr De Vere

The Colour Problem

Recorded 4 January 1972, broadcast 5 March 1972, with Anthony Sharp as the Doctor, Jo Manning Wilson as Muriel Duddy and William Eedle as the Policeman

And Afterwards At ...

Recorded 14 January 1972, broadcast 12 March 1972, with Pat Coombs as Auntie Ethel, Patricia Hayes as Auntie May and Margot Boyd, Sheila Grant, Katherine Parr, Edward Kelsey and Martin Friend as the Steptoe Wedding Party

Any Old Iron?

Recorded 10 Janaury 1972, broadcast 19 March 1972, with Richard Hurndall as Timothy Stanhope, John Samson as Edgar and Stephanie Turner as Dolly Miller

Series Five

26 May–30 June 1974, Sunday 2–2.30 p.m., Radio 2, repeated the following Saturday 7–7.30 p.m.

Starring Wilfrid Brambell as Albert and Harry H. Corbett as Harold

Written and adapted for radio by Ray Galton and Alan Simpson Produced by Bobby Jaye

The Desperate Hours

Recorded 11 September 1973, broadcast 26 May 1974, with Leonard Rossiter as John Spooner and Paddy Joyce as Frank Ferris

Come Dancing

Recorded 11 September 1973, broadcast 2 June 1974, with Clifford Norgate as the Milkman

A Star is Born

Recorded 14 September 1973, broadcast 9 June 1974, with Trevor Bannister as Rupert Faines Muir, Jo Manning Wilson, Michael McClain and Nicolette McKenzie as the am. drams and Jimmy Young as himself

A Winter's Tale

Recorded 14 September 1973, broadcast 16 June 1974

Men of Property

Recorded 16 September 1973, broadcast 23 June 1974, with Norman Bird as Mr Wood the Bank Manager, Jeanne Cook as Mrs Wood and Michael McClain as the Waiter

Men of Letters

Recorded 16 September 1973, broadcast 30 June 1974, with Anthony Sharp as the Vicar

Series Six

8 February–28 March 1976, Sunday 2–2.30 p.m., Radio 2, repeated the following Saturday 7–7.30 p.m.

Starring Harry H. Corbett as Harold and Wilfrid Brambell as Albert

Written and adapted for radio by Ray Galton and Alan Simpson Produced by Bobby Jaye

Loathe Story

Recorded 2 December 1975, broadcast 8 February 1976, with Graham Stark as the Psychiatrist, Margot Boyd as Mrs Kennington-Stroud and Jo Manning Wilson as Bunty Kennington-Stroud

Oh, What a Beautiful Mourning

Recorded 17 November 1975, broadcast 15 February 1976, with George A. Cooper as Uncle Arthur and Michael Burlington, David Graham, Anne Jameson, Norma Ronald and Marianne Stone as the Steptoe Family Mourners

Live Now, PAYE Later

Recorded 29 November 1975, broadcast 22 February 1976, with Edward Kelsey as Mr Greenwood, Michael Shannon as the Man from the Ministry and Peter Williams as Norman

Upstairs, Downstairs, Upstairs, Downstairs

Recorded 25 November 1975, broadcast 29 February 1976, with Michael McClain as the Doctor

And So to Bed

Recorded 25 November 1975, broadcast 7 March 1976, with Norma Ronald as Merrissa and Michael Burlington as the Salesman

Porn Yesterday

Recorded 17 November 1975, broadcast 14 March 1976, with Anthony Sharp as the Vicar and Norma Ronald as the Vicar's Wife

The Seven Steptoerai

Recorded 2 December 1975, broadcast 21 March 1976, with Henry Woolf as Frankie Barrow and, uncredited, Alan Simpson as Robin and Ray Galton as Eric

Seance in a Wet Rag and Bone Yard

Recorded 29 November 1975, broadcast 28 March 1976, with Patricia Routledge as Madame Fontana, Gwen Nelson as Dorothy Duddy and Edward Kelsey as Mr Weldon

David Jacobs' Crackers

Recorded 30 November 1976, broadcast 25 December 1976, Radio 4, 10.30 a.m.–1 p.m.

Starring Harry H. Corbett as Harold and Wilfrid Brambell as Albert, with Douglas Blackwell as the Immigration Officer and Nicolette McKenzie as the Girl

Written and adapted for radio by Ray Galton and Alan Simpson Compiled and produced by Bobby Jaye and Geoffrey Perkins

An invitation to celebrate Christmas morning in the company of Woody Allen, Alan Bennett, Michael Bentine, *Dad's Army*, Windsor Davies, Les Dawson, The Goons, Tony Hancock, Hinge and Brackett, Kenneth Horne, The King's Singers, Morecambe and Wise and many others. David Jacobs introduces a seasonal selection of wildly varied entertainment, including a special Christmas edition of *Steptoe and Son*

FEATURE FILMS

Steptoe and Son
Released March 1972, 98 minutes

Starring Wilfrid Brambell as Steptoe and Harry H. Corbett as Son
Scriptwriters Ray Galton and Alan Simpson

Carolyn Seymour as Zita, Arthur Howard as Albert the Vicar, Victor Maddern as the Chauffeur, Fred Griffiths as the Barman, Joan Heath and Fred McNaughton as Mr and Mrs Smith, Zita's Parents, Lon Satton as the Pianist, Perri St Claire as Arthur, Patsy Smart as Mrs Hobbs, Mike Reid as the Compère, Alec Mango as the Hotel Doctor, Michael da Costa as the Hotel Manager, Enys Box as the Traffic Warden, Neil Wilson as the Airline Clerk, Bart Allison as the Tramp, Caroline Eves as the Flamenco Dancer, Julian Alonson as the Guitarist, Julia Goodman as the Lady Courier, Vivien Lloyd as the Bride and Gary Wraight and Selina Becket as the Babies, with, uncredited, Barrie Ingham as Terry

The Steptoes leave a London divorce court and Harold is outraged that his father has successfully ruined his marriage. The scene flashes back three years, with Harold preparing to go out to a football-club stag night for the evening. On hearing that there are strippers on the bill as well as a comic and a drag act, the old man wants to tag along. The two get ready for their big night, with Albert bathing in the kitchen sink and terrifying a neighbour when he emerges naked from the suds. At the club, Harold meets one of the strippers before the show and buys her a drink. During her routine the stripper, Zita, gives Harold a note inviting him to meet her for a drink afterwards. Albert goes too and unwittingly gets chatting to the drag act as Harold and Zita get it together. Returning to Oil Drum Lane the next morning, Harold announces he is engaged. Although Albert tries to scupper the marriage plans, Harold and Zita tie the knot and head off to Spain on their honeymoon ... with the old man in tow. While abroad, Albert eats lobster and, suffering from food poisoning, begs Harold to take him back home to die. They get the last two seats on the plane to England. Zita is left behind, and she is soon shacked up with Terry, a comic she used to work with on the stripper circuit. Harold is heartbroken and furious, but, when he tracks her down back in England, she reveals she is pregnant and that Harold is the father. He attempts to take her back, but Albert refuses to welcome her to the house. Later, Harold discovers a baby boy in the stables and, assuming Zita has abandoned him, looks after the child. Working all the hours God sends to provide enough money for his son's future education, Harold returns home exhausted, to find the pram empty. Albert is asleep and hasn't realized that the mother has returned to take the child back. Harold is livid and searches out Zita once more. But her baby is not the missing one, nor is it Harold's. It is the black daughter of the pianist with the stripper show. Reflecting again on the aftermath of the divorce, father and son drive the horse and cart up Pall Mall and infringe the passage of a right royal traveller.

Nat Cohen presents an Anglo-EMI film, Associated London Films production released through MGM-EMI Distributors Limited, in Technicolor Made on location and at Lee International Studios, London, England Director of photography John Wilcox B.S.C. Production designer Peter Mullins Art director Bernard Sarron Editor Bernard Gribble Production supervisor Christopher Sutton Music composed and arranged by Roy Budd and Jack Fishman *Steptoe* Theme by Ron Grainer End title music played by

Mr Acker Bilk Assistant director Ariel Levy Camera operator Chic Waterson
Continuity Zelda Baron Sound recordist Kevin Sutton Sound editor Frank Goulding
Make-up supervisor Heather Nurse Hairdressing supervisor Pat McDermot
Wardrobe supervisor Dora Lloyd Set construction by Jack Carter and Terry Apsey
Dubbing mixer Trevor Pyke Property master John Leuenberger Striptease routine
Vi Tye Executive producer Beryl Vertue Producer Aida Young Director Cliff Owen

Steptoe and Son Ride Again
Released July 1973, 99 minutes

Starring Wilfrid Brambell as Steptoe and Harry H. Corbett as Son

Scriptwriters Ray Galton and Alan Simpson

Diana Dors as the Woman in the Flat, Milo O'Shea as Dr Popplewell, Neil McCarthy
as Lennie, Bill Maynard as George, George Tovey as Percy, Sam Kydd as Claude,
Yootha Joyce as Lennie's Wife, Olga Lowe as Percy's Wife, Joyce Hemson as Claude's
Wife, Henry Woolf as Frankie Barrow, Geoffrey Bayldon as the Vicar, Frank Thornton as
Mr Russell the Insurance Agent, Richard Davies as the Butcher, Eamonn Boyce as
Frankie Barrow's Crony, Hilda Barry as the Woman with the Carrot, Joan Ingram as the
Lady in the Butcher's, Rafiq Anwar as the Doctor, Siobhan Quinlan as the Nurse, Peter
Thornton as the Landlord, Stewart Bevan as the Vet, Grazina Frame as the Dolly Bird
and Peter Newby as the Boy

While Albert is tracking down his neighbour's chicken for supper, Harold is enduring a fraught day on his round. He climbs up to see an old lady in a block of flats
only to receive a carrot for his horse, is seduced by a recently widowed blonde and
finally falls asleep and drives the cart into an open-backed removal van heading for
York. By the time he arrives home – three days later – the chicken is ancient history
and Hercules the horse is pronounced lame and unable to work. Harold retires him
off to an old horses' home and Albert digs out his life savings – £89 – for a new
horse. But Harold gets drunk with local tough guy Frankie Barrow and ends up putting the money towards a greyhound he buys from Barrow for £200. Worse still, the
dog performs badly at his trial race, refusing to even leave the trap, and Barrow is
pushing hard for the rest of his money. While out training Harold loses the dog,
Hercules the Second, who runs home to Oil Drum Lane in record-breaking time.
He surmises that the dog is short-sighted and, sure enough, a suitable pair of
glasses improves his performance tenfold. Harold sells everything in the house to
raise the stake money for the dog's first race, but the evening is another disaster:
while well in the lead, the dog spots Albert in the audience and runs towards him
instead. With nothing left and the heavies on their way, Albert reveals that he has a
life insurance policy. Harold decides to fake his father's death and calls in well-
known drunk Dr Popplewell to sign a death certificate. With Albert officially
deceased, he and Harold plan a quiet funeral but the Shepherd's Bush totters
gather to give Albert a traditional totter's farewell. During the pre-funeral party, the
insurance man arrives to inform Harold that his father's policy was signed over to
an old girlfriend and that all family rights to the money have been forfeited. Instead
of leaving the country, Harold plans to bring his father miraculously back to life but,
with the party in full swing and Albert dozing in the comfortable coffin, the opportunity doesn't present itself. On his way to the funeral Harold, still desperately trying
to wake up his sleeping father, is bashed on the head by an opening lorry door and
rushed to casualty. Making a speedy exit and heading towards the graveyard, he

crash-lands in a crypt just as the old man wakes up and gives the vicar and congregation the shock of their lives. Harold's mournful, shroud-clad appearance from the crypt doesn't help to relieve the tension either. The insurance man reveals that the ex-girlfriend's claim on the money was forfeited when she married and pays out the surrender amount to the Steptoes. With a new horse for the business, Harold has invested the rest of the money in a part share in a racehorse that Frankie Barrow 'sold' him. Driving to the first race meeting on the horse and cart, the other owner is a certain 'H.M. Queen', and the Steptoes and their greyhound find themselves in the royal parade.

An Associated London Films production released through MGM-EMI Distributors Limited, in Technicolor Made on location and at Lee International Studios, London, England Director of photography Ernie Steward B.S.C. Production supervisor Christopher Sutton Art director Bernard Sarron Editor Bernard Gribble Assistant director Graham Ford Camera operator Neil Binney Continuity Josie Fulford Sound recordist Kevin Sutton Sound editor Frank Goulding Dubbing mixer Trevor Pyke, Make-up Heather Nurse Hairdressing Katie Dawson Costume supervisor Emma Porteous Construction manager Peter Verard Set construction by Jack Carter and Terry Apsey Set dresser Philip Cowlam Property master Tommy Raeburn Buyer Dennis Maddison Gaffer Len Crowe Animal trainer Danny Graber Music composed and arranged by Roy Budd and Jack Fishman *Steptoe* theme by Ron Grainer Executive producer Beryl Vertue Producer Aida Young Director Peter Sykes

VIDEO

Classic Comedy of the Sixties
Features 'The Wooden Overcoats' extract. WSP 1054, 1991

Classic Moments from BBC Comedy
includes 'Porn Yesterday' extract, 2000

The Golden Years of Comedy 1966
Features 'Pilgrim's Progress'. BBCV 5783, 1996, deleted 1998

Radio Times' Funny Faces on BBC Video
Includes 'And So to Bed' extract, RT001, 1993

Steptoe and Son
Warner Home Video/Weintraub Entertainment Group WTB 38149, 1989, deleted 1993, re-released Warner Home Video/Lumiere SO 38149, 1993, repackaged 1996

Steptoe and Son Ride Again
Warner Home Video/Weintraub Entertainment Group PES 38179, 1989, deleted 1993, re-released Warner Home Video/Lumiere SO 38179, 1993, repackaged 1996

Steptoe and Son/Steptoe and Son Ride Again/Till Death Us Do Part
Film Triple Bill. Braveworld Video STV 4021, 1992, deleted 1994

Steptoe and Son/Steptoe and Son Ride Again
Film Double Bill. Warner Home Video SO 38363, 1995, deleted 1996

Steptoe and Son: Divided We Stand
With 'The Desperate Hours' and 'Porn Yesterday'. BBCV 4041, 1985

Steptoe and Son: Men of Letters
With 'Live Now, PAYE Later' and Christmas Special 1973. BBCV 4042, 1985, deleted 1998

Steptoe and Son: A Star is Born
With 'Upstairs, Downstairs, Upstairs, Downstairs' and 'Cuckoo in the Nest'. BBCV 4059, 1985, deleted 1998

Steptoe and Son: Oh, What a Beautiful Mourning
With 'Loathe Story' and 'And So to Bed'. BBCV 4060, 1985, deleted 1998

Steptoe and Son W.H. Smith Exclusive Video
Box Set. 4 tapes with 12 episodes. BBCV 4041, 4042, 4059 and 4060, 1995

Steptoe and Son: The Seven Steptoerai
With 'Seance in a Wet Rag and Bone Yard' and 'Back in Fashion'. BBCV 4601, 1991, deleted 1998

Steptoe and Son: The Piano
With 'The Bath' and 'The Holiday'. BBCV 4602, 1991, deleted 1998

Steptoe and Son: Sixty-Five Today
With 'The Lodger' and 'The Bird'. BBCV 4797, 1992

Steptoe and Son: The Stepmother
With 'Full House' and 'The Wooden Overcoats'. BBCV 4798, 1992

Steptoe and Son: A Winter's Tale
With 'Steptoe and Son – and Son!' and 'Two's Company'. BBCV 4830, 1992, deleted 1998

Steptoe and Son: Tea for Two
With 'Without Prejudice' and 'The Three Feathers'. BBCV 4831, 1993

Steptoe and Son: Is That Your Horse Outside?
With 'Steptoe à la Cart' and 'Those Magnificent Men and Their Heating Machines'. BBCV 5345, 1994, deleted 1998

Steptoe and Son: The Siege of Steptoe Street
With 'Crossed Swords' and 'The Bonds That Bind Us'. BBCV 5373, 1994, deleted 1998

Steptoe and Son: The Offer
With 'The Economist' and 'The Lead Man Cometh'. BBCV 5582, 1995, deleted 1998

Steptoe and Son: Wallah-Wallah Catsmeat
With 'And Afterwards At ...' and 'Homes Fit for Heroes'. BBCV 5638, 1995

Steptoe and Son: The Diploma
With 'A Musical Evening' and 'A Box in Town'. BBCV 5856, 1996, deleted 1998

Steptoe and Son: Come Dancing

With Christmas Special 1974. BBCV 6167, 1997

The Very Best of Steptoe and Son

'Upstairs, Downstairs, Upstairs, Downstairs', 'The Bath', 'Seance in a Wet Rag and Bone Yard', 'Porn Yesterday' and 'And So to Bed'. BBCV 5102, 1993

The Very Best of Steptoe and Son Volume 2

'A Star is Born', 'Oh, What a Beautiful Mourning', 'Men of Letters', 'The Desperate Hours' and 'Back in Fashion'. BBCV 5395, 1995

DVD

The Very Best of Steptoe and Son

'Men of Letters', 'A Star is Born', 'Oh, What a Beautiful Mourning', 'The Desperate Hours' and 'Back in Fashion'. BBCDVD 1056, 2001

The Very Best of Steptoe and Son Volume 2

'The Bath', 'And So to Bed', 'Porn Yesterday', 'Upstairs, Downstairs, Upstairs, Downstairs', 'Seance in a Wet Rag and Bone Yard'. BBCDVD 1122, 2002

BBC RADIO COLLECTION

Radio Times' Comedy Classics

With 'Two's Company' extract. 1993

Steptoe and Son Volume 1, The Lead Man Cometh

With 'The Offer', 'Pilgrim's Progress', 'Homes Fit for Heroes'. 1990, repackaged 1997 as *Steptoe and Son Gold*

Steptoe and Son Volume 2, Two's Company

With 'Crossed Swords', 'Tea for Two', 'TB or not TB?'. 1992

Steptoe and Son Volume 3, Is That Your Horse Outside?

With 'Without Prejudice', 'Robbery with Violence', 'And Afterwards At ...'. 1993

Steptoe and Son Volume 4, Cuckoo in the Nest

With 'A Death in the Family', 'Full House', 'The Colour Problem'. 1995

Steptoe and Son Volume 5, Any Old Iron?

With 'The Lodger', 'A Box in Town', 'The Three Feathers'. 1996

Steptoe and Son Volume 6, The Seven Steptoerai

With 'Men of Letters', 'Live Now, PAYE Later', 'Seance in a Wet Rag and Bone Yard'. 1997

Steptoe and Son Volume 7, And So to Bed

With 'A Winter's Tale', 'Oh, What a Beautiful Mourning', 'Porn Yesterday'. 1998, volumes 1–7 repackaged and released in 1999

Steptoe and Son Volume 8, Come Dancing

With 'The Desperate Hours', 'Upstairs, Downstairs, Upstairs, Downstairs', 'A Star is Born'. 1999

Steptoe and Son Volume 9, Men of Property

With 'The Economist', 'Steptoe and Son – and Son!', 'Loathe Story'. 2001

Steptoe and Son, Any Old Iron?, BBC Experience Exhibition Audio Birthday Card

A65BBC011, 1999

RECORDINGS

Old Ned/Happy Joe

Ron Grainer and his group. Pye 7N.15411, 1962

Steptoe and Son

Ron Grainer and his group. Pye 7N 45141, 1962

Steptoe and Son (Old Ned)/Over the Backyard Fence

Geoff Love and His Orchestra. Columbia 45-DB 4881, 1962

Steptoe and Son/Phase Four

Joe Loss and His Orchestra. HMV POP 1192, 1963

Steptoe and Son/Ragtime Tuba

Alexander Murray Smith & the Mack O'Town Syncopators. Decca 45-F.11604, 1963

On The Air – 60 Years of BBC Theme Music

Features 'Old Ned'. BBC ZCD 454, 1982

TV Times – Name That Tune

Features 'Old Ned'. MACCD366, 1998

Steptoe and Son

Pye NPL 18081, 1962, reissued Golden Guinea GGL 0278, 1962, Marble Arch MAL 1160, 1969, Hallmark HMA 238

Steptoe & Son at Buckingham Palace

Pye 7N.15588, 1963

The Facts of Life from Steptoe & Son

Pye NEP.24169, 1963

The Wages of Sin

Pye NEP.24180, 1963

More Junk from Steptoe and Son

Pye 1964, reissued Golden Guinea GGL 0278, 1964, Marble Arch MAL 1214, 1969

Steptoe à la Cart
Pye Popular NPL 18101, 1964

Love and Harold Steptoe
Pye NPL 18135, 1965

Gems from the Steptoe Scrap Heap
Pye NPL 18153, 1966

A Golden Hour of Steptoe and Son
Features 'Is That Your Horse Outside?'. 'The Lodger', 'The Siege of Steptoe Street', 'And Afterwards At ...' and 'Full House' extracts. Pye GH527

40 Years of Television – Comedy Spectacular
Features 'The Facts of Life', (extract from 'Is That Your Horse Outside?') BBC REB 249, 1976

Carrying On
Features 'Steptoe & Son at the Palace'. EMI, 1993

A Pye in the Face
Features 'Steptoe & Son at the Palace'. Diamond Recordings GEMCD007, 1996

Laughing Stock
Features 'Steptoe & Son at the Palace'. Sanctuary Records, CMDDD403, 2002

BOOKS

All Above Board by Wilfrid Brambell, W. H. Allen 1976

The Best of Steptoe and Son by Ray Galton and Alan Simpson, Robson Books 1993

No More Curried Eggs For Me by Roger Wilmut, Methuen 1982

Steptoe and Son by Gale Pedrick, Hodder 1964

Steptoe and Son at the Palace by Gale Pedrick, Hodder 1966

Steptoe and Son – Four Television Scripts by Ray Galton and Alan Simpson, Longman Group Limited 1971

The Very Best of Steptoe and Son by Ray Galton and Alan Simpson, 1989

The Official Steptoe & Son Appreciation Society
23 Surrey Road, Peckham, London SE15 3AS, e-mail: steptoesss@yahoo.co.uk

http://www.achilles.net/~howardm/sasas/

http://www.galtonandsimpson.com

Index